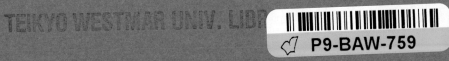

Basic Functional Japanese

Basic Functional Japanese

Pegasus Language Services

日本語

The Japan Times

Audio cassette tape data of *Basic Functional Japanese*
Pack 1 — Pack 6 (60 minutes each)
Recordings: Bunji Shono, Yumi Mizusawa, Hisao Oyama, Shingo Hiromori, Sakiko Tamagawa and Mary Blaber
Recording studio: Churoku Creation Co., Ltd., Tokyo
Produced by The Japan Times, Ltd.
ISBN4-7890-0373-6

Illustrations: Junko Shimizu
Cover art: Koji Detake
Photographs: Janet Perkins

Published in 1987 by The Japan Times, Ltd.
5-4 Shibaura 4-chome, Minato-ku, Tokyo 108, Japan

ISBN4-7890-0372-8

91 90   8

Printed in Japan

PREFACE

Basic Functional Japanese is designed for beginning students as well as those who have studied a little Japanese. Students who have begun their studies with traditional grammar-oriented textbooks but who now wish to make a fresh start using a different approach will find this text ideal. Those who wish to learn Japanese for business purposes will find the emphasis on practical communication well-suited to their needs. The text will be both useful and approachable for native speakers of English or those who know English as a second language. After completing this text, estimated to take 90–120 classroom hours, the student will be able not only to handle practical daily transactions but also to exchange information about themselves, their families, jobs, and special interests. People in business will be able to break the ice and chat with their Japanese counterparts before beginning business discussions in English.

Basic Functional Japanese takes an approach different from traditional textbooks which are primarily grammar based. The authors feel strongly that communication skills should take precedence over the learning of grammatical patterns for their own sake. This means that the emphasis in the classroom must shift from a traditional teacher-centered approach to a student-centered approach in which students can learn Japanese which is meaningful, relevant and above all, useful. Using recent findings in language learning, the authors of this textbook present communicative Japanese through a combination of functions and situations with the minimum amount of grammar required for everyday conversation.

Although the grammatical presentations in this text are unlike traditional approaches, material is carefully arranged for beginning students. The conversation drills are based on discourse analysis of the conversation situations beginning students frequently encounter, and are designed in such a way that even students at the earliest stages can complete the entire conversation. For example, a Japanese person will often follow up ''When did you come to Japan?'' with the question: ''How do you like Japan?'' To cover such frequent conversational situations, the drills include exercises that teach students not only how to tell when they came to Japan but also to make comments about Japan. The drill then goes on to show how ''enthusiastic listening'' (using *aizuchi* to show interest in what the speaker is saying) is a natural part of spoken Japanese and smooths the conversational flow.

Where appropriate, the text introduces various useful ways to show politeness when speaking Japanese. For instance, Japanese peopole often feel it is more polite to be approximate or indirect when speaking. Since such intentionally vague ways of speaking are an important feature of the language, it is important to know how and when to use them to communicate appropriately. Using this textbook, students can acquire such techniques and thus learn useful expressions, not as disconnected phrases without rhyme or reason, but as a logical part of communicative language.

The Culture Notes convey useful information about Japanese social and linguistic behavior, and an abundance of illustrations and photographs portrays Japanese lifestyles.

ACKNOWLEDGEMENTS

The publication of this textbook would not have been possible without the help and encouragement of the Pegasus Language Services Japanese and English teaching staff, both past and present, who contributed their ideas, comments and time. Particular thanks go to the three instructors who created, compiled and wrote *Basic Functional Japanese:*

    Keiko Kawai

    Kanae Miura

    Hiromi Suzuki

Others who assisted in this effort are (in alphabetical order):

    William Boletta

    Yumiko Hama

    Shirley Miyasaki

    James Moore

    Reiko Nakajima

    Hiroko Shimbo

    Chieko Takasaki

    Douglas Tomlinson

    Susan Ueno

    Susan Wanwig

    Anne Ward

    Clare Williams

    Yoshiko Yoshimatsu

Pegasus Language Services

CONTENTS

Contents of Cassette Tapes

Pack 1
    Side A   From Lesson 1 to Drill 1, Lesson 5
    Side B   From Drill 4, Lesson 5 to Drill 5, Lesson 8
Pack 2
    Side A   From Drill 6, Lesson 8 to Lesson 10
    Side B   From Lesson 11 to Lesson 12
Pack 3
    Side A   From Lesson 13 to Drill 6, Lesson 14
    Side B   From Drill 7, Lesson 14 to Drill 5, Lesson 15
Pack 4
    Side A   From Drill 7, Lesson 15 to Lesson 16
    Side B   From Lesson 17 to Lesson 18
Pack 5
    Side A   From Lesson 19 to Drill 1, Lesson 21
    Side B   From Drill 2, Lesson 21 to Lesson 22
Pack 6
    Side A   Lesson 23
    Side B   Lesson 24

INTRODUCTION

ORGANIZATION OF THE TEXTBOOK

The lessons are divided into seven units according to function. Each unit has three or four lessons based on specific situations and sentence structures. There are twenty-four lessons in all.

1. Scope of the Units
   The scope of each unit appears at the beginning of the unit and gives a summary of what is covered.

2. Dialogues
   The dialogue utilizes the structures and functions of each lesson in everyday conversation. The material is presented in such a way that the student can readily use it.

   Japanese script accompanies the dialogue and is basically written in *kana* for the beginning student's convenience except for proper nouns (*e.g.*, personal names, place names). Pronunciation for these *kanji* is written underneath in *hiragana*.

3. Grammar Notes
   Grammatical explanations relating to each function appear along with several examples illustrating the new structures.
   Vocabulary lists (excluding the vocabulary attached to the dialogue) are also presented. The students need not memorize all the vocabulary listed, but may choose according to their needs.

4. Drills
   There are mainly two types of drills in this textbook: 1) item drills and 2) discourse drills. Item drills consist of substitution drills, transformation drills, questions and answers, expansion exercises, fill-ins, translations and short dialogues. Discourse drills use the material of the opening dialogue.

5. Culture Notes
   Culture notes are at the end of each unit. They will give you some insight into the Japanese language and culture.

6. Review Quizzes
   Quizzes are at the end of every two units. After Lesson 24, there is a final review quiz.

JAPANESE WRITING SYSTEM

Japanese is normally written in a mixture of Chinese characters (*kanji*) and two phonetic syllabaries (*hiragana* and *katakana*):

Example

"American embassy" "to"   "please"
Amerika taishikan made onegaishimasu.   "Take me to the American Embassy."
—for taking a taxi—

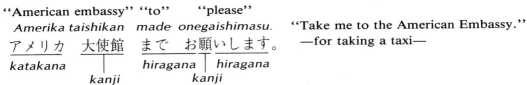

1. *Kanji* represent meaning plus sound and are used for writing nouns, main parts of verbs, adjectives, adverbs, and other parts of speech. Each *kanji* ordinarily has two or more pronunciations (readings).
2. *Hiragana* symbols represent sounds and are used for writing the parts which *kanji* do not cover. Books for very young children, station names, *etc.,* are often written entirely in *hiragana*.
3. *Katakana* symbols represent sounds and are used for writing words borrowed from foreign languages.

For the student's convenience, this textbook uses the Hepburn system of Romanization (*rōmaji*). However, the opening dialogues are also given in Japanese writing.

JAPANESE SYLLABARY CHART

rōmaji *hiragana* *katakana*

a	あ	ア	ka	か	カ	sa	さ	サ	ta	た	タ	na	な	ナ	ha	は	ハ
i	い	イ	ki	き	キ	shi	し	シ	chi	ち	チ	ni	に	ニ	hi	ひ	ヒ
u	う	ウ	ku	く	ク	su	す	ス	tsu	つ	ツ	nu	ぬ	ヌ	fu	ふ	フ
e	え	エ	ke	け	ケ	se	せ	セ	te	て	テ	ne	ね	ネ	he	へ	ヘ
o	お	オ	ko	こ	コ	so	そ	ソ	to	と	ト	no	の	ノ	ho	ほ	ホ
			kya	きゃ	キャ	sha	しゃ	シャ	cha	ちゃ	チャ	nya	にゃ	ニャ	hya	ひゃ	ヒャ
			kyu	きゅ	キュ	shu	しゅ	シュ	chu	ちゅ	チュ	nyu	にゅ	ニュ	hyu	ひゅ	ヒュ
			kyo	きょ	キョ	sho	しょ	ショ	cho	ちょ	チョ	nyo	にょ	ニョ	hyo	ひょ	ヒョ

			ga	が	ガ	za	ざ	ザ	da	だ	ダ				ba	ば	バ
			gi	ぎ	ギ	ji	じ	ジ	ji	ぢ	ヂ				bi	び	ビ
			gu	ぐ	グ	zu	ず	ズ	zu	づ	ヅ				bu	ぶ	ブ
			ge	げ	ゲ	ze	ぜ	ゼ	de	で	デ				be	べ	ベ
			go	ご	ゴ	zo	ぞ	ゾ	do	ど	ド				bo	ぼ	ボ
			gya	ぎゃ	ギャ	ja	じゃ	ジャ							bya	びゃ	ビャ
			gyu	ぎゅ	ギュ	ju	じゅ	ジュ							byu	びゅ	ビュ
			gyo	ぎょ	ギョ	jo	じょ	ジョ							byo	びょ	ビョ

PRONUNCIATION AND WRITING

1. Vowels: *a i u e o*
   あ い う え お
   ア イ ウ エ オ

2. Long vowels:
   ā   ii   ū   ē   ō
   ああ いい うう ええ おお／おう
   アー イー ウー エー オー

3. Consonants + vowel:
   e.g., ka ki ku ke ko
   　　　か き く け こ
   　　　カ キ ク ケ コ
   e.g., ga gi gu ge go
   　　　が ぎ ぐ げ ご
   　　　ガ ギ グ ゲ ゴ

4. Consonant + Consonant + Vowel:
   e.g., kya kyu kyo
   　　　きゃ きゅ きょ
   　　　キャ キュ キョ
   e.g., gya gyu gyo
   　　　ぎゃ ぎゅ ぎょ
   　　　ギャ ギュ ギョ

5. Double consonant:
   e.g., ikko   kissaten   matte
   　　　いっこ きっさてん まって
   　　　ippon   hotto doggu
   　　　いっぽん   ホットドッグ

6. Single /n/: *n*
   　　　　　　ん
   　　　　　　ン

	ma ま マ	ya や ヤ	ra ら ラ	wa わ ワ	n ん ン
	mi み ミ		ri り リ		
	mu む ム	yu ゆ ユ	ru る ル		
	me め メ		re れ レ		
	mo も モ	yo よ ヨ	ro ろ ロ	o を ヲ	
	mya みゃ ミャ		rya りゃ リャ		
	myu みゅ ミュ		ryu りゅ リュ		
	myo みよ ミョ		ryo りょ リョ		

pa ぱ パ				
pi ぴ ピ			N.B. This syllabary chart does not	
pu ぷ プ			cover all the syllables needed	
pe ぺ ペ			to express loan words from foreign	
po ぽ ポ			languages.	
pya ぴゃ ピャ				
pyu ぴゅ ピュ				
pyo ぴょ ピョ				

ABBREVIATIONS, NOTATIONS AND SYMBOLS

( )		Words which can be omitted in the Japanese version
[ ]	(1)	Denotes explanation
	(2)	Unspecified term or words to be inserted
" "		English equivalent
⟶	(1)	Transformations
⟵	(2)	Drill cues
⇄ ⇩		Modifiers
⟵⟶		Negative versions or antonyms
↗ ↘		Intonation
Ø		No marker needed
X		Negative cues
Lit.		Literal translation
[EL]		Enthusiastic Listening sign
[C]		Confirmation
[M]		Marker (Particle)
[SM]		Marker (Particle) at the end of the sentence
[A]		Adjective
[AN]		Adjectival Noun
[N]		Noun
⊟		Taped dialogues and drills (where ⊟ appears beside an example in a drill, only the example is recorded, not the drill itself.)

Unit I

Meeting People

SCOPE OF UNIT I

The main function of Unit I is INTRODUCTIONS, beginning with introducing yourself and then extending to include others, using the appropriate Japanese manner.

Lesson 1   covers how to introduce yourself, others, including your family, using appropriate greetings and the custom of bowing.

Lesson 2   presents daily greetings and how to start a conversation by making comments on the weather.

Lesson 3   gives pointers on expanding conversation after having introduced yourself and others and how to use and incorporate *aizuchi*—"enthusiastic listening" into your speech.

Lesson 4   describes how to apologize for serious mistakes—using "I'm sorry,"—as well as for minor breaches of etiquette—using "Excuse me."

1

Lesson 1

INTRODUCING YOURSELF AND OTHERS 1

DŌZO YOROSHIKU
"NICE TO MEET YOU"

Dialogue I

[Mr. Tanaka and Mr. Smith meet for the first time. They introduce themselves.]

Tanaka:　Hajimemashite.
　　　　　Tanaka desu.
Sumisu:　Hajimemashite.
　　　　　Sumisu desu.
Tanaka:　Dōzo yoroshiku.
Sumisu:　Kochira koso dōzo yoroshiku.

> Mr. Tanaka:　How do you do.
> 　　　　　　　I'm Tanaka.
> Mr. Smith:　How do you do.
> 　　　　　　I'm Smith.
> Mr. Tanaka:　Nice to meet you.
> Mr. Smith:　Nice to meet you, too.

Dialogue II

[Mr. Smith introduces Mr. Yamashita, his colleague to Mr. Tanaka at his (Mr. Smith's) office.]

Sumisu:　　　[To Mr. Tanaka]
　　　　　　　Tanaka-san, Yamashita desu.
　　　　　　　[To Mr. Yamashita]
　　　　　　　Mōbiru Sekiyu no Tanaka-san desu.
Tanaka:　　　[To Mr. Yamashita]
　　　　　　　Tanaka to mōshimasu. Dōzo yoroshiku.
Yamashita:　[To Mr. Tanaka]
　　　　　　　Yamashita to mōshimasu. Dōzo yoroshiku.

> Mr. Smith:　　　Mr. Tanaka, this is Mr. Yamashita.
> 　　　　　　　　This is Mr. Tanaka from Mobil.
> Mr. Tanaka:　　I'm Tanaka. [*Lit.* I'm called Tanaka.] Nice to meet you.
> Mr. Yamashita:　I'm Yamashita. [*Lit.* I'm called Yamashita.] Nice to meet you.

Vocabulary

Tanaka: Japanese surname
desu: is/am/are
Sumisu: Smith
Hajimemashite: How do you do.
Dōzo yoroshiku: Nice to meet you.

Yamashita: Japanese surname
Mōbiru Sekiyu: Mobil Oil
____ to mōshimasu: I'm ____ .
Kochira koso dōzo yoroshiku: Nice to meet you, too.

▦Dialogue III

[Mr. Tanaka introduces his wife to Mr. Smith of Esso.]

Tanaka: Sumisu-san, kanai desu.

        [To his wife] *Esso no Sumisu-san desu.*

Tanaka: Hajimemashite. Dōzo yoroshiku onegai
[okusan] itashimasu.

Sumisu: Kochira koso dōzo yoroshiku.

Mr. Tanaka:	Mr. Smith, (this is) my wife. (This is) Mr. Smith from Esso.
Mrs. Tanaka:	How do you do. I'm very pleased to meet you.
Mr. Smith:	Pleased to meet you, too.

I

田中　：はじめまして。　田中です。

スミス：はじめまして。　スミスです。

田中　：どうぞ　よろしく。

スミス：こちらこそ　どうぞ　よろしく。

II

スミス：田中さん、　山下です。　モービル石油の　田中さんです。

田中　：田中と　もうします。　どうぞ　よろしく。

山下　：山下と　もうします。　どうぞ　よろしく。

III

田中　　　　　：スミスさん、　かないです。

             エッソの　スミスさんです。

田中(おくさん)：はじめまして。　どうぞ　よろしく　おねがい　いたします。

スミス　　　　：こちらこそ　どうぞ　よろしく。

Vocabulary

kanai: (my) wife

Esso Sekiyu: Esso Oil

Okusan: (your/his) wife

Dōzo yoroshiku onegai itashimasu: I'm very pleased to meet you.

Grammar Note 1 — Introducing yourself

[Name] *desu.*

Tanaka desu.   I'm Tanaka.

a. **Desu**

When introducing yourself, add **desu** after your name.

Desu ''am/is/are'' preceded by a noun, is used to identify people or things.

Predicate*		
[Surname]	[Given Name]	*desu*
Tanaka	Ichirō	*desu*

''I'm Ichiro Tanaka.''

In both formal and informal situations, a Japanese uses a speaker's full name or surname only. In business situations, the surname only is usually used.

In Japanese, the surname always comes before the given name. When you introduce yourself, you can do it either in the Japanese or Western way. However, a Japanese may not know which is your surname. Therefore, for a Westerner, it is better to introduce himself/herself in the Western order; *i.e.,* given name then surname, to minimize confusion for the Japanese listener.

Examples

Tanaka desu.	''I'm (Mr./Ms.) Tanaka.''
Tanaka Ichirō desu.	''I'm (Mr.) Ichiro Tanaka.''
Tanaka Mariko desu.	''I'm (Ms.) Mariko Tanaka.''
Sumisu desu.	''I'm (Mr./Ms.) Smith.''
Jon Sumisu desu.	''I'm (Mr.) John Smith.''
Merī Sumisu desu.	''I'm (Ms.) Mary Smith.''

* Predicate

In this textbook we call the following ''Predicates'' in English.

English	1.	Be Verb + Noun	*e.g.*	am Smith
	2.	Be Verb + Adjective	*e.g.*	is expensive
	3.	Verb	*e.g.*	ate, is running

Therefore, the pattern **Tanaka Ichiro desu** shown in the example belongs to the first kind of Predicate.

b. In more formal situations, **to mōshimasu** is often used rather than **desu**.

Example

Tanaka <u>desu</u>.

↓

Tanaka <u>to mōshimasu</u>.

c. Any information can be eliminated when it is understood or clear from the context. For example, in the sentence **Tanaka desu**, ''I am Tanaka,'' **watashi wa** (''I'') is eliminated because in self-introduction, ''I'' is obvious.

d. Here are some expressions used when people meet for the first time:

Hajimemashite.	''How do you do.''
Dōzo yoroshiku.	''Nice to meet you.''
Kochira koso dōzo yoroshiku.	''Nice to meet you, too.''

Grammar Note 2 — Introducing others

[Name]-san desu. . . . . .for "non-in-group" person*
Tanaka-san desu.   "This is Mr./Ms. Tanaka."

[Name] desu.   . . . . for "in-group" person*
Tanaka desu.   "This is Mr./Ms. Tanaka."

[Relationship] desu. . . . . for one's family (in-group*)
Kanai desu.   "This is my wife."

*cf. Culture Note 3

a.   -san
San is a formal and honorific suffix added to one's surname, given name or full name. When you introduce "non-in-group*"people, say **X-san desu**, "This is Mr./Ms. X." In business situations, the surname plus **san** is used.

Examples
Tanaka-san desu.	"This is Mr./Ms. Tanaka."
Ichirō-san desu.**	"This is Ichiro."
Mariko-san desu.**	"This is Mariko."
Tanaka Ichirō-san desu.	"This is Mr. Ichiro Tanaka."
Tanaka Mariko-san desu.	"This is Ms. Mariko Tanaka."
Sumisu-san desu.	"This is Mr./Ms. Smith."
Jon Sumisu-san desu.	"This is Mr. John Smith."
Merī Sumisu-san desu.	"This is Ms. Mary Smith."

**Using the given name only is for casual situations.

b.   without -san
When you talk about yourself or your "in-group" members to "non-in-group" members (_e.g._, customers, strangers) do not add **san**, because it is slightly honorific and should not be used for your "in-group."

c.   -sen'sei
Here we introduce one more suffix similar to **san**. For teachers, medical doctors, politicians, and very prominent people, use the more respectful suffix — **sen'sei**, which originally meant "a person born before me."

d.   Introducing your family members
When a Japanese introduces his family members as his "in-group" members, he introduces them in terms of his relationship between them using the vocabulary below rather than referring to their names:

Vocabulary
kazoku	"(my) family"
shujin	"(my) husband"
kanai	"(my) wife"
kodomo (tachi)	"(my) child(ren)"
musuko	"(my) son"
musume	"(my) daughter"
ryōshin	"(my) parents"
chichi	"(my) father"
haha	"(my) mother"

e.   Additional— More about introducing your family members

[First name] *desu.*

Jēn desu.   "This is Jane."

[Relationship] *no* **[First name]** *desu.*

Kanai no Jēn desu.   "This is my wife, Jane."

When a Japanese introduces his/her family members, it is perfectly all right to use only the relationship word.
(*cf.* Grammar Note 2-d)

For those who want to mention their family members' first name, another way would be to use the same structure as in Grammar Note 3,
"_____*no*_____*desu.*"

Grammar Note 3 — Introducing yourself/others as a member of a group

[Group name] *no* **[Surname]** *desu.*

Mōbiru Sekiyu no Tanaka desu.   "I'm Tanaka from Mobil Oil."

[Group name] *no* **[Surname]**-*san desu.*

Esso Sekiyu no Sumisu-san desu.   "This is Mr. Smith from Esso Oil."

When a Japanese introduces himself or others in business situations, mentioning which group (*i.e.*, company, department, *etc.*) the person belongs to is important.

(*cf.* Culture Note 3)

Examples

Tōkyō Gin'kō no Takahashi desu.
   "I'm Takahashi from the Bank of Tokyo."

Tōkyō Gin'kō no Takahashi-san desu.
   "This is Mr. Takahashi from the Bank of Tokyo."

Eigyō no Yamada desu.
   "I'm Yamada from the sales department."

Drill 1   Introduce yourself and offer a greeting.

(1)	Tape:	*Hajimemashite. Abe desu.*
Mr. Abe You	You:	_____.
	Tape:	*Dōzo yoroshiku.*
	You:	_____.

(2) [This time you start first.]	You:	_____.
You Mr. Mizuno	Tape:	*Hajimemashite. Mizuno to mōshimasu.*
	You:	_____.
	Tape:	*Kochira koso dōzo yoroshiku.*

Drill 2   Listen to the self-introduction of the characters in this text. Listen to the difference in pronunciation and notice the difference in the way of writing.

(1)	*Tanaka Ichirō* Mr. Ichiro Tanaka	(2)	*Burūsu Howaito* Mr. Bruce White
(3)	*Jon Sumisu* Mr. John Smith	(4)	*Ōno Yuriko* Ms. Yuriko Ono
(5)	*Kyasarin Ton'puson* Ms. Catherine Thompson	(6)	*Han'su Shuwarutsu* Mr. Hans Schwartz
(7)	*Yamashita Yoshio* Mr. Yoshio Yamashita		

Drill 3   Introduce the following people:

1. as your "in-group" members first;
2. as "non-in-group" members next.

(1) Mr. Oishi   (2) Miss Mori   (3) Mrs. Ide
(4) Ms. Okuda (a teacher)   (5) Mr. Togo (a doctor)

Drill 4   Introduce the person indicated by the mark.

(1) Ms. Nakada	You: _____. Tape: *Dōzo yoroshiku.*
(2) Mr. Tanaka	You: _____. Tape: *Tanaka desu.* *Dōzo yoroshiku.*
(3) Mrs. Maetani	You: _____. Tape: *Hajimemashite. Maetani desu.* *Dōzo yoroshiku.*
(4) Mr. Kawasaki	You: _____. Tape: *Kawasaki desu.* *Dōzo yoroshiku.*
(5) Mrs. Nakamura	You: _____. Tape: *Hajimemashite. Nakamura desu.* *Dōzo yoroshiku.*

Drill 5   Introduce these people as your family members.

e.g.,   my husband   ⟶   *Shujin desu.*

(1) my wife   (2) my child(ren)   (3) my son   (4) my daughter
(5) my parents   (6) my father   (7) my mother

Drill 6   Introduce the people with their group name as your "non-in-group" member.

e.g.,

Mr. Tanaka
Mobil Oil   ⟶   *Mōbiru Sekiyu no Tanaka-san desu.*

(1) Mr. Smith Esso Oil	(2) Ms. Ono Mobil Oil
(3) Mr. Schwartz Bank of Tokyo	(4) Ms. Thompson Canadian Embassy *Kanada Taishikan*

Drill 7   Introduce yourself and your company and offer a greeting.

(1)	
Mr. Kato — You Sumitomo Trading Co.	Tape: *Hajimemashite. Sumitomo Shōji no Katō desu.* You: _____. Tape: *Dōzo yoroshiku onegaishimasu.* You: _____.
(2) [This time you start first.]	
You — Mr. Togo Mitsui Bank	You: _____. Tape: *Mitsui Gin'kō no Tōgō to mōshimasu.* You: _____. Tape: *Kochira koso dōzo yoroshiku.*

Drill 8   Listen to the characters of this textbook introducing their family members and spell out their names.

(1)   Mr. Tanaka

Mrs. Tanaka ⟶ _____

His daughter ⟶ _____

His son ⟶ _____

His daughter ⟶ _____

(2)   Mr. Smith

Mrs. Smith ⟶ _____

His son ⟶ _____

His daughter ⟶ _____

(3)   Mr. White

Mrs. White ⟶ _____

His daughter ⟶ _____

Drill 9   Show pictures of your family and introduce them.

Lesson 2

GREETINGS — HELLO AND GOOD-BYE

KON'NICHIWA
''HELLO''

📻 Dialogue

[Mr. Smith and Ms. Inoue meet at the tennis club. They regularly come to the club, but they aren't well acquainted.]

Sumisu: *Kon'nichiwa.*
Inoue: *Kon'nichiwa.*
Sumisu: *Ii ten'ki desu nē.*
Inoue: *Sō desu nē.*

      *   *   *

[After a day's practice, they part.]
Inoue: *Sore jā, osakini shitsurei shimasu.*
Sumisu: *Shitsurei shimasu.*

      *   *   *

Mr. Smith: Hello.
Ms. Inoue: Hello.
Mr. Smith: It's fine weather, isn't it?
Ms. Inoue: Yes, it is.

Ms. Inoue: Well then, [*Lit.* before you] good-bye.
Mr. Smith: Good-bye.

スミス：こんにちは。
井上　：こんにちは。
スミス：いい　てんきですねえ。
井上　：そうですねえ。

      *   *   *

井上　：それじゃあ、　おさきに　しつれいします。
スミス：しつれいします。

Vocabulary

kon'nichiwa: hello, good afternoon
ii: good, fine
ten'ki: weather
nē [SM]:   [Asking for agreement and exclamation]

Sō desu nē: [Agreement with exclamation to the previous statement]
sore jā: well then
osakini: *Lit.* before you
shitsurei shimasu: good-bye

Grammar Note 1 — Daily greetings

Japanese greet each other with a bow (*ojigi*) or a nod. (*cf.* Culture Note 1)

Expressions :   Daily greetings

–Responses–

L. 1   *Ohayō.*   "Good morning."

L. 2⎫
L. 3⎭ *Ohayō gozaimasu.*   "Good morning."

L. 1⎫
L. 2⎭ *Kon'nichiwa.** ··"Hello."   [Respond by repeating]

L. 3   *Kon'nichiwa.*   "Good afternoon."

L. 1⎫
L. 2⎭ *Kon'ban'wa.** "Hello."

L. 3   *Kon'ban'wa.*   "Good evening."

*__Kon'nichiwa__ and __kon'ban'wa__ are rarely used among family members.

L.1 = Speech Level 1
L.2 = Speech Level 2
L.3 = Speech Level 3 (*cf.* Culture Note 3)

Grammar Note 2 — Commenting on the weather I

[State of the weather] *desu nē* ↘.
Ii ten'ki desu nē.   "It's fine weather, isn't it?"

a.   After saying "good morning" or "good afternoon" *etc.,* Japanese usually mention the weather. (They do not say *Ogen'ki desu ka* "How are you?" unless it is after a long absence or the person has been sick.)

b.   *Ten'ki* means weather. *Ii ten'ki* means fine weather/day. Women often say *Ii o-ten'ki*, adding *o* for the sake of elegance.

c.   *Nē* ↘ [Exclamation/Agreement Marker]   "isn't it?"
The final *nē* ↘, a sentence marker coming at the end of a sentence, pronounced with falling intonation, asks for the listener's agreement to the comment, or shows a strong feeling. The response to this should also be followed by *nē* ↘. Thus, *So desu nē* ↘ "Yes, it is." (*Lit.* That's so, isn't it?) is said to give agreement with emphasis to the previous statement.

Expressions
Commenting on the weather (I)

–Responses–

L. 2   *Ii ten'ki desu nē.*
        "It's fine weather, isn't it?"

                                    Sō desu nē.
                                    "Yes, it is."

L. 2   *Iya na ten'ki desu nē.*
        "It's terrible weather, isn't it?"

Grammar Note 3 — Commenting on the weather II — Seasonal greetings

The Japanese language has a variety of words and expressions for each season. Appropriate greetings should be expressed for each seasonal occasion.

The weather expressions below are a few typical examples of these seasonal greetings. These expressions can be used instead of **Ii/Iyana ten'ki desu nē** "Good/Awful weather, isn't it?"

Expressions

fuyu "winter"	*Ichi-gatsu* "January" *Ni-gatsu* "February"	*Samui desu nē.* "It's cold, isn't it?"
haru "spring"	*San-gatsu* "March" *Shi-gatsu* "April" *Go-gatsu* "May"	*Atatakaku narimashita nē.* "It's gotten warm, hasn't it?"
natsu "summer"	*Roku-gatsu* "June" *Shichi-gatsu* "July" *Hachi-gatsu* "August"	*Atsuku narimashita nē.* "It's gotten hot, hasn't it?" *Mushimasu nē.* "It's humid, isn't it?" *(Mushi)atsui desu nē.* "It's hot (and humid) isn't it?"
aki "autumn"	*Ku-gatsu* "September" *Jū-gatsu* "October" *Jūichi-gatsu* "November"	*Suzushiku narimashita nē.* "It's gotten cool, hasn't it?" *Samuku narimashita nē.* "It's gotten cold, hasn't it."
fuyu "winter"	*Jūni-gatsu* "December"	*Samui desu nē.* "It's cold, isn't it?" –Response– *Sō desu nē.* "It sure is (has)!"

Vocabulary

samui	"cold"	*mushimasu←musu*	"to be humid"
atatakaku←atatakai	"warm"	*mushiatsui*	"hot and humid"
narimashita←naru	"has become/gotten"	*suzushiku←suzushii*	"cool"

Grammar Note 4 — Additional expressions

Greetings for persons you haven't seen for a while:

Expressions   –Responses–

Shibaraku } *desu nē.*   *Sō desu nē.*
Hisashiburi }   "It sure has!"
   "It's been a long time since
    I saw you last."

Sonogo ikaga desu ka.   *Okagesama de (gen'ki desu).*
   "How have you been since I   "Thank you for asking.
    saw you last."   (I've been well)."

Sonogo ogen'ki desu ka.   *Okagesama de (gen'ki desu).*
   "Have you been well since I   "Thank you for asking.
    saw you last?"   (I've been well)."

Example Dialogue

Tanaka: *Kon'nichi wa.*   "Good afternoon."
Sumisu: *Kon'nichi wa.*   "Good afternoon."
Tanaka: *Shibaraku desu nē.*   "It's been a long time
                                                        (since I saw you last)!"
Sumisu: *Sō desu nē.*   "It sure has!"
Tanaka: *Sonogo ikaga desu ka.*   "How have you been?"
Sumisu: *Okagesama de,*   "Oh, fine thank you.
              Tanaka-san wa   And how are you,
              ikaga desu ka.   Mr. Tanaka?"
Tanaka: *Okagesama de gen'ki desu.* "I'm fine (too), thank you."

Grammar Note 5 — Leave taking

a. **Sayōnara** "good-bye"
   Shitsurei shimasu "good-bye"
   These are the key farewell expressions which are shown in Diagram III in the chart
   on the next page. In Diagram III, there are two cases:
   (1)   is for non-business or less formal situations.
   (2)   is for business or more formal situations.

b. **Mata ashita:** "See you tomorrow."
   The expressions in Diagram III alone are sufficient for farewell, but the expressions
   in Diagram II add some modification to the farewell. Expressions in Diagram II
   precede those in Diagram III. The expressions in Diagram II alone will be acceptable
   for Levels 1 or 2.

c. **Jā** "well, then"
   Diagram I shows the "signal for breaking off or changing activities." This is used
   when people part from each other after some kind of involvement; for example, after
   finishing a conversation, when leaving a meeting, *etc.* This is also used just before
   changing the activity like *(Sore) jā, hajimemashō* "Well, then, let's start."

d. Possible combinations of Diagrams I, II, and III are:

I	*Sore jā.*	"Well, then..."
I ⇒ II	*Sore jā, mata raishū.*	"Well then, see you next week."
I ⇒ II ⇒ III	*Sore jā, mata raishū. Shitsurei shimasu.*	"Well then, see you next week. Good-bye."
II	*Mata raishū.*	"See you next week."
II ⇒ III	*Mata raishū. Shitsurei shimasu.*	"See you next week, good-bye."
II	*Shitsurei shimasu.*	"Good-bye."

e. ***Osaki ni*** "(I'm leaving) before you."

Osaki ni (in Diagram II) is often heard at work, at clubs, *etc.,* when a person leaves before his colleagues.

Observe the following examples:

Expressions: Leave taking

I.   Signal for breaking off or changing activities

L.1	*Jā* "Well then"
L.2	*Sore jā* "Well then"
L.3	*Sore dewa* "Well then"

II.   Modifier to III

L.1	*Mata*	"See you again."
	atode	"See you later."
	ashita	"See you tomorrow."
	raishū	"See you next week."
L.2	*getsu-yōbi*	"See you on Monday."
	jūgo-nichi	"See you on the 15th."
	Osakini	[*Lit.*] "Before you."

L.3	*Mata*	"See you again."
	nochihodo	"See you later."
	myōnichi	"See you tomorrow."
	raishū	"See you next week."
	getsu-yōbi	"See you on Monday."
	jūgo-nichi	"See you on the 15th."
	Osakini	[*Lit.*] "Before you."

III.   Key farewell expressions

(1)

L.1	*Sayonara* "Bye."
L.2	*Sayōnara* "Good-bye."
L.3	

[Non-business]

(2)

L.1	
L.2	*Shitsurei shimasu* "Good-bye."
L.3	*Shitsurei itashimasu* "Good-bye."

[Business/social, more formal]

Drill 1   Give the right greetings for the times of day.

e.g.	A: [To your friend] *Ohayō.* B: *Ohayō.*
(1)	Tape [Your superior] : *Ohayō.* You: _____.
(2)	You: [To your neighbor] _____. Tape: *Kon'nichiwa.*
(3)	Tape [Your neighbor]: *Kon'ban'wa.* You: _____.

Drill 2   Make small talk about the weather.

e.g.	A: *Ii ten'ki desu nē.* B: *Sō desu nē.*
(1)	You: _____. Tape: *Sō desu nē.*
(2)	Tape: *Iya na ten'ki desu nē.* You: _____.
(3)	You: _____. Tape: *Sō desu nē.*
(4) —In the morning—	You: [To your neighbor] _____. Tape: *Ohayō gozaimasu.* You: _____. Tape: *Sō desu nē.*
(5) —In the afternoon—	Tape [Your neighbor]: *Kon'nichiwa.* You: _____. Tape: *Ii ten'ki desu nē.* You: _____.

15

Drill 3   Give the right expression for the time and the season.

e.g., —In the morning in winter— It's cold, isn't it? Level 2	**A:** *Ohayō gozaimasu.* **B:** *Ohayō gozaimasu.* **A:** *Samui desu nē.* **B:** *Sō desu nē.*
(1) —In the afternoon in early spring— It's gotten warm, hasn't it? Level 2	Tape: *Kon'nichiwa.* You: _____ . Tape: *Atatakaku narimashita nē.* You: _____ .
(2) —In the afternoon in midsummer— It's hot and humid, isn't it? Level 2	You: _____ . Tape: *Kon'nichiwa.* You: _____ . Tape: *Sō desu nē.*
(3) —In the morning in early winter— It's gotten cold, hasn't it? Level 2	You: _____ . Tape: *Ohayō gozaimasu.* You: _____ . Tape: *Sō desu nē.*

Drill 4   Expand the expressions for saying farewell.

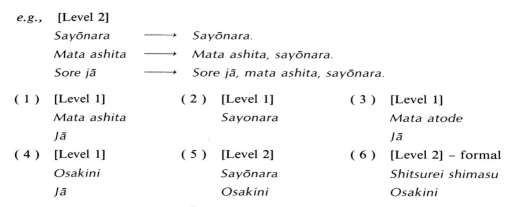

e.g.,   [Level 2]
Sayōnara   ⟶   Sayōnara.
Mata ashita   ⟶   Mata ashita, sayōnara.
Sore jā   ⟶   Sore jā, mata ashita, sayōnara.

(1)   [Level 1]   (2)   [Level 1]   (3)   [Level 1]
Mata ashita   Sayonara   Mata atode
Jā   Jā

(4)   [Level 1]   (5)   [Level 2]   (6)   [Level 2] – formal
Osakini   Sayōnara   Shitsurei shimasu
Jā   Osakini   Osakini

(7)   [Level 2] – formal   (8)   [Level 2] – formal   (9)   [Level 3] – formal
Shitsurei shimasu   *Shitsurei shimasu*   *Shitsurei itashimasu*
Mata raishū   *Osakini*   *Sore dewa*
Sore jā

Drill 5   What would you say in the following situations?

(1)   You are leaving the office before your colleague.

(2)   You and your colleague part. You will see each other tomorrow.

(3)   You say good-bye to your acquaintance.

(4)   You say good-bye to your teacher. Your next lesson is on Wednesday.

(5)   You say good-bye to your business customer after having dinner with him.

Lesson 3

INTRODUCING YOURSELF AND OTHERS 2
TALKING ABOUT YOURSELF

O-KUNI WA DOCHIRA DESU KA
"WHERE DO YOU COME FROM?"

Dialogue

[At a party, Mr. Smith introduces Mr. Tanaka to Ms. Marilyn Clark and Mr. Michael Brown.]

Sumisu:	[To Ms. Clark and Mr. Brown] *Kochira wa Tanaka-san desu.*
Tanaka:	[To Ms. Clark and Mr. Brown] *Hajimemashite.*
	Tanaka desu. Dōzo yoroshiku.
Sumisu:	[To Mr. Tanaka] *Kochira wa Maririn-san desu.*
Kurāku:	*Hajimemashite. Maririn Kurāku desu.*
Sumisu:	[To Mr. Tanaka] *Kochira wa Maikeru-san desu.*
Buraun:	[To Mr. Tanaka] *Maikeru Buraun desu. Dōzo yoroshiku.*

       *   *   *

Tanaka:	*Maririn-san wa o-kuni wa dochira desu ka.*
Kurāku:	*Ōsutoraria desu.*
Tanaka:	*Buraun-san wa dochira desu ka.*
Buraun:	*Watashi mo Ōsutoraria desu.*
Tanaka:	*Ā, Buraun-san mo desu ka.*
Buraun:	*Ē.*

Mr. Smith:	This is Mr. Tanaka.
Mr. Tanaka:	How do you do.
	I'm Tanaka. Nice to meet you.
Mr. Smith:	This is Marilyn.
Ms. Clark:	How do you do. I'm Marilyn Clark.
Mr. Smith:	This is Michael.
Mr. Brown:	I'm Michael Brown. Nice to meet you.

       *   *   *

Mr. Tanaka:	Marilyn, where do you come from?
	[*Lit.* Marilyn, as for your country,
	where (do you come from)?]
Ms. Clark:	(I'm from) Australia.

Vocabulary

kochira: this person, this side
wa [M]: [Contrast]
Maririn: Marilyn
Kurāku: Clark
Maikeru: Michael
Buraun: Brown

o-kuni: (your/his/her) country
Ōsutoraria: Australia
mo [M]: [Inclusion] also
ā: oh
ē: yes

Mr. Tanaka: Mr. Brown, where do you come from?
[*Lit.* Mr. Brown, (as for your country), where (do you come from)?]
Mr. Brown: I'm also from Australia.
Mr. Tanaka: Oh, you're also from Australia.
Mr. Brown: That's right.

* * *

Tanaka: *Buraun-san wa o-shigoto wa nan desu ka.*
Buraun: *Tōkyō Gin'kō ni tsutomete imasu.*
  Tanaka-san wa.
Tanaka: *Watashi wa Mōbiru Sekiyu ni tsutomete imasu.*
Buraun: *Mōbiru desu ka.*
Tanaka: *Maririn-san wa o-shigoto wa nan desu ka.*
Kurāku: *Watashi wa ei-go no kyōshi desu.*
Tanaka: *Ei-go no sen'sei desu ka.*

* * *

Mr. Tanaka: Mr. Brown, what do you do?
[*Lit.* Mr. Brown, as for your job, what do you do?]
Mr. Brown: I work for the Bank of Tokyo.
How about you, Mr. Tanaka?
Mr. Tanaka: I work for Mobil Oil.
Mr. Brown: Oh, (you're with) Mobil Oil.
Mr. Tanaka: Marilyn, what do you do? [*Lit.* Marilyn, as for your job, what is it?]
Ms. Clark: (I'm) an English teacher.
Mr. Tanaka: Oh, you're an English teacher.

スミス　：こちらは　田中さんです。
田中　　：はじめまして。　田中です。　どうぞ　よろしく。
スミス　：こちらは　マリリンさんです。
クラーク：はじめまして。　マリリン・クラークです。
スミス　：こちらは　マイケルさんです。
ブラウン：マイケル・ブラウンです。　どうぞ　よろしく。

Vocabulary

o-shigoto: (your/his/her) job
nan: what
Tōkyō Gin'kō: the Bank of Tokyo
—ni tsutomete imasu: work for—
Mōbiru: Mobil

sō: so
ei-go: the English language
kyōshi: teacher [refers only to you]
sen'sei: teacher [refers only to someone else]

19

＊　　＊　　＊

田中　　　：マリリンさんは　おくには　どちらですか。
たなか

クラーク：オーストラリアです。

田中　　　：ブラウンさんは　どちらですか。

ブラウン：わたしも　オーストラリアです。

田中　　　：ああ、　ブラウンさんもですか。

ブラウン：ええ。

＊　　＊　　＊

田中　　　：ブラウンさんは　おしごとは　なんですか。

ブラウン：東京銀行に　つとめています。　田中さんは。
とうきょうぎんこう

田中　　　：わたしは　モービル石油に　つとめています。
せきゆ

ブラウン：モービルですか。

田中　　　：マリリンさんは　おしごとは　なんですか。

クラーク：わたしは　えいごの　きょうしです。

田中　　　：えいごの　せんせいですか。

Grammar Note 1 — Introducing others individually

[Person to be introduced] *wa* **[Name]-*san desu*.**

<u>Kochira</u> wa <u>Tanaka</u>-san desu.　　　''This is Mr./Ms. Tanaka.''

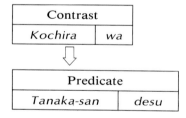

a.　***Kochira***　　''this person''
　　Kochira literally means ''this side,'' and is used to indicate direction, place or person.

b.　***Wa***　　[Contrast Marker]
　　It is almost impossible to give an English equivalent to this word. Here, we call ***wa*** a marker which functions to make the preceding noun contrast with, or be set apart from, something (*or* someone) else.

In Lesson 1, you learned that ***watashi wa*** ''I'' is eliminated when introducing yourself because any information understood or clear from the context is eliminated. Here, when introducing two or more people one by one, gesture toward the one you are introducing and start by saying ***Kochira wa*** ''This person'' and say the person's name, ***Tanaka-san desu***.

Grammar Note 2 — Asking or telling others about your job, country, residence, hobby, *etc.*

[Job, country, *etc.*, **as topic]** *wa* **[Actual information]** *desu.*

Kuni wa *America* desu.   "I'm from the U.S. [*Lit.* As for my country, it's the U.S.]"

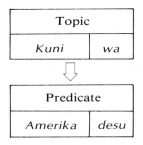

Topic	
Kuni	*wa*

⇩

Predicate	
Amerika	*desu*

a. **Wa**   [Topic Marker]

The marker **wa** also works as a topic marker. The noun (*or* noun phrase) followed by **wa** is the "topic" of a statement or question. The words following **wa** give information on the topic.

Examples

Uchi wa Hiroo desu.	"I live in Hiro. [*Lit.* As for my house, it's Hiro.]"
Shumi wa chesu desu.	"My hobby is chess. [*Lit.* As for my hobby, it's chess.]"
Kuni wa Ōsutoraria desu.	"I'm from Australia. [*Lit.* As for my country, it's Australia.]"
Shigoto wa Mōbiru ni tsutomete imasu.	"I work for Mobil. [*Lit.* As for my job, I work for Mobil.]"

b. Questions

[Interrogative Pronoun] *desu ka* ↗.

Dochira ⎫
Doko   ⎬ *desu ka.*   "Where is it?"

Nan   *desu ka.*   "What is it?"

Ka is a question marker added to the end of a sentence with rising intonation.

Dochira, an interrogative pronoun, means "which direction, which place or where," and has polite nuance.

Doko, an interrogative pronoun, means "where."

Nan, an interrogative pronoun, means "what."

c. Series of honorific and neutral words

O-kuni "your (*or* his/her) country" [Honorific]

Kuni "my (*or* his/her) country" [Neutral]

O in **o-kuni** is an honorific prefix.

When you talk about job, hobby, residence or nationality:

(1)   use "honorific" words from the list below when talking to or asking about

    i)   the listener

    ii)   a person who is a member of the listener's "in-group" and a member of the speaker's "non-in-group" at the same time; *e.g.*, the listener's family or colleagues.

(2)   use "neutral" words when discussing or asking about
    i)   yourself (the speaker)
    ii)   a third person who is **not** included in (1) ii).

	[Neutral]	[Honorific]	[Question Forms]
Job	*shigoto*	*o-shigoto*	*nan desu ka* [Neutral & Honorific]
Hobby	*shumi*	*(go-)shumi*	*nan desu ka* [Neutral & Honorific]
Residence	*uchi*	*otaku*	*doko desu ka* [Neutral] *dochira desu ka* [Honorific]
Nationality	*kuni*	*o-kuni*	*doko desu ka* [Neutral] *dochira desu ka* [Honorific]

Examples

A: *Otaku wa dochira desu ka.*   "Where do you live?
                                       [*Lit*. As for your residence, where is it?]"
B: *Shibuya desu.*   "I live in Shibuya. [*Lit*. It's Shibuya.]"

A: *Go-shumi wa nan desu ka.*   "What is your hobby?"
                                       [*Lit*. As for your hobby, what is it?]"
B: *Tenisu desu.*   "It's tennis."

d.   Telling someone about your occupation
Here we introduce two ways to tell someone about your occupation.

(1)   *(Shigoto wa)* **[Organization]** *ni tsutomete imasu.*
           Mōbiru Sekiyu ni tsutomete imasu.   "I work for Mobil Oil."

(2)   *(Shigoto wa)* **[Profession]** *desu.*
           Ben'goshi desu.   "I'm a lawyer."

The pattern (1) is very widely used among Japanese rather than telling what your specific occupation is because it is important for them to say which group they belong to.

Vocabulary

a.   Job

For vocabulary concerning occupations I, apply the same rule as in Grammar Note 2-c.

Job		*Shigoto*	*O-shigoto*
		[Neutral]	[Honorific]
I	teacher	*kyōshi*	*sen'sei*
	doctor	*isha*	*o-isha-san*
	lawyer	*ben'goshi*	*ben'goshi-san*
	student	*gakusei*	*gakusei-san*
II	company employee	*kaishain*	—
	bank employee	*gin'kōin*	—
	engineer	*en'jinia*	—
	housewife	*shufu*	—

b.   Countries

Country	*Kuni*
Japan	*Nihon*
U.S.A.	*Amerika*
U.K.	*Eikoku, Igirisu*
Canada	*Kanada*
Australia	*Ōsutoraria*
France	*Furan'su*
Germany	*Doitsu*
Spain	*Supein*
Italy	*Itaria*
Korea	*Kan'koku*
China	*Chūgoku*
The Philippines	*Firipin*
Indonesia	*In'doneshia*
India	*In'do*
U.S.S.R.	*Soren*

c.   Hobbies

Hobby	*Shumi*
sports	*supōtsu*
squash	*sukasshu*
tennis	*tenisu*
golf	*gorufu*
jogging	*joggin'gu*
sailing	*yotto*
ski	*sukī*
swimming	*suiei, oyogu koto*
fishing	*tsuri*
mountain climbing	*yama (nobori)*
reading	*dokusho*
gardening	*niwa ijiri*
photography	*shashin*
travelling	*ryokō*
cooking	*ryōri*

Grammar Note 3 — Having more than two *wa*'s in one sentence

[Person] *wa*, [Job/Nationality/Residence/Hobby] *wa*, · · · , —————— *desu*.

<u>*Watashi*</u> *wa,* <u>*kuni*</u> *wa, Amerika desu.*   "I'm from the U.S. [*Lit.* As for me, as for my country, it's the U.S.]"

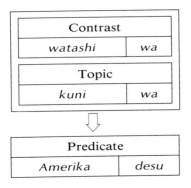

You can have many topics or as many topics with contrasting nuance as you need in one sentence. (See the first sentence in the example.)

From the second sentence on, the information already understood is eliminated as shown below:

Examples

    Watashi wa uchi wa Roppon'gi desu.   "I live in Roppongi.
                      [*Lit.* As for me, as for my house, it's in Roppongi.]"

    Ton'puson-san wa Shibuya desu.   "Ms. Thompson lives in Shibuya.
                      [*Lit.* As for Ms. Thompson, it's in Shibuya.]"

    Howaito-san wa Minami Azabu desu.   "Mr. White lives in Minami Azabu.
                      [*Lit.* As for Mr. White, it's in Minami Azabu.]"

    Maririn-san wa o-kuni wa dochira desu ka.   "Where do you come from,
                                            Marilyn?"

When asking the listener about himself/herself, Japanese normally do not use the pronoun **anata** which corresponds to English "you." Instead, the second person's
(sur)name plus **san** is used.

Grammar Note 4 — *Mo* [Inclusion Marker] "also"

[Person] *mo* **[Actual information]** *desu.*
<u>*Watashi*</u> *mo* <u>*Ōsutoraria*</u> *desu.*   "I'm also from Australia."

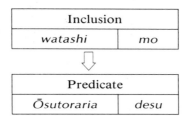

The marker **mo** after a noun corresponds to "also" or "too." It indicates that the same
question or statement is being repeated in reference to someone or something else.

Examples
    Tanaka-san wa shumi wa chesu desu.   "Mr. Tanaka's hobby is chess.
                                        [*Lit.* As for Mr. Tanaka, as for his
                                          hobby, it's chess.]"
    Takahashi-san mo chesu desu.   "Mr. Takahashi's hobby is also chess.
                                            [*Lit.* Also Mr. Takahashi, it's chess.]"

Grammar Note 5 — *Aizuchi* or "Enthusiastic listening" sign

(Ā,) **[Key word]** *desu ka* ↘.
(Ā,) <u>*Buraun-san mo Ōsutoraria*</u> *desu ka* ↘.   "Oh, you're also from Australia,
                                                  Mr. Brown."

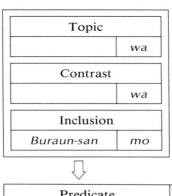

Aizuchi is one of the most common characteristics in the Japanese language. To encourage the conversation to continue or simply to show interest in the conversation, Japanese often repeat the important part of the conversation partner's answer or statement, or say *(Ā,) sō desu ka* ↘ "Oh, is that right?", *ē* or *hai* "yes", or nod enthusiastically. This is a kind of pleasantry in carrying on the conversation smoothly. You may feel interrupted as you talk, but Japanese feel uneasy when they do not hear *aizuchi.* In this textbook we will call it an "Enthusiastic Listening" sign.

The following are two types of *aizuchi*:

(1) *(Ā,)* [key word] *desu kā* ↘ .

Repeat a key word, especially if it is something impressive, or familiar. Also when the speaker has said something unexpected, or expected, the key word can be repeated.

(2) *(Ā,) sō desu kā* ↘ .

Use this expression when there is no particular key word to single out for repetition. This phrase also provides variation from the pattern of repeating key words.

Examples

A:	*Uchi wa <u>Shirogane</u> desu.*	"I live in Shirogane."
B:	*<u>Shirogane</u> desu ka.*	"Oh, (you live in) Shirogane!
	Watashi mo desu.	I live there, too."
A:	*Go-shumi wa nan desu ka.*	"What's your hobby?
B:	*<u>Tsuri</u> desu.*	"Fishing."
A:	*Ā, <u>tsuri</u> desu ka.*	"Oh, fishing!"
B:	*Ē. A-san wa nan desu ka.*	"Right. What's your hobby, Mr. A?"
A:	*<u>Watashi</u> mo tsuri desu.*	"I like fishing, too."
B:	*Ā, <u>A-san</u> mo desu ka.*	"Oh, you, too, Mr. A."

Underlined parts are the key words.

25

Drill 1   Introduce the people indicated with the mark ▼.

e.g.		
You ▼ Mr. Tanaka	A:	*Kochira wa Tanaka-san desu.*
	B:	*Tanaka desu.*
(1) You ▼ Mr. Takahashi	You:	_____.
	Tape:	*Takahashi desu.*
		Dōzo yoroshiku.
(2) You ▼ Mr. Suzuki	You:	_____.
	Tape:	*Dōzo yoroshiku.*
(3) You ▼ Ms. Nakada	You:	_____.
	Tape:	*Nakada desu. Dōzo yoroshiku.*

Drill 2   Substitute the underlined part.

1. *Kuni wa A̲o̲y̲a̲m̲a̲* *Amerika desu.*

   (1)   *Nihon*　　　　(2)   *Kanada*　　　　(3)   *Firipin*
   (4)   *Kan'koku*　　　(5)   *Chūgoku*　　　(6)   *Furan'su*

2. *Uchi wa A̲o̲y̲a̲m̲a̲ desu.*

   (1)   *Shibuya*　　(2)   *Roppon'gi*　　(3)   *Minami Azabu*　　(4)   *Ogikubo*

3. *Shumi wa c̲h̲e̲s̲u̲ desu.*

   (1)   *gorufu*　　(2)   *dokusho*　　(3)   *ryokō*　　(4)   *tsuri*

4. *Shigoto wa E̲s̲s̲o̲ ni tsutomete imasu.*

   (1)   *gin'kō*　　　　　　　　(2)   *sekiyu-gaisha*
   (3)   *shōsha*　　　　　　　　　　　　"oil company"
   　　"large trading company"

Drill 3   Make questions and answers.

　　e.g.,   job   ⟶   *O-shigoto wa nan desu ka.*
　　　　　　　　　　　Gin'kōin desu.

   (1)   hobby　　(2)   residence　　(3)   country　　(4)   job

Drill 4   Talk about each person's job, nationality, residence and hobby.

e.g.

	Job	Nationality	Residence	Hobby
White	Mobil Oil	U.S.A.	Minami Azabu	Tennis

Howaito-san wa (shigoto wa) Mōbiru Sekiyu ni tsutomete imasu.

Kuni wa Amerika desu.

Uchi wa Minami Azabu desu.

Shumi wa tenisu desu.

(1)

Thompson	Canadian Embassy	Canada	Shibuya	Bird Watching

(2)

Schwartz	Bank of Tokyo	Germany	Yoyogi	Personal computer

(3)

Clark	English Teacher	Australia	Aoyama	Tennis and photography

Drill 5   Talk about these people's jobs, nationalities, *etc.,* using **mo** if necessary.

	Job	Nationality	Residence	Hobby
Ms. Ford	Mobil	U.S.A.	Minami Azabu	tennis
Mr. White	Mobil	U.S.A.	Minami Azabu	tennis
Mr. Moore	Mobil	U.S.A.	Minami Azabu	tennis

e.g., Jobs ⟶ *Fōdo-san wa (shigoto wa) Mōbiru ni tsutomete imasu.*

Howaito-san mo Mōbiru ni tsutomete imasu.

Mūa-san mo Mōbiru ni tsutomete imasu.

(1)   Nationality   (2)   Residence   (3)   Hobby

Drill 6   Fill in the blank with your personal information. Talk about job, nationality, *etc.*, using **wa** and **mo**.

	Job	Nationality	Residence	Hobby
You				
White	Mobil	U.S.A.	Minami Azabu	tennis
James	I.B.M.	U.S.A.	Shibuya	tennis
Williams	I.B.M.	U.K.	Shibuya	bird watching

e.g., Nationalities ⟶ *Watashi wa kuni wa Amerika desu.*
Howaito-san mo Amerika desu.
Jēmuzu-san mo Amerika desu.
Uiriamuzu-san wa Eikoku desu.

(1)   Job   (2)   Residence   (3)   Hobby

Drill 7   Ask your conversation partner about his/her nationality and so on.

e.g.,   Ask Mr. Smith his hobby.⟶ *Sumisu-san wa go-shumi wa nan desu ka.*

(1)   Ask Mr. White his nationality.
(2)   Ask Ms. Thompson where she lives.
(3)   Ask Ms. Sachie Fujii about her job.

Drill 8   Give *Aizuchi* "Enthusiastic Listening" to the underlined part.

e.g.,   Kuni wa Amerika desu. ⟶ Ā, Amerika desu ka.

(1)   *Mōbiru ni tsutomete imasu.*
(2)   *Isha desu.*
(3)   *Nihon-go* "Japanese language" *no kyōshi desu.*
(4)   *Maririn-san wa o-kuni wa Ōsutoraria desu.*
(5)   *Maririn-san wa o-kuni wa Ōsutoraria desu.*
(6)   *Maririn-san wa o-kuni wa Ōsutoraria desu.*
(7)   *Buraun-san mo Ōsutoraria desu.*
(8)   *Buraun-san mo Ōsutoraria desu.*

Drill 9 Complete the following, using the dialogue as a model.

```
( 1 )  Tape:  Kochira wa Inoue-san desu. Kochira wa Sasaki-san desu.
       You:   _____ .
       You:   [Ask Ms. Inoue where she lives.] _____ .
       Tape:  Den'en'chōfu desu.
       You:   [EL]* _____ .
       Tape:  Ē.
       You:   [Ask Mr. Sasaki where he lives.] _____ .
       Tape:  Kamakura desu.
       You:   [EL] _____ .
       Tape:  Ē. Anata** wa dochira desu ka.
       You:   _____ .
       Tape:  [EL] Ā, sō desu ka.
       You:   _____ .
       *[EL] = Enthusiastic Listening, Aizuchi.
       **Anata = In this drill anata is used because the name of the student is not known.
```

```
( 2 )  Tape:  Kochira wa Howaito-san desu. Kochira wa Sumisu-san desu.
       You:   _____ .
       You:   [Ask Mr. White where he comes from.] _____ .
       Tape:  Amerika desu.
       You:   [EL] _____ .
       Tape:  Ē.
       You:   [Ask Mr. Smith where he comes from.] _____ .
       Tape:  Amerika desu. Anata wa o-kuni wa dochira desu ka.
       You:   _____ .
       Tape:  Ā, sō desu ka.
       You:   [Ask Mr. White what he does.] _____ .
       Tape:  Esso ni tsutomete imasu.
       You:   [EL] _____ .
       Tape:  Ē. Anata wa o-shigoto wa nan desu ka.
       You:   _____ .
       Tape:  Ā, sō desu ka.
       You:   _____ .
```

— At the same party —

(3) Tape: *Kochira wa Dagurasu-san no okusan no Rūsu-san desu.*

Kochira wa Maririn-san desu.

You: _____.

You: [Ask Ruth where she lives.] _____.

Tape: *Aoyama desu.*

You: [EL] _____.

Tape: *Ē.*

You: [Ask Marilyn where she lives.] _____.

Tape: *Watashi mo Aoyama desu.*

You: [EL] _____.

Tape: *Ē, anata wa dochira desu ka.*

You: _____.

Tape: *Ā, sō desu ka.*

You: [Ask Marilyn what she does.] _____.

Tape: *Ei-go no kyōshi desu.*

You: [EL] _____.

Tape: *Ē.*

You: [Ask Ruth what she does.] _____.

Tape: *(Watashi wa) shufu desu.*

You: [EL] _____.

Lesson 4

EXPRESSING APOLOGIES

DŌMO SUMIMASEN
"I AM VERY SORRY"

Dialogue I

[At a party, Mr. Tanaka introduces Mr. Wong to Mr. Smith.]

Tanaka: Sumisu-san, kochira wa Wan-san desu.
Wan: Wan desu. Dōzo yoroshiku.
Sumisu: Sumisu desu. Dōzo yoroshiku.
Wan-san wa o-kuni wa Chūgoku desu ka.
Wan: Iie. Amerika desu.
Sumisu: A, Amerika desu ka. Dōmo sumimasen.
Wan: Iie.

No, I'm from the States.

Mr. Tanaka:	Mr. Smith, this is Mr. Wong.
Mr. Wong:	I'm Wong. Nice to meet you.
Mr. Smith:	I'm Smith. Nice to meet you.
	Are you from China?
	[*Lit.* As for your country, is it China?]
Mr. Wong:	No, I'm from the States.
Mr. Smith:	Oh, (you are) from the States. Excuse me.
Mr. Wong:	That's all right.

Dialogue II

– *riin . . . riin . . . riin . . .* –
[Mrs. Smith answers the phone at home.]

Sumisu: Moshimoshi . . .
Nihon-jin: Yamada-san no otaku desu ka.
Sumisu: Iie, chigaimasu kedo . . .
Nihon-jin: A, dōmo sumimasen.
Sumisu: Iie.

Vocabulary

Wan: Chinese surname
Chūgoku: China
moshimoshi: hello [usually on the phone]
Yamada: Japanese surname

otaku: residence
Iie: No, that's all right.
chigaimasu: (that's) wrong
dōmo sumimasen: I'm sorry

31

– Ring . . . ring . . . –

Mrs. Smith:	Hello.
Japanese:	Is this the Yamada residence?
Mrs. Smith:	No, I'm sorry, you've got the wrong number.
	[*Lit.* No, (the number) is wrong . . .]
Japanese:	Oh, I'm very sorry.
Mrs. Smith:	That's all right.

I

田中　：スミスさん、　こちらは　ワンさんです。
たなか

ワン　：ワンです。　どうぞ　よろしく。

スミス：スミスです。　どうぞ　よろしく。

　　　　ワンさんは　おくには　中国ですか。
　　　　　　　　　　　　　　ちゅうごく

ワン　：いいえ。　アメリカです。

スミス：あ、　アメリカですか。　どうも　すみません。

ワン　：いいえ。

II

　　　　―リーン、リーン―

スミス：もしもし…

日本人：山田さんの　おたくですか。
にほんじん　やまだ

スミス：いいえ、　ちがいますけど…

日本人：あ、　どうも　すみません。

スミス：いいえ。

Grammar Note 1 — Yes/No question

You have seen two ways of using *ka*, a sentence marker:

    i)   WH question (*cf*. Lesson 3, Grammar Note 2)
        O-kuni wa dochira desu ka ↗.   "Where do you come from?"

    ii) Enthusiastic Listening (*cf*. Lesson 3, Grammar Note 5)
        Ā, sō desu ka ↘.   "Oh, is that right?"

Here we introduce another type of question using *ka*.

    iii) Yes/No question (*or* confirmation)
        O-kuni wa Amerika desu ka ↗.   "Is your country the U.S.?"

Grammar Note 2 — Answering yes/no questions

Interjective	Predicate	
Ē/Hai,	Amerika ↓ sō	desu

"Yes, it's the U.S."
"Yes, it is."

Interjective	Predicate	
Iie,	Amerika ↓ sō	ja arimasen

"No, it isn't the U.S."
"No, it isn't."

a. **Ē/Hai** "Yes", **Iie** "No"

Answers to yes/no questions begin with **Ē/Hai** "Yes" or **Iie** "No". **Ē** and **Hai** are both formal, yet the formality of **Hai** is higher than that of **Ē**.

b. **··· ja arimasen**

The negative form of **[Noun]** **desu** is **[Noun]** **ja arimasen.**

Examples

Amerika desu.	⟷	Amerika ja arimasen.
"It's the U.S."		"It isn't the U.S."
Sumisu desu.	⟷	Sumisu ja arimasen.
"I'm Smith."		"I'm not Smith."

c. **Chigaimasu** "That's wrong."

This could be used instead of **[Noun]** **ja arimasen**, but this has a definite negative tone.

d. **Kedo** ··· "— but ···"

Japanese tend not to finish negative sentences with a full stop. Instead they add **kedo** or **ga** "but" at the end of the sentence to avoid sounding totally negative or discouraging.

Examples

[on the phone]

A: Moshimoshi, Sumisu-san desu ka. "Hello, is this Mr. Smith?"

B: Iie, {Sumisu ja arimasen / chigaimasu} kedo ··· "No, this is not Smith ···"

A: Otaku wa Aoyama desu ka. "Do you live in Aoyama?"

B: Iie, {Aoyama ja arimasen / chigaimasu} kedo ··· "No, I don't live in Aoyama but ···"

Grammar Note 3 — Apologizing

When you make a rather serious mistake, apologize with the following expressions. Choose the right level according to the relative relationship between you and the person to whom you are apologizing.

There are, of course, other ways to express apologies, but the most significant and simplest ways are introduced for each level.

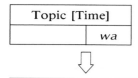

	Apologizing for accidents or unavoidable circumstances	Meaning	Acknowledging
	in the non-past		
L.1 L.2 L.3	Gomen(nasai) (Dōmo) su(m)imasen (Dōmo) mōshiwake gozaimasen	I'm sorry.	L.1 Uun L.2/3 Iie "Don't mention it."
	in the past		
L.1 L.2 L.3	Gomen(nasai) (Dōmo) su(m)imasen deshita (Dōmo) mōshiwake gozaimasen deshita	I'm sorry (for what I have done).	L.1 Uun L.2/3 Iie "Don't mention it."

a.   *(Dōmo) sumimasen.*   "I'm sorry."

　　　　　　　　　vs.

** *(Dōmo) sumimasen deshita.*   "I'm sorry (for what I have done)."**

"Past" tense in this textbook mainly covers the past tense as used in English grammar, and "Non-past" tense roughly covers the rest.   One example of how to use the "Non-past" and "Past" tenses is shown below.

While you are in another person's house, if you drop and break something, you immediately say *A, dōmo sumimasen* "Oh, I'm sorry (that I have just broken it)." Later, when you leave, say *Dōmo sumimasen deshita* "I'm sorry (that I broke it)." Apologizing twice for the same thing is not unusual for Japanese people.

b.   *Dōmo* · · ·

You may often hear this unfinished phrase. *Dōmo* sometimes is a part of *Dōmo sumimasen, Dōmo arigatō* "Thank you" (*cf.* Lesson 5), *etc.*, and can have variety in nuance.

c.   [For what you are apologizing] *wa* · · ·

Sometimes, time expressions followed by the Topic Marker *wa,* for example, *sakihodo wa* "earlier today," *kyō wa* "today" or *kinō wa* "yesterday," may precede the apology.

d.   *Iie*　　"Don't mention it ."

Iie literally means "no," and *Uun* is a casual equivalent of *Iie.* You may also hear *Hai* "certainly [*Lit.* Yes.]" to acknowledge the apology.

e. *Dōitashimashite* "Don't mention it."

You may hear **Iie**, **dōitashimashite**, "Don't mention it," which is a more formal equivalent of **Hai**. This is not on the list, because it often sounds rather inappropriate when it is not said exactly when it is expected. This politely indicates that you were hurt or offended but it is all right.

Examples
[Level 1]

Woman A:	*Gomen nasai.*	"I'm sorry."
Woman/Man B:	*Uun.*	"O.K."

Man A:	*A, gomen.*	"Oh, I'm sorry."
Woman/Man B:	*Uun, daijōbu.*	"O.K., it's all right."

[Level 2]

A:	*Dōmo sumimasen.*	"I'm sorry."
B:	*Iie.*	"Don't mention it."

A:	*Kinō wa dōmo sumimasen deshita.*	"I'm sorry (for what I did yesterday)."
B:	*Iie.*	"Don't mention it."

[Level 3]

A:	*Dōmo mōshiwake gozaimasen.*	"I'm terribly sorry."
B:	*Iie.*	"Don't mention it."

Grammar Note 4 — More usage of *no*

[Name]-*san no otaku desu ka.*
Tanaka-san no otaku desu ka. "Is this the Tanaka residence?"

X *no* Y
Using this pattern you have learned the following usages so far:

i) **[Company name]** *no* **[Surname]**
    Mōbiru no Tanaka "Tanaka from Mobil." (Lesson 1)

ii) **[Relationship]** *no* **[Name]**
    kanai no Jēn "Jane, my wife." (Lesson 1)

The new usage is:
iii) **[X]** *no* **[Y]** "X's Y"

Examples

Sumisu-san no otaku	"the Smith residence"
Sumisu-san no ofisu	"Mr. Smith's office"
Sumisu-san no o-kuni	"Mr. Smith's country"
Okusan no go-shumi	"your wife's hobby"
Sumisu-san no otaku desu ka.	"Is this the Smith residence?"
Sumisu-san no otaku wa dochira desuka.	"Where is Mr. Smith's house?"

Drill 1   Make yes/no questions.

> e.g.,   *Kan'koku desu.* ⟶ *Kan'koku desu ka.*

(1) *Chūgoku desu.*   (2) *Furan'su desu.*   (3) *Ogawa-san desu.*

(4) *Ōkawa-san desu.*   (5) *Samui desu.*   (6) *Atsui desu.*

Drill 2   Confirm the underlined parts.

> e.g.,   *Kuni wa Kan'koku desu.* ⟶ *Kan'koku desu ka.*

(1) *Kuni wa Ōsutoraria desu.*   (2) *Watashi wa Ōkawa desu.*

(3) *Mōbiru no Howaito desu.*   (4) *Mōbiru no Howaito desu.*

(5) *Mōbiru no Howaito desu.*   (6) *Samui desu.*

Drill 3   Answer.

> e.g.,   *Yamada-san desu ka. (Ē)* ⟶ *Ē, Yamada desu.*
>
> (Iie) ⟶ *Iie, Yamada ja arimasen kedo...*

(1) *O-kuni wa Ōsutoria desu ka.   (Ē)*

(2) *Go-shumi wa gorufu desu ka.   (Iie)*

(3) *Otaku wa Tōkyō desu ka.   (Iie)*

(4) *O-shigoto wa ei-go no sen'sei desu ka.   (Ē)*

Drill 4   What would you say if...

(1) —You were late for a business meeting—
You: [Apologize] _____ .   Tape: *Iie.*

(2) —You entered the home of your Japanese acquaintance without taking off your shoes— *
 Tape: *Anō...kutsu "shoes" wa...*   You: [Apologize] _____ .   Tape: *Iie.*

(3) Continued from (2)

—You spilled tea on the *tatami* [floor]—

You: [Apologize] _____ .

Tape: *A, iie. Daijōbu desu ka.* "Are you all right?"

You: [Say you're all right and apologize again.]

_____ .

(4) —You visited another Japanese acquaintance.

You spilled soup on the pretty *zabuton* [cushion]—

You: [Apologize] _____ .

Tape: *A, iie. Daijōbu desu ka.*

You: [Say you're all right and apologize again.]

_____ .

—After the cushion has been cleaned—

You: [Apologize for the accident]

_____ .

Tape: *Iie.*

(5) You visited another Japanese acquaintance.

—You broke a fine *yunomi* [tea cup]—

You: [Apologize] _____ .

Tape: *A, iie. Daijōbu desu ka.*

You: [Say you're all right and apologize again.]

_____ .

—The next day—

You: [Apologize for what happened yesterday.]

_____ .

Tape: *Iie.*

* When entering a Japanese house it is customary to take off one's shoes at the entrance way.

Drill 5 What would you say in these situations?

(1) —You are introduced to Ms. Ogawa—

Tape 1: *Ogawa-san desu.*

You: [Confirm her name.] _____ .

Tape 2: *Ē, Ogawa desu. Dōzo yoroshiku.*

You: _____ .

(2)   —You are introduced to Mr. Okawa—

Tape: *Ōkawa-san desu.*

You: [Confirming his name (but you say <u>Ogawa</u>).]

_____ .

Tape: *Iie, Ogawa ja arimasen. Ōkawa desu kedo...*

You: [EL] _____ .

Tape: *Ē, sō desu.*

You: [Apologize.] _____ .

Tape: *Iie.*

(3)   —You are introduced to Ms. Chang—

Tape: *Chan-san desu.*

You: [Ask if she's from China.] _____ .

Tape: *Iie, Chūgoku ja arimasen. Firipin desu.*

You: [EL] _____ .

Tape: *Ē, sō desu.*

You: [Apologize] _____ .

Tape: *Iie.*

Drill 6   Make a telephone call to the following, saying *Moshimoshi, _____ desu ka.*

e.g.,   Mr. Tanaka ⟶   *Moshimoshi, Tanaka-san desu ka.*

the Tanaka residence ⟶   *Moshimoshi, Tanaka-san no otaku desu ka.*

(1)   Mr. Smith   (2)   the Inoue residence   (3)   the Yamashita residence

Drill 7   Answer the telephone.

e.g., *Moshimoshi, Takahashi-san no otaku desu ka.*

(Hai) ⟶   *Hai, sō desu.*

(Iie) ⟶   *Iie, chigaimasu kedo ...*

(1)   *Moshimoshi, Takahashi-san desu ka. (Iie)*

(2)   *Moshimoshi, Mōbiru Sekiyu desu ka. (Hai)*

(3)   *Moshimoshi, Yamada-san no otaku desu ka. (Iie)*

Drill 8   Complete the telephone conversation using the dialogue as a model.

(1)	You:	_____ .
Fujii	Tape:	*Fujii-san no otaku desu ka.*
wrong number	You:	_____ .
	Tape:	*A, dōmo sumimasen.*
	You:	_____ .
(2)	You:	_____ .
Yamamoto	Tape:	*Yamamoto-san no otaku desu ka.*
wrong number	You:	_____ .
	Tape:	*A, dōmo shitsurei shimashita.*
	You:	_____ .

Culture Note 1 — A Land of *Ojigi* "bowing"

Traditionally, in formal situations Japanese people bow to each other on occasions where westerners might shake hands — for example, when meeting someone or when saying goodbye. Nowadays, more and more Japanese use the handshake, especially when meeting westerners. Some people use the bow and the handshake together.

If you aren't sure whether to bow or shake hands with a Japanese, the best thing to do is simply watch the other person and be ready to do as he or she does. If the other person makes no move, he/she is probably watching to see what you do! In that case, you can take the initiative. If you don't want to bow, nodding with a smile will do.

But for those who want to make a perfect *ojigi*, bend from the waist at the angle shown in the picture. Don't change the angle of your head or direction of eyesight — you should be looking slightly downward. The legs are kept straight, and the heels should be together. A man's arms are held close to his sides; a woman brings her hands together in front to lightly touch each other.

The lower ranking person (age, social status, business relationship, *etc.*, determines rank) holds the bow lower and longer than the higher ranking person.

Life in Japan is full of *ojigi*. People bow not only when meeting and parting, but also when expressing gratitude and apologizing. You may see many bows for business sake in an office corridor or lobby. Waiters, waitresses, and sales clerks bow to customers. You may even see people who are bowing while talking on the phone. A common sight in the street is two little old ladies endlessly bowing to each other as they exchange seasonal greetings, thanks, apologies, and good-byes, going up and down just like a seesaw. They have so many things to express gratitude about, so many people to send regards to, or so much respect to show one another that neither wants to be the first to raise her head.

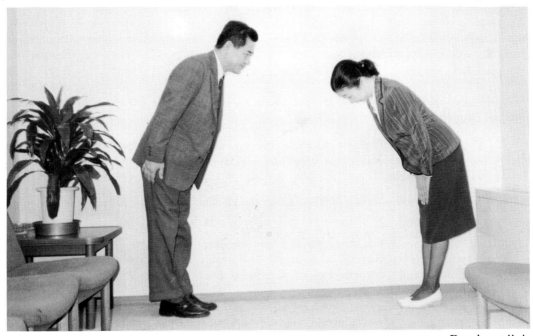

Bowing *ojigi*

Culture Note 2 — The Magic of *Meishi*

A *meishi* is a business card or other name card or calling card. Exchanging *meishi* is a universal ritual in the Japanese business world when intorducing oneself. Whenever anyone in a business or professional field meets another person for the first time, *meishi* must be exchanged.

The information printed on the *meishi* is intended to clarify each person's social rank, relative to the other. This is necessary to guide each person in finding the right level of speech and the appropriate mannerisms to use. For example, in making an *ojigi*, or bow, the social rank expressed on the calling cards determines which person should hold the bow the longest.

The information printed will include the name of the person's company or organization, the position held, the person's name, and the address and telephone number of the organization. Although the person's name may appear in the boldest print, the most important information on the card is the name of the company or organization. Even a young employee from a large and famous company is quite highly ranked by virtue of his prestigious company. The next most important information is the person's position in the organization. However, even an executive of a small or unknown company will not command the high respect given the junior employee of a famous company. Thus, the all-important rank can be established at a glance.

People also exchange *meishi* in non-business situations. This may be because people feel more at ease identifying themselves as members of groups. The information on the card may provide a conversation topic or may be useful for a future business contact.

All this emphasis on prestigious organizations and title may sound to westerners like a shallow, or even hypocritical, basis on which to begin a relationship. However, remember that *meishi* are exchanged in business introductions or when making acquaintances which are still at a superficial level. Remember too, that the Japanese language is oriented to vertical relationships. It does not have polite forms which are universally appropriate between people of all rank. It is impossible to use the language properly and politely without knowing the rank of each person. Between friends, the ranking, if never quite forgotten, is greatly de-emphasized.

When you exchange *meishi,* be careful about how you handle the cards. These points are important:

1. If you are meeting more than one person, exchange cards with each one before going on to the next. You should not look as though you are dealing from a deck of playing cards.

2. After receiving a card, study it a moment, handling it carefully.
    You can place it on the table or hold it during the meeting.
    (This also helps you remember names.)

3. If you have to introduce yourself and don't have a *meishi*, mention your organization or job when you give your name.

After the meeting is over, place the *meishi* in your wallet or in a special *meishi* case or notebook that most Japanese use. Then, if you want to contact that person again, you will not be a total stranger.

Name
Title
Department/Section
Company Name

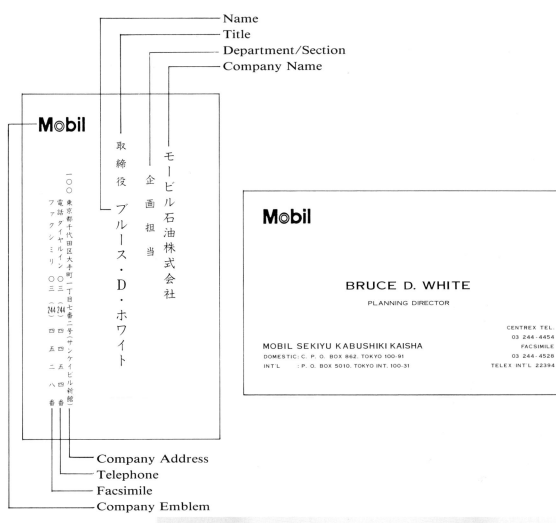

モービル石油株式会社

企 画 担 当

取締役　ブルース・Ｄ・ホワイト

一〇〇　東京都千代田区大手町一丁目七番二号（サンケイビル新館）

電話 ダイヤルイン 〇三（244）四五四番

ファクシミリ 〇三（244）四五二八番

Company Address
Telephone
Facsimile
Company Emblem

BRUCE D. WHITE
PLANNING DIRECTOR

MOBIL SEKIYU KABUSHIKI KAISHA
DOMESTIC: C. P. O. BOX 862. TOKYO 100-91
INT'L   : P. O. BOX 5010. TOKYO INT. 100-31

CENTREX TEL.
03 244-4454
FACSIMILE
03 244-4528
TELEX INT'L 22394

Exchanging *meishi* cards

Culture Note 3 — Japanese Outlook on Relationships

(1)   Group consciousness: *uchi*, the "in-group," and *soto* or *yoso*, the "non-in-group"

A Japanese normally identifies him/herself in terms of relationships to others. It is very important for Japanese to make it known to what group they belong. In other words, they place themselves within a frame together with the other group member. The concept of being inside the frame is called *uchi*, which corresponds to one's "in-group"; *soto* or *yoso* corresponds to the "non-in-group." *Uchi* can be used in reference to many kinds of groups, such as family, company (or department), school, organization, club, and so on. You may hear people refer to *yoso mono* or *yoso no hito,* which means outsider or stranger; in other words, one who does not belong to the group.

(2)   Vertical organization

Inside every "frame," relationships tend to be vertical rather than horizontal. That is, courtesy, status, and sometimes power are accorded to various group members in a kind of hierarchy. Position, age, educational background, tenure in the group, *etc.*, determine ranking within the group. However, the function of these vertical relationships is not to put down junior members. In fact, real power is shared by junior members with high ranking members who try to get the consensus of lower ranking members before making decisions. In addition, the senior members have a responsibility to provide for and even to protect the junior members.

(3)   Speech levels

These concepts permeate every aspect of Japanese life. Language is also determined by the relationships mentioned above. For example, Japanese tend to speak formally to "in-group" members with whom they have vertical relationships, and to "non-in-group" members; and speak informally to "in-group" members with whom they do not have such vertical relationships — such as family members, friends and so on. In this textbook, the informal level of speech is called "Level 1" and the formal levels of speech are called "Level 2" and "Level 3." Most of the conversation in this textbook is at Level 2.

Both Levels 2 and 3 are formal but Level 2 is used toward strangers or between those who have not established a close relationship, whereas Level 3 is used toward customers, superiors, *etc.*, when deference and respect are required.

Communication at Level 3 involves the use of "Honorific" and "Humble" terms. "Honorific" words and expressions are used when Japanese talk about "non-in-group" people (*e.g.,* customers); and "Humble" words and expressions are used when they talk about themselves or their "in-group" members to "non-in-group" people (*e.g.,* talking to a client about one's family).

Each level of speech is illustrated below:

Level 1	Level 2	Level 3
(speaker) You — The circle indicates "in-group."	(speaker) You	(speaker) You

Unit II

Requesting

SCOPE OF UNIT II

The main function of Unit II is REQUESTS and how to make them in a variety of situations. You will be introduced to numbers and the secondary functions necessary in asking about prices and paying for services.

You will also learn important expressions of gratitude—"Thank you very much"; how to attract someone's attention—"Excuse me"; and other uses of "Excuse me."

Lesson 5   provides an introduction to and practice of Japanese numbers, which is necessary in this and later lessons.

Lesson 6   will take you through the language functions at a restaurant—from ordering food in a simple way and requesting something extra, to paying the check individually.

Lesson 7   supplies useful patterns and expressions in directing a taxi driver through city streets.

Lesson 8   will acquaint you with the language you may need in shopping.

Lesson 5

NUMBERS
EXPRESSING GRATITUDE

IKURA DESU KA
"HOW MUCH IS IT?"

Dialogue I

[At the station, Mr. Smith is asking a station employee how much a ticket to Ueno costs.]

Sumisu: Sumimasen. Ueno made ikura desu ka.
Ekiin: Ēto · · ·, hyaku hachijū-en desu.
Sumisu: Hyaku hachijū-en desu ne.
Ekiin: Ē.
Sumisu: Dōmo.
Ekiin: Iie.

Mr. Smith:	Excuse me, how much is it to Ueno?
Station Employee:	Well, err ..., let me see, 180 yen.
Mr. Smith:	It's 180 yen, right?
Station Employee:	That's correct. [*Lit.* Yes.]
Mr. Smith:	Thanks.
Station Employee:	You're welcome.

Dialogue II

[At a newspaper stand on a station platform, Mr. Smith is holding a newspaper.]

Sumisu: Sumimasen, ikura desu ka.
Ten'in: Hyaku-en desu.
Sumisu: [Pointing to *The Japan Times*]
          Japan Taimuza wa ikura desu ka.
Ten'in: Hyaku yon'jū-en desu.
Sumisu: Ryōhō de nihyaku yon'jū-en desu ne.
Ten'in: Hai.
Sumisu: [Handing the clerk the money]
          Sore jā, hai.
Ten'in: Arigatō gozaimashita.
Sumisu: Dōmo.

Vocabulary

Ueno: place name
made [M]:   [Destination]
ikura: how much
ryōhō: both, together
de [M]:   [Total]

ne [SM]:   [Confirming]
hai: here (you are)
arigatō gozaimashita: thank you (for what
          you've done)

Mr. Smith: Excuse me, how much is it?
Sales Clerk: (It's) 100 yen.
Mr. Smith: How much is *The Japan Times*?
Sales Clerk: (It's) 140 yen.
Mr. Smith: Then, it's 240 yen altogether/for both, isn't it?
Sales Clerk: Yes.
Mr. Smith: Here.
Sales Clerk: Thank you.
Mr. Smith: Thank you.

I

スミス　：すみません。　上野まで　いくらですか。

えきいん：ええと…、　180えんです。

スミス：：180えんですね。

えきいん：ええ。

スミス　：どうも。

えきいん：いいえ。

II

スミス　：すみません、　いくらですか。

てんいん：100えんです。

スミス　：ジャパン・タイムズは　いくらですか。

てんいん：140えんです。

スミス　：りょうほうで　240えんですね。

てんいん：はい。

スミス　：それじゃあ、　はい。

てんいん：ありがとうございました。

スミス　：どうも。

Grammar Note 1 — Cardinal numbers

Here we introduce Japanese cardinal numbers and the counting system:

I   1)   1-10
           Memorize the pronunciation.
           1   *ichi*   2   *ni*   3   *san*   4   *yon/shi*   5   *go*
           6   *roku*   7   *nana/shichi* 8   *hachi*   9   *kyū/ku*   10   *jū*

      2)   11-19
           11 is pronounced   10, 1   *jū-ichi*
           12   10, 2   *jū-ni*
           .
           .
           .
           19   10, 9   *jū-kyū / jū-ku*

      3)   20-90
           20 is pronounced   2, 10   *ni-jū*
           30   3, 10   *san-jū*
           .
           .
           .
           90   9, 10   *kyū-jū*

      4)   21-99
           21 is pronounced   2, 10, 1   *ni-jū-ichi*
           53   5, 10, 3   *go-jū-san*
           99   9, 10, 9   *kyū-jū-kyū*
                                                 kyū-jū-ku

II   5)   Memorize the pronunciation.
           100   *hyaku*   1,000   *sen*

      6)   101 is pronounced   100, 1   *hyaku-ichi*
           1,002   1,000, 2   *sen-ni*
            113   100, 10, 3   *hyaku-jū-san*
           1,114   1,000, 100, 10, 4   *sen-hyaku-jū-yon*

      7)   200 is pronounced   2, 100   *ni-hyaku*
            300   3, 100   *san-byaku*
             .
             .
             .
            900   9, 100   *kyū-hyaku*
           2,000   2, 1,000   *ni-sen*
           3,000   3, 1,000   *san-zen*
             .
             .
             .
           9,000   9, 1,000   *kyū-sen*

8) 2,215 is pronounced   *ni-sen ni-hyaku jū-go*

      .

      .

      .

   9,999   *kyū-sen kyū-hyaku kyū-jū kyū/ku*

III   9)   When counting from 10,000 to 99,999,999 put *man* after the ten thousandth digit. (Look at the chart.)

10,000 is pronounced	1 *man*	*ichi-man*
20,000	2 *man*	*ni-man*
100,000	10 *man*	*jū-man*
1,000,000	100 *man*	*hyaku-man*
10,000,000	1000 *man*	*sen-man*

Numbers lower than 10,000 are counted in the way shown in I and II.

Thus,

99,999,999 is pronounced 9,999 *man* 9,999

                kyū-sen kyū-hyaku kyū-jū kyū man kyū-sen kyū-hyaku kyū-jū kyū/ku

15,678,400 is pronounced 1,567 *man* 8,400

                sen go-hyaku roku-jū nana-man ha-ssen yon-hyaku

10)   Likewise, put *oku* after the hundred millionth digit.

100,000,000 is pronounced 1 *oku*		*ichi-oku*
3,500,000,000	35 *oku*	*san-jū-go-oku*
10,000,000,000	100 *oku*	*hyaku-oku*
100,000,000,000	1,000 *oku*	*sen-oku*
222,222,222,222	2,222 *oku* 2,222 *man* 2,222	*ni-sen ni-hyaku ni-jū ni-oku*
		ni-sen ni-hyaku ni-jū ni-man
		ni-sen ni-hyaku ni-jū ni

After every four digits, the name for the unit (*e.g., man, oku*) changes. Now, try and read the numbers in the drills applying the rules.

Cardinal Numbers

kanji characters

1	ichi	一
10	jū	十
100	hyaku	百
1000	sen	千
1 0000	ichi-man	一万
10	jū-man	十万
100	hyaku-man	百万
1000	sen-man	千万
1 0000 0000	ichi-oku	一億
10	jū-oku	十億
100	hyaku-oku	百億
1000	sen-oku	千億
1 0000 0000 0000	i-t-chō	一兆
10	ju-t-chō	十兆
100	hyaku-chō	百兆
1000	sen-chō	千兆

Pronunciation Exceptions

	1 一	2 二	3 三	4 四	5 五	6 六	7 七	8 八	9 九
10	*			yon-			nana-		kyū-
100	*		-byaku	yon-		ro-p-pyaku	nana-	ha-p-pyaku	kyū-
1000	*		-zen	yon-			nana-	ha-s-sen	kyū-
10000				yon-			nana-		kyū-
100000000				yon-			nana-		kyū

* In the pronunciation of ten, hundred and thousand in Japanese, one is normally not pronounced, while the rest of the numbers are pronounced; *i.e.,* ni-jū "20," go-hyaku "500" and yon-hyaku "400."

1 *ichi*	10 *jū*	100 *hyaku*	1,000 *sen*
2 *ni*	20 *ni-jū*	200 *ni-hyaku*	2,000 *ni-sen*
3 *san*	30 *san-jū*	300 *san-b̊yaku*	3,000 *san-z̊en*
4 *yon/shi*	40 *yon-jū*	400 *yon-hyaku*	4,000 *yon-sen*
5 *go*	50 *go-jū*	500 *go-hyaku*	5,000 *go-sen*
6 *roku*	60 *roku-jū*	600 *ro-p̊-pyaku*	6,000 *roku-sen*
7 *nana/shichi*	70 *nana-jū*	700 *nana-hyaku*	7,000 *nana-sen*
8 *hachi*	80 *hachi-jū*	800 *ha-p̊-pyaku*	8,000 *ha-s̊-sen*
9 *kyū/ku*	90 *kyū-jū*	900 *kyū-hyaku*	9,000 *kyū-sen*
10 *jū*	100 *hyaku*	1,000 *sen*	10,000 *ichi-man*

10,000 *ichi-man*	100,000 *jū-man*	1,000,000 *hyaku-man*	10,000,000 *sen-man*
20,000 *ni-man*	200,000 *ni-jū-man*	2,000,000 *ni-hyaku-man*	20,000,000 *ni-sen-man*
30,000 *san-man*	300,000 *san-jū-man*	3,000,000 *san-b̊yaku-man*	30,000,000 *san-z̊en-man*
40,000 *yon-man*	400,000 *yon-jū-man*	4,000,000 *yon-hyaku-man*	40,000,000 *yon-sen-man*
50,000 *go-man*	500,000 *go-jū-man*	5,000,000 *go-hyaku-man*	50,000,000 *go-sen-man*
60,000 *roku-man*	600,000 *roku-jū-man*	6,000,000 *ro-p̊-pyaku-man*	60,000,000 *roku-sen-man*
70,000 *nana-man*	700,000 *nana-jū-man*	7,000,000 *nana-hyaku-man*	70,000,000 *nana-sen-man*
80,000 *hachi-man*	800,000 *hachi-jū-man*	8,000,000 *ha-p̊-pyaku-man*	80,000,000 *ha-s̊-sen-man*
90,000 *kyū-man*	900,000 *kyū-jū-man*	9,000,000 *kyū-hyaku-man*	90,000,000 *kyū-sen-man*
100,000 *jū-man*	1,000,000 *hyaku-man*	10,000,000 *sen-man*	100,000,000 *ichi-oku*

* *cf.* Pronunciation exception list

Grammar Note 2 — Asking/Telling — Price of an item

[The item] *wa ikura desu ka* ↗.

<u>Japan Taimuzu</u> *wa ikura desu ka.*   "How much is *The Japan Times*?"

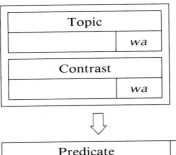

a. ***Ikura desu ka*** ↗.   "How much is it?"

   Ikura is the equivalent of "how much."
   When it is clear which item you are referring to, omit **[The item]** *wa.*

   Examples
     Kōhī wa ikura desu ka.   "How much is coffee?"

     — Pointing to the article —
     Ikura desu ka.   "How much is it?"

b. *X-en desu.*   ''It's X yen.''

Answers to the questions would be:

Examples

     Yon-hyaku-nana-jū-en desu.   ''It's 470 yen.''

     Ichi-man-ni-sen-en desu.   ''It's 12,000 yen.''

Grammar Note 3 — Asking/Telling — Total price

[Item(s)] *de ikura desu ka* ↗.

<u>*X to Y*</u> *de ikura desu ka.*   ''How much is (the total price) of X and Y?''

Total			Predicate	Final
X to Y	de		ikura desu	ka ↗

a. **[Noun 1]** *to* **[Noun 2]**   ''and''

To is a conjunction connecting two or more nouns. It means ''and.''
Never use *to* to connect adjectives, verbs or sentences.

Examples

     Tanaka-san to okusan   ''Mr. Tanaka and his wife''

     Japan Taimuzu to gamu   ''*The Japan Times* and gum''

b. *De*   [Total Marker]

De, following a noun or noun phrase, is a marker indicating the total of a number of items.

Examples

     X to Y de ikura desu ka.   ''How much is (the total price of) X and Y?''

     X to Y to Z de sen-en desu.   ''The total price of X, Y and Z is 1,000 yen.''

     Ryōhō de gohyaku-en desu.   ''The total price of both is 500 yen.''

     Zen'bu de san'zen-en desu.   ''Altogether, it's 3,000 yen.''

Grammar Note 4 — Asking/Telling — Transportation fees

[Place] *made ikura desu ka* ↗.

<u>*Ueno*</u> *made ikura desu ka.*   ''How much is it to Ueno?''

Destination			Predicate		Final
Ueno	made		ikura	desu	ka ↗

Made   [Destination Marker]

    The ending point of time, place, deed or thought, *etc.,* is indicated by *made.* In this lesson, *made* is introduced as a destination marker.

Grammar Note 5 — Confirming

[Key word] *desu ne* ↗.

<u>San'byaku-en</u> *desu ne.*   "Is it 300 yen?"

You learned **[Key word]** *desu ka* as a Yes/no question (*or* confirmation) in Lesson 4. This time, instead of *ka* add *ne* with a rising intonation. The markers *ne* and *ka* are both question markers, but *ne* indicates that the speaker is more certain about his utterance than when using *ka*.

Examples

Salesclerk:	*Kyū-hyaku-en desu.*	"It's 900 yen."
Customer:	*Kyū-hyaku-en desu ne* ↗.	"900 yen?"
Station Employee:	*Shin'juku made ni-hyaku-en desu.*	"It's 200 yen to Shinjuku."
Passenger:	*Ni-hyaku-en desu ne* ↗.	"200 yen?"

Grammar Note 6 — Attracting someone's attention

Sumimasen or Shitsurei shimasu.   "Excuse me."

In Lesson 4 you have seen *sumimasen* for apologizing earnestly "I'm sorry," and apologizing for etiquette's sake "excuse me." *Sumimasen* is also used to attract someone's attention. Variations and responses are shown below.

	Attracting Attention	Response	Meaning
L.1	Name + *san* ↗	*Nāni* ↗	
L.2	Name + *san* ↗ *(Chotto) su(m)imasen* *(Chotto) shitsurei shimasu*	*Hai* *Nan deshō ka* ↘	"Excuse me." "Yes, what is it?" [*Implies* "May I help you?"]
L.3	*Shitsurei itashimasu*	*Hai* ↘	

Grammar Note 7 — Offering

a. *Dōzo*   "Please . . ."

When offering a person a gift, cup of tea, a chair, or some act of courtesy, say *dōzo* as you hand the person the object or as you gesture to indicate the chair, the door, *etc.* When offering an object, *dōzo* is enough for Levels 2 and 3. Occasionally, a few other words are needed to indicate what you are offering.

b. *Hai*   "Here you are."

When offering something casually, you can say *Hai* as you hand it over. *Hai* is also used when handing money to sales clerks, *etc.*

51

Grammar Note 8 — Expressing gratitude

Dōmo arigatō gozaimasu.   "Thank you very much."

Below are expressions to express thanks.   Use the non-past expressions as soon as you receive a gift, favor, or service. Usually, if you have received hospitality, special help, or a gift of some value, you should say thank you again when you say good-bye, or perhaps the next day. At that time you should use one of the past tense expressions. Notice that ***gozaimasu*** becomes ***gozaimashita***:

Topic (Time)		
kyō	"today"	
kinō	"yesterday"	
kono aida	"the other day" L-1,2	*wa*
sen'jitsu	"the other day" L-2,3	

Expressing Gratitude		Meaning	Acknowledging	
In the non-past				
L.1	*Dōmo*		L.1	*Uun*
	(Dōmo) arigatō			
L.2	*Dōmo*	Thank you.	L.2/3 *Iie*	
	(Dōmo) arigatō gozaimasu		"You're welcome	
L.3	*Dōmo arigatō gozaimasu*		[*Lit.* No]."	
In the Past				
L.1	*Dōmo*	Thank you	L.1	*Uun*
	(Dōmo) arigatō	(for what you		
L.2	*Dōmo*	have done	L.2	*Iie*
	(Dōmo) arigatō gozaimashita	for me).		
L.3	*Dōmo arigatō gozaimashita*			

For acknowledging gratitude, *Un* [L.1] *or Hai* [L.2/3] "Certainly [*Lit.* Yes]." can also be used.

Examples

A:	[Handing over a present] *Dōzo* . . .	"Please."
B:	*A, dōmo arigatō gozaimasu.*	"Oh, thank you very much."

— A few days later —

B:	*A-san, kono aida wa arigatō gozaimashita.*	"Mr. A, thank you for (the present) the other day."
A:	*Iie.*	"You're welcome."

Drill 1 1. Repeat the names of the items you can buy at a newspaper stand.
2. Ask the price and answer.

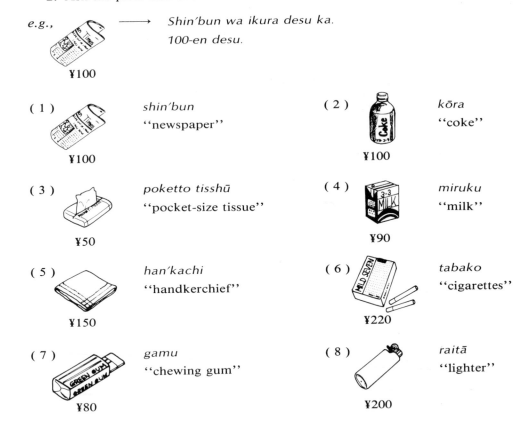

e.g., ⟶ *Shin'bun wa ikura desu ka.*
    100-en desu.

¥100

(1) *shin'bun*
  "newspaper"

¥100

(2) *kōra*
  "coke"

¥100

(3) *poketto tisshū*
  "pocket-size tissue"

¥50

(4) *miruku*
  "milk"

¥90

(5) *han'kachi*
  "handkerchief"

¥150

(6) *tabako*
  "cigarettes"

¥220

(7) *gamu*
  "chewing gum"

¥80

(8) *raitā*
  "lighter"

¥200

Drill 2 Ask the price and answer.

e.g.,

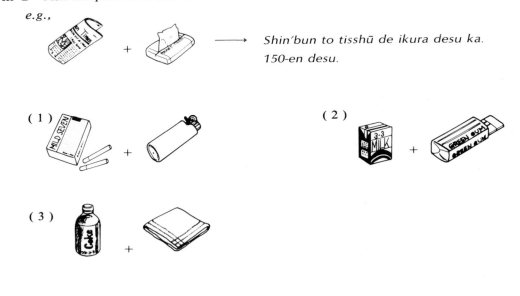

+ ⟶ *Shin'bun to tisshū de ikura desu ka.*
    150-en desu.

(1)   +

(2)   +

(3)   +

(4) the two together

(5) altogether

Drill 3   Confirm the price.

  e.g.,   *Shin'bun wa 100-en desu.* ⟶ *100-en desu ne.*

(1)   *Tisshū wa 50-en desu.*   (2)   *Kōra wa 100-en desu.*

(3)   *Tabako wa 200-en desu.*   (4)   *Gamu wa 80-en desu.*

Drill 4   Using the place names, make questions and answers.

  e.g.,   *Gin'za* ⟶ *Gin'za made ikura desu ka.*
                              140-en desu.

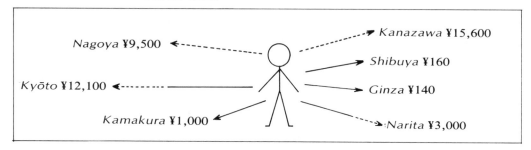

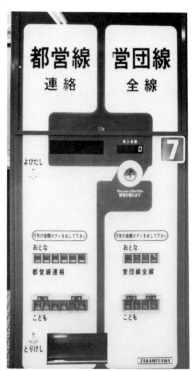

Drill 5 Using Dialogue I as a model, complete the following.

(1) You want to go to Tokyo Tower, *Tōkyō Tawā*. —On a bus— to Tokyo tower ¥? ¥160	You: _____ . Tape: *Hyaku-rokujū-en desu.* You: _____ . Tape: *Ē.* You: _____ . Tape: *Hai.*
(2) You want to go to Enoshima. [Stop a passer-by and ask.] —At the station, in front of the ticket machine— to Enoshima ¥? ¥580	You: _____ . Tape: *Chotto matte kudasai.* "Wait a moment." *Ēto . . . gohyaku-hachijū-en desu.* You: _____ . Tape: *Ē, sō desu.* You: _____ . Tape: *Iie.*

Drill 6 Using Dialogue II as a model, complete the following conversations.

(1) —At a liquor store— [a] How much is this? [b: Confirm the price.]	Tape: *Irasshaimase.* You: [Holding up a bottle of wine.] [a] _____ . Tape: *San'zen-en de gozaimasu.* You: [b] _____ . Tape: *Hai.* You: [Hand the clerk the money.] _____ . Tape: *Dōmo arigatō gozaimashita.* You: _____ .
(2) —At a sandwich counter— [a] How much . . . ? [b] How much . . . ? [c: Confirm, two together]	You: [Holding up a package of sandwiches] [a] _____ . Tape: *Yon'hyaku-san'jū-en desu.* You: [b] _____ . Tape: *Hyaku-en desu.* You: [c] _____ . Tape: *Hai.* You: [Hand over the money.] _____ . Tape: *Arigatō gozaimashita.* "Thank you." You: _____ .

Drill 7   How would you express gratitude and so on, in the following situations?

e.g.,	Your business associate Mr. A gives you a present *o-miyage* from his trip to Hokkaido.	*Hokkaidō* [Place name]
	— When you receive the present—	
	A: *Hokkaidō no o-miyage desu. Dōzo.*	*o-miyage* "souvenir"
	B: *Dōmo arigatō gozaimasu.*	
	A: *Iie.*	
	— A few days later —	
	B: *Sen'jitsu wa dōmo arigatō gozaimashita.*	*sen'jitsu* "the other day"
	A: *Iie.*	

(1) You are invited to the Kabuki Theater by your business associate.	
— When you meet at the theater —	
You: [Say "thank you" for being invited. *Lit.* Today, thank you.]	
_____ .	*kyō* "today"
Tape: *Iie, kochira koso.*	
— The next day —	
You: [Say "thank you" for yesterday's entertainment. *Lit.* Yesterday, thank you.]	
_____ .	*kinō* "yesterday"
Tape: *Iie, kochira koso arigatō gozaimashita.*	

(2) Your business associate visits you on New Year's Day as a formal annual visit.

— At the door —

Tape: *Akemashite omedetō gozaimasu.*

You: [Return the New Year's greeting.]

_____ .

— When you receive a present —

Tape: *Tsumaranai mono desu ga, dōzo.*

You: [Say "thank you" as you accept the present.]

_____ .

— When you offer sake as you formally receive guests on New Year's Day —

You: [Offer sake.]

_____ .

Tape: *Dōmo arigato gazaimasu.*

— When the visitor leaves —

Tape: *Kyō wa dōmo arigatō gozaimashita.*

You: [Acknowledge the gratitude and express gratitude in return.]

_____ .

Tape: *Sore dewa shitsurei itashimasu.*

You: [Say "good-bye" formally.]

_____ .

— A week later —

Tape: *Sen'jitsu* "the other day" *wa dōmo arigatō gozaimashita.*

You: [Acknowledge the gratitude and express gratitude in return.]

_____ .

akemashite omedetō gozaimasu "Happy New Year"

"This is really nothing, but please accept it."

Lesson 6

AT A RESTAURANT

RAN'CHI SETTO (O) HITOTSU ONEGAISHIMASU
"ONE LUNCH SPECIAL, PLEASE."

▣ Dialogue

[Mr. Smith and Mr. Yamashita, colleagues, go to lunch together.]

[At the entrance of the restaurant]
Ueitā: *Irasshaimase.*
Yamashita: *Futari desu.*
Ueitā: [Showing the way] *Dōzo kochira e.*
[At the table]
Ueitoresu: [Bowing] *Irasshaimase.*
              [Puts glasses of water on the table,
               hands them menus, and walks away.]

              *   *   *

Yamashita: *Sumimasen.*
Ueitoresu: *Hai.*
Yamashita: *Ran'chi-setto (o) hito-tsu onegai shimasu. Sorekara mikkusu-san'do to*
              tomato-jūsū (o) onegai shimasu.
Ueitoresu: *Hai, kashikomarimashita.*

Waiter:	Hello.
Mr. Yamashita:	Table for two, please.
Waiter:	This way, please.
Waitress:	Hello.
	* * *
Mr. Yamashita:	Excuse me, Miss . . .
Waitress:	Ready to order! [*Lit.* Yes!]
Mr. Yamashita:	We'd like the lunch special,
	the assorted sandwich plate
	and a glass of tomato juice, please.
Waitress:	OK. Thank you. [*Lit.* Certainly. I've understood.]

Vocabulary

ueitā: waiter
ueitoresu: waitress
irasshaimase: Hello. [*Lit.* Welcome.]
futari: two people
Dōzo kochira e: This way, please.
sumimasen: excuse me
hai: yes, OK, I understand
ran'chi-setto: lunch special

hito-tsu: one
mikkusu-san'do: sandwich assortment
tomato-jūsu: tomato juice
o [M]: [Object]
onegai shimasu: I ask you to . . . for me
sorekara: and then
kashikomarimashita: certainly, I've
                    understood.

* * *

—At the cashier—

Yamashita: *O-kan'jō onegai shimasu. Sumimasen kedo, betsubetsu ni onegai dekimasu ka.*

Kaikei: *Hai.*

Yamashita: *Ran'chi-setto wa ikura desu ka.*

Kaikei: *Happyaku-en de gozaimasu.*

Sumisu: *Mikkusu-san'do to tomato jūsu de ikura deshō ka.*

Kaikei: *Kyūhyaku-en de gozaimasu.*

Sumisu: *Kyūhyaku-en desu ne.*

Kaikei: *Hai.*

Sumisu / Yamashita: [Handing the money to the cashier] *Hai.*

Kaikei: *Dōmo arigatō gozaimashita.*

Sumisu / Yamashita: *Dōmo.*

Mr. Yamashita: Here's our check. Excuse me, but could you ring it up separately?
Cashier: Certainly, sir.
Mr. Yamashita: How much is it for the lunch special?
Cashier: That will be 800 yen.
Mr. Smith: How much do I owe you for the assorted sandwich plate and a glass of tomato juice?
Cashier: That'll be 900 yen.
Mr. Smith: Oh, OK, 900 yen.
Cashier: That's right, sir.
Mr. Smith / Mr. Yamashita: Here you are.
Cashier: Thank you very much (for having come).
Mr. Smith / Mr. Yamashita: Thank you.

ウェイター　：いらっしゃいませ。

山下　　　　：ふたりです。

ウェイター　：どうぞ　こちらへ。

ウェイトレス：いらっしゃいませ。

* * *

山下　　　　：すみません。

ウェイトレス：はい。

Vocabulary

o-kan'jō: check, bill
kedo: although
betsubetsu ni: separately
de gozaimasu: Humble* equivalent of *desu*

de [M]: [Total]
deshō: is, will be
ne [SM]: [Confirmation]
　　**cf.* Culture Note 3

山下 : ランチセット（を）　ひとつ　おねがいします。
やました
　　　　　　それから　ミックスサンドと　トマトジュース（を）
　　　　　　おねがいします。

ウェイトレス：はい、　かしこまりました。

＊　　　＊　　　＊

山下 : おかんじょう　おねがいします。
　　　　　　すみませんけど、　べつべつに　おねがいできますか。

かいけい：はい。

山下 : ランチセットは　いくらですか。

かいけい：800えんでございます。

スミス : ミックスサンドと　トマトジュースで　いくらでしょうか。

かいけい：900えんでございます。

スミス : 900えんですね。

かいけい：はい。

スミス
山下 } : はい。

かいけい：どうも
　　　　　　ありがとうございました。

スミス
山下 } : どうも。

Noodle restaurant *sobaya*
with the sign 営業中*(ei-gyō-chū)* ''open''

Plastic samples in a display case
at a *sushi* shop

Japanese restaurant
with the sign 準備中*(jun-bi-chū)* ''closed''

Grammar Note 1 — Requests to people serving you

[Item you want to order] *o onegai shimasu.*

Kōhī o onegai shimasu. "(I'd like to have) coffee, please."

Object			Predicate
			Verb
kōhī	*(o)*	⟹	*onegai shimasu*

a. **Onegai shimasu** "I ask you to . . . for me." *or* "I'd like to have . . ."

When you make a request — for example, when you order food in a restaurant — use **onegai shimasu.**

b. **O** [Object Marker]

O, following a noun, is a marker indicating that the noun is the Object of the Predicate. As *o* is easily omitted **kōhī onegai shimasu** is quite often heard.

c. **Kore** "this one"

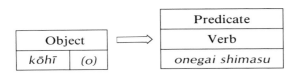

speaker	*kore*	"this thing" near the speaker	
listener speaker	*sore*	"that thing" near the listener	
speaker listener	*are*	"that thing over there" far from both the speaker and the listener	
?	*dore*	"which thing"	

Examples

Kore (o) onegai shimasu. "(I'd like) this, please."

Are (o) onegai shimasu. "(I'd like) that, please."

San'doitchi to kōhī (o) onegai shimasu. "(I'd like) a sandwich and coffee, please."

Grammar Note 2 — How to order using numbers

[Item] *o* **[Number]** *onegai shimasu.*

Kōhī o futatsu onegai shimasu. "(I'd like) two coffees, please."

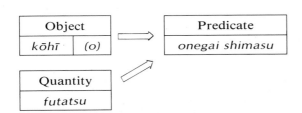

Object			Predicate
kōhī	*(o)*	⟹	*onegai shimasu*

Quantity	
futatsu	

a. If you want two cups of coffee say **kōhī (o) futatsu onegai shimasu** "(I'd like to have) two coffees, please." No marker follows a quantity word such as **futatsu** "two."

b. Counters

When counting objects in Japanese, special suffixes called counters are added to the numbers. There are a variety of these counting suffixes, each used with a different category of objects. For example, long objects such as pencils, trees, bottles, or even films and tapes, are counted with **-hon**. Thin or flat things like paper, tickets, or stamps are counted with the number plus **-mai**. Japanese money is counted with **-en** "yen."

Examples

ni-mai	"two sheets (of paper, *etc.*)"
san-en	"three yen"

The counter should never be deleted not even in a short answer or a situation where it is obvious what kind of thing is being counted.

There are two types of pronunciation when counting:

Type 1 — Use **ichi** (1), **ni** (2), **san** (3) series plus counter.

Type 2 — Use **hito** (1), **futa** (2), **mi** (3) series plus counter and with higher numbers use **ichi**, **ni**, **san** series plus or without counter.

The chart below shows the numbers one through twelve with several types of counters:

OBJECT	Type 1			Type 2	
	-en	-mai	-hon	miscellaneous items -tsu	-nin
1	ichi-en	ichi-mai	ip-*pon	hito-tsu	hito-*ri
2	ni-en	ni-mai	ni-hon	futa-tsu	futa-*ri
3	san-en	san-mai	san-*bon	mit-tsu	san-nin
4	yo-en	yon-mai	yon-hon	yot-tsu	yo-nin
5	go-en	go-mai	go-hon	itsu-tsu	go-nin
6	roku-en	roku-mai	rop-*pon	mut-tsu	roku-nin
7	nana-en	nana-mai	nana-hon	nana-tsu	shichi⎫ nana⎭-nin
8	hachi-en	hachi-mai	hap-*pon	yat-tsu	hachi-nin
9	kyū-en	kyū-mai	kyū-hon	kokono-tsu	kyū-nin
10	jū-en	jū-mai	jup-*pon	tō	jū-nin

11	*jūichi-en*	*jūichi-mai*	*jūip-*pon*	*jūichi*	*jūichi-nin*
12	*jūni-en*	*jūni-mai*	*jūni-hon*	*jūni*	*jūni-nin*
How many	*nan-en* or *ikura*	*nan-mai*	*nan-*bon*	*iku-tsu*	*nan-nin*

* pronunciation exceptions

Grammar Note 3 — Connecting two sentences

[Sentence 1]. **Sorekara** [Sentence 2].   "And"

Sorekara is a conjunction connecting two sentences. It means "and." In Lesson 1 you have seen **to** "and" which connects two nouns.

Examples

Sutēki to sarada (o) onegai shimasu.   "I'd like a steak and a salad."
Sorekara, kōhī (o) onegai shimasu.   "And, coffee, please."

Grammar Note 4 — Requesting extra work

Onegai dekimasu ka ↗.   "Could I ask you to . . . for me?"

When requesting extra work, special service, or service under rather difficult conditions, use **onegai dekimasu ka** "Could I ask you to . . .?" which is the humble equivalent of **onegai shimasu**. Situations when this form is appropriate are, for example, when asking for another glass of water, when asking for a knife and fork instead of chopsticks in a Japanese restaurant, or when the person looks busy.

Examples

Mizu (o) onegai dekimasu ka.   "(Could I ask you to bring) water, please?"

Naifu to fōku (o) onegai dekimasu ka.   "(Could I ask you to bring) a knife and fork please?"

Grammar Note 5 — Expressing gratitude with apologies

Sumimasen   "Thank you for your trouble." *or* "I'm sorry that you have to do it."

Japanese people sometimes use **sumimasen** which expresses gratitude with a nuance of apology, instead of using the straightforward expression of gratitude **dōmo arigatō gozaimasu**.   To express this type of gratitude refer to the same list for expressing apologies.

Grammar Note 6 — Asking the price

Ikura deshō ka ↘.   "How much will it be?"

In Lesson 5 you learned **Ikura desu ka** "How much is it?"   **Deshō ka** with falling intonation is an indirect equivalent of **desu ka**. Therefore, **ikura deshō ka** sounds more polite than **ikura desu ka**. Apply the same idea as in Grammar Note 4 (**onegai shimasu** *vs.* **dekimasu ka**.)

Grammar Note 7 — More about "thank you," "sorry," and "excuse me."

a.   Humble phrase preceding/following a "minor indulgence"

One reason the Japanese seem to be constantly apologizing is that **sumimasen** is used as a humble phrase accompanying many actions which require nothing in English. Just as the Japanese often end their thanks with an apologetic tone, they say **sumimasen** when doing anything that could involve indulgence or intrusion on another person. Some situations that require **sumimasen** (or in business or formal situations, **shitsurei shimasu**) in recognition of the other person's consideration or tolerance: when taking a seat (after saying **dōmo** "thank you"); when entering a room; when someone holds an elevator for you; when interrupting a conversation to answer the phone or door; when going ahead of someone through a door or passageway. There is considerable overlap with expressions of thanks and apology for rudeness. After a minor indulgence, use the same expressions in the past tense, **sumimasen deshita** or **shitsurei shimashita**, *etc.*

	Humble phrase	Acknowledging the humble phrase	Meaning
	Preceding a minor indulgence		
L.1	*Gomen (nasai)*		
L.2	*Su(m)imasen or Shitsurei shimasu*	*Dōzo* ↘	Excuse me. Yes, go ahead.
L.3	*Shitsurei itashimasu*		
	Following a minor indulgence		
L.1	*Gomen (nasai)*	*Uun* ↗	
L.2	*Su(m)imasen (deshita) or Shitsurei shimashita*		Excuse me. That's quite all right.
L.3	*Shitsurei itashimashita*	*Iie* ↗	

Shitsurei (shimashita) is more formal or business like than **sumimasen (deshita)**.

Example dialogues

1.   [A telephone rings during a conversation with an acquaintance.]
        —*Rīn, rīn . . .* "Ring, ring."—
Host: *Chotto shitsurei shimasu.* or *Chotto sumimasen.*
Guest: *Dōzo.*
            —When the host returns—
Host: *Shitsurei shimashita.*
Guest: *Iie.*

        Host: Excuse me for a moment.
        Guest: Yes [*Lit.* Go ahead.]

        Host: I'm sorry. [*Lit.* I was sorry.]
        Guest: That's all right.

2. [Mr. Tanaka is in a conference room having a meeting. His secretary interrupts the meeting to say there is a telephone call for him.]

—*Ton, ton.* . . . "Knock, knock."—

Mr. Tanaka:	*Hai.*
Secretary:	*Shitsurei shimasu. Oden'wa desu.*
Mr. Tanaka:	[To the others] *Shitsurei shimasu.*
Others:	*Dōzo.*
	—When he returns—
Mr. Tanaka:	*Shitsurei shimashita.*
Others:	*Iie.*

Mr. Tanaka:	Yes.
Secretary:	Excuse me, there's a telephone call (for you).
Mr. Tanaka:	Will you excuse me for a moment?
Others:	Certainly.

Mr. Tanaka:	I'm sorry. [*Lit.* I was sorry.]
Others:	Not at all.

3. [Mr. Smith accidentally steps on a stranger's toe.]

Mr. Smith:	*A, sumimasen. or A, shitsurei (shimashita).*
Stranger:	*Iie.*

Mr. Smith:	Oh, I'm sorry *or* Excuse me.
Stranger:	That's all right.

b. Here is a simpler list of thank you or sorry or excuse me expressions in Level 2 speech introduced in this and previous lessons.

		Responses
Gratitude	*Arigatō gozaimasu* "Thank you."	*Iie*
Gratitude with apology	*Sumimasen* "Thank you."	*Iie*
Apology	*Sumimasen* *or Mōshiwake arimasen* "I'm sorry."	*Iie*
Attracting attention	*Sumimasen* *or Shitsurei shimasu* "Excuse me."	*Hai*
Humble phrase preceding *or* following a minor indulgence	*Shitsurei shimasu* *Shitsurei shimashita* "Excuse me."	*Iie*

Grammar Note 8 — Paying at the cashier

Here are some phrases to use when you pay a bill:

Ikura desu ka.	"How much is it?"
Ikura deshō ka.	"How much would it be?"
O-kanjō onegai shimasu.	"Check, please."
Issho ni onegai shimasu.	"(We'd like to pay) all together, please."
Betsubetsu ni onegai dekimasu ka.	"Could we pay separately, please?"

Grammar Note 9 — Shopkeepers' *or* waiters' expressions

Here are some expressions you may hear:

—To a customer entering a store or approaching a counter—

Irasshaimase.	"Welcome (to the shop)."
Irasshai! (infomral)	*or* "May I help you?"

—After taking the order—

Kashikomarimashita.	"Certainly."
Shōshō omachi kudasai.	"Could you please wait a little while?"

—When presenting a customer the requested items or food—

Omatase itashimashita.	"[Sorry.] You've been kept waiting."
or	
Omachidōsama deshita.	

—To a customer leaving the store—

(Maido) arigatō gozaimashita.	"Thank you for coming."

It is usually not necessary to reply to these except perhaps with a nod.

Drill 1   Repeat the names of the items you can order in a restaurant.

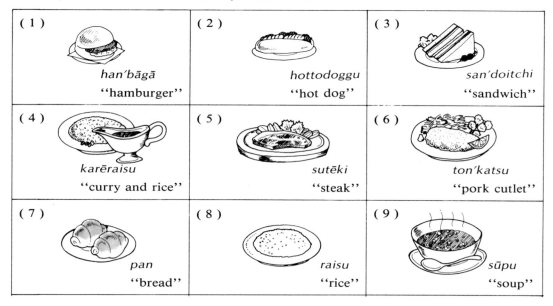

(1) han'bāgā "hamburger"	(2) hottodoggu "hot dog"	(3) san'doitchi "sandwich"
(4) karēraisu "curry and rice"	(5) sutēki "steak"	(6) ton'katsu "pork cutlet"
(7) pan "bread"	(8) raisu "rice"	(9) sūpu "soup"

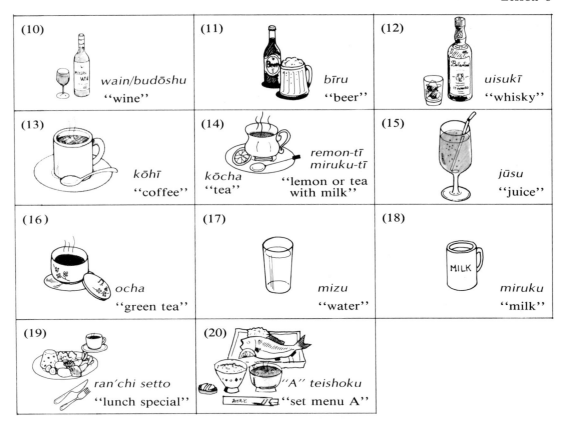

(10) *wain/budōshu* "wine"	(11) *bīru* "beer"	(12) *uisukī* "whisky"
(13) *kōhī* "coffee"	(14) *kōcha* "tea" *remon-tī* *miruku-tī* "lemon or tea with milk"	(15) *jūsu* "juice"
(16) *ocha* "green tea"	(17) *mizu* "water"	(18) *miruku* "milk"
(19) *ran'chi setto* "lunch special"	(20) "A" *teishoku* "set menu A"	

Drill 2   Order something.

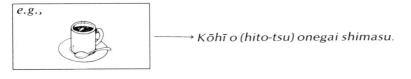

e.g.,
⟶ *Kōhī o (hito-tsu) onegai shimasu.*

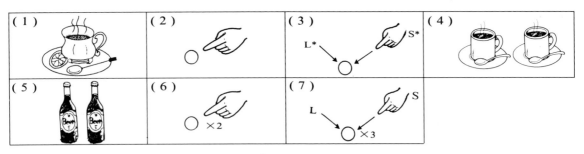

(1)	(2)	(3)	(4)
		L* ⟶ ○ ⟵ S*	
(5)	(6) ○ ×2	(7) L ⟶ ○ ⟵ S ×3	

*S = Speaker   *L = Listener

Drill 3 Order something using *to* "and".

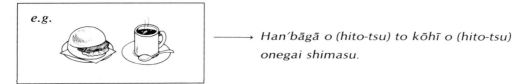

→ *Han'bāgā o (hito-tsu) to kōhī o (hito-tsu)*
onegai shimasu.

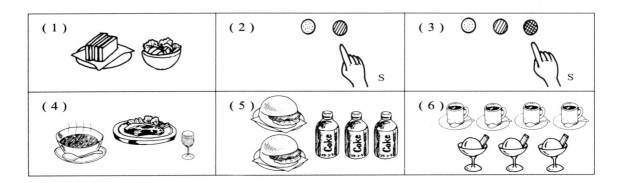

Drill 4 Order something using *sorekara* "and".

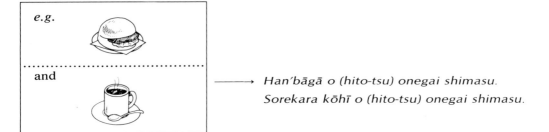

→ *Han'bāgā o (hito-tsu) onegai shimasu.*
Sorekara kōhī o (hito-tsu) onegai shimasu.

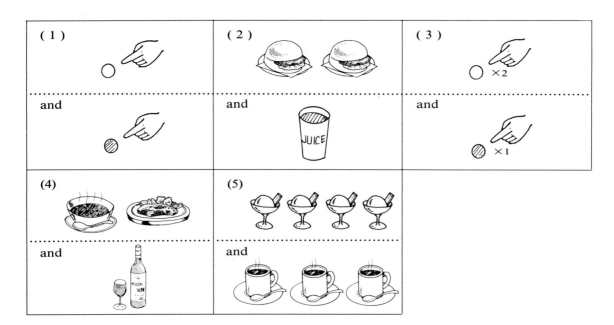

Drill 5   Give the price.

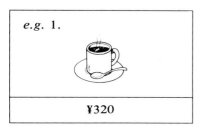

e.g. 1.

¥320

⟶   *Kōhī wa san'byaku-nijū-en desu.*

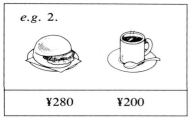

e.g. 2.

¥280   ¥200

⟶   *Han'bāgā to kōhī de yon'hyaku-hachijū-en desu.*

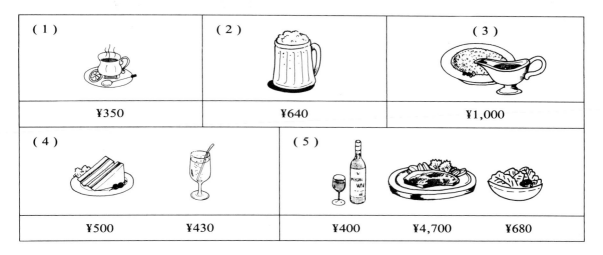

(1)	(2)	(3)
¥350	¥640	¥1,000

(4)		(5)		
¥500	¥430	¥400	¥4,700	¥680

Drill 6   Tell the waiter how large your group is using *-nin.*

e.g.

⟶   Waiter: *Irasshaimase. Nan-nin desu ka.*
       Customer: *Hito-ri desu.*

(1) 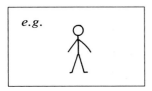   (2)   (3)    (4)

Drill 7   Complete the following using the dialogue as a model.

(1)	
[a]	Tape: *Irasshaimase.* You: [a] _____ . Tape: *Dōzo kochira e.* :
[b]	—Waiter approaches for order— Tape: *Irasshaimase.* You: [b] _____ . Tape: *Hai. Kashikomarimashita.*
(2)	
[a]	Tape: *Irasshaimase.* You: [a] _____ . Tape: *Dōzo kochira e.* :
[b]	Tape: *Irasshaimase.* You: [b] _____ . Tape: *Hai. Kashikomarimashita.*
(3)	
[a]	Tape: *Irasshaimase.* You: [a] _____ . Tape: *Dōzo kochira e.* :
[b] and 	Tape: *Irasshaimase* —Hands over menu and leaves— : You: [A]* _____ . Tape: *Hai.* You: [b] _____ . Tape: *Hai. Kashikomarimashita.*

* [A] = Attract the waiter's attention.

Drill 8   Complete the dialogues. Pay careful attention to the usage of *onegai shimasu* and *onegai dekimasu ka.*

(1) —You go to a local Japanese restaurant—		
[a] Pork cutlet entrée	Tape: *Irasshaimase.*	*ton'katsu*
	You: [a] _____ .	*teishoku*
	Tape: *Hai.*	
	:	
	Tape: *Omatase shimashita.*	
—The waiter brings you the *ton'katsu* dinner with chopsticks—		
	You: [A]* _____ .	*naifu* "knife"
[b]	You: [b] _____ .	*fōku* "fork"
	Tape: *Hai.*	
	:	
	Tape: *Hai, dōzo.*	
[c] Thank you for the trouble.	You: [c] _____ .	

* [A] = Attract (waitress's) attention

(2) —You go to a *ten'puraya* "tempura restaurant"—		
	Tape: *Iresshaimase.*	
[a] Tempura set menu	You: [a] _____ .	*ten'pura* teishoku
	Tape: *Hai.*	
	:	
—You drop your chopsticks on the floor while eating—		
	You: [A] _____ .	*hashi* [m]*
[b]	You: [b] _____ .	*o-hashi* [w]*
	Tape: *Hai.*	
	:	
	Tape: *Hai, dōzo.*	
[c] Thank you for the trouble.	You: [c] _____ .	

*Expressions used by men [m] and women [w].

Drill 9   Complete the following, using the dialogue as a model.

(1) —You go to a restaurant with your colleague— [a] separately [b] raw fish set 	You: [a] _____ . Tape: *Hai.* You: [b] _____ . Tape: *Sen-san'byaku-en de gozaimasu.* You: [Confirm the price.] _____ . Tape: *Hai.* You: [Hand over the money.] _____ . Tape: *Dōmo arigatō gozaimashita.* You: _____ .	*sashimi teishoku*
(2) [a] separately [b] lunch special "A" 	You: [a] _____ . Tape: *Hai.* You: [b] _____ . Tape: *Happyaku-kyūjū-en desu.* You: _____ . Tape: *Hai.* You: _____ . Tape: *Arigatō gozaimashita.* You: _____ .	*"A" ran'chi*

(3)
[a]   separately
 	
[b]   the deluxe
       sushi
       assortment
       and a red
       miso soup
 	
	You: [a] _____ .
	Tape: *Hai.*
	You: [b] _____ .
	Tape: *Sen-happyaku-en desu.*
	You: _____ .
	Tape: *Hai.*
	You: _____ .
	Tape: *Maido arī. . .*
	You: _____ .
		*jōzushi,
		akadashi*
		
		"Thank you
		for coming
		often."

Lesson 7

TAKING A TAXI

SHIN'JUKU EKI NO NISHI-GUCHI MADE ONEGAI SHIMASU
"TAKE ME TO THE WEST EXIT OF SHINJUKU STATION"

Dialogue

Sumisu:	*Shin'juku Eki no nishi-guchi made onegai shimasu.*
Un'ten'shu:	*Hai.*
	* * *
Sumisu:	*Meiji Dōri o tōtte kudasai.*
	* * *
Sumisu:	*Tsugi o migi e magatte kudasai.*
	* * *
Sumisu:	*Koko de ii desu.* [Handing the driver the fare as the taxi stops] *Hai.*
Un'ten'shu:	*Dōmo.*
Sumisu:	*Dōmo.*

ta-ku-shī-no-ri-ba   "Taxi stand"
タクシーのりば

Mr. Smith:	(Take me to) the west exit of Shinjuku Station, please.
Driver:	All right.
	* * *
Mr. Smith:	Go by way of Meiji Avenue, please.
	* * *
Mr. Smith:	Turn right at the next street, please.
	* * *
Mr. Smith:	Stop here, please. [*Lit.* Just here will be fine.]
Driver:	Thank you.
Mr. Smith:	Thank you.

Vocabulary

eki: station
nishi-guchi: west exit
made [M]: [Ending Point]
un'ten'shu: driver
Meiji Dōri: Meiji Avenue

tōtte kudasai: please go by way of
koko [N]: here
de [M]: [Place of Action]
ii: good, fine

スミス　　　：新宿駅の　にしぐちまで　おねがいします。
　　　　　　　しんじゅくえき
うんてんしゅ：はい。

　　　　　　　　＊　　　＊　　　＊

スミス：明治通りを　とおってください。
　　　　めいじどお

　　　　　　＊　　　＊　　　＊

スミス：つぎを　みぎへ　まがってください。

　　　　　　＊　　　＊　　　＊

スミス　　　：ここで　いいです。　はい。
うんてんしゅ：どうも。
スミス　　　：どうも。

Grammar Note 1 — Giving the destination

[Place to go] *made onegai shimasu.*
Roppongi made onegai shimasu.　　　"Take me to Roppongi, please."

Destination			Predicate	Final
Roppongi	*made*	$\Rightarrow$	*onegai shimasu*	∅
			onegai dekimasu*	*ka*↗

　　　*Humble equivalent of **onegai shimasu** (see Lesson 6)

a.　Made　[Destination Marker]　(*cf.* Lesson 5)

When you tell the driver where you want to go, use **made.**

Examples
　　Roppongi made onegai shimasu.　　"(Take me) to Roppongi, please."
　　Ōtemachi no San'kei Biru made　　"(Take me) to the Sankei Building in
　　　onegai shimasu.　　　　　　　　　Otemachi, please."

b.　Nishi-guchi　　"West exit"

When you want to say the west exit/entrance of a station, say **[Station name]-eki no
nishi-guchi. Nishi** means "west" and **-guchi** means "exit or entrance."

Vocabulary

北
kita
N

西 *nishi* W ——————— E *higashi* 東

S
minami
南

kita-guchi	"north exit/entrance"
nishi-guchi	"west exit/entrance"
minami-guchi	"south exit/entrance"
higashi-guchi	"east exit/entrance"
chūō-guchi	"central exit/entrance"

c. **[Landmark]** *no chikaku*   "Near the [landmark]"

When you cannot give an exact destination, say **[Landmark]** *no chikaku made onegai shimasu* "Take me to the vicinity of [landmark]."

Example

Amerika taishikan no chikaku made onegai shimasu.	"(Take me) to the vicinity of the American Embassy, please."

Grammar Note 2 — Giving directions I

[Where to turn] *o* **[Direction]** *e onegai shimasu.*
Tsugi o migi e onegai shimasu.   "Turn right at the next (corner), please."

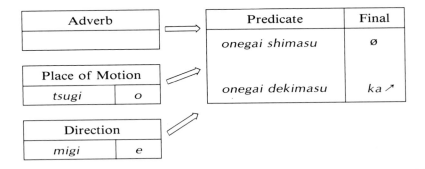

a. Adverbs

"Straight" *massugu*, as in "Go straight, please," is an adverb here, and adverbs do not take any marker.

Examples

Massugu onegai shimasu.	"(Go) straight, please."
Yukkuri onegai shimasu.	"(Go) slowly, please."
Isoide onegai shimasu.	"(Go) faster, please."

b. *E* [Direction Marker] "to"

"(Turn) right, please" is *migi e onegai shimasu*. Left is *hidari*.

c. *O* [Place of Motion Marker]

"(Turn) right at the next intersection, corner or traffic light, please" is *tsugi o migi e onegai shimasu*.

Examples

Tsugi o hidari e onegai shimasu.	"(Turn) left at the next (intersection), please."
Tsugi no tsugi o migi e onegai shimasu.	"(Turn) right at the one after the next, please."
Shin'gō o hidari e onegai shimasu.	"(Turn) left at the traffic light."
Aoyama Dōri o tōtte*kudasai.	"(Go) by way of Aoyama Avenue, please."

(**cf.* Grammar Note 4)

Grammar Note 3 — Telling the driver where to stop

[Place to stop] *de ii desu.*

<u>Koko</u> *de ii desu.* "Stop here, please. [*Lit.* Just here will be fine.]"

Place of Action			Predicate	
koko *kono hen*	*de*	$\Rightarrow$	*ii* *kekkō*	*desu*

a. **Koko** "this place or here"
   Kono hen "around this place or about here"

b. **De** [Place of Action Marker]

   Actions like "to stop" takes a place word plus **de** to indicate the point of action.

c. **Ii desu.** "this is fine"
   Ii means good, fine, or all right. Therefore, **koko de ii desu** means "(To stop) here is fine."
   kekkō desu, a humble equivalent of **ii desu**, is also used.

   Examples

   Koko de ii desu. "Just here will be fine."
   Kono hen de kekkō desu. "Just about here would be fine."
   Shin'gō no temae de ii desu. "Just before the traffic light will be fine."

Grammar Note 4 — Additional — Giving directions II

The following verbs replace **onegai shimasu** by indicating actual actions in giving directions to a driver, such as to go, stop, turn, *etc.*

   Examples

   Nakameguro made itte kudasai. "Take me [*Lit.* Go] to Nakameguro, please."
   Kono hen de tomatte kudasai. "Stop around here, please."
   Tsugi o migi e magatte kudasai. "Turn to the right at the next (intersection), please."
   Yamate Dōri o tōtte kudasai. "Go by way of Yamate Avenue, please."

The verbs (more strictly called the **Te** form), such as **itte** "to go," **tomatte** "to stop," **magatte** "to turn," and **tōtte** "to go through or by way of," with **kudasai** can replace **onegai shimasu** with more exact meaning of what to do.

Grammar Note 5 — Additional settings for requesting

The main function of this unit, Requesting, can be applied in many other settings. For example, at a barber or beauty shop, a dry cleaning shop, and in making a telephone call.

   Examples

   Shan'pū to katto to burō onegai shimasu. "(I'd like) a shampoo, a haircut and blow dry, please."

   Moshimoshi, Jon'son desu ga, Tanaka-san onegai shimasu. "Hello, this is Johnson calling, . . . Mr. Tanaka, please."

Drill 1 Tell the driver where you want to go.

> e.g., *Shinjuku Eki made onegai shimasu.*
> (1) *Tōkyō Tawā*　　　　　　　　(2) *Shibuya Eki no nishi-guchi*
> (3) *Shibuya Eki no minami-guchi*　(4) *Roppon'gi (no) kōsaten* "crossing"
> (5) *Ōtemachi no San'kei Biru*　　(6) *Amerika Taishikan* "embassy"
> 　　　　　　　　　　　　　　　　　　　　*no chikaku*

Drill 2 Tell the driver the specific street/area to go to or by way of.

> e.g., *Yamate Dōri* "Yamate Avenue"　⟶　*Yamate Dōri o tōtte kudasai.*
> (1) *Aoyama Dōri*　　　　　　　(2) *Shuto Kōsoku*
> 　　　"Aoyama Avenue"　　　　　　　　"metropolitan expressway"
> (3) *Azabu Jūban*　　　　　　　(4) *Gin'za*

Drill 3 Vocabulary I—Repeat and memorize the vocabulary.

(1) ↑ *massugu* "straight"	(2) *migi e* "to the right"
(3) ← *hidari e* "to the left"	(4) *kōsaten* "intersection"
(5) *shin'gō* "traffic light"	(6) *tsukiatari* "T junction"

Drill 4 Give directions, using Vocabulary I.

e.g.,

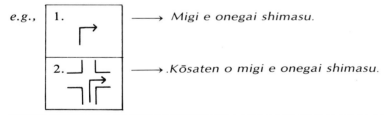

> 1. ⟶ *Migi e onegai shimasu.*
> 2. ⟶ *Kōsaten o migi e onegai shimasu.*

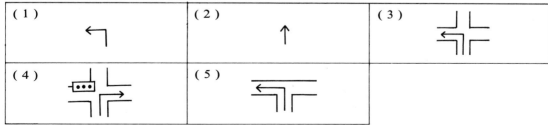

Drill 5 Vocabulary II—Repeat and momorize the vocabulary.

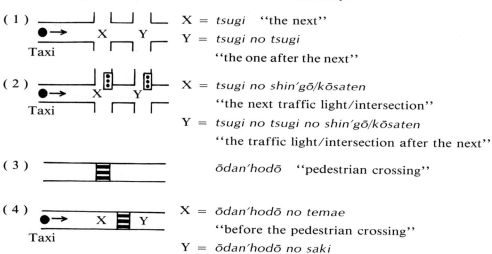

(1) X = *tsugi* "the next"

Taxi

Y = *tsugi no tsugi*
"the one after the next"

(2) X = *tsugi no shin'gō/kōsaten*
"the next traffic light/intersection"

Taxi

Y = *tsugi no tsugi no shin'gō/kōsaten*
"the traffic light/intersection after the next"

(3) *ōdan'hodō* "pedestrian crossing"

(4) X = *ōdan'hodō no temae*
"before the pedestrian crossing"

Taxi

Y = *ōdan'hodō no saki*
"after the pedestrian crossing"

Drill 6 Give directions, using Vocabulary II.

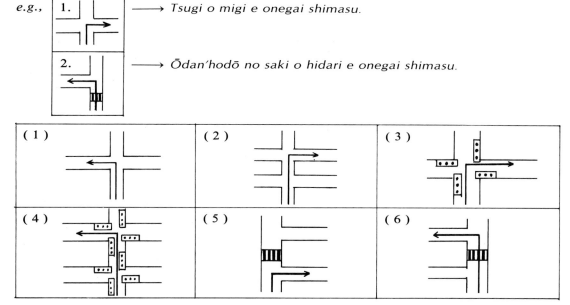

e.g., 1. ⟶ *Tsugi o migi e onegai shimasu.*

2. ⟶ *Ōdan'hodō no saki o hidari e onegai shimasu.*

(1) (2) (3)

(4) (5) (6)

Drill 7 Tell the driver where to stop.

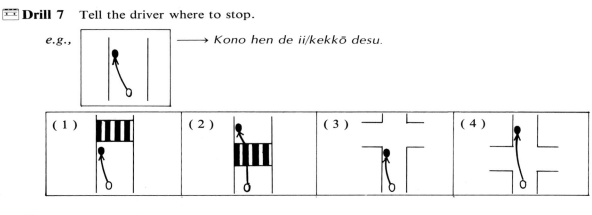

e.g., ⟶ *Kono hen de ii/kekkō desu.*

(1) (2) (3) (4)

Drill 8 Begin at A, tell your taxi driver to go to Z; then direct him through the stress, using the map.

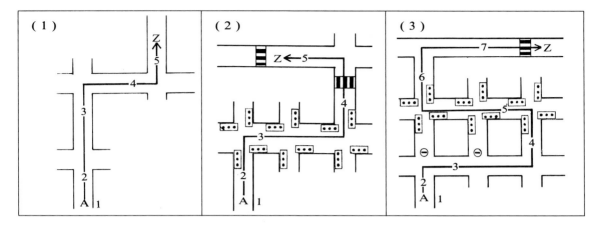

Drill 9 Continue giving directions, referring to the landmarks on the map.

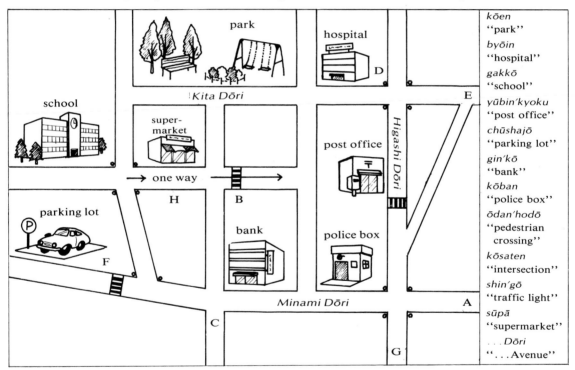

kōen	"park"
byōin	"hospital"
gakkō	"school"
yūbin′kyoku	"post office"
chūshajō	"parking lot"
gin′kō	"bank"
kōban	"police box"
ōdan′hodō	"pedestrian crossing"
kōsaten	"intersection"
shin′gō	"traffic light"
sūpā	"supermarket"
. . .Dōri	". . .Avenue"

(1) You are at (A) and you want to go to (B).

(2) You are at (C) and you want to go to (D).

(3) You are at (E) and you want to go to (F).

(4) You are at (G) and you want to go to (H).

Drill 10 Draw a map of your own neighborhood and practice giving directions between your home and various points. (You may be able to get a map from a city or ward office or from a police box.)

Lesson 8

SHOPPING

SONO KUROI SĒTĀ O MISETE KUREMASEN KA
"WILL YOU SHOW ME THAT BLACK SWEATER, PLEASE?"

🔲 Dialogue

[Ms. Thompson goes to buy a sweater.]

Ten'in:	*Irasshaimase. Yoroshikattara otori itashimasu.*
Ton'puson:	*Sono kuroi sētā o misete kuremasen ka.*
Ten'in:	*Hai. Dōzo.*
Ton'puson:	*Dōmo.*
Ten'in:	*Ikaga de gozaimasu ka.*
Ton'puson:	[In a negative tone] *Sō desu nē. . .*
	Ano midori no o misete kuremasen ka.
Ten'in:	*Hai, kashikomarimashita. Dōzo.*
Ton'puson:	*Dōmo. Kore wa ikura desu ka.*
Ten'in:	*Ichi-man-ni-sen-en de gozaimasu.*
Ton'puson:	*Ii desu kedo, chotto takai desu nē.*
	Mō sukoshi yasui no wa arimasen ka.
Ten'in:	*Hai. Kore wa ikaga de gozaimasu ka.*
	Nana-sen-go-hyaku-en de gozaimasu ga. . .

Ton'puson:	*Ā, ii desu nē. Sore jā,* ⟵⟶	Ton'puson:	[She doesn't want the sweater]
	kore kudasai.		*. . . Sō desu nē . . .*
Ten'in:	*Arigatō gozaimasu.*		*Dōmo. Mata kimasu.*
			[and leaves the shop.]
		Ten'in:	*Arigatō gozaimashita.*

Vocabulary

yoroshikattara: if it's all right with you . . . [Humble]

otori itashimasu: I'll show it to you. [Humble]

sono [P]:   that (near the listener)

kuroi: black

sētā: sweater

misete kuremasen ka: Could you please show me. . .?

ikaga: how [Humble]

sō desu nē: let me see

midori [N]:   green

no [Pronoun]:   one

kedo: although

takai: expensive

mō sukoshi yasui: a little less expensive

yasui: inexpensive

arimasen ka: Do you have...?

kudasai: please give me

mata: again

kimasu: will come

Salesclerk:	Hello. [*Lit.* Welcome.]
	If you'd like [*Lit.* If it's all right with you],
	I'll show that to you.
Ms. Thompson:	Thank you. Could I see that black sweater?
Salesclerk:	Yes, ma'am. Here you are. [*Lit.* Please.]
Ms. Thompson:	Thank you.
Salesclerk:	How is it? [*Lit.* How do you like it?]
Ms. Thompson:	Well. . . , let me see. . .
	Could I see that green one over there?
Salesclerk:	Certainly. Here you are.
Ms. Thompson:	Thank you. How much is this one?
Salesclerk:	It's 12,000 yen.
Ms. Thompson:	I like it [*Lit.* It's good], but it's expensive, isn't it?
	Do you have one a little less expensive?
Salesclerk:	Yes. . . How do you like this one?
	It's 7,500 yen.

Ms. Thompson:	Ah, I like it.	⟷	Ms. Thompson:	Hmm. . .
	[*Lit.* It's good, isn't it?]			Well. . . (I don't
	Well, I'll take this one.			know. . .), Thank
				you.
Salesclerk:	Thank you.			I'll come again.
			Salesclerk:	Thank you (for
				coming).

てんいん　　：いらっしゃいませ。　よろしかったら　おとりいたします。

トンプソン：その　くろい　セーターを　みせてくれませんか。

てんいん　　：はい。　どうぞ。

トンプソン：どうも。

てんいん　　：いかがでございますか。

トンプソン：そうですねえ…。　あの　みどりのを　みせてくれませんか。

てんいん　　：はい、　かしこまりました。　どうぞ。

トンプソン：どうも。　これは　いくらですか。

てんいん　　：12,000えんでございます。

トンプソン：いいですけど、　ちょっと　たかいですねえ。

　　　　　　　もう　すこし　やすいのは　ありませんか。

てんいん　　：はい。　これは　いかがでございますか。

　　　　　　　7,500えんでございますが…。

トンプソン：ああ、　いいですね。　⟷　トンプソン：そうですねえ…。

　　　　　　　それじゃあ、　　　　　　　　　　どうも。

　　　　　　　これ　ください。　　　　　　　　また　きます。

てんいん　　：ありがとうございます。　　てんいん：　ありがとう

　　　　　　　　　　　　　　　　　　　　　　　　　　ございました。

Grammar Note 1 — Asking to see something at a shop

[The item] *o misete kudasai.*
Sētā o misete kudasai.   "Show me a sweater, please."

[The item] *o misete kuremasen ka.*
Sētā o misete kuremasen ka.   "Could you show me a sweater, please?"

Object			Predicate	Final
sētā	*o*	⟹	*misete kudasai* *misete kuremasen*	∅ *ka* ↗

a.   *Misete kudasai.*   "Show me, please."

When asking to see something addressing people helping you at a store, use this verb. This pattern is polite but it is a mild command form.

b.   *Misete kuremasen ka.*   "Could you show me, please?"

Misete kuremasen ka is a rather indirect way of making a request, therefore, more polite than *misete kudasai.*

c.   Variation
   X wa arimasen ka.   "Do you have X?"

Here we mention this just as a variation. The verb *arimasen* is a negative form of the verb *arimasu* "have," which will be discussed later.

Grammar Note 2 — Noun modifiers

Here, we introduce the way to modify nouns. With noun modifiers you can refer to, describe or explain the noun.

Examples   The underlined parts are the noun modifiers.
   a.   *kono*   *hon*   "this book"
   b.   *omoshiroi hon*   "interesting book"
   c.   *kirei na*   *hon*   "pretty book"
   d.   *Nihon no*   *hon*   "book on Japan"

a.   Pre-Nouns [PN]

Noun Phrase		
Pre-noun	Noun	
kono	*hon*	"this book"
sono	*hon*	"that book [near the listener]"
ano	*hon*	"that book [far from the speaker and the listener]"
dono	*hon*	"which book"

Pre-nouns are never used alone.   They always precede nouns.

Examples
   Sono hon o misete kuremasen ka.   "Could you show me that book, please?"
   Ano sētā o misete kudasai.   "Show me that sweater, please."
   Kono kamera wa ikura desu ka.   "How much is this camera?"
   Ano sētā o onegai shimasu.   "(I'd like to take) that sweater, please."

b. Adjectives [A]

Noun Phrase	
Adjective	Noun
tak-ai	*hon*
ōk-ii	*hon*
yas-ui	*hon*
omoshir-oi	*hon*

"expensive book"
"large book"
"inexpensive/cheap book"
"interesting book"

Adjectives are recognizable by their ending -*ai*, -*ii*, *ui*, or -*oi*.

Examples

Ōkii sētā o misete kudasai.   "Show me a large sweater, please."
Kore wa ōkii sētā desu.   "This is a large sweater."
Are wa omoshiroi hon desu nē.   "That's an interesting book, isn't it?"
Chiisai kamera wa arimasu ka.   "Do you have a small camera?"

c. Adjectival Nouns [AN]

Noun Phrase		
Adjectival Noun		Noun
kan'tan	*na*	*hon*
kirei	*na*	*hon*

"simple/easy book"
"pretty book"

Examples

Kan'tan na kamera o misete kudasai.   "Show me a simple camera, please."
Kan'tan na kamera wa arimasu ka.   "Do you have a simple camera?"

d. Nouns [N]

Noun Phrase		
Noun		Noun
saisho	*no*	*hon*
hoka	*no*	*hon*
ei-go	*no*	*hon*
Nihon	*no*	*hon*
Tanaka-san	*no*	*hon*
watashi	*no*	*hon*

"the first book"
"the other book"
"English book"
"book on Japan"
"Mr. Tanaka's book"
"my book"

Words like "first" or "other", *etc.*, are adjectives in English grammar, but the equivalent are nouns in Japanese grammar. They need *no* after them when they modify other nouns.

Following are the patterns using this structure, **[Noun]** *no* **[Noun]**. You have already learned:

Mōbiru Sekiyu no Tanaka desu.
     "I'm Tanaka from Mobil." (Lesson 1)
Kanai no Jēn desu.
     "This is Jane, my wife." (Lesson 1)
Sumisu-san no o-taku wa dochira desu ka.
     "Where is Mr. Smith's residence?" (Lesson 4)
Tsugi no shin'gō o migi e onegai shimasu.
     "Turn right at the next traffic light." (Lesson 7)

e.

Adjective + Noun

Pre-noun + Adjectival Noun + **na** + Noun

Noun + **no** + Noun

Observe the following:

Kono ōkii kamera [PN] [AN] [N]	"this large camera"
Sono kirei na sētā [PN] [AN] [N]	"that pretty sweater"
Ano ei-go no hon [PN] [N] [N]	"that English book"

Example

Sono kirei na sētā o misete   "Could you show me that pretty sweater,
kuremasen ka.   please?"

Ano ei-go no hon wa ikura desu ka. "How much is that English book?"

Grammar Note 3 — Making comments

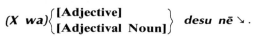

(X wa)$\left\{\begin{matrix}\textbf{[Adjective]}\\\textbf{[Adjectival Noun]}\end{matrix}\right\}$ ***desu nē*** ↘.

(Kore wa) ii desu nē.   "I like it!" *or* "It's good, isn't it?"

(Kore wa) kirei desu nē.   "It's pretty, isn't it?"

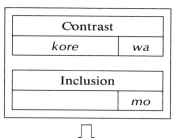

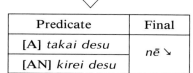

a.   When making a comment, add ***desu*** after an adjective or adjectival noun. ***Nē*** is added after ***desu*** when you want to get the listener's involvement or agreement with your comment.

b.   **[Comment 1]** *kedo/ga,* **[Comment 2]**   "but, although"

If you have a paradoxical comment to the main comment, use ***kedo*** or ***ga*** to link two thoughts. Observe the following, paying attention to the order of the two comments:

Comment 1 Paradoxical Comment	Conjunction	Comment 2 Main Comment
Takai desu	*kedo/ga,*	*ii desu nē.*
Kirei desu	*kedo/ga,*	*takai desu nē.*

"Although it's expensive, it's good, isn't it?"

"Although it's pretty, it's expensive, isn't it?"

Keredomo or *keredo* can be used instead of *kedo* with the same meaning and position. Note the difference in formality.

ga	[most formal]
keredomo	[more formal]
keredo	[less formal than *keredomo*]
kedo	[less formal than *keredo*]

Examples

Ii desu kedo, chotto takai desu nē.   "Although I like it, it's a little expensive, isn't it?"

Ano resutoran wa takai desu ga, ben'ri desu nē.   "Although that restaurant is expensive, it's convenient, isn't it?"

Grammar Note 4 — Asking to see an alternative item

Mō sukoshi $\left\{ \begin{array}{l} \textbf{[Adjective]} \\ \textbf{[Adjectival Noun]} \ \textit{na} \end{array} \right\}$ *no o misete kuremasen ka.*

Mō sukoshi <u>*yasui*</u> *no o misete kuremasen ka.*   "Could you show me a slightly cheaper one?"

a. *No* "the one"

This *no* is different from *no* in Grammar Note 2 b.

This *no* is used instead of the noun when you do not want to repeat the same noun again, or the noun is understood from the context.

Observe the following:

Sono akai sētā o misete kudasai.   "Show me that red sweater, please."

Then later

Ano kuroi no o misete kuremasen ka.   "Could you show me that black one, please?"

Study how *no* is substituted for the noun:

yasui <u>*sētā*</u> [A] ↓ *yasui* <u>*no*</u>	"an inexpensive sweater" "an inexpensive one"
kirei na <u>*sētā*</u> [AN] ↓ *kirei na* <u>*no*</u>	"a pretty sweater" "a pretty one"
hoka no <u>*sētā*</u> [N] ↓ *hoka* <u>*no*</u>	"another sweater" "another, some others"

b. *Mō sukoshi/chotto* "slightly" *or* "a little more"

Examples

mō sukoshi yasui sētā	"a slightly cheaper sweater"
mō sukoshi yasui no	"a slightly cheaper one"
Mō sukoshi yasui no o misete kuremasen ka.	"Could you show me a little cheaper one?"
Mō sukoshi kan'tan na no o misete kuremasen ka.	"Could you show me a slightly simpler one?"
Mō sukoshi ōkii no wa arimasu ka.	"Do you have a slightly bigger one?"

Grammar Note 5 — Indicating that you will take something

[The item you want to buy] *(o)* {**kudasai.**
                                       onegai shimasu.

Kore (o) kudasai.   "(I'd like to take) this one, please."

Object			Predicate
kore	*o*	⟹	*kudasai* *onegai shimasu*

Onegai shimasu is, in this lesson, used when you want to buy something. **Kudasai**, which literally means "give me," is also used to mean that you will take the item.

In shopping, expressing likes/dislikes often corresponds to the indication that you will or will not buy.

Observe the example:

Ā, ii desu nē.   "Ah, I like it. [*Lit*. It's good.]
   Kore onegai shimasu.   I'll take this one, please."

Grammar Note 6 — Indicating that you will not buy something

Sō desu nē . . .   "Hmm . . . , well . . . , Let me see . . ."
Mata kimasu.   "I'll come again."

When you express a dislike or a negative decision, don't use the negative forms explicitly. Japanese usually do not directly say, "I don't want to buy it." Instead, they express hesitation using **Ūn . . . , sō desu nē . . .** "Well . . . , let me see . . ." Then they leave the shop saying **Dōmo . . . Mata kimasu** "Thank you, I'll be back again," or they ask for an alternative item.

Grammar Note 7 — Color words

Words for color are divided into two groups:
   I.   Those which are adjectives
   II. Those which are nouns

I. [Adjectives]

akai	"red"
aoi	"blue"
kuroi	"black"
shiroi	"white"
kiiroi	"yellow"
chairoi	"brown"

II. [Nouns]

midori, guriin	"green"
gurē	"gray"
murasaki	"purple"
pin'ku	"pink"
bēju	"beige"
oren'ji	"orange"

Examples

Ano akai sētā o misete kudasai.   "Show me that red sweater, please."
Kono midori no sētā wa ikura desu ka.   "How much is this green sweater?"
Kore wa akai desu.   "This is red."
Sore wa midori desu.   "This is green."

Grammar Note 8 — Recommending

[Thing to be recommended] *wa ikaga de gozaimasu ka* ↗.

<u>Kore</u> *wa ikaga de gozaimasu ka.*   "How about this one?"

Ikaga means "how." *De gozaimasu* is a humble equivalent of *desu*, and often used by the people serving you, or respected people.

X wa ikaga de gozaimasu ka can be a real question, meaning "How do you like X?" or a recommendation "I recommend X . . . How about it?"

Grammar Note 9 — Additional vocabulary

These words will be used in "Requesting" and "Making Comments" when shopping but you need not memorize them all now. Notice the parts of speech:

a.

Meaning	[A]	[A]	Meaning
good	ii ↔	warui	bad
expensive	takai	yasui	inexpensive, cheap
big	ōkii	chiisai	small
heavy	omoi	karui	light
long	nagai	mijikai	short
spacious, wide	hiroi	semai	small in space, narrow
thick (cylindrical things)	futoi	hosoi	thin (cylindrical things)
thick (things like books)	atsui	usui	thin (things like books)
deep (color) strong tasting (beverages)	}koi	usui {	light (color) weak tasting (beverages)
far	tōi	chikai	near
difficult	muzukashii	yasashii	easy

b.

	[A]	[AN]	
noisy	urusai ↔	shizuka	quiet
difficult, complicated	muzukashii	kan'tan	easy, simple
dirty	kitanai	kirei	clean, pretty

c.

	[AN]	[AN]	
convenient	ben'ri ↔	fuben	inconvenient
simple, easy	kan'tan	fukuzatsu	complicated
subdued, plain	jimi	hade	flamboyant, loud

d.

	[N]	[N]	
first	saisho ↔	saigo	last
second	niban'me		
next	tsugi		
other	hoka		
men's	otoko mono	on'na mono	women's
adult	otona	kodomo	child, children
facing south	minami muki		

e.

Meaning	[N]
silk	*kinu, shiruku*
wool	*ūru*
cotton	*(mo)men, kotton*
linen	*asa*
synthetic fabric	*kasen*
nylon	*nairon*
polyester	*poriesuteru*
rayon	*rēyon*

Examples

kinu no sukāfu	"silk scarf"
momen no shatsu	"cotton shirt"
ūru no sūtsu	"wool suit"

Drill 1   Vocabulary 1—Repeat and learn the items for shopping.

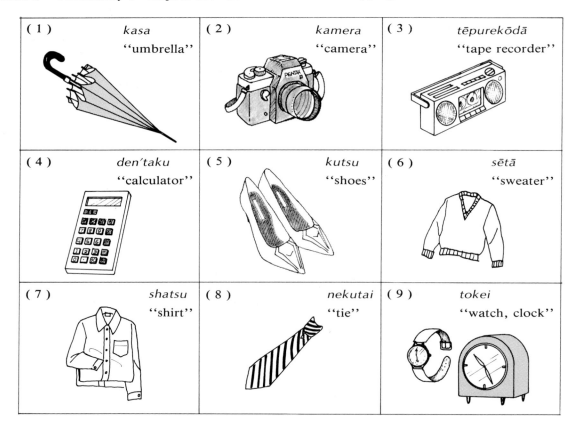

Drill 2   Ask to see the item.

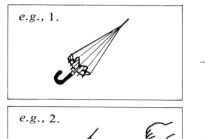

e.g., 1. ⟶ *Kasa o misete kudasai.*

e.g., 2. ⟶ *Sono kasa o misete kudasai.*

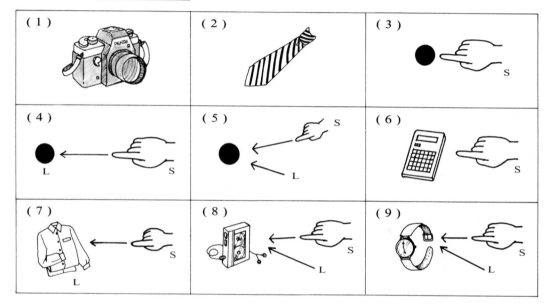

(1)   (2)   (3)

(4)   (5)   (6)

(7)   (8)   (9)

Drill 3   Ask to see the item, using adjectives.

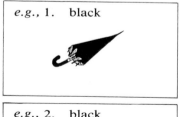

e.g., 1.   black ⟶ *Kuroi kasa o misete kuremasen ka.*

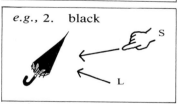

e.g., 2.   black ⟶ *Ano kuroi kasa o misete kuremasen ka.*

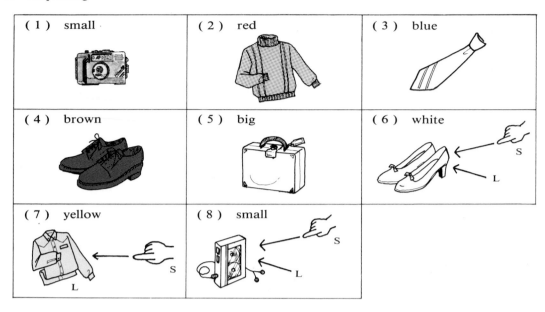

Drill 4   Ask to see the item, using nouns or adjectival nouns.

Drill 5   Transform the following using *no*.

    e.g.,   *Chiisai kamera o misete kuremasen ka.*

          ⟶ *Chiisai no o misete kuremasen ka.*

(1)   *Ōkii sētā o misete kuremasen ka.*

(2)   *Kan'tan na den'taku o misete kuremasen ka.*

(3)   *Hoka no "other" nekutai o misete kuremasen ka.*

(4)   *Ano midori no sētā o misete kuremasen ka.*

(5)   *Mō sukoshi kan'tan na kamera o misete kuremasen ka.*

(6) *Mō sukoshi yasui tokei "watch, clock" wa arimasu ka.*

(7) *Kyanon no kamera wa arimasu ka.*

(8) *Saisho no "the first" tokei wa ikura desu ka.*

(9) *Sono kuroi kutsu wa ikura desu ka.*

(10) *Kono Sonī "Sony" no tēpurekōdā wa ikura desu ka.*

Drill 6 Make comments.

> *e.g.,* 1. *ii.* ⟶ *Ii desu nē.*
>
> 2. *ii, takai* ⟶ *Ii desu kedo, takai desu nē.*

(1) *kirei*   (2) *ben'ri*

(3) *takai*   (4) *kirei, takai*

(5) *takai, ben'ri*   (6) *ii, chotto hade*

Drill 7 Complete the following, using the dialogue as a model.

You are the customer:

[a] Ask to see the article or the price.

[b] Make a comment.

[c] Show that you do not like it.

[d] Take the article or leave the shop.

(1) —At a chinaware shop—			
[a]	Tape:	*Irasshaimase.*	*kabin*
		Yoroshikattara odashi itashimasu.	"vase"
	You:	[a] _____ .	
	Tape:	*Hai. Dōzo.*	
		Ikaga de gozaimasu ka.	
[b] It's beautiful.	You:	[b] _____ .	
[d] Take it.	You:	[d] _____ .	
	Tape:	*Dōmo arigatō gozaimasu.*	
(2) —At a shop—	Tape:	*Irasshaimase.*	
		Yoroshikattara odashi itashimasu.	
[a]	You:	[a] _____ .	
	Tape:	*Hai. Kashikomarimashita. Dōzo.*	
		Ikaga de gozaimasu ka.	
[c] You don't like it.	You:	[c] _____ .	
[a] other one	You:	[a] _____ .	*hoka* [N]
	Tape:	*Hai. Dōzo. Kore wa ikaga de*	
		gozaimasu ka.	
[a] Ask the price.	You:	[a] _____ .	
	Tape:	*San'zen-en de gozaimasu.*	
[d] Take it.	You:	[d] _____ .	
	Tape:	*Dōmo arigatō gozaimasu.*	

(3)—At an electric appliance shop—

	Tape:	*Irasshaimase.*
		Yoroshikattara otori itashimasu.
[a]	You:	[a] _____ .
	Tape:	*Hai. Dōzo.*
	You:	[Say thank you.] _____ .
	Tape:	*Ikaga de gozaimasu ka.*
[b] It's good but slightly complicated.	You:	[b] _____ .
[a] a slightly simpler one	You:	[a] _____ .
	Tape:	*Hai. Kore wa ikaga de gozaimasu ka.*
[a] Ask the price.	You:	[a] _____ .
	Tape:	*Yon'sen-happyaku-en de gozaimasu ga . . .*
[d] Take it.	You:	[d] _____ .
	Tape:	*Hai, dōmo arigatō gozaimasu.*

fukuzatsu [AN]

kan'tan [AN]

(4)—At a shirt counter—

	Tape:	*Irasshaimase.*
		Yoroshikattara odashi itashimasu.
[a]	You:	[a] _____ .
	Tape:	*Hai. Dōzo.*
[b] It's good but expensive.	You:	[b] _____ .
[a] a slightly cheaper one	You:	[a] _____ .
	Tape:	*Hai. Kore wa ikaga de gozaimasu ka.*
[b] It's pretty but a little small.	You:	[b] _____ .
	Tape:	*Ā, sayō de gozaimasu ka.*
[c] You don't like it either.	You:	[c] _____ .
[d] Leave the shop.	You:	[d] _____ .
	Tape:	*Arigatō gozaimashita.*
		Mata dōzo.

"Oh, is that so?"

"Please come again."

Culture Note 4 — *"Tsumaranai mono desu ga . . ."*

Gift giving is an important part of Japanese life — and as is the case with many facets of Japanese life — there is a set way in which to go about this. The following is intended as a simple guide to a rather complex system.

A gift of money is the appropriate gift for many occasions. This is usually given in brand new bills in amounts of ¥3,000, ¥5,000, ¥10,000, and ¥20,000 and so on. (It's a good idea to consult a Japanese friend as to when and what amount you should give.) Money is always handed or mailed to the recipient in special envelopes (**noshibukuro**), and is given as an award, a wedding or housewarming gift, when attending a funeral, and as a gift on entering school or a company, on graduation or promotion, and as a New Year gift to children. On many occasions, you will receive a gift in return for the one you have given.

When visiting someone in the hospital, again money is appropriate, or flowers or fruit. Only remember that cut flowers are more popular than plants — as they imply the putting down of roots — and that's something no one wants to do in a hospital! Neither will a bunch of those beautiful chrysanthemums be appreciated — they're funeral flowers!

Seasonal gifts — given in summer (**ochūgen**) and winter (**oseibo**) — are traditional in Japan, but as this can turn into a long exchange of gifts, escalating in cost with each season, it is better not to initiate this exchange unless required to for business reasons. These gifts are usually impersonal household goods, and during these seasons department stores have displays of appropriately boxed gifts for you to select from. Their staff will then affix a **noshigami** to the gift (a slip of paper on which greetings and the name of the recipient are written), and arrange for it to be delivered.

When visiting someone, it is customary to take a gift of flowers, or a gift wrapped box of cookies or fruit. A gift of food, also, some local specialty, or a sample of some local craft, should be brought back from a trip, to friends and office staff. Of course, upon receiving a gift, thanks are in order. However, in Japan, once is not enough! The next time you meet, you must once again thank the giver.

Not governed by the bounds of tradition, although popular, is the comparatively recent custom of exchanging birthday and Christmas gifts. A personal gift may be presented in any way you like. Here department store gift wrap is quite acceptable. It does not appear impersonal, but, on the contrary, shows that you have taken the trouble to shop at a prestigious store.

Another western custom that has been enthusiastically adopted — be it with some changes — is that of giving chocolate on St. Valentine's Day. At this time the stores ring up millions of yen in sales of chocolate and cards — to young girls — who bestow these gifts upon their boyfriends, classmates and office colleagues — who anxiously await these tokens as proof of their popularity.

So, now all that remains is for you to be initiated into the rites of gift giving. Don't be daunted by all the do's and don'ts. Next time you visit a friend, arm yourself with a "name brand" box of rice crackers, or one of those melons that cost thousands of yen, and present your host or hostess with it, while murmuring hesitantly **Tsumaranai mono desu ga** . . . "just a little something . . ."

Money envelopes *noshibukuro*

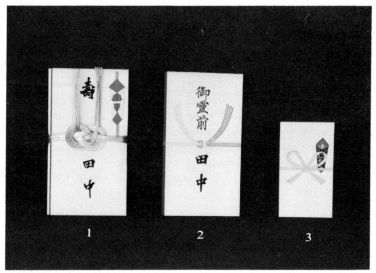

1. for a wedding
2. for a funeral
3. for a small gift of money such as a New Year gift to children

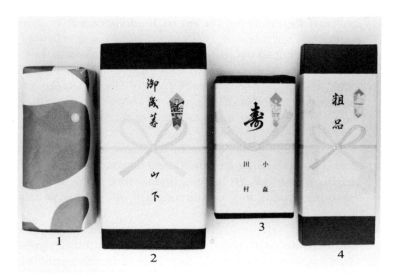

1. The usual gift wrapping from a prestigious department store.
2. A winter gift *oseibo.*
3. A thank-you gift to a wedding guest.
4. A formal gift for other occasions.

Under the wrapping paper (1), you will see a paper affixed to the box, on which the occasion and the giver's name are stated.

Katakana has various functions but the overwhelming use of **katakana** is for foreign words. Nowadays, most foreign words come from English, so if you speak English you may think this is a godsend. Having once learned the phonetic symbols you can now read menus of Western-style restaurants, some signs and most of many advertisements. But the catch comes when, having proudly and laboriously figured out the word *binīru* or *u-o-k-ka* or *gādoru*, you find yourself left, like Alice, with your head full of ideas without quite knowing what they are.

But don't despair — there are guidelines to follow in attacking such words. With judicious manipulation they yield vinyl, vodka and girdle. The guidelines will also tell you how a one-syllable word in English — strike — becomes a five-syllable word — *su-to-ra-i-ku* — in Japanese.

The key word, of course, is syllable. Japanese is syllabic and the only consonant that stands alone is "n." Every other consonant acquires a vowel and attains thereby full syllabic status as well. Other factors that contribute to the distortion in the import process are: one, the 14 or so vowel sounds of English that must be channeled through the five vowels of Japanese; and two, the consonants of English that don't exist in Japanese must be rendered through whatever is available locally.

Taking the last first, let's look at consonant changes. "Ca" of cabbage becomes *kya* as in *kyabetsu*, "who" of "Who's Who" becomes *fū* as in *fūzu fū*, "ci" as in city becomes *shi* as in *shitī* (don't laugh — it's true), "ti" often becomes *chi* as in *chiketto*, ticket, "wo" of woman becomes *u* as in *ūman ribu*, women's lib, where you may also note that "l" becomes "r." "Th" becomes "s/z" and "v" becomes "b" as in *rabu*, love (or rub!). "Gu" of penguin and "qu" of banquet become *gi* and *ke* giving *pengin* and *ban' ketto*. These are the main changes.

But now we have a different problem. To make consonants into syllables we have to add a vowel, but what vowel? Well, it's usually "u," except for "t/d" which become "tsu/ju" in Japanese so they take "o" instead. Witness: *supai* — spy, *sukurīn* — screen, *kōto* — coat, and *suriru* — thrill. There are occasional exceptions: final consonant "k" can be seen as *ki* as well as *ku*, as in *kēki* — cake and *burēki* — break, and then we get *sutoraiku* as in baseball but *sutoraiki* as in going on strike.

And what about the vowels themselves? We could go into exquisite detail but we'll just add a couple of simple comments. First, every "o" sound in English becomes something resembling the American pronunciation of "aw" (flaw). Thus, the vowels sounds in "John," "front" and "coat" all come out the same in Japanese. Then, all the "er" sounds as in "bird" and "a" sounds as in "apple" come out *a*, giving words like *fāsuto* — first. In addition, because there is no pattern of stressed and unstressed syllables in Japanese, even the unstressed vowels end up having their full values. Hence *rondon* — London, and *bābon* — bourbon.

The last thing to consider is the doubling of the vowels and consonants. The rule is fuzzy and seems to depend on patterns of stress in English which are then reflected in Japanese in terms of long and short vowels and single and double consonants.

Complicated? You'll get used to it. Anyway, let us leave you with the following:

hanbāgā ハンバーガー — hamburger

fasshon ファッション — fashion

kāten カーテン — curtain

damu ダム — dam

passhibu パッシブ — passive

tēburu テーブル — table

makudonarudo マクドナルド — McDonald's

wārudo ワールド — world

uisukī ウイスキー — whisky

katto カット — cut

sutoppu ストップ — stop

kādo カード — card

McDonald's マクドナルド
(ma-ku-do-na-ru-do)
ハンバーガー
(ha-n-bā-gā)

Review Quiz (Lesson 1 — Lesson 8)

I. Give the prices of the following items using _____ *wa* _____ *desu*.

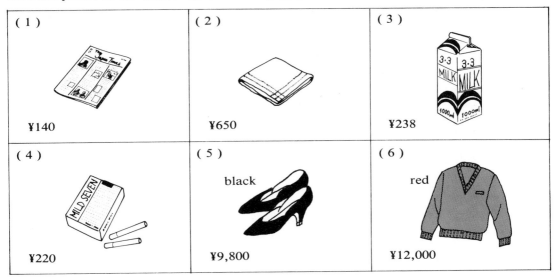

(1)	(2)	(3)
¥140	¥650	¥238
(4)	**(5)** black	**(6)** red
¥220	¥9,800	¥12,000

II. Match the expressions on the left with those in the column on the right.

1. *Esso Sekiyu no*
2. *O-kuni wa*
3. *Tsugi o migi e*
4. *O-kan'jō wa*
5. *Ii desu kedo,*
6. *Sore jā*

a. *dochira desu ka.*
b. *mata getsu-yōbi.*
c. *betsubetsu ni onegai shimasu.*
d. *Sumisu-san desu.*
e. *magatte kudasai.*
f. *chotto takai desu nē.*

III. Fill in the blanks with the Japanese equivalents given in English.

1. *Sono (   ) sētā o misete kuremasen ka.*   [red]
2. *Are wa (   ) hon desu ka.*   [interesting]
3. *(   ) kamera o misete kudasai.*   [simple]
4. *Sono (   ) shatsu o kudasai.*   [green]
5. *(   ) nekutai o misete kudasai.*   [silk]

IV. Fill in the blanks with the words from below.

1. *Kochira (   ) Maikeru Buraun-san desu.*
2. *Ueno (   ) ikura desu ka.*
3. *San'doitchi (   ) tomato jūsu onegai shimasu.*
4. *Kono hen (   ) ii desu.*
5. *Shin'gō o hidari (   ) onegai shimasu.*
6. *Moshimoshi, Sumisu-san (   ) otaku desu ka.*

   [*to,   made,   no,   de,   e,   wa*]

V. What Japanese expressions would you use in the following situations?

1. When you are introduced to a club member for the first time . . .
2. When you want to attract a waiter's attention at a restaurant . . .
3. When you meet the person who invited you to the *Kabuki* theater yesterday . . .

4. When you feel that you have inconvenienced someone by asking them to do something for you ...
5. When you want a taxi driver to go by way of Aoyama Avenue ...
6. When you want a taxi driver to stop before the pedestrian crossing ...
7. When you want to indicate that you will not buy something at a store ...
8. When you want to express gratitude for (being invited) to a party before leaving ...
9. When you want to express that you are impressed when someone says, *Uchi wa Roppon'gi desu* "I live in Roppongi" ...
10. When you leave the room in the middle of a conversation, and when you come back to the room a few minutes later ...

VI. Express in Japanese —

1. I'm Mr. Tanaka from Mobil Sekiyu.
2. I'll take this. [At a store]
3. I live in Minami Azabu, Minato-ku.
4. Good weather, isn't it?
5. Bye. [*Lit.* I'm leaving before you.] — to your colleague.
6. Well then, see you next week. — to your teacher.
7. Two coffee and one tea, please.
8. Stop about here, please. [*Lit.* About here is fine.]
9. Could you show me that green sweater?
10. Could you show me a slightly less expensive one?

Unit III

Expressing What You Did and What You Will Do

SCOPE OF UNIT III

The main function of Unit III is DESCRIBING, ASKING ABOUT and COMMENTING ON ACTIVITIES in the past and the future.

Lesson 9 presents both general and specific time words enabling you to talk about birthdays, store — restaurant operating hours and plans or engagements during the week.

Lesson 10 introduces three verbs: *ikimasu* "go," *kimasu* "come," and *kaerimasu* "go/come home," in conjunction with the time words (introduced in Lesson 9). This lesson also teaches you how to give your impression of Japan.

Lesson 11 covers the language you need to discuss and comment on an upcoming trip or a holiday. It also introduces you to some of the nuances evident in different combinations of the markers *wa*, *mo*, *ga*, *e*, *de*, *etc*.

Lesson 12 further discusses holidays but this time focuses on how the holiday went. You will be able to tell your friends how you enjoyed your holiday, from general remarks to a detailed description, and from exciting to disappointing situations.

Lesson 9

TIME EXPRESSIONS

NAN-JI KARA NAN-JI MADE DESU KA
"WHAT ARE THE HOURS?"

Dialogue I

[Mr. Smith asks Mr. Tanaka.]

Sumisu: *Tanaka-san, futsū depāto wa nan-ji kara nan-ji made desu ka.*

Tanaka: *Futsū gozen jū-ji kara gogo roku-ji made desu.*

Sumisu: *Jū-ji kara roku-ji made desu ka.*

Tanaka: *Ē.*

Sumisu: *Dōmo.*

Mr. Smith: Mr. Tanaka, what are the usual hours of a department store?
[*Lit.* from what time to what time]

Mr. Tanaka: Ordinarily from 10 a.m. to 6 p.m.

Mr. Smith: From 10 to 6?

Mr. Tanaka: Right.

Mr. Smith: Thanks.

Dialogue II

[As Mr. Smith leaves a restaurant he asks the waitress . . .]

Sumisu: *Koko wa nan-ji kara nan-ji made deshō ka.*

Ueitoresu: *Asa no jū-ji han kara yoru no ichi-ji made de gozaimasu.*

Sumisu: *Asa no jū-ji han kara yoru no ichi-ji made desu ka.*

Ueitoresu: *Hai.*

Sumisu: *Dōmo.*

Ueitoresu: *Dōmo arigatō gozaimashita.*

Mr. Smith: What are the hours of this restaurant?
[*Lit.* from what time to what time]

Waitress: We're open from half past ten in the morning to one o'clock in the morning.
[*Lit.* to one o'clock at night]

Mr. Smith: From half past ten in the morning to one o'clock in the morning?
[*Lit.* to one o'clock at night]

Vocabulary

futsū: usually

depāto: department store

kara [M]: [Starting Point] from

made [M]: [Ending Point] to

gozen: a.m.

gogo: p.m.

asa: morning

yoru: night

Waitress: Yes.
Mr. Smith: Thank you.
Waitress: Thank you.

I

スミス：田中さん、　ふつう　デパートは　なんじから　なんじまでですか。

田中　：ふつう　　ごぜん　10じから　ごご　6じまでです。

スミス：10じから　6じまでですか。

田中　：ええ。

スミス：どうも。

II

スミス　　　　：ここは　なんじから　なんじまででしょうか。

ウェイトレス：あさの　10じはんから　よるの　1じまででございます。

スミス　　　　：あさの　10じはんから　よるの　1じまでですか。

ウェイトレス：はい。

スミス　　　　：どうも。

ウェイトレス：どうも　ありがとうございました。

Time words are introduced in this lesson. Use the pattern from Unit I, _____ **wa** _____
desu. Add **desu** "is/are" right after the time word. For the past tense use **deshita**
"was/were."

Grammar Note 1 — General time

The type of words like yesterday, today, tomorrow, last week, or this week are called
"general time" in this textbook.

Vocabulary

Year Month Week	*kyonen* "last year" *sen′getsu* "last month" *sen′shū* "last week"	*kotoshi* "this year" *kon′getsu* "this month" *kon′shū* "this week"	*rainen* "next year" *raigetsu* "next month" *raishū* "next week"
Day	*kinō* "yesterday"	*kyō* "today"	*ashita* "tomorrow"
Morning Noon Evening	*kinō no asa* "yesterday morning" *kinō no hiru* "yesterday noon" *kinō no ban* "yesterday evening"	*kesa* "this morning" *kyō no hiru* "this noon" *kon′ban* "this evening"	*ashita no asa* "tomorrow morning" *ashita no hiru* "tomorrow noon" *ashita no ban* "tomorrow evening"
When?	*itsu*		

Examples
A: *Pātī wa itsu desu ka.*   "When is the party?"
B: *Ashita desu.*   "It's tomorrow."

101

Grammar Note 2 — Specific time

The type of words like 1986, January, one o'clock are called "specific time" in this book.

Year -nen			
Western Calendar			Japanese Calendar
1868	sen-happyaku-rokujūhachi-nen	*Meiji Gan-nen	Meiji Era first year
:	:	:	
1912	sen-kyūhyaku-jūni-nen	*Taishō Gan-nen	Taisho Era first year
:	:	:	
1926	sen-kyūhyaku-nijūroku-nen	*Shōwa Gan-nen	Showa Era first year
:	:	:	
1945	sen-kyūhyaku-yon'jūgo-nen	Shōwa nijū-nen	20th year
:	:	:	
1980	sen-kyūhyaku-hachijū-nen	Shōwa gojūgo-nen	55th year
1981	sen-kyūhyaku-hachijūichi-nen	Shōwa gojūroku-nen	56th year
1982	sen-kyūhyaku-hachijūni-nen	Shōwa gojūnana/shichi-nen	57th year
1983	sen-kyūhyaku-hachijūsan-nen	Shōwa gojūhachi-nen	58th year
1984	sen-kyūhyaku-hachijūyo-nen	Shōwa gojūkyū/ku-nen	59th year
1985	sen-kyūhyaku-hachijūgo-nen	Shōwa rokujū-nen	60th year
1986	sen-kyūhyaku-hachijūroku-nen	Shōwa rokujūichi-nen	61st year
1987	sen-kyūhyaku-hachijūnana/shichi-nen	Shōwa rokujūni-nen	62nd year
1988	sen-kyūhyaku-hachijūhachi-nen	Shōwa rokujūsan-nen	63rd year
1989	sen-kyūhyaku-hachijūkyū/ku-nen	Shōwa rokujūyo-nen	64th year
1990	sen-kyūhyaku-kyūjū-nen	Shōwa rokujūgo-nen	65th year
What year?	nan-nen		

Examples

A: Souru orin'pikku wa nan-nen desu ka.   "What year will the Seoul Olympics be held?"

B: Sen-kyūhyaku-hachijūhachi-nen desu.   "(In) 1988."

*The Japanese count years by historical periods as well as by the western system. The Japanese system numbers the years of an emperor's reign. This is the period of **Shōwa** (Hirohito).

	Months -gatsu	Days of the Month -ka/-nichi	Hours of the Day -ji	Minutes -fun/-pun
1	ichi-gatsu "January"	tsuitachi	ichi-ji	ip-pun
2	ni-gatsu "February"	futsu-ka	ni-ji	ni-fun
3	san-gatsu "March"	mik-ka	san-ji	san-pun
4	shi-gatsu "April"	yok-ka	yo-ji	yon-pun
5	go-gatsu "May"	itsu-ka	go-ji	go-fun
6	roku-gatsu "June"	mui-ka	roku-ji	rop-pun
7	shichi-gatsu "July"	nano-ka	⎰shichi-ji ⎱nana-ji	⎰shichi-fun ⎱nana-fun
8	hachi-gatsu "August"	yō-ka	hachi-ji	⎰hachi-fun ⎱hap-pun
9	ku-gatsu "September"	kokono-ka	ku-ji	kyū-fun
10	jū-gatsu "October"	tō-ka	jū-ji	⎰jup-pun ⎱jip-pun
11	jūichi-gatsu "November"	jūichi-nichi	jūichi-ji	jūip-pun
12	jūni-gatsu "December"	jūni-nichi	jūni-ji	jūni-fun
:				
14	—	jūyok-ka	jūyo-ji	jūyon-pun
:				
20	—	hatsu-ka	nijū-ji	⎰nijup-pun ⎱nijip-pun
:				
24	—	nijūyok-ka	nijūyo-ji	⎰nijūyon-pun ⎱nijūyon-fun
?	nan-gatsu "what month?"	nan-nichi "what day of the month?"	nan-ji "what time?"	nan-pun "how many minutes?"

	Day of the Week -yōbi
Sunday	nichi-yōbi
Monday	getsu-yōbi
Tuesday	ka-yōbi
Wednesday	sui-yōbi
Thursday	moku-yōbi
Friday	kin-yōbi
Saturday	do-yōbi
?	nan-yōbi "what day of the week?"

Examples

A: Sumimasen, ima nan-ji deshō ka.   "Excuse me, what time is it now?"
B: Chōdo ku-ji desu.   "It's exactly 9."

A: Ressun wa nan-yōbi desu ka.   "Which days do you have your lessons?"
B: Sui-yōbi to kin'yō-bi desu.   "Wednesdays and Fridays."

Grammar Note 3 — Period of time

	Number of Years -nen	Number of Months -kagetsu	Number of Weeks -shūkan	Number of Days -nichi/-ka
0.5	han-toshi	han-tsuki	—	han-nichi
1	ichi-nen	ik-kagetsu	is-shūkan	ichi-nichi
1.5	ichi-nen-han	ik-kagetsu-han	is-shūkan-han	ichi-nichi-han
2	ni-nen	ni-kagetsu	ni-shūkan	futsu-ka
3	san-nen	san-kagetsu	san-shūkan	mik-ka
4	yo-nen	yon-kagetsu	yon-shūkan	yok-ka
5	go-nen	go-kagetsu	go-shūkan	itsu-ka
6	roku-nen	rok-kagetsu	roku-shūkan	mui-ka
7	⎰ nana-nen ⎱ shichi-nen	⎰ nana-kagetsu ⎱ shichi-kagetsu	nana-shūkan	nano-ka
8	hachi-nen	⎰ hachi-kagetsu ⎱ hak-kagetsu	⎰ hachi-shūkan ⎱ has-shūkan	yō-ka
9	⎰ kyū-nen ⎱ ku-nen	⎰ kyū-kagetsu ⎱ ku-kagetsu	kyū-shūkan	kokono-ka
10	jū-nen	⎰ juk-kagetsu ⎱ jik-kagetsu	⎰ jus-shūkan ⎱ jis-shūkan	tō-ka
11	jūichi-nen	⎰ jūichi-kagetsu ⎱ jūik-kagetsu	⎰ jūichi-shūkan ⎱ jūis-shūkan	jūichi-nichi
12	jūni-nen	jūni-kagetsu	jūni-shūkan	jūni-nichi
?	nan-nen "how many years?"	nan-kagetsu "how many months?"	nan-shūkan "how many weeks?"	nan-nichi "how many days?"
?	dono gurai "how long?"			

	Number of Hours -jikan	Number of Minutes -pun/-fun
1	ichi-jikan	ip-pun
2	ni-jikan	ni-fun
3	san-jikan	san-pun
4	yo-jikan	yon-pun
5	go-jikan	go-fun
6	roku-jikan	rop-pun
7	⎰ shichi-jikan ⎱ nana-jikan	⎰ shichi-fun ⎱ nana-fun
8	hachi-jikan	⎰ hachi-fun ⎱ hap-pun
9	⎰ ku-jikan ⎱ kyū-jikan	kyū-fun
10	jū-jikan	⎰ jup-pun ⎱ jip-pun
11	jūichi-jikan	jūip-pun
12	jūni-jikan	jūni-fun
?	nan-jikan "how many hours?"	nan-pun "how many minutes?"
?	dono gurai "how long?"	

Example

A: *Kyūka wa dono gurai desu ka.*　　　"How long is your vacation?"

B: *Is-shūkan desu.*　　　"One week."

Grammar Note 4 — Starting point and ending point

[Time] *kara* [Time] *made desu.*

Jū-ji kara roku-ji made desu.   "(It's) from 10 to 6."

a. ***Kara*** [Starting Point Marker]   "from"
    Starting point of time, place, deed or thought, *etc,* is indicated by ***kara.***

b. ***Made*** [Ending Point Marker]   "to"
    (*cf.* Lesson 5, Grammar Note 4; Lesson 7, Grammar Note 1-a)

    Remember, ***Shinjuku eki made onegai shimasu.*** "Take me to Shinjuku station, please."
    [X] *made* indicates the ending point of time, place, deed or thought, *etc.*

    Examples

    A: *Kaisha wa nan-ji kara nan-ji*   "What are your office hours?"
        made desu ka.
    B: *Ku-ji kara go-ji made desu.*   "9 to 5."

**Drill 1**   Make short dialogues.

1. *e.g.,* A: *Pātī* "party" *wa itsu desu ka.*

    B: *Ashita desu.*

    (1) *kaigi* "conference", *kyō*   (2) *shutchō* "business trip", *ashita*

    (3) *ryokō* "trip", *raishū*   (4) *tsugi no yasumi* "next vacation", *rainen*

2. *e.g.,* A: *Pātī wa itsu desu ka.*

    B: *Kinō deshita.*

    (1) *kon'sāto* "concert", *sen'shū*   (2) *tan'jōbi* "birthday", *sen'getsu*

    (3) *shiken* "examination", *kyō*   (4) *okusan/go-shujin no tan'jōbi, ashita*

    (5) *kodomo-san no tan'jōbi, kinō*

Dril 2   Give the time.

e.g.,   A: *Sumimasen, ima nan-ji deshō ka.*

    B: *Chōdo 12-ji desu.*

    A: *Dōmo.*

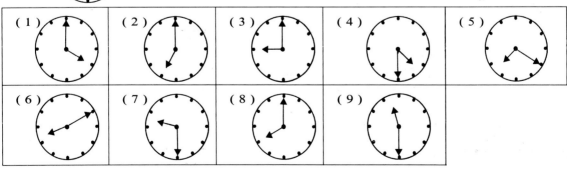

Drill 3   Substitute.

e.g.,   9:00 a.m. ⎫
          ↓   ⎬ ⟶   <u>Gozen ku-ji kara</u>
      5:00 p.m. ⎭   <u>gogo go-ji</u> made desu.

(1)   10:00 a.m.   (2)   12:00   (3)   9:30 a.m.   (4)   7:00 in the morning
        ↓   ↓   ↓   ↓
     6:00 p.m.   1:30   5:15 p.m.   11:00 in the evening

Drill 4   Use Dialogue I as a model.

(1) supermarket? You	You: _____ . Tape: *Futsū gozen jū-ji kara gogo roku-ji han made desu yo.* You: [EL] _____ . Tape: *Ē.* You: _____ .	*sūpā*
(2) bank? You	You: _____ . Tape: *Futsū ku-ji kara san-ji made desu yo. Kyasshusābisu wa shichi-ji made desu kedo.* You: [EL] _____ . Tape: *Ē.* You: _____ .	*gin'kō* "cash card service"

Drill 5   Use Dialogue II as a model.

(1) —At a supermarket—	You: _____ . Tape: *Asa no go-ji kara yoru no ni-ji made desu.* You: [EL] _____ . Tape: *Hai.* You: _____ .	*asa* "morning" *yoru* "evening"
(2) —At a gas station—	You: _____ . Tape: *Ku-ji kara yoru no jūni-ji made desu.* You: [EL] _____ . Tape: *Hai.* You: _____ .	

Drill 6 Talk about the following people's birthdays.

Name	Tanaka	Sumisu	Ōno	Ton'puson	Howaito
Birthday	Jan. 11	Oct. 30	April 21	July 25	Sept. 12

🔲 *e.g.,*   A: *Tanaka-san no tan'jōbi wa itsu desu ka.*

B: *Ichi-gatsu jūichi-nichi desu.*

Drill 7 Ask and answer which days the department stores, *etc.,* are closed (*yasumi*).

Names (Dept. stores, museums, *etc.*)	Mitsukoshi Depāto "department store"	Matsuya/ Tōkyū Depāto	biyōin "beauty shop"	toshokan "library" bijutsukan "museum" tokoya "barber shop"	byōin "hospital"
yasumi Days Closed	Monday	Thursday	Tuesday	Monday	Sunday

🔲 *e.g.,*   A: *Mitsukoshi wa yasumi wa nan-yōbi desu ka.*

B: *Getsu-yōbi desu.*

(1) *Matsuya Depāto*   (2) *biyōin*   (3) *toshokan*

(4) *byōin*   (5) *bijutsukan*   (6) *tokoya*

Drill 8 Answer the questions using the engagement calendar.

Mon.	Tues.	Wed.	Thu.	Fri.	Sat.	Sun.
8:15 *Nihon-go* ≀ *no* 9:15 *ressun* "Japanese lesson"	10:00 *Kaigi* ≀ "meeting" 12:00	8:15 *Nihon-go* ≀ *no* 9:15 *ressun*		8:15 *Nihon-go* ≀ *no* 9:15 *ressun* 6:30 *pātī* ≀ "party" 8:30	2:00 *Tenisu* ≀ 3:00	

(1) *Nihon-go no ressun wa nan-yōbi desu ka.*

(2) *Nan-ji kara nan-ji made desu ka.*

(3) *Kaigi wa nan-yōbi desu ka.*

(4) *Nan-ji kara nan-ji made desu ka.*

(5) *Tenisu wa nan-yōbi desu ka.*

(6) *Nan-ji kara nan-ji made desu ka.*

(7) *Pātī wa nan-yōbi desu ka.*

(8) *Nan-ji kara nan-ji made desu ka.*

Drill 9   Talk about vacations (*kyūka or yasumi*).

> e.g.,   A: *Kyūka wa nan-gatsu desu ka.*
>
> B: <u>*Go-gatsu*</u> *desu.*
>
> A: *Dono gurai desu ka.*
>
> B: <u>*Go-shūkan*</u> *desu.*

(1) *jūni-gatsu, yon-shūkan*   (2) *roku-gatsu, is-shūkan*

(3) *san-gatsu, ik-kagetsu*   (4) *shichi-gatsu, itsu-ka*

Lesson 10

COMING, GOING AND RETURNING MAKING COMMENTS ON JAPAN

ITSU NIHON E KIMASHITA KA
"WHEN DID YOU COME TO JAPAN?"

▣ Dialogue

[Mr. Takahashi has met Mr. Smith and Mr. White.]

Takahashi:	Sumisu-san, itsu Nihon e kimashita ka.
Sumisu:	Kyonen no shi-gatsu ni kimashita.
Takahashi:	Howaito-san wa itsu kimashita ka.
Howaito:	Ni-nen mae ni kimashita.
Takahashi:	Ni-nen mae no nan-gatsu desu ka.
Howait:	Shichi-gatsu desu.
Takahashi:	Nihon wa dō desu ka.
Howaito:	Bukka ga takai desu nē.
Sumisu:	Sō desu nē.
Takahashi:	Howaito-san wa itsu goro (Amerika e) kaerimasu ka.
Howaito:	Tabun rainen no ku-gatsu goro desu.
Takahashi:	Sumisu-san wa.
Sumisu:	Mada wakarimasen.
Takahashi:	Sō desu ka.

Mr. Takahashi:	Mr. Smith, when did you come to Japan?
Mr. Smith:	In April last year.
Mr. Takahashi:	What about you, Mr. White?
Mr. White:	(I came here) two years ago.
Mr. Takahashi:	What time of year [*Lit*. what month] was it?
Mr. White:	It was July.
Mr. Takahashi:	How do you like Japan? [*Lit*. How is Japan?]
Mr. White:	Well, prices are high, aren't they?
Mr. Smith:	You can say that again. [*Lit*. That's so.]
Mr. Takahashi:	When are you possibly going back to the States?
Mr. White:	Maybe in September of next year.
Mr. Takahashi:	What about you, Mr. Smith?
Mr. Smith:	I don't know yet.
Mr. Takahashi:	I see. [*Lit*. Is that so?]

Vocabulary

kimashita ← kuru: came
bukka: cost of living
goro: approximately [with specific time]
kaerimasu ← kaeru: return, go back

tabun: maybe
mada: yet [with the negative form]
wakarimasen: don't know
[*Lit*. don't understand]

高橋　　　：スミスさん、　いつ　日本へ　きましたか。
たかはし

スミス　　：きょねんの　4がつに　きました。

高橋　　　：ホワイトさんは　いつ　きましたか。

ホワイト：2ねんまえに　きました。

高橋　　　：2ねんまえの　なんがつですか。

ホワイト：7がつです。

高橋　　　：日本は　どうですか。
にほん

ホワイト：ぶっかが　たかいですねえ。

スミス　　：そうですねえ。

高橋　　　：ホワイトさんは　いつごろ　（アメリカへ）　かえりますか。

ホワイト：たぶん　らいねんの　9がつごろです。

高橋　　　：スミスさんは。

スミス　　：まだ　わかりません。

高橋　　　：そうですか。

Grammar Note 1 — Coming, going, returning

Three verbs are introduced in this lesson:

ikimasu　　　"to go"　(motion away from the speaker's home base)
kimasu　　　"to come"　(motion toward the speaker's home base)
kaerimasu　　"to go/come back"

a.　In ordinary, polite speech (Level 2), verbs end in *-masu* or its variation. (There are different endings of verbs due to different speech levels or structures of the sentence, but they are not discussed in this textbook.)

b.　Tenses

Note that the tenses in Japanese are different from those in English.

| *-masu* | [Non-Past Affirmative] — has two possible meanings:

　i)　what you generally or habitually do
　ii)　**what you will do**

| *-masen* | [Non-Past Negative] — has three possible meanings:

　i)　what you generally or habitually do not do
　ii)　**what you will not do**
　iii)　what you have not done

110

| -mashita | [Past Affirmative] — has two possible meanings:

i) what you have done
ii) **what you did in the past**

| -masen deshita | [Past Negative]

It generally means **what you did not do in the past**.

In this lesson, the meanings in bold letters are introduced.

When the subject of the sentence is the speaker, **-masu** or **-masen** can express the speaker's will.

Non-Past		Past	
Aff.	Neg.	Aff.	Neg.
iki-masu	*iki-masen*	*iki-mashita*	*iki-masen deshita*
ki-masu	*ki-masen*	*ki-mashita*	*ki-masen deshita*
kaeri-masu	*kaeri-masen*	*kaeri-mashita*	*kaeri-masen deshita*

Grammar Note 2 — Places

[Place] *kara* [Place] *e/made* [Verb].
Kyōto kara Nara e/made ikimasu.   "(I) will go from Kyoto to Nara."

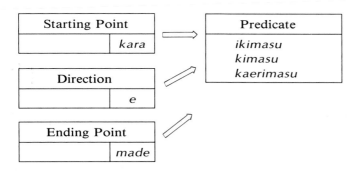

a.   **E**   [Direction Marker]   "to"
Remember in "Taking a taxi," you learned **migi e onegai shimasu** "Turn to the right, please."
[X] e indicates direction or the place you are moving toward.

Examples

Hokkaidō e ikimasu.	"(I) will go (*or* am going) to Hokkaido."
Sapporo made ikimasu.	"(I) will go (*or* am going to go) as far as Sapporo."
Yokohama kara Nagoya made ikimashita.	"(I) went from Yokohama to Nagoya."
Tanaka-san wa uchi e kaerimashita.	"Mr. Tanaka went home."

b.   **Doko**   "where"

Example

Doko e ikimashita ka.   "Where did you go?"

Vocabulary: Places to go

Meaning	
immigration office	*shutsunyūkoku kan'ri jimusho*
ward office	*kuyakusho*
city office	*shiyakusho*
embassy	*taishikan*
church	*kyōkai*
department store	*depāto*
supermarket	*sūpā (māketto)*
bank	*gin'kō*
hospital	*byōin*
beauty parlor	*biyōin*
barber shop	*tokoya*
school	*gakkō*
office, company	*kaisha*
office	*ofisu*
(my) house, home	*uchi*
(my) friend's house, home	*tomodachi no uchi*
(your/his/her) house, home	*otaku*
Mr./Ms. Tanaka's house, home	*Tanaka-san no otaku*
where?	*doko*

Grammar Note 3 — Time

[Time] *ø, ni [Verb].   *φ = "zero" No marker is needed.
Kyonen kimashita.   "(I) came (here) last year."
San-gatsu ni kimashita.   "(I) came (here) in March."

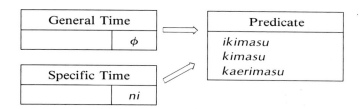

a.   **ø ***   [General Time]

General time words (*e.g.,* **kyonen** "last year," **ashita** "tomorrow") were introduced in Lesson 9.
When you use them with a verb, they do not take a marker.

b.   ***Ni***   [Specific Time Marker]   "at, in, on"
The marker ***ni*** indicates the point of time with specific time words introduced in Lesson 9 (*e.g.,* **1986-nen, ichi-gatsu** "January," **go-ji** "five o'clock").

Examples

Kyonen ikimashita.	"(I) went (there) last year."
Ichi-gatsu ni ikimashita.	"(I) went (there) in January."
Kyonen no ichi-gatsu ni ikimashita.	"(I) went (there) in January last year."
Go-ji ni kaerimasu.	"(I) will go/come back at five o'clock."
Raishū no getsu-yōbi ni ikimasu.	"(I) will go on Monday next week."

c. **_Itsu_**   "when"

Itsu does not take **_ni_**, a specific time marker.

d. **_Nan-nen_**   "which year"
   Nan-gatsu   "which month"
   Nan-nichi   "what day of the month"
   Nan-yōbi   "what day of the week"
   Nan-ji   "what time"
   Nan-pun   "what time, [_Lit._ how many minutes]"

These words take **_ni_** to mean "at what time," _etc._

e. **[Time]** **_goro_**   "around [Time]"

The word **_goro_** after a specific time word indicates an approximate time.

Examples

Tanaka-san wa ni-ji goro kaerimashita.	"Mr. Tanaka went home around two o'clock."
Tanaka-san wa ni-ji goro ni kaerimashita.	"Mr. Tanaka went home at around two o'clock."
Itsu Nihon e kimashita ka.	"When did (you) come to Japan?"
Itsu goro kaerimasu ka.	"When (approximately) are you going to go home?"
Nan-ji ni ikimasu ka.	"At what time are you going to go?"
Nan-ji goro ikimasu ka.	"About what time are you going to go?"

f. **[Period of time]** **_mae (ni)_**   " ~ago/before"

   ni-nen mae (ni)   "two years ago"

Use the time period words in Lesson 9.

Examples

Ni-nen mae (ni) kimashita.	"(I) came (here) two years ago."
San-kagetsu mae (ni) kimashita.	"(I) came (here) three months ago."
Tanaka-san wa yon-shūkan mae (ni) Kyōto e ikimashita.	"Mr. Tanaka went to Kyoto four weeks ago."
Sumisu-san wa go-jikan mae (ni) uchi e kaerimashita.	"Mr. Smith went home five hours ago."

g. **[Period of time]** **_go (ni)_**   " ~later/after"

   ni-nen go (ni)   "two years later, in two years"

Examples

Ichi-jikan go ni ikimasu.	"I will be there in one hour."
Ni-nen go ni kaerimasu.	"I will go back (to my country) in two years."

Grammar Note 4 — Subject

[Person] **_ga_** **[Verb].**

Tanaka-san ga ikimashita.   "Mr. Tanaka went (there)."

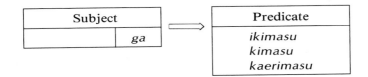

a.   ***Ga***   [Subject Marker]

The marker ***ga*** indicates that the preceding noun is the subject of the sentence. Very often, these sentences are narrative or descriptive. Sentences which answer "who" questions also have the subject marked by ***ga***. (There can also be a topic, marked by ***wa***, in addition to the subject, marked by ***ga***.)

b.   ***Dare***   "who"

Examples

Nichi-yōbi ni tomodachi ga uchi e kimashita.	"On Sunday, a friend of mine came to my house."
A: *Dare ga ikimasu ka.*	"Who is going?"
B: *Tanaka-san ga ikimasu.*	"Mr. Tanaka is going."

Grammar Note 5 — Answering questions

a.   Answering WH questions (Answering when, where, who, *etc.*)

Examples

A: *Itsu Nihon e kimashita ka.*	"When did you come to Japan?"
B: *Kyonen kimashita.*	"I came (here) last year."
A: *Kinō doko e ikimashita ka.*	"Where did you go yesterday?"
B: *Nara e ikimashita.*	"I went to Nara."
A: *Ashita dare ga kimasu ka.*	"Who is coming tomorrow?"
B: *Ono-san ga kimasu.*	"Mr. Ono is coming."

b.   Answering Yes/No questions

***Ē,* [Verb].**

or

***Iie,* [Verb].**

When answering, use the same main verb as in the question.

Examples

A: *Kyōto e ikimashita ka.*	"Did you go to Kyoto?"
B: *Ē, ikimashita.*	"Yes, I did."
Iie, ikimasen deshita.	"No, I didn't."
A: *Sen'shū kyōto e ikimashita ka.*	"Did you go to Kyoto last week?"
B: *Ē, ikimashita.*	"Yes, I did."
Iie, ikimasen deshita.	"No, I didn't."

Grammar Note 6 — Replacing the verb with ***desu***

A verb can be replaced by ***desu*** when it is understood from the context. Note that the marker preceding the verb is eliminated:

Examples

A: *Itsu Nihon e kimashita ka.*	
B: *Ni-nen mae ni kimashita.*	
Ni-nen mae desu.	

A: *Kinō doko e ikimashita ka.*
B: *Nara e ikimashita.*
    ↓
   Nara desu.

A: *Ashita dare ga kimasu ka.*
B: *Ono-san ga kimasu.*
    ↓
   Ono-san desu.

The tense of the replaced verb does not matter here — use **desu** for all tenses.

Grammar Note 7 — Asking for comments on Japan

$$X wa \begin{Bmatrix} d\bar{o} \\ ikaga \end{Bmatrix} desu\ ka \nearrow.$$ "How do you like X?" [*Lit.* "How is X?"]

Dō means "how." **Ikaga** (*cf.* Lesson 8, Grammar Note 8) is a humble equivalent of **dō**.

Examples

Nihon wa dō desu ka.	"How do you like Japan?"
Tōkyō wa ikaga desu ka.	"How do you like Tokyo?"
Nihon no tabemono wa dō desu ka.	"How do you like Japanese food?"
— Variations —	
Nihon no tabemono wa oishii desu ka.	"Is Japanese food tasty?"
Nihon-go wa muzukashii desu ka.	"Is Japanese (language) difficult?"
Nihon wa nagai desu ka.	"Have you been in Japan for a long time?" (*cf.* "Is Japan long?")

Grammar Note 8 — Making comments on Japan

Here, we introduce two ways to make comments:

a. **[Item] ga [A/AN] desu (nē ↘).**
  Bukka ga takai desu (nē).   "Prices (cost of living) are high, (aren't they?)"

Subject			Predicate		Final
bukka	ga	⟹	takai	desu	nē ↘

Examples

Hito ga ōi desu (nē).	"There are many people, (aren't there?)" [*Lit.* "People are many, aren't they?"]
Yachin ga takai desu (nē).	"The (house) rent is high, (isn't it?)"
Tabemono ga oishii desu (nē).	"The food is delicious, (isn't it?)"
Hito ga shin'setsu desu (nē).	"People are nice and kind, (aren't they?)"

Nē is often added at the end of these types of comments.
(*cf.* Lesson 2, Grammar Note 2–c)

b. **(_____ wa) _____ desu (nē ↘).**
  Nihon wa ii kuni desu (nē).   "Japan is a nice country, (isn't it?)"

Topic	
Nihon	wa

⇓

Predicate		Final
ii kuni	desu	nē ↘

Examples

(Nihon wa) omoshiroi kuni desu (nē).	"Japan is an interesting country, (isn't it?)"
(Nihon wa) kirei na kuni desu (nē).	"Japan is a beautiful country, (isn't it?)"
(Kyōto wa) ii tokoro desu (nē).	"Kyoto is a good place, (isn't it?)"
(Tōkyō wa) an'zen na tokoro desu (nē).	"Tokyo is a safe place, (isn't it?)"
(Nihon wa) tsumaranai kuni desu (nē).	"Japan is a boring country, (isn't it?)"

Grammar Note 9 — Expressing agreement or disagreement to a comment

You have learned small but important techniques of showing agreement or enthusiastic listening signs to allow you to converse smoothly. They are:

Sō desu nē ↘.   "Yes, it is." (*cf.* Lesson 2)
Sō desu ka ↘.   "Is that so?" (*cf.* Lesson 3)

Now, for expressing mild disagreement:

Sō desu ka ↗.   "Is that so?"

Examples

A:	Nihon wa bukka ga takai desu nē.	"Prices (cost of living) are expensive in Japan, aren't they?"
B:	Sō desu nē.	"They (it) sure are (is)!"
A:	Tōkyō wa kirei na tokoro desu nē.	"Tokyo is a pretty/clean place, isn't it?"
B:	Sō desu ka ↗.	"Is that so?" [*Implies* "I doubt it."]

Grammar Note 10 — Expressing uncertainty

Here we introduce two examples to express that you are not certain:

a. **Tabun +** _____ .   "Probably _____ ."
b. **Mada wakarimasen.**   "I don't know yet."

Examples

A:	Itsu goro okuni e kaerimasu ka.	"(Around) when are you going back to your country?"
B:	1. Tabun rainen no shi-gatsu goro kaerimasu.	"I'll probably go next April."
	2. Tabun rainen no shi-gatsu goro desu.	"It will probably be next April."
	3. Mada wakarimasen.	"I don't know yet."

Drill 1   Answer the questions.

    e.g.,   *Ikimasu ka.* ⟶ $\begin{cases}\bar{E}, \textit{ikimasu.}\\ \textit{Iie, ikimasen.}\end{cases}$

   (1) *Kimasu ka.*   (2) *Kimashita ka.*   (3) *Kaerimasu ka.*
   (4) *Kaerimashita ka.*   (5) *Ikimasu ka.*   (6) *Ikimashita ka.*

Drill 2   Substitute the underlined parts.

    1. <u>*Kyonen*</u> *Nihon e kimashita.*

      (1) *kotoshi*   (2) *sen'getsu*   (3) *sen'shū*
      (4) *kinō*   (5) *kinō no asa*   (6) *kesa*

    2. <u>*Rainen*</u> *Amerika e kaerimasu.*

      (1) *kotoshi*   (2) *raigetsu*   (3) *raishū*
      (4) *kon'shū*   (5) *ashita*   (6) *ashita no ni-ji goro*

    3. <u>*Ichinen mae*</u> *ni Hiroshima made ikimashita.*

      (1) *ni-nen mae*   (2) *ni-gatsu*   (3) *kotoshi no ni-gatsu*
      (4) *shi-gatsu*   (5) *jū-ji*   (6) *Shōwa gojū-nen*

    4. <u>*San-ji*</u> *ni tomodachi no uchi e ikimasu.*

      (1) *sui-yōbi*   (2) *raishū no kin-yōbi* (3) *raigetsu no mik-ka*
      (4) *ichi-gatsu tō-ka* (5) *kyō no go-ji*   (6) *roku-ji goro*

Drill 3   Expand the sentences.

    e.g., *kimashita* ⟶ *Kimashita.*
            Nihon e ⟶ *Nihon e kimashita.*
            kyonen ⟶ *Kyonen Nihon e kimashita.*

   (1) *ikimasu*   (2) *kimashita*
        tomodachi no uchi e   *Nihon e*
        raishū   *shi-gatsu ni*

   (3) *kimashita*   (4) *kimashita*
        Nihon e   *Nihon e*
        kyonen no shichi-gatsu ni   *san-nen mae ni*

   (5) *kaerimasu*   (6) *kaerimasu*
        kuni e   *Igirisu e*
        rainen   *ni-nen go ni*
        tabun "probably"   *moshikashitara* "possibly"

   (7) *kaerimashita*   (8) *kimashita*
        uchi e   *uchi e*
        ku-ji goro   *Amerika no tomodachi ga*
        kinō   *nichi-yōbi ni*

   (9) *kimasu*   (10) *ikimasu*
        tomodachi ga   *Kyōto e*
        Amerika kara   *kanai/shujin ga*
        ashita   *nichi-yōbi made*
                               ashita kara

Drill 4   Make questions which ask for the underlined parts.

e.g.,   *Raishū ikimasu.*   ⟶   *Itsu ikimasu ka.*

(1)   *Go-gatsu ni ikimasu.*

(2)   *Hachi-ji ni kimashita.*

(3)   *Ni-nen mae ni kimashita.*

(4)   *Hokkaidō e ikimasu.*

(5)   *Tanaka-san ga kimashita.*

(6)   *Ashita kara ikimasu.*

(7)   *Gin'za made ikimashita.*

Drill 5   Abbreviate the sentence using **desu**, supposing the underlined parts are understood.

e.g.,   *Ni-gatsu ni kimashita.*   ⟶   *Nigatsu desu.*

(1)   *Sen'shū ikimashita.*

(2)   *Sen-kyūhyaku-hachijū-nen ni kimashita.*

(3)   *Kanai ga kimasu.*

(4)   *Nikkō e ikimasu.*

(5)   *Rainen no roku-gatsu ni kaerimasu.*

(6)   *Ni-nen mae ni kimashita.*

(7)   *Roppongi made ikimashita.*

Drill 6   Make comments on Japan.

1. e.g.,   *bukka, takai*   ⟶   *Bukka ga takai desu nē.*

(1)   *bukka, yasui*   (2)   *yachin, takai*

(3)   *hito, ōi*   (4)   *hito, shin'setsu*

(5)   *tabemono, oishii*

2. e.g.,   *ii[A], kuni*   ⟶   *Ii kuni desu nē.*

(1)   *omoshiroi [A], kuni*   (2)   *kirei [AN], kuni*

(3)   *ii [A], tokoro*   (4)   *an'zen [AN], kuni*

(5)   *iya [AN], tokoro*   (6)   *tsumaranai [A], kuni*

Drill 7   Agree or disagree or offer an enthusiastic listening sign to each comment.

e.g.,   *Nihon wa bukka ga takai desu nē.*

(Agree)   ⟶   *Sō desu nē* ↘.

(Disagree)   ⟶   *Sō desu ka* ↗.

(Offer EL*)   ⟶   [Key word] *desu ka* ↘. or *Sō desu ka* ↘.

   *EL = Enthusiastic Listening sign

(1)   *Tōkyō wa hito ga ōi desu nē.*

(2)   *Ōsaka wa omoshiroi tokoro desu nē.*

(3)   *Nihon wa ii kuni desu nē.*

(4)   *Nihon wa iya na kuni desu nē.*

Drill 8   Using the dialogue as a model, complete the following according to the cues.

When you do [d] choose one of these:

Agreement	⟶	*Sō desu nē* ↘.
Disagreement	⟶	*Sō desu ka* ↗.
Enthusiastic listening	⟶	*Sō desu ka* ↘.

---

(1)   —You are asking Mr. Smith—

[a]   *itsu*
      Nihon   ⟶

[b]   *nan-gatsu*

[c]   *dō*

[d]

[e]   *itsu*
      Amerika   USA   ⟵

You: [a] _____ .
Tape: *Kyonen kimashita.*
You: [b] _____ .
Tape: *Shi-gatsu desu.*
You: [c] _____ .
Tape: *Ii kuni desu nē.*
You: [d] _____ .
You: [e] _____ .
Tape: *Mada wakarimasen.*
You: [d] _____ .

---

(2)   —You are asking Mr. Schwartz—

[a]   *itsu*
      Nihon   ⟶

[b]   *nan-gatsu*

[c]   *dō*

[d]

[e]   *itsu*
      Doitsu   Germany   ⟵

You: [a] _____ .
Tape: *San-nen mae ni kimashita.*
You: [b] _____ .
Tape: *Ku-gatsu desu.*
You: [c] _____ .
Tape: *Bukka ga takai desu nē.*
You: [d] _____ .
You: [e] _____ .
Tape: *Tabun rainen no shi-gatsu goro desu.*
You: [d] _____ .

---

(3)   —Now you answer about yourself—

Tape: *Itsu Nihon e kimashita ka.*
You: _____ .
Tape: *Nihon wa dō desu ka.*
You: _____ .
Tape: *Sō desu ka.*
Tape: *Itsu goro o-kuni e kaerimasu ka.*
You: _____ .

Lesson 11

GOING ON A HOLIDAY

DEN'SHA DE IKIMASU
"WE WILL GO BY TRAIN"

🎞 **Dialogue** ──────────────────────────────────

[Mr. Tanaka and Mr. Smith are talking about their plans for the up-coming holidays.]

Tanaka: Kon'do no yasumi ni dokoka e ikimasu ka.

Sumisu: Ē, kazoku to tomodachi to Nikkō e ikimasu. ⟷ | S: Iie, doko e mo
                                                              | ikimasen.

Tanaka: Ii desu nē. Asakusa kara den'sha desu ka.

Sumisu: Iie, kon'do wa den'sha ja arimasen. Kuruma de | T: Ā, sō desu ka.
         ikimasu. Tanaka-san mo dokoka e ikimasu ka.

Tanaka: Ē, Goten'ba e gorufu ni ikimasu.

Sumisu: Goten'ba desu ka.

Mr. Tanaka:	Are you planning to go somewhere for the up-coming holidays?
Mr. Smith:	Yes, I'm planning to go to Nikko ⟷ | S: No, I'm not planning with my family and friends. | to go anywhere.
Mr. Tanaka:	That's great. Are you going to take | T: I see. the train from Asakusa station?
Mr. Smith:	No, this time we're not taking the train, we'll drive. Are you also planning to go somewhere, Mr. Tanaka?
Mr. Tanaka:	Yes, I'm going to Gotenba to play golf.
Mr. Smith:	Oh. (You're going) to Gotenba!

Vocabulary ──────────────────────────────────

kon'do:	up-coming, this time	den'sha:	train
yasumi:	holiday, weekend, day off	de [M]:	[Means] by
dokoka:	somewhere, anywhere	Asakusa:	place name
ikimasu:	will go	Goten'ba:	place name
tomodachi:	(my) friends	gorufu:	golf
kazoku:	(my) family	ni [M]:	[Purpose]
Nikkō:	place name		

田中　：こんどの　やすみに　どこかへ　いきますか。
たなか

スミス：ええ、　かぞくと　ともだちと ⟷ スミス：いいえ、　どこへも

日光へ　いきます。 いきません。
にっこう

田中　：いいですねえ。 田中　：ああ、　そうですか。

浅草から　でんしゃですか。
あさくさ

スミス：いいえ、　こんどは

でんしゃじゃありません。

くるまで　いきます。

田中さんも　どこかへ　いきますか。

田中　：ええ、　御殿場へ　ゴルフに　いきます。
ごてんば

スミス：御殿場ですか。

○Grammar Note 1 — Accompaniment

[Person] *to* [Verb].

Tomodachi *to* *ikimasu*.　　"I will go (*or* am going) with my friend."

Accompaniment		Predicate
tomodachi	*to*	*ikimasu*

a.　***To***　[Accompaniment Marker]　　"with"
The marker ***to*** means "with."

Notice the difference:
Kanai to ikimasu.　　"I will go (*or* am going) with my wife."
Kanai ga ikimasu.　　"My wife will go."

Examples
Kazoku to Nikkō e ikimasu.　　"I will go (*or* am going) to Nikko
with my family."

Kazoku to tomodachi to　　"I will go (*or* am going) to Nikko
Nikkō e ikimasu.　　with my family and friends."

b.　**[Person] *to* *issho ni***　　"together with"
To emphasize that you are going "with" somebody, you can add ***issho ni*** "together"
after ***to***.

Example
Kazoku to issho ni Nikkō e ikimasu.　　"I will go (*or* am going) to Nikko
together with my family."

c.　Family words (*cf.* Lesson 1, Grammar Note 2)
Family words for your "in-group" members were introduced in Lesson 1. Here we introduce the family words for your "non-in-group" acquaintances.

Examples

| A: | *Musume to Kyōto e ikimasu.* | "I am going to Kyoto with my daughter." |
| B: | *Ojōsan to desu ka.* | "Oh, with your daughter." |

| A: | *Okusan to ikimasu ka.* | "Are you going with your wife?" |
| B: | *Ē, kanai to issho ni ikimasu.* | "Yes, I'm going with my wife." |

Vocabulary: Family

Meaning	In-group [Humble/Neutral]	Non-in-group [Honorific]
family	*kazoku*	*go-kazoku*
husband	*shujin*	*go-shujin*
wife	*kanai*	*okusan*
child	*kodomo*	*okosan*
son	*musuko*	*musuko-san*
daughter	*musume*	*ojōsan*
parents	*ryōshin*	*go-ryōshin*
father	*chichi*	*otōsan*
mother	*haha*	*okāsan*
brothers & sisters	*kyōdai*	*go-kyōdai*
elder brother	*ani*	*onīsan*
elder sister	*ane*	*onēsan*
younger brother	*otōto*	*otōto-san*
younger sister	*imōto*	*imōto-san*
who?	*dare*	*donata*

d.   Words for other people

For choosing neutral or honorific words for people, apply the same rule for country, job, residence, *etc.* (*cf.* Lesson 3, Grammar Note 2–c)

Example

| A: | *Tomodachi to Ōsaka e ikimashita.* | "I went to Osaka with my friend." |
| B: | *O-tomodachi to desu ka.* | "Oh, with your friend." |

Vocabulary: People

Meaning	[Neutral]	[Honorific]
friend	*tomodachi*	*o-tomodachi*
acquaintance	*shiriai*	*shiriai no kata*
person in the company	*kaisha no hito*	*kaisha no kata*
secretary	*hisho*	*hisho no kata*
guest/customer	*kyaku*	*o-kyaku-san*
supervisor	*jōshi*	
subordinate	*buka*	
colleague	*dōryō*	
who?	*dare*	*donata*

e.   ***Dare* or *Donata***   "who"

Donata is an honorific equivalent of ***dare***.

Example

| A: | *Dare/Donata to ikimashita ka.* | "Who did you go with?" |
| B: | *Dōryō to ikimashita.* | "With my colleague." |

Grammar Note 2 — Purpose

[Noun] *ni* [Verb].

Pātī ni ikimasu.   "I will go (*or* am going) to a party."

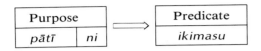

Purpose		Predicate
pātī	*ni*	*ikimasu*

a. ***Ni***   [Purpose Marker]   "(in order) to, for"
This ***ni*** following an activity noun like party, shopping, *etc.,* indicates the purpose of going, coming and going/coming back.

   Example
      Ashita Shin'juku e kaimono ni ikimasu.   I'm going shopping in Shinjuku."

   Vocabulary: Purpose

Meaning	
party	*pātī*
movie	*eiga*
Kabuki play	*Kabuki*
travel	*ryokō*
driving	*doraibu*
hiking	*haikin'gu*
golf	*gorufu*
tennis	*tenisu*
meal	*shokuji*
shopping	*kaimono*
work	*shigoto*
study	*ben'kyō*
doing what?	*nani o shi*

b. ***Nani o shi ni***   "to do what?"
To ask the reason or purpose for doing something, you can say ***nani o shi ni*** plus ***ikimasu/kimasu/kaerimasu*** plus ***ka.*** However, this should only be used among acquaintances because it sounds too inquisitive.

Grammar Note 3 — Means

[Means of Transportation] *de* [Verb].

Den'sha de ikimasu.   "I will go (*or* am going) by train."

Means		Predicate
den'sha	*de*	*ikimasu*

a. ***De***   [Means Marker]   "by"
De, indicates the "means", any kind of means, but in this lesson, means of transportation is introduced.

   Example
      Shin'kan'sen de Niigata e ikimasu.   "I'm going to Niigata by 'bullet train'."

123

Vocabulary: Means of transportation

Meaning	
car	*kuruma*
taxi	*takushī*
bus	*basu*
train, street car	*den'sha*
subway	*chikatetsu*
bullet train [new trunk line]	*shin'kan'sen*
. . . line	*. . . sen*
The Ginza Line	*Gin'za-sen*
The Marunouchi Line	*Marunouchi-sen*
airplane	*hikōki*
. . . airline	*. . . kōkū*
Japan Airlines	*Nihon-kōkū*
ship	*fune*
on foot	*aruite**
what?, how?	*nan, dōyatte**

* These words do not take the marker **de**.

b.   ***Nan de***   ''by what (means),''   ***Dōyatte***   ''how''
Nan de means ''by what (means),'' but it can mean ''why.'' Therefore, ***dōyatte*** ''(doing) how'' is more precise when asking the means.

Grammar Note 4 — ***Doko*** vs. ***Dokoka***

Doko means ''where'' but ***dokoka*** means ''somewhere.''

Compare:
1. *Ashita doko e ikimasu ka.*   ''Where are you going tomorrow?''
2. *Ashita dokoka e ikimasu ka.*   ''Are you going somewhere tomorrow?''

Answers to question 2 are:
   Ē, (Hakone e) ikimasu.   ''Yes, I'm going (to Hakone).''
      or
   Iie, (betsu ni) doko e mo ikimasen.   ''No, I'm not going anywhere (especially).''

Subway platform

Bus Terminal at Shibuya Station

Grammar Note 5 — How to use the diagram

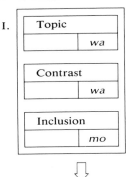

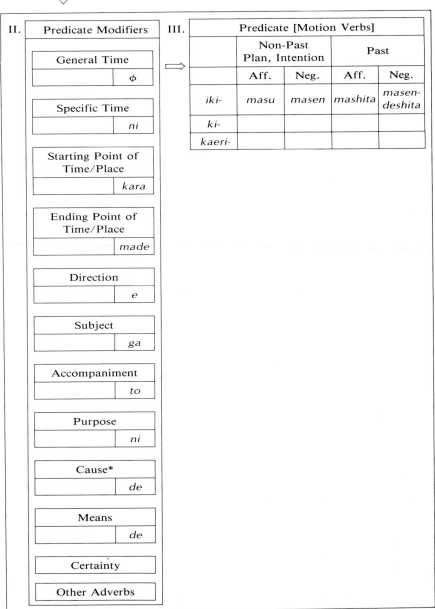

	Non-Past Plan, Intention		Past	
	Aff.	Neg.	Aff.	Neg.
iki-	masu	masen	mashita	masen-deshita
ki-				
kaeri-				

* Cause Marker **de** will be introduced in Lesson 12.

Here, let's learn how to read the diagram with the markers introduced so far:

a.   Predicate

The key part of a sentence is the predicate (III in the diagram). It normally comes at the end of the sentence.

It sometimes does not require anything else to complete the sentence, for example, ''I will go'' can be expressed by only *Ikimasu.*

b.   Predicate modifiers

If you want to add more information to the predicate to complete the thought, put the elements (II), such as Specific Time or Direction, before the predicate. As these elements modify the predicate they are called predicate modifiers in this textbook.

The order of the predicate modifiers can be at random, but often comes in the order given, from top to bottom of the diagram.

Examples

Kinō Yokohama e ikimashita.	''(I) went to Yokohama yesterday.''
Kinō san-ji goro Yokohama e ikimashita.	''(I) went to Yokohama around three yesterday.''
Kinō Yokohama e shujin to shokuji ni ikimashita.	''(I) went to Yokohama for dinner with my husband yesterday.''

c.   Topic or Contrast (*cf.* Lesson 3)

If you want to choose one or more predicate modifiers as the topics of the sentence, or the topics to be contrasted, put *wa* after the predicate modifier.

[Predicate Modifier]	+ *wa* +	[Predicate]	
kyonen φ	*wa*	*ikimashita*	''(I) went last year.''.
shi-gatsu ni	*wa*	*ikimashita*	''(I) went in April.''
Kyōto e	*wa*	*ikimashita*	''(I) went to Kyoto.''
watashi	*wa*	*ikimashita*	''I went.''
kanai to	*wa*	*ikimashita*	''(I) went with my wife.''
kaimono ni	*wa*	*ikimashita*	''(I) went shopping.''
den'sha de	*wa*	*ikimashita*	''(I) went by train.''

* The marker *ga* is eliminated when *wa* follows.

Topics and topics with contrast usually come at the beginning of the sentence.

Examples

Basic information:

Kinō	*Yokohama e*	*Tanaka-san ga*	*den'sha de*	*ikimashita.*
''Yesterday''	''to Yokohama''	''Mr. Tanaka''	''by train''	''went''

''Mr Tanaka went to Yokohama by train yesterday.''

1.   Choose *Tanaka-san ga* as a topic, and you will get:

   Tanaka-san wa kinō Yokohama e den'sha de ikimashita.
   ''As for Mr. Tanaka, he went to Yokohama by train yesterday.''

2.   Choose *kinō* as a topic, and you will get:

   Kinō wa Yokohama e Tanaka-san ga den'sha de ikimashita.
   ''As for yesterday, Mr. Tanaka went to Yokohama by train.''

3. Choose **Yokohama e** as a topic, and you will get:

> *Yokohama e wa kinō Tanaka-san ga den'sha de ikimashita.*
> "As for to Yokohama, Mr. Tanaka went there by train yesterday."

4. Choose **den'sha de** as a topic, and you will get:

> *Den'sha de wa, kinō Yokohama e Tanaka-san ga ikimashita.*
> "As for going by train, Mr. Tanaka went to Yokohama yesterday."

5. Choose **Tanaka-san ga** and **kinō** as topics, and you will get:

> *Tanaka-san wa kinō wa Yokohama e den'sha de ikimashita.*
> "As for Mr. Tanaka, as for yesterday, he went to Yokohama by train."

You can use more than two **wa**'s in a sentence depending on what you need to say.

(Note that these examples are not very natural sounding. This is because they do not have any elimination which normal sentences in ordinary circumstances usually have. However, we included these examples to explain the idea of **wa**.)

When the subject of the sentence is **watashi**, the topic **watashi wa** is often eliminated, because it is understood from the context. (*cf.* Lesson 1, Grammar Note 1–c)

Example

Kinō wa den'sha de Yokohama e ikimashita.	"As for yesterday, (I) went to Yokohama by train."

d. Inclusion

If you want to add "also" or "too" to some elements of the sentence (excluding the predicate), use **mo** instead of **wa**.

Examples

Tanaka-san ga kimasu.	"Mr. Tanaka will come (here)."
Sumisu-san mo kimasu.	"Mr. Smith will also come (here)."
Kyonen ikimashita.	"(I) went (there) last year."
Kotoshi mo ikimashita.	"(I) went (there) this year also."
Tanaka-san wa Kyōto e ikimashita.	"Mr. Tanaka went to Kyoto."
Sumisu-san mo ikimashita.	"Mr. Smith also went there."
Tanaka-san wa Kyōto e ikimashita.	"Mr. Tanaka went to Kyoto."
Nara e mo ikimashita.	"He went to Nara also."

When you want to say "not _____, either," use **mo**.

Examples

Tanaka-san wa Kyūshū e ikimashita.	"Mr. Tanaka went to Kyushu (Island)."
Demo, Nagasaki* e wa ikimasen deshita.	"However, he did not go to Nagasaki."
Kumamoto* e mo ikimasen deshita.	"He did not go to Kumamoto, either."
Ashita Ōno-san to watashi ga Ōsaka e ikimasu.	"Tomorrow, Mr. Ono and I will go to Osaka.
Kon'do wa Tanaka-san wa ikimasen.	"This time, Mr. Tanaka is not going."
Yamashita-san mo ikimasen.	"Mr. Yamashita is not going, either."

* Cities in Kyushu.

e.   Questions and answers with nuance.
Observe the examples using **wa** or **mo**.

Examples

A: *Yōroppa e ikimashita ka.*   "Did you go to Europe?"
B: *Ē . . ., Doitsu e wa ikimashita.*   "Yes, I went to Germany."
                                              (Implies this person did not go to any
                                              other countries.)

A: *Doitsu e ikimashita.*   "I went to Germany."
B: *Furan'su e mo ikimashita ka.*   "Did you also go to France?"
        or
    Furan'su e wa ikimashita ka.   "Did you go to France?"
                                              (This person may have some special in-
                                              terest in France.)

A: *Ē, Furan'su e mo ikimashita.*   "Yes, I went to France also."
        or   (Implies this person **did** go to other
    Iie, Furan'su e wa ikimasen   places, or is sorry/happy about not
        deshita.   having been to France.)
                                              "No, I didn't go to France."

Grammar Note 6 — Replacing the negative form of the verb with **ja arimasen**

As you know, **ja arimasen** is the negative form of **desu**. Observe how the verb is replaced
by **desu** or **ja arimasen** when it is clear from the context.

Examples

A: *Mae wa nan de ikimashita ka.*   "How did you go (there) before?"
B: *Den'sha de ikimashita.*   "I went by train."
                ↓
    Den'sha desu.   "By train."

A: **Kon'do mo den'sha de*   "Are you going by train this time
        ikimasu ka.   also?"
B: *Iie, kon'do wa den'sha de wa ikimasen.* "No, I'm not going by train this
                        ↓   time."
    Iie. kon'do wa den'sha ja arimasen.   "No, not by train this time."

    ***Kon'do** means "this time" or "this coming time."*

Drill 1   Substitute the underlined parts.

1.   *Yasumi "holiday" ni kazoku to Kyūshū e ikimasu.*
       (1) *kanai/shujin*   (2) *kodomo*   (3) *tomodachi*
       (4) *kaisha no hito*   (5) *dōryō*   (6) *Tanaka-san*
2.   *Ashita pātī ni ikimasu.*
       (1) *eiga*   (2) *kon'sāto "concert"*   (3) *gorufu*
       (4) *tenisu*   (5) *ryokō*   (6) *doraibu*

3. *Gin'za e shokuji ni ikimasu.*
    (1) *Roppon'gi*   (2) *kaimono*   (3) *Shin'juku*
    (4) *shokuji*   (5) *Ōtemachi*   (6) *Nihongo* ''Japanese''
                                                            no ben'kyō

4. *Sen'dai made shin'kan'sen de ikimasu.*
    (1) *hikōki*   (2) *Nagoya*   (3) *kuruma*
    (4) *Ikebukuro*   (5) *takushī*   (6) *basu*
    (7) *chikatetsu*   (8) *den'sha*   (9) *aruite*

Drill 2   Expand the sentences.

    e.g.,   *ikimasu* ⟶ *Ikimasu.*
              eiga ni ⟶ *Eiga ni ikimasu.*
              ashita ⟶ *Ashita eiga ni ikimasu*

    (1) *ikimasu*   (2) *ikimashita*
           doraibu ni   *kaimono ni*
           Hakone e   *Gin'za no Mitsukoshi made*
           do-yōbi ni   *nichi-yōbi ni*
    (3) *ikimasu*   (4) *ikimasu*
           ryokō ni   *tomodachi no uchi no pātī ni*
           shujin to   *Ikeda-san to*
           raishū   *kon'ban*
    (5) *ikimasu*   (6) *ikimashita*
           gorufu ni   *Okinawa e*
           kyaku to   *fune de*
           kon'do no nichi-yōbi ni   *yasumi ni*
    (7) *ikimashita*   (8) *ikimasu*
           Takao-san ''Mt. Takao'' *made*   *haikin'gu ni*
           aruite   *Hakone e*
           kazoku to   *Shin'juku kara*
           sen'shū no do-yōbi ni   *kon'do no yasumi ni*

Drill 3   Change the underlined ''in-group'' words to ''non-in-group'' words. Also change the forms of the sentences.

    e.g.,   *Shujin ga kimasu.* ⟶ *Go-shujin wa kimashita ka.*
              ''My husband will come (here).'' ⟶ ''Did your husband come (here)?''

    (1) *Kanai ga kimasu.*   (2) *Kodomo ga kimasu.*
    (3) *Musume ga kimasu.*   (4) *Musuko ga kimasu.*
    (5) *Haha ga kimasu.*   (6) *Chichi ga kimasu.*
    (7) *Kanai no ryōshin ga kimasu.*   (8) *Shujin no ryōshin ga kimasu.*

Drill 4   Following the example, first take A's part and then B's part.

    e.g.,   Cue: today, 'my parents,' to Japan
              A: *Kyō ryōshin ga Nihon e kimasu.*
              B: *Sō desu ka. Ii desu nē.*
                  — The next day —
              B: *Kinō go-ryōshin wa kimashita ka.*
              A: *Ē, kimashita.*

(1)   tomorrow, my father, to Japan

A: _____ .

B: *Sō desu ka. Ii desu nē.*

— Next week —

B: _____ .

A: *Ē, kimashita.*

(2)   Saturday, my mother, from U.S.

A: _____ .

B: *Sō desu ka. Ii desu nē.*

— On Sunday—

B: _____ .

A: *Ē, kimashita.*

(3)   Next Monday, my wife's parents, from U.K.

A: _____ .

B: *Sō desu ka. Ii desu nē.*

— On Tuesday —

B: _____ .

A: *Ē, kimashita.*

Drill 5   Make questions which ask for the underlined parts.

e.g.,   *Shujin to ikimasu.* ⟶ *Donata/Dare to ikimasu ka.*

(1)   *Kanai to kodomo to ikimasu.*   (2)   *Shokuji ni ikimashita.*

(3)   *Chikatetsu de kimasu.*   (4)   *Kaisha no kuruma de kimashita.*

(5)   *Nikkō eki kara renta kā "rental car" de ikimashita.*

Drill 6   Make up dialogues according to the cues. Note how **de** and **de wa** are used.

e.g.,   *Nikkō*

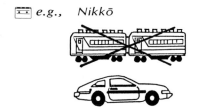

A: *Raishū Nikkō e ikimasu.*

B: *Ii desu nē.*

Den'sha de *ikimasu ka.*

A: *Iie, kon'do wa den'sha* de wa *ikimasen.*

Kuruma de *ikimasu.*

B: *Ā, sō desu ka.*

(1)   *Niigata*

Shinkansen

(2)   *Okinawa*

(3)   *Kyōto*

(4)   *Kawaguchiko "Lake Kawaguchi(-ko)"*

*   ✕   mark indicates negative cues.

Drill 7   Use the same dialogues as in Drill 6, and substitute *desu* or *ja arimasen* for the verbs wherever possible.

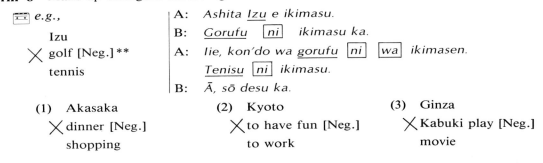

e.g., | A: *Raishū Nikkō e ikimasu.*
       | B: *Ii desu nē.*
       | *Den'sha desu ka.*
       | A: *Iie, kon'do wa den'sha ja arimasen.*
       | *Kuruma desu.*
       | B: *Ā, sō desu ka.*

Drill 8   Make up dialogues according to the cues. Note how *ni* and *ni wa* are used.

e.g.,

Izu
✕ golf [Neg.]**
tennis

A: *Ashita Izu e ikimasu.*
B: *Gorufu* ni *ikimasu ka.*
A: *Iie, kon'do wa gorufu* ni wa *ikimasen.*
     Tenisu ni *ikimasu.*
B: *Ā, sō desu ka.*

(1) Akasaka
     ✕ dinner [Neg.]
     shopping

(2) Kyoto
     ✕ to have fun [Neg.]
     to work

(3) Ginza
     ✕ Kabuki play [Neg.]
     movie

** [Neg.] indicates negative cues.

Drill 9   Use the same dialogues as in Drill 8, and substitute *desu* or *ja arimasen* for the verbs wherever possible.

e.g., | A: *Ashita Izu e ikimasu.*
       | B: *Gorufu desu ka.*
       | A: *Iie, kon'do wa gorufu ja arimasen.*
       | *Tenisu desu.*
       | B: *Ā, sō desu ka.*

Drill 10   Make up dialogues according to the cues. Note how *to* and *to wa* are used.

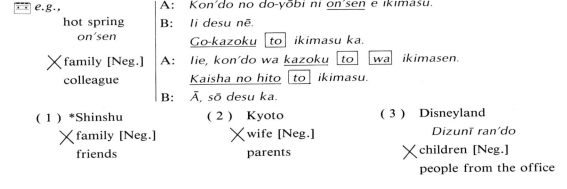

e.g.,

hot spring
on'sen

✕ family [Neg.]
colleague

A: *Kon'do no do-yōbi ni on'sen e ikimasu.*
B: *Ii desu nē.*
     Go-kazoku to *ikimasu ka.*
A: *Iie, kon'do wa kazoku* to wa *ikimasen.*
     Kaisha no hito to *ikimasu.*
B: *Ā, sō desu ka.*

(1) *Shinshu
     ✕ family [Neg.]
     friends

(2) Kyoto
     ✕ wife [Neg.]
     parents

(3) Disneyland
     Dizunī ran'do
     ✕ children [Neg.]
     people from the office

* Shinshu is another name for Nagano Prefecture.

Drill 11   Use the same dialogues as in Drill 10, and substitute **desu** or **ja arimasen** for the verbs wherever possible.

Notice the marker **to** remains. (*cf.* Drills 8, 11)

e.g.,

A: *Kon'do no do-yōbi ni on'sen e ikimasu.*

B: *Ii desu nē.*

     Go-kazoku | to | *desu ka.*

A: *Iie, kon'do wa kazoku* | to | *ja arimasen.*

     Kaisha no hito | to | *desu.*

B: *Ā, sō desu ka.*

Drill 12   Look at the map and make up dialogues. Note how **wa** and **mo** are used.

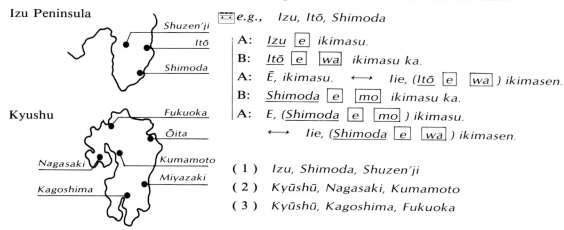

Izu Peninsula

Shuzen'ji
Itō
Shimoda

e.g.,   Izu, Itō, Shimoda

A: *Izu* | e | *ikimasu.*

B: *Itō* | e | | wa | *ikimasu ka.*

A: *Ē, ikimasu.* ⟷ *Iie, (Itō* | e | | wa |) *ikimasen.*

B: *Shimoda* | e | | mo | *ikimasu ka.*

A: *E, (Shimoda* | e | | mo |) *ikimasu.*

     ⟷ *Iie, (Shimoda* | e | | wa |) *ikimasen.*

Kyushu

Fukuoka
Ōita
Kumamoto
Nagasaki
Miyazaki
Kagoshima

(1)   *Izu, Shimoda, Shuzen'ji*

(2)   *Kyūshū, Nagasaki, Kumamoto*

(3)   *Kyūshū, Kagoshima, Fukuoka*

Drill 13   Use the markers **ga, e, ni, de, to, wa,** and **mo** correctly.

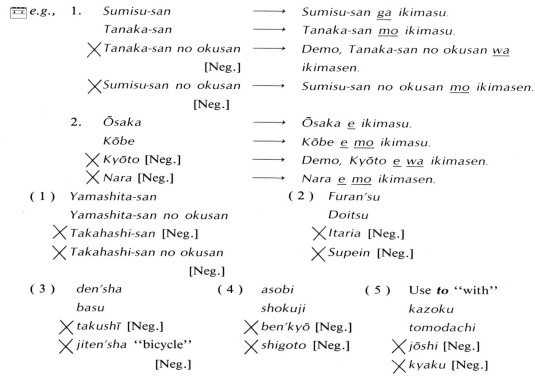

e.g.,   1.   *Sumisu-san* ⟶ *Sumisu-san ga ikimasu.*

Tanaka-san ⟶ *Tanaka-san mo ikimasu.*

✗*Tanaka-san no okusan* ⟶ *Demo, Tanaka-san no okusan wa*
[Neg.]   *ikimasen.*

✗*Sumisu-san no okusan* ⟶ *Sumisu-san no okusan mo ikimasen.*
[Neg.]

2.   *Ōsaka* ⟶ *Ōsaka e ikimasu.*

Kōbe ⟶ *Kōbe e mo ikimasu.*

✗*Kyōto* [Neg.] ⟶ *Demo, Kyōto e wa ikimasen.*

✗*Nara* [Neg.] ⟶ *Nara e mo ikimasen.*

(1)   *Yamashita-san*   (2)   *Furan'su*

Yamashita-san no okusan   *Doitsu*

✗*Takahashi-san* [Neg.]   ✗*Itaria* [Neg.]

✗*Takahashi-san no okusan*   ✗*Supein* [Neg.]
[Neg.]

(3)   *den'sha*   (4)   *asobi*   (5)   Use **to** ''with''

basu   *shokuji*   *kazoku*

✗*takushī* [Neg.]   ✗*ben'kyō* [Neg.]   *tomodachi*

✗*jiten'sha* ''bicycle''   ✗*shigoto* [Neg.]   ✗*jōshi* [Neg.]
[Neg.]   ✗*kyaku* [Neg.]

Drill 14 Using the Dialogue as a model, complete the following conversation between you and Mr. Tanaka.

---

(1)

[a] → Kamakura

[b]

[c] Mr. Tanaka?

[d] EL

Tape:	*Ashita dokoka e ikimasu ka.*
You:	[a]_____.
Tape:	*Ii desu nē. Kuruma desu ka.*
You:	[b]_____.
Tape:	*Ā, sō desu ka.*
You:	[c]_____.
Tape:	*Watashi wa tenisu ni ikimasu.*
You:	[d]_____.

---

(2)

[a] → Kyushu

[b]

[c] Yes.

[d] No.

[e] Mr. Tanaka?

[f] Where?

[g] EL

Tape:	*Kon'do no yasumi ni dokoka e ikimasu ka.*
You:	[a]_____.
Tape:	*Ii desu nē. Hikōki desu ka.*
You:	[b]_____.
Tape:	*Nagasaki e wa ikimasu ka.*
You:	[c]_____.
Tape:	*Kagoshima e mo ikimasu ka.*
You:	[d]_____
Tape:	*Ā, sō desu ka.*
You:	[e]_____.
Tape:	*Watashi mo kazoku to ryokō ni ikimasu.*
You:	[f]_____.
Tape:	*Hawai desu.*
You:	[g]_____.

---

(3)

[a] No.

[b] Mr. Tanaka?

[c] EL

Tape:	*Kon'do no yasumi ni dokoka e ikimasu ka.*
You:	[a]_____.
Tape:	*Ā, sō desu ka.*
You:	[b]_____.
Tape:	*Watashi mo doko e mo ikimasen.*
You:	[c]_____.

Drill 15 Answer about yourself.

(1) *Kon'do no yasumi ni dokoka e ikimasu ka.*

(2) *Nani o shi ni ikimasu ka.*

(3) *Donata to ikimasu ka.*

(4) *Nan de ikimasu ka.*

(5) *Kyō wa dokoka e ikimasu ka.*

Lesson 12

AFTER THE HOLIDAY

NIKKŌ WA DŌ DESHITA KA
"HOW WAS THE TRIP TO NIKKO?"

📼 Dialogue

[One morning after the holiday]

Tanaka: *Sumisu-san, Nikkō wa dō deshita ka.*

Sumisu: *Yokatta desu yo.* ⟷ | *S:*   *Jitsu wa kyūyō de ikimasen deshita.*

Tanaka: *Tokuni doko ga* | *T:*   *Sō desu ka. Sore wa zan'nen deshita nē.*
            yokatta desu ka.

Sumisu: *Tōshōgū ga subarashikatta desu. Soreni, yama mo kirei deshita.*

Tanaka: *Sore wa yokatta desu nē.*

Mr. Tanaka:	How was the trip to Nikko, Mr. Smith?	
Mr. Smith:	It was nice. ⟷ | S:	Sorry, but I didn't go because of urgent business.
	T:	That's too bad.
Mr. Tanaka:	What part of Nikko was good, particularly?	
Mr. Smith:	Toshogu Shrine was just gorgeous, and the mountains were beautiful.	
Mr. Tanaka:	That's good.	

Vocabulary

dō deshita ka: how was . . . ?

yokatta ← *ii, yoi:* was good

jitsu wa: to tell the truth, by the way

kyūyō: urgent business

de [M]: [Cause] because of

ikimasen deshita: didn't go

zan'nen deshita: That's too bad.
                    [*Lit.* that was too bad]

doko: where

Tōshōgū: Toshogu Shrine

subarashikatta ← *subarashii:* was superb,
                                   fantastic, gorgeous

soreni: and, in addition

yama: mountain(s)

田中　：スミスさん、　日光は　どうでしたか。
たなか　　　　　　　　　にっこう

スミス：よかったですよ。　⟵⟶　｜スミス：じつは　きゅうようで

田中　：とくに　どこが　　　　　　｜　　　　　いきませんでした。

　　　　よかったですか。　　　　　｜田中　：そうですか。

スミス：東照宮が　　　　　　　　　　　　　　それは　ざんねんでしたねえ。
　　　　とうしょうぐう

　　　　すばらしかったです。

　　　　それに、　やまも　きれいでした。

田中　：それは　よかったですねえ。

Grammar Note 1 — Asking generally how the holiday went

X wa {**dō** / **ikaga**} **deshita ka** ↗.　　"How was X?"

In Lesson 10 you learned **X wa dō desu ka** "How do you like X?"
In this lesson, you learn to use **deshita**, the past equivalent of **desu**.

Yasumi wa dō deshita ka.　　　"How was your holiday?"
Nikkō wa ikaga deshita ka.　　"How was Nikko?"

Grammar Note 2 — Making a general comment on your holiday

(X wa) {**A-katta desu** / **AN　deshita**} **(yo** ↗**)**

(*Yasumi wa*) *yokatta desu* (*yo*).　　"The holiday was nice [*Lit.* good]."
(*Nikkō wa*) *kirei deshita* (*yo*).　　"Nikko was beautiful."

a. Past tense of Adjectives and Adjectival Nouns [Level 2]
Notice the different conjugations between [A] — Adjectives and [AN] — Adjectival Nouns —

	Non-Past		Past		Meaning
	Aff.	Neg.	Aff.	Neg.	
[A] omoshiro tanoshi subarashi tsumarana 　　i*	-i desu	-ku arimasen yo-	-katta desu yo-	-ku arimasen 　deshita yo-	interesting enjoyable, fun wonderful boring, worthless good
[AN] 　kirei shizuka dame	desu	-ja arimasen	deshita	-ja arimasen 　deshita	pretty, clean quiet no good

*The adjective **ii** "good" has an exceptional conjugation.
　　Non-Past Aff.　　**ii** *desu*
　　Non-Past Neg.　　**yoku** *arimasen*
　　Past Aff.　　　　**yokatta** *desu*
　　Past Neg.　　　　**yoku** *arimasen deshita*

b. *Yo* ↗ [Emphasis Marker]

Yo, like *ka*, is a sentence marker which comes at the end of a sentence. *Yo* indicates the speaker's assurance that his/her statement is correct. It is often used in informative explanations, warnings, contradictions, *etc.* Although it is difficult to give an English equivalent for this marker, sometimes it corresponds to "you know," "I tell you," "I'll say!" *etc.*

By *yo* ↗, with rising intonation, the speaker is emphatic but also trying to avoid sounding pompous.

By *yo* ↘, with falling or low intonation, the speaker is just being emphatic.

Examples

A: *Yasumi wa dō deshita ka.*	"How was your holiday?"
B: *Tanoshikatta desu (yo ↗).*	"We had fun (!)"

A: *Nikkō wa dō deshita ka.*	"How was Nikko?"
B: *Ē, yokatta desu (yo ↗).*	"Oh, yes, it was fine (!)"

A: *Yama wa ikaga deshita ka.*	"How were the mountains?"
B: *Taihen/Totemo kirei deshita (yo ↗).*	"They were very beautiful (!)"

Grammar Note 3 — Giving reasons why you could not go somewhere

(Jitsu wa) **[Reason]** *de* **[Verb].**

(Jitsu wa) <u>*kyūyō* de *ikimasen deshita.*</u>　　"To tell the truth, I didn't go because of urgent business."

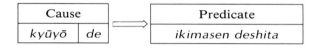

Cause		Predicate
kyūyō	*de*	*ikimasen deshita*

a. *Jitsu wa* "to tell the truth"

This phrase is often used when you give an excuse, or when you explain that something unexpected has happened.

b. *De* [Cause Marker] "because of"

The marker *de* indicates why you do/did something or do/did not do something.

Examples

Shutchō de Sapporo e ikimashita.	"I went to Sapporo on business."
Kyūyō de pātī ni wa ikimasen deshita.	"I didn't go to the party because of urgent business."

A: *Kinō wa dō deshita ka.*	"How did it go yesterday?"
B: *Jitsu wa kaze de ikimasen deshita.*	"To tell the truth, I didn't go because I had a cold."

A: *Ashita gorufu ni ikimasu ka.*	"Are you going to play golf tomorrow?"
B: *Iie, jitsu wa, ashita wa kaigi de gorufu ni wa ikimasen.*	"No, to tell the truth, I'm not going to play golf because I have to attend a conference."

Vocabulary — Cause

Meaning	
business	*shigoto*
business trip	*shutchō*
conference	*kaigi*
urgent business	*kyūyō*
errand	*yōji*
rain	*ame*
sickness	*byōki*
cold	*kaze*
why?	*dōshite**

* ***Dōshite*** does not take the marker **de**.

c. **Dōshite**   "why"

In formal situations, Japanese tend to avoid asking questions with **dōshite** "why" because it sounds too inquisitive or too straightforward.

Naze "why" or **nan de** "for what reason" is also used for asking for a reason. Note that **nan de** can also mean "by what means." (*cf.* Lesson 11, Grammar Note 3-b)

Examples

| *Kinō wa nan de kimasen deshita ka.* | "Why didn't you come (here) yesterday?" |
| *Dōshite ashita Kyūshū e ikimasu ka.* | "Why are you going to Kyushu tomorrow?" |

Grammar Note 4 — More ways to give "Enthusiastic Listening"

a. ***Sore wa yokatta desu nē*** ↘ .   "I'm glad to hear that.
[*Lit.* That was good, wasn't it.]"
Say this if you hear somebody has had a nice time, or had a nice experience. You should say this in a happy, encouraging high tone.

b. ***Sore wa zan'nen deshita nē*** ↘ .   "That's too bad.
[*Lit.* That was disappointing, wasn't it?]"
Say this when you hear somebody missed something which he/she had been looking forward to. Say this in an unhappy, low tone.

c. ***Sore wa ikemasen nē*** ↘ .   "I'm sorry to hear that.
[*Lit.* That's no good, is it?]"
Say this in an unhappy, low tone when you hear somebody is/was ill.

Examples

| A: *Ryokō wa tanoshikatta desu.* | "I had a nice trip." |
| B: *Sore wa yokatta desu nē.* | "Oh, good!" |

| A: *Kinō wa kyūyō de kon'sāto ni wa ikimasen deshita.* | "I didn't go to the concert because of urgent business." |
| B: *Sore wa zan'nen deshita nē.* | "Oh, that's too bad." |

137

— Some expressions for inquiring/answering about someone's health are shown below —

A:	*Nichi-yōbi wa kaze de doko e mo ikimasen deshita.*	"I didn't go anywhere on Sunday because of a cold."
B:	*Sore wa ikemasen nē.*	"Oh, I'm sorry to hear that."
	Mō daijōbu desu ka.	"Are you all right now [*Lit.* already]?"
A:	*Ē, mō daijōbu desu.*	"Yes, I'm all right now."

A:	*Kinō wa kaze de gakkō ni wa ikimasen deshita.*	"I didn't go to school yesterday because of a cold."
B:	*Sore wa ikemasen nē.*	"Oh, I'm sorry to hear that."
	Mō daijōbu desu ka.	"Are you all right now?"
A:	*Iie, mada chotto . . .*	"Well, not yet . . ."
B:	*Dōzo odaiji ni . . .*	"Please take care."
A:	*Dōmo.*	"Thank you."

Grammar Note 5 — Asking for detailed comments

Tokuni **[Interrogative]** *ga* $\left\{ \begin{array}{l} \textbf{[A]-}\textit{katta desu} \\ \textbf{[AN]} \qquad \textit{deshita} \end{array} \right\}$ *ka* ↗.

Tokuni doko ga yokatta desu ka.   "Which/what part was particularly nice?"

This is one type of question you can use when you want to ask for detailed comments.

Examples

Tokuni doko ga omoshirokatta desu ka.	"Which place was particularly interesting?"
Tokuni nani ga oishikatta desu ka.	"What was particularly delicious?"
Tokuni nan-ji goro ga kirei deshita ka.	"Around what time was it particularly beautiful?"

Grammar Note 6 — Giving detailed comments

In answering the question "what was particularly good?," give more detailed comments using _____ *ga* _____.

Examples

Umi ga kirei deshita.	"The ocean was beautiful."
Hoteru no sābisu ga yokatta desu.	"The hotel service was good."
O-tera ga in'shōteki deshita.	"The temples were impressive."

Vocabulary

Detailed comments on a trip — for reference (You don't need to memorize all of these. Just choose the ones you need.)

[The item]		*ga*	[Predicate]		
Meaning					Meaning
scenery	*keshiki*	*ga*	[A]	*yokatta*	*desu*	good, nice
ocean, sea	*umi*			*utsukushikatta*	*desu*	beautiful
beach (sea, ocean)	*kaigan*			*subarashikatta*	*desu*	wonderful
river	*kawa*			*kitanakatta*	*desu*	dirty
water	*mizu*		[AN]	*kirei deshita*		pretty, clean
air	*kūki*					
mountain	*yama*					
forest	*mori*					
greenery	*midori*					

tree	ki				
flower	hana				
rice field	ta(n'bo)				
other grain *or* vegetable fields	hatake				
uncultivated field	nohara				
country side	inaka				
town	machi				
buddhist temple	(o-)tera				
shinto shrine	jin'ja				
the price of ____ prices	____ no nedan bukka	ga	[A]	takakatta desu yasukatta desu	expensive cheap
people car	hito kuruma	ga	[A]	ōkatta desu sukunakatta desu	many few
food beverages	tabemono nomimono	ga	[A] [AN]	oishikatta desu mazukatta desu shin'sen deshita	delicious tastes bad fresh
service weather	sābisu ten'ki	ga	[A]	yokatta desu warukatta desu	good bad

Grammar Note 7 — Adding more comments

In Lesson 8, you learned:

[Comment 1] *kedo/ga*, [Comment 2]

Kirei desu ga takai desu nē.   "Although it's pretty, it's expensive, isn't it?"

Here we introduce two ways to offer further comments:

a.

Detailed Comment 1
[Item] *ga* **[Predicate]**

Conjunction	Detailed Comment 2
Soreni,	**[Item]** *mo* **[Predicate]**

Tōshōgū ga yokatta desu.
"The Toshogu Shrine was nice."

Soreni, *yama mo kirei deshita.*
"In addition to that, the mountains were beautiful, too."

Soreni means "in addition to that" or "furthermore."

b.

Further Comment 1
[Item] *ga/wa* **[Predicate]**

Conjunction	Further Comment 2
Demo,	**[Item]** *ga/wa* **[Predicate]**

Yama ga kirei deshita.
"The mountains were beautiful."

Demo, *hito ga ōkatta desu.*
"However, there were too many people."
[*Lit.* People were many.]

Examples

Umi ga kirei deshita.   "The sea was beautiful."
Soreni, tabemono mo oishikatta desu.   "In addition to that, the food was
                                 delicious too."

Keshiki wa yokatta desu.   "The scenery was nice."
Demo, sābisu wa warukatta desu.   "However, the service was bad."

If you apply the pattern from Lesson 8, you will get:

Keshiki wa yokatta desu ga, sābisu wa warukatta desu.

Drill 1   Substitute the underlined parts.

1. _Sumisu-san, Nikkō wa dō deshita ka._
   (1)   Tanaka   gorufu   (2)   Inoue   nichi-yōbi
   (3)   Ōno |yasumi   (4)   Takahashi   pātī
2. _Yokatta desu_ yo.
   (1)   tanoshikatta desu   (2)   omoshirokatta desu
   (3)   kirei deshita   (4)   dame deshita
3. Tokuni _doko_ ga _yokatta desu_ ka.
   (1)   doko, omoshirokatta desu (2)   nani, oishikatta desu
   (3)   doko kirei deshita   (4)   nani, yokatta desu
4. _Yama_ ga kirei deshita.
   (1)   umi   (2) keshiki   (3)   otera
5. Jitsu wa, _kyūyō_ de ikimasen deshita.
   (1)   shutchō   (2) yōji   (3)   ame   (4)   kaze

Drill 2   Expand the sentences.

_e.g.,_   ikimasen deshita ⟶ Ikimasen deshita.
          pātī ni wa   ⟶ Pātī ni wa ikimasen deshita.
          yōji de   ⟶ Yōji de pātī ni wa ikimasen deshita.

(1)   ikimasen deshita   (2)   ikimasen deshita
        tenisu ni wa   gakkō e wa
        kaze de   byōki de
        nichi-yōbi wa   sen'shū
                                           kodomo wa
(3)   ikimasu   (4)   ikimasu
        Shikoku e   Ōsaka e
        shutchō de   kaigi de
        sui-yōbi ni   raishū

Drill 3   Fill in the appropriate forms in the blank, and give the meaning in English.

Meaning	Non-Past		Past	
	Aff.	Neg.	Aff.	Neg.
expensive	takai desu	takaku arimasen	takakatta desu	takaku arimasen deshita
	yasui desu			
		oishiku arimasen		
			tanoshikatta desu	
				omoshiroku arimasen deshita
	ii desu			
		waruku arimasen		

			tsumaranakatta desu	
				mazuku arimasen deshita
	ōi desu			
		sukunaku arimasen		
pretty, clean	kirei desu	kirei ja arimasen	kirei deshita	kirei ja arimasen deshita
	shizuka desu			
		in'shōteki ja arimasen		
			dame deshita	

⊞ Drill 4　Change the affirmative sentences to negative. Notice the tense.

e,g.,　1.　*Bukka ga takai desu.* ⟶ *Bukka wa takaku arimasen.*

　　　2.　*Bukka ga takakatta desu.* ⟶ *Bukka wa takaku arimasen deshita.*

(1)　*Tabemono ga oishii desu.*

(2)　*Ten'ki ga ii desu.*

(3)　*Ten'ki ga yokatta desu.*

(4)　*Hoteru ga yasukatta desu.*

(5)　*Machi ga kirei desu.*

(6)　*Umi ga kirei deshita.*

(7)　*O-tera ga in'shō-teki deshita.*

(8)　*Hito ga ōkatta desu.*

⊞ Drill 5　Give "Enthusiastic Listening" to the comment. Choose one of the following:

Sore wa yokatta desu nē ↘.

Sore wa zan'nen deshita nē ↘.

Sore wa ikemasen nē ↘.

Sō desu ka ↘.

e.g.,　A:　*Ryokō wa tanoshikatta desu.*

　　　B:　*Sore wa yokatta desu nē.*

(1)　*Nikkō wa kirei deshita yo.*

(2)　*Ame de haikin'gu ni wa ikimasen deshita.*

(3)　*Tabemono ga oishikatta desu.*

(4)　*Ashita shutchō de Kōbe e ikimasu.*

(5)　*Kodomo wa kaze de kyō wa gakkō e ikimasen deshita.*

(6)　*Ten'ki ga warukatta desu.*

(7)　*Yasumi wa yokatta desu yo.*

(8)　*Jitsu wa, shujin wa shigoto de ikimasen deshita.*

Drill 6   Put *wa*, *mo* or *ga* in the blank _____, and *Soreni* or *Demo* in the box ⬜ .

📼 *e.g.,* | A: *Yasumi ni Shin'gapōru e ikimasu.*
| | — After Mr. A's return from Singapore —
| B: *Shin'gapōru <u>wa</u> dō deshita ka.*
| A: *Yokatta desu yo.*
| *Machi <u>ga</u> kirei deshita.*
| ⬜Sore ni *tabemono <u>mo</u> oishikatta desu.*
| ⬜Demo *bukka <u>wa</u> takakatta desu.*

(1) | A: *Ashita Makishimu e shokuji ni ikimasu.*
| | — The next day —
| B: *Makishimu _____ dō deshita ka.*
| A: *Oishikatta desu yo.*
| ⬜ *takakatta desu.*

(2) | A: *Do-yōbi ni Asakusa e ikimasu.*
| | — Next Monday —
| B: *Do-yōbi _____ dō deshita ka.*
| A: *Omoshirokatta desu yo.*
| ⬜ *hito _____ ōkatta desu.*

(3)   — At lunch time —
| A: *Kyō ano resutoran e ikimasu.*
| | — After Mr. A has returned from the restaurant —
| B: *Resutoran _____ dō deshita ka.*
| A: *Oishiku arimasen deshita.*
| ⬜ *takakatta desu.*

(4) | A: *Yasumi ni Marēshia e ikimasu.*
| | — After Mr. A's return from Malaysia —
| B: *Marēshia _____ dō deshita ka.*
| A: *Yokatta desu yo.*
| *Tabemono _____ yasukatta desu.*
| ⬜ *ten'ki _____ yokatta desu.*

(5) | A: *Shōgatsu ni Kamakura e ikimasu.*
| "The New Year's"
| | — On the 15th of January —
| B: *Kamakura _____ dō deshita ka.*
| A: *Samukatta desu.*
| ⬜ *hito _____ ōkatta desu.*
| ⬜ *omoshirokatta desu yo.*

Drill 7 Using the Dialogue as a model, complete the following conversation. Use the cue just as a hint and make sentences as you like.

(1) — Before the holiday —		
[a] *Kyōto*	You:	[a] _____.
ikimasu	Tape:	*Ii desu nē.*
— After the holiday —		
	Tape:	*Kyōto wa dō deshita ka.*
[b] *ii*	You:	[b] _____.
	Tape:	*Tokuni doko ga yokatta desu ka.*
[c] *Arashiyama*	You:	[c] _____
(hill)		_____
Ryōan'ji		_____.
(temple)	Tape:	*Sore wa yokatta desu nē.*

(2) — Before the holiday —		
[a] *Firipin*	You:	[a] _____.
ikimasu	Tape:	*Ii desu nē.*
— After the holiday —		
	Tape:	*Firipin wa dō deshita ka.*
[b] *ii*	You:	[b] _____.
	Tape:	*Tokuni doko ga yokatta desu ka.*
[c] *umi*	You:	[c] _____
tabemono		_____.
bukka	Tape:	*Sore wa yokatta desu nē.*

(3) — Before the holiday —		
[a] *Hokkaidō*	You:	[a] _____.
ikimasu	Tape:	*Ii desu nē.*
— A few days later —		
	Tape:	*Hokkaidō wa dō deshita ka.*
[b] *kyūyō*	You:	[b] _____.
	Tape:	*Sore wa zan'nen deshita nē.*

Drill 8 Answer about yourself.

(1) *Yasumi ni dokoka e ikimashita ka.*

(2) *Dare to ikimashita ka.*

(3) *Dōyatte ikimashita ka.*

(4) *(Yasumi wa) dō deshita ka.*

(5) *Toku ni doko ga yokatta desu ka.*

(6) *Tabemono wa oishikatta desu ka.*

(7) *Kon'do wa doko e ikimasu ka.*

Culture Note 6— *"Nihon wa dō desu ka"*

The Japanese language has its own unique set of appropriate phrases when it comes to small talk with foreigners. Some may seem amusing, others annoying when taken at face value — out of the cultural context — and translated directly, particularly if the other language is English.

Probably the most commonly heard expression anywhere, once you begin to speak in Japanese is **Nihon-go (ga) jōzu desu nē** "Oh, how good your Japanese is!" usually said with complimentary surprise. Even though your fluency may be a mere handful of useful phrases and your pronunciation far from native naturalness, you'll encounter this expression over and over again. Don't feel it's false praise, rather consider it a friendly gesture, a conversational opener. You can respond with a simple thank you **Dōmo** . . . , but a more culturally appropriate response would be **Iie, mada heta desu** "No, I'm still poor at Japanese." accompanied by a humble lowering of the eyes. "No, it's not." would be abrupt and because it is contradictory in tone, though perfectly honest, it would put your native speaker off.

Once it's been established that your Japanese is **jōzu** "fluent," you'll probably be asked a number of questions which may seem very personal, but again are meant as friendly, pretty impersonal inquiries or asked out of curiosity. For example, you may be asked your age **Ikutsu desu ka** "How old are you?" and then whether you're married **Kekkon shite imasu ka** "Are you married?" If you're a woman over 25 and unmarried you may be asked why you're not **Dōshite kekkon shinai-n desu ka** "Why aren't you married?" Or if you've been married several years and have no children you'll be asked why **Dōshite okosan (ga) inai-n desu ka** "Why don't you have children?" and probably encouraged to hurry up and have a family so you won't be lonely **Hayaku kodomo o tsukutta hō ga ii desu yo** "You'd better have children as soon as possible." Please don't respond with "It's none of your business." Rather, you can avoid any response with a vague smile, or if your conversational ability allows, provide a witty rejoinder that lets you off the "embarrassed hook." If you're a man, the above questions about marriage and family probably won't be asked. You may just be asked what you do and what company you work for. If you answer with a well-known company's name — regardless of your position — don't be surprised at the high estimation of your importance your answer brings.

In social gatherings these personal questions will crop up predictably. Usually your age and what you do will be solicited first. However, you may first be asked where you're from **Okuni wa dochira desu ka** "Where are you from?" This is often asked **Amerika-jin desu ka** "Are you American?" Though this may lead you to believe that all foreigners are regarded as Americans, it's the culture's way of establishing your nationality. If you are American, a further probe will be made to find out which part **Amerika wa dochira desu ka** "Which part of the States are you from?" You can reply by asking whether your questioner has ever been there **Amerika e itta koto arimasu ka**.

Other common questions will include:

How long will you stay?   **Ato dono gurai imasu ka.**
How long have you been in Japan?   **Nihon wa nagai-n desu ka.** [*Lit.* Is (your) stay in) Japan long?]
How is Japan?   **Nihon wa dō desu ka.**

Many people are annoyed when Japanese comment on their ability to use chopsticks or inquire whether the foreigners can eat raw fish. Again, these are mentioned only casually in conversational passing and carry no more value than the usual social chit-chat we fill our lives with in our own cultures.

Keeping our responses light and humorous is basically what's expected.

Culture Note 7 — ...Hai?

The way to say "yes" in Japanese, as every beginner in the language knows, is **hai** or **ē**. But what the beginner doesn't know is that the innocuous **hai** has a variety of other usages that don't concur at all with the English "yes."

For example, while you are talking, your Japanese listener will interpolate **hai** every time you pause for breath. A frequent reaction on the part of the speaker is to think that the listener is losing interest, and is trying not so politely to end the conversation. Another reaction is to think that your demands and proposals have a favorable reception and you are accordingly surprised to hear a refusal after so many **hai**'s.

In reality, this **hai** merely means "I hear you. Go on." It is a form of **aizuchi**, or short expressions that reassure the speaker that the listener is still listening. (*cf.* Lesson 3, Grammar Note 5) In Japan, if you listen silently, the speaker may think you are not listening or don't understand. To assure the speaker, you must constantly be "encouraging." You are bound to have heard a telephone conversation that consisted on one end of "**Hai** ... **hai** ... **ē, ē** ... **ē** ... **hai**."

Hai with a question mark means "What did you say?" and usually indicates a degree of surprise. You are then expected to repeat what you have just said. This shock reaction can often be avoided by prefacing your statement/question with a softening **Anō** ... to which you will hear **Hai** again. This means "What is it *or* What can I do for you?"
A further, rather informal, meaning of **Hai** is "Here you are." When you are served tea, given change, handed something, it is accompanied by **Hai** or **Hai, dōzo**. And your reply? **Hai** again. But as **Hai** alone doesn't express gratitude, you should usually reply **Hai, dōmo** ...

Hai is used at roll call time to reply to your name, and when you are called upon to answer a question, **hai** is what you say whether answering or admitting you don't know the answer.

Last of all, again informally, **Hai, hai** means "I'm coming *or* Wait a second, I know you're there."

So now that you know "yes" doesn't always mean "yes," it should come as no surprise to you to learn there are some problems with "no." But that's another story.

Rock garden in Ryoanji Temple (Kyoto)

Toshogu Shrine (Nikko)

Expressing What You Usually Do

SCOPE OF UNIT IV

The main function of Unit IV is TALKING ABOUT ROUTINE ACTIVITIES.

Lesson 13 deals with the activities and things you do in your spare time, giving you an insight into Japanese habits and behavior.

Lesson 14 covers eating, drinking and shopping, giving you a glimpse of the traditional and modern lifestyle of the Japanese people.

Lesson 15 concerns daily activities and routines, such as getting up, going to bed, leaving and arriving. After this lesson, you will be able to talk about your daily and weekly engagements.

Lesson 13

WHAT YOU USUALLY DO IN YOUR SPARE TIME

YORU WA ITSUMO NANI O SHIMASU KA
"WHAT DO YOU USUALLY DO AT NIGHT?"

Dialogue I

Sumisu: Tanaka-san, yoru wa itsumo
nani o shimasu ka.

Tanaka: Sō desu nē, taitei terebi o
mimasu.

Sumisu: Don'na mono o mimasu ka.

Tanaka: Yoku eiga o mimasu.

Sumisu: Kinō wa nani o mimashita ka.

Tanaka: 'Sen'sō to Heiwa' o mimashita.

Sumisu: 'Sen'sō to Heiwa' desu ka.
Are wa ii desu nē.

Tanaka: Ē. Sumisu-san wa terebi wa
mimasu ka.

Sumisu: Ē, tokidoki mimasu.

Mr. Smith:	What do you usually do at night?
Mr. Tanaka:	Well..., I watch television most nights.
Mr. Smith:	What kind of programs [*Lit.* things] do you usually watch?
Mr. Tanaka:	I often watch movies.
Mr. Smith:	What did you see last night?
Mr. Tanaka:	I saw the movie 'War and Peace.'
Mr. Smith:	Did you? [*Lit.* Is it 'War and Peace'?]
	I liked that (movie). [*Lit.* That's a good movie, isn't it?]
Mr. Tanaka:	Yes. Do you watch television?
Mr. Smith:	Yes, I sometimes do.

Vocabulary

itsumo: always, usually
shimasu ← *suru:* do
taitei: mostly
mimasu ← *miru:* watch, look at, see
don'na mono: what kind of things

yoku: often
eiga: movies
sen'sō: war
heiwa: peace
tokidoki: sometimes

Dialogue II

Tanaka:	*Sumisu-san wa shigoto no ato nani o shimasu ka.*
Sumisu:	*Taitei sugu uchi e kaerimasu ga, is-shūkan ni ni-kai Nihon-go no ressun ga arimasu.*
Tanaka:	*Doko de naratte imasu ka.*
Sumisu:	*Ōtemachi no Pegasasu Ran'gēji Sābisu de naratte imasu.*
Tanaka:	*Pegasasu Ran'gēji Sābisu desu ka.*
Sumisu:	*Ē, sō desu.*
Tanaka:	*Nihon-go wa omoshiroi desu ka.*
Sumisu:	*Ē, omoshiroi desu. Watashi wa Nihon-go ga heta desu ga . . .*
Tanaka:	*Son'na koto wa arimasen yo.*

Mr. Tanaka:	What do you usually do after work, Mr. Smith?
Mr. Smith:	I go home right away most days, but I have Japanese lessons twice a week (in the evening).
Mr. Tanaka:	Where are you taking lessons? [*Lit.* Where are you learning?]
Mr. Smith:	At Pegasus Language Services in Otemachi (Tokyo).
Mr. Tanaka:	Oh, at Pegasus Language Services!
Mr. Smith:	Yes, that's right.
Mr. Tanaka:	Are the lessons interesting? [*Lit.* Is the Japanese language interesting?]
Mr. Smith:	Yes, they're interesting. My [*Lit.* it's] Japanese is not good, though.
Mr. Tanaka:	Oh, don't say that! [*Lit.* It cannot be so.]

I

スミス：田中さん、　よるは　いつも　なにを　しますか。

田中　：そうですねえ、　たいてい　テレビを　みます。

スミス：どんな　ものを　みますか。

田中　：よく　えいがを　みます。

スミス：きのうは　なにを　みましたか。

田中　：「戦争と平和」をみました。

スミス：「戦争と平和」ですか。　あれは　いいですねえ。

田中　：ええ。　スミスさんは　テレビは　みますか。

スミス：ええ、　ときどき　みます。

Vocabulary

ato: after	*arimasu* ← *aru:* have
sugu: immediately	*naratte* ← *narau:* learn
is-shūkan: a week	*heta:* not skillful
ni-kai: twice	*son'na koto:* such a fact
ressun: lessons	

II

田中　：スミスさんは　しごとの　あと　なにを　しますか。

スミス：たいてい　すぐ　うちへ　かえりますが、　1しゅうかんに　2かい
　　　　日本語の　レッスンが　あります。

田中　：どこで　ならっていますか。

スミス：大手町の　ペガサス・ランゲージ・サービスで　ならっています。

田中　：ペガサス・ランゲージ・サービスですか。

スミス：ええ、　そうです。

田中　：日本語は　おもしろいですか。

スミス：ええ、　おもしろいです。　わたしは　日本語が　へたですが…。

田中　：そんな　ことは　ありませんよ。

▮ Grammar Note 1 ▮ — Verbs

a.　The following verbs are introduced in this lesson:

	Meaning	
I.	see, watch	*mimasu*
	listen	*kikimasu*
	read	*yomimasu*
	do	*shimasu*
	learn, take lessons	*naratte imasu**
	teach	*oshiete imasu**
II.	have	*arimasu*

　　　　*combined verb:　This form is not discussed in this lesson.

b.　Remember the meaning which goes with verb endings, **-masu, -masen, -mashita, -masen deshita**. (*cf.* Lesson 11, Grammar Note 1)

In this Unit, we mainly introduce for the first time the following meanings, which were not introduced in Lesson 11:

| *-masu* |　[Non-Past Affirmative]

What you generally or habitually do.

| *-masen* |　[Non-Past Negative]

What you generally or habitually do **not** do.

▮ Grammar Note 2 ▮ — Object of the verb

a.　All the verbs introduced in this lesson take objects. The verb **arimasu** ''have'' takes **ga** as an object marker but the other verbs take **o**.

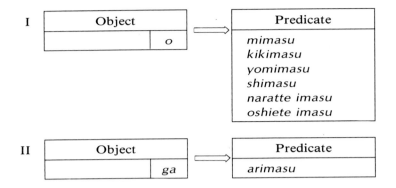

I

Object			Predicate
	o	⟶	*mimasu* *kikimasu* *yomimasu* *shimasu* *naratte imasu* *oshiete imasu*

II

Object			Predicate
	ga	⟶	*arimasu*

Examples

I *Terebi o mimasu.*   "(I) watch TV."

  Yoru* on'gaku o kikimasu.   "(I) listen to music in the evening."

  Mainichi hon o yomimasu.   "(I) read books every day."

  Do-yōbi wa tenisu o shimasu.   "(I) play tennis on Saturdays."

  Nihon-go o naratte imasu.   "(I) take Japanese (lessons)."

  Ei-go o oshiete imasu.   "(I) teach English."

II *Nihon-go no ressun ga arimasu.*   "(I) have a Japanese lesson."

  *Although the meaning of **ban** and **yoru** overlaps, **ban** is rather early evening and **yoru** is rather late in the evening.

b. ***Nani*** "what", ***Nanika*** "something, anything"

Note that when you make a question using ***nanika***, do not put the object marker ***o*** or ***ga***.

Examples

A: *Nichi-yōbi wa nani o shimasu ka.*   "What do you do on Sundays?"

B: *Gorufu o shimasu.*   "I play golf."

A: *Nichi-yōbi wa nanika shimasu ka.* "Do you do anything on Sundays?"

B: *Ē, gorufu o shimasu.*   "Yes, I play golf."

A: *Sui-yōbi wa nani ga arimasu ka.* "What do you do [*Lit.* have] on Wednesdays?"

B: *Nihon-go no ressun ga arimasu.* "I have a Japanese lesson."

A: *Sui-yōbi wa nanika arimasu ka.* "Do you do [*Lit.* have] anything on Wednesdays?"

B: *Ē, Nihon-go no ressun ga arimasu.* "Yes, I have a Japanese lesson."

Grammar Note 3 — Place of action

[Place] *de* [Verb].

Shin'juku de mimasu.   "I (usually) see (it) in Shinjuku."

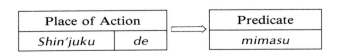

Place of Action			Predicate
Shin'juku	*de*	⟶	*mimasu*

De [Place of Action Marker]   "at" *or* "in"

These verbs also take the place of action, which is indicated by the marker ***de***.

Vocabulary: Places of action (*cf.* Places to go in Lesson 10)

Place names in Tokyo	*Shin'juku* *Shibuya* *Ikebukuro* *Gin'za* *Yūrakuchō* *Ōtemachi* *Aoyama* *Omotesan'do*
on the train	*den'sha (no naka)*
where?	*doko*

Examples

Shibuya de eiga o mimasu.	"I see movies in Shibuya."
Uchi de on'gaku o kikimasu.	"I listen to music at home."
Ōtemachi de ressun ga arimasu.	"I have a lesson in Otemachi."
Den'sha no naka de hon o yomimasu.	"I read books on the train."

Grammar Note 4 — Expressing how often you do something

To express frequency there are two ways:
  a)   using adverbs of frequency
  b)   telling how many times you do something in a week, month, *etc.*

a.   **[Time]** *wa* **[Frequency] [Item]** *o/ga* **[Verb]**.

Yoru wa *itsumo nani o shimasu ka*.	"What do you usually [*Lit.* almost always] do in the evening?"
(*Yoru* wa) *taitei terebi o mimasu*.	"I usually watch TV (in the evening)."

Adverb of Frequency	Predicate
itsumo *taitei*	*shimasu* *mimasu*

The following are adverbs of frequency:

	Meaning	
I.	(almost) always usually often sometimes occasionally	*itsumo** *taitei* *yoku* *tokidoki* *tamani*
II.	not so often seldom not at all	*amari* *mettani* *zen'zen*
	how often?	*dono gurai*

I.   —— used with affirmative form of the verb
II.   —— used with negative form of the verb

  Itsumo is not taken literally as "always" when talking about everyday activities; the meaning is closer to "almost always."

Use *itsumo* "always" when you ask about someone's routine activities. However, it's more common to use *taitei* "usually" or "mostly" in response. The meaning of *itsumo* and *taitei* overlaps somewhat.

Examples

A: *Yoru wa itsumo nani o shimasu ka.*	"What do you usually do in the evening?"
B: *Taitei terebi o mimasu.*	"I usually watch TV."
A: *Shūmatsu wa itsumo nani o shimasu ka.*	"What do you usually do over the weekend?"
B: *Yoku tenisu ni ikimasu.*	"I often play tennis."
A: *Hima na toki wa itsumo nani o shimasu ka.*	"What do you usually do in your spare time?"
B: *Taitei hon o yomimasu.*	"I usually read books."
A: *Yoku eiga o mimasu ka.*	"Do you often go to the movies?"
B: *Iie, amari mimasen.*	"No, I don't go very often."
A: *Terebi o mimasu ka.*	"Do you watch TV?"
B: *Ē, tokidoki mimasu yo.*	"Yes, I sometimes watch it. (you know)."

b.

Frequency
[Period of Time]* *ni* [Times]

[Item] *o/ga* **[Verb]**.

Shū ni *ni-kai* *ressun* ga *arimasu.*   "I have lessons twice a week."

*cf. Lesson 9

When you want to express frequency in terms of how many times in an hour, week, month and so on, use the phrases listed in the table below:

	Period of Time*			*ni*	Times	
	[day]	[week]	[others]			
1	ichi-nichi	is-shūkan			ik-kai "once"	ichi-ni-kai "once or twice"
2	futsu-ka	ni-shūkan			ni-kai "twice"	ni-san-kai "two or three times"
3	mik-ka	san-shūkan		ni	san-kai "three times"	san-yon-kai "three or four times"
4	yok-ka	yon-shūkan			yon-kai "four times"	shi-go-kai "four or five times"
5	. . .	. . .			go-kai "five times"	
?	nan-nichi	nan-shūkan			nan-kai "how many times" dono gurai "how often"	
	dono gurai	"how often"				

Examples

ichi-nichi ni ik-kai	"once a day"
is-shūkan ni ni-kai	"twice a week"
ichi-nen ni ni-san-kai	"two or three times a year"
futsu-ka ni ik-kai	"once in two days"

is-shūkan ni ni-kai Nihon-go no ressun ga arimasu.	"I have Japanese lessons twice a week."

A:	*Yoku Roppongi e ikimasu ka.*	"Do you often go to Roppongi?"
B:	*Ē, shū ni ni-san-kai ikimasu.*	"Yes, two or three times a week."

c.   *Gurai*   "about"

The word ***gurai*** indicates approximate extent. It follows the noun which indicates quantity — number of times, people, things, or amount of things.

Remember that ***goro*** "around" follows specific time words.

Examples

san-kai gurai	"about three times"
Ik-kagetsu ni ni-kai gurai tsuri ni ikimasu.	"I go fishing about twice a month."

d.   *Dono gurai*   "How often",
***Nan-kai (gurai)*   "About how many times?"**

With ***dono gurai***, you can ask not only frequency but also many other things like "how much/far/long/heavy, *etc.*"

On the other hand, ***is-shūkan ni nan-kai (gurai)*** asks specifically "(about) how many times a week" you do something.

Examples

A:	*Eiga wa dono gurai mimasu ka.*	"How often do you go to the movies? [*Lit.* As for movies, how often do you see them?]"
B:	*Ik-kagetsu ni ik-kai gurai mimasu.*	"I go (see) about once a month."
A:	*Kinō Shibuya e ikimashita. Kyō mo ikimasu.*	"I went to Shibuya yesterday. I'm also going today."
B:	*Yoku ikimasu nē. Is-shūkan ni nan-kai gurai ikimasu ka.*	"You go there quite often! About how many times a week do you go there?"
A:	*San-yon-kai desu.*	"Three or four times."

Grammar Note 5 — Replacing the object marker with ***wa*** or ***mo***

You often use ***wa*** [Topic *or* Contrast Marker] when making a yes/no question or a negative sentence. When using ***wa*** or ***mo*** [Inclusion Marker] after the object, omit ***o*** or ***ga*** [Object Marker].

Note that you do the same thing with ***ga*** [Subject Marker].
(*cf.* Lesson 11, Grammar Note 4 – c)

Examples

Terebi o mimasu.	"I watch TV."
Eiga mo mimasu.	"I go to the movies, too. [*Lit.* I see movies.]"

154

Terebi wa mimasen.	"I don't watch TV. [*Lit.* As for TV, I don't watch it.]"
Eiga mo mimasen.	"I don't go to (see) movies, either."
Terebi wa mimasu ka.	"Do you watch TV? [*Lit.* As for TV, do you watch it?]"
Eiga mo mimasu ka.	"Do you also go to (see) movies?"
Kyō wa kaigi ga arimasu.	"I have a meeting today."
Nihon-go no ressun mo arimasu.	"I have a Japanese lesson, too."
Kyō wa kaigi wa arimasen.	"I don't have a meeting today. [*Lit.* As for meeting, I don't have it today.]"
Nihon-go no ressun mo arimasen.	"I don't have a Japanese lesson, either."
Kyō wa kaigi wa arimasu ka.	"Do you have a meeting today? [*Lit.* As for meeting, do you have it today?]"
Nihon-go no ressun mo arimasu ka.	"Do you also have a Japanese lesson?"

Grammar Note 6 — Not any . . .

[Interrogatives] *mo* [Verb (Negative)].

Nani mo yomimasen.   "I don't read anything."

The interrogative **nani** "what," **dare** "who," and **doko** "where" followed by **mo** plus the negative form of a verb mean "not any . . ."

Examples

Shūmatsu wa nani mo shimasen deshita.	"I didn't do anything on the weekend."
Sono hon wa dare mo yomimasen.	"Nobody reads that book."
Kinō wa doko e mo ikimasen deshita.	"I didn't go anywhere yesterday."
A: Do-yōbi wa nani o shimasu ka.	"What are you going to do on Saturday?"
B: Betsu ni nani mo shimasen.	"Nothing special."

Sumo on TV

Here is the diagram for the verbs and other elements of this lesson:

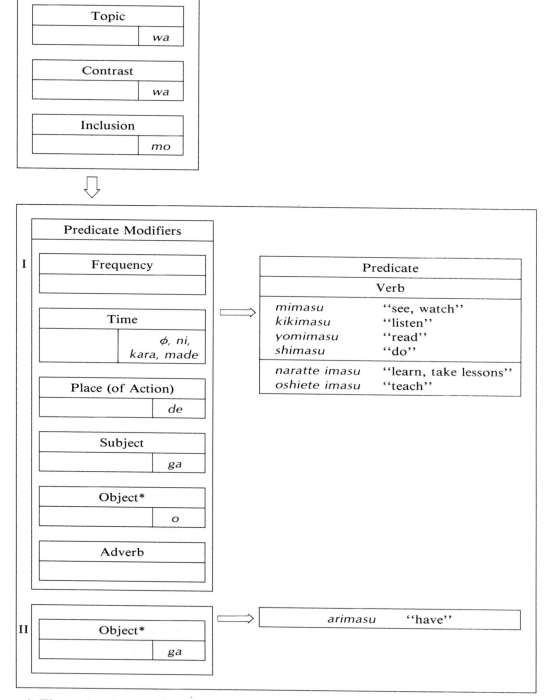

* The verb **arimasu** takes the object marker **ga** instead of the marker **o**.

Grammar Note 7 — Asking/Answering further questions

Don'na [Item/Thing] o [Verb] ka ↗.
Don'na <u>hon o yomimasu</u> *ka.*   "What kind of books do you read?"

Don'na plus words like **koto** "(abstract) thing," **mono** "(tangible) thing," or **hon** "book" enables you to ask further questions about somebody's activities.

Examples

A: *Hima na toki wa itsumo nani o shimasu ka.*   "What do you usually do in your spare time?"
B: *Taitei hon o yomimasu.*   "I usually read books."
A: *Don'na hon o yomimasu ka.*   "What kind of books do you read?"
B: *Shōsetsu o yomimasu.*   "I read novels."

A: *Yoru wa itsumo nani o shimasu ka.*   "What do you usually do in the evening?"
B: *Yoku terebi o mimasu.*   "I often watch TV."
A: *Don'na mono o mimasu ka.*   "What kind of program do you watch?"
B: *Supōtsu nyūsu desu.*   "Sports news."

Compare:
Nichi-yōbi wa nani o shimasu ka.   "What do you do on Sundays?"
Nichi-yōbi wa don'na koto o shimasu ka.   "What kind of things do you do on Sundays?"

Grammar Note 8 — Expressing like/dislike in general

[Person] wa [Item/Thing] ga suki desu.
Watashi wa <u>sumō*</u> *ga suki desu.*   "I like *sumo*."

*Japanese traditional sport.

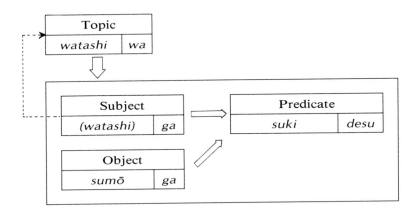

a. **Suki desu**   "like"
Suki is translated as a verb in English, but it is an adjectival noun in Japanese grammar.

Examples
(Eiga wa) seibugeki ga suki desu.   "(As for movies,) I like cowboy movies."

A:	B-san wa don'na on'gaku ga suki desu ka.	"What kind of music do you like, Mr./Ms. B?"
B:	Kurasshikku ga suki desu.	"I like classical music."
A:	Jazu wa suki desu ka.	"Do you like jazz?"
B:	Ē, (jazu mo) suki desu.	"Yes, I do."
	or	
	Iie, (jazu wa) amari* suki ja arimasen.	"No, I don't like it very much."

Amari + **negative form** here means "not very much." In Grammar Note 4 in this Lesson, it means "not very often."

b.   Kirai desu   "dislike"

Kirai is also an adjectival noun. You could say **kirai desu** "I dislike it," but this shows strong hatred. Therefore, we recommend that you use **amari suki ja arimasen**.

c.   Suki desu vs. **Ii desu**

With **suki desu** you express your general taste. To express that you like something for specific cases, do not use **suki desu**, but use **ii desu**. (*cf.* Shopping, Lesson 8)

Compare:

Watashi wa kōhī ga suki desu.	"I like coffee (in general)."
Kyō wa kōhī ga ii desu.	"(As for) today, I would like (to have) coffee."

Grammar Note 9 — Expressing being good/poor at doing something
                     Expressing compliments

[Person] wa [Thing] ga heta desu.
Watashi wa Nihon-go ga heta desu.   "I'm poor at Japanese."

[Person] wa [Thing] ga jōzu desu nē.
Sumisu-san wa Nihon-go ga jōzu desu nē.   "Mr. Smith, you are good at Japanese!"
                                             or
                                            "Mr. Smith is good at Japanese, isn't he?"

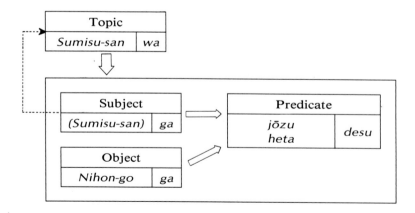

a.   Jōzu desu "be good at",   **Heta desu**   "be poor at"
Both **jōzu** and **heta** are adjectival nouns. **Jōzu desu nē** is often used for a compliment.

b. *Son'na koto wa arimasen (yo).*   "That's not true(!)"
Use this when someone has modestly said that he/she is poor at something.

Examples

	Takahashi-san wa Ei-go ga jōzu desu.	"Mr. Takahashi is good at English."
Nihon-jin:	*Sumisu-san, Nihon-go ga jōzu nē.*	"You are good at Japanese, Mr. Smith."
Sumisu:	*Iie, mada heta desu.*	"No. I'm still poor at it."
Sumisu:	*Watashi wa Nihon-go ga heta desu.*	"I'm poor at Japanese."
Nihon-jin:	*Son'na koto wa arimasen yo.*	"Oh, that's not true!"

Here is the vocabulary list for each verb. You do not need to memorize them all:

1. _____ *o mimasu.* _____ *ga suki desu.*

Vocabulary: Things to watch/see at home

Meaning	
Movies	*eiga*
Japanese movies	*Nihon no eiga*
American movies	*Amerika no eiga*
French movies	*Furan'su no eiga*
Kurosawa's movies	*Kurosawa no eiga*
samurai movies	*samurai (no) eiga, jidaigeki*
western (cowboy) movies	*kābōi (no) eiga, seibugeki*
action movies	*akushon-eiga*
comedies	*komedī*
what kind of {things? / movies?} what?	*don'na* {*mono* / *eiga*} *nani*

Meaning	
video	*bideo*
television (set)	*terebi*
news program	*nyūsu*
weather forecast	*ten'ki-yohō*
documentaries	*dokyumen'tarī*
soap operas	*hōmu-dorama*
cartoons	*man'ga*
sports programs	*supōtsu ban'gumi*
sumo matches	*sumō*
baseball games	*yakyū*
kabuki plays	*kabuki*
what kind of {thing? / program?} what?	*don'na* {*mono* / *ban'gumi*} *nani*

2. _____ *o kikimasu.* _____ *ga suki desu.*

Vocabulary: Things to enjoy listening to

Meaning	
radio	*rajio*
FM	*efu-emu*
stereo (set)	*sutereo*
record	*rekōdo*
tape	*tēpu*
music	*on'gaku*
Japanese music	*Nihon no on'gaku*
classical music	*kurashikku*
jazz	*jazu*
what kind of { thing? / music? } what?	*don'na* { *mono* / *on'gaku* } *nani*

Example

  Efu-emu de* on'gaku o kikimasu.   "I listen to music on FM radio."

  *This *de* is a Means Marker.

3. _____ *o yomimasu.* _____ *ga suki desu.*

Vocabulary: Things to read

Meaning	
book	*hon*
reference book on a specific subject	*sen'mon'sho*
essay	*essei*
novel	*shōsetsu*
mystery	*suiri-shōsetsu*
what kind of { thing? / books } what?	*don'na* { *mono* / *hon* } *nani*

Meaning	
magazine	*zasshi*
Japanese magazine	*Nihon no zasshi*
newspaper	*shin'bun*
English newspaper	*Ei-go no shin'bun*
Japanese (language) newspaper	*Nihon-go no shin'bun*
document	*shorui*
business documents	*shigoto no shorui*
materials for business	*shigoto no shiryō*
what kind of { thing? / magazine? / newspaper? / document? } what? what newspapers?	*don'na* { *mono* / *zasshi* / *shin'bun* / *shorui* } *nani* *nani shin'bun*

4. _____ *o shimasu*. _____ *ga suki desu*.

Vocabulary: Things to do [VN]*

Meaning	
sports	*supōtsu*
squash	*sukasshu*
tennis	*tenisu*
golf	*gorufu*
jogging	*jogin'gu*
ski	*sukī*
swimming	*suiei*
fishing	*tsuri*
gardening	*niwaijiri*
study	*ben'kyō*
reading	*dokusho*
knitting	*amimono*
carpentry (during leisure time)	*nichiyō-daiku*
house work	*kaji*
shopping	*kaimono*
preparing a meal	*shokuji no shitaku*
cooking	*ryōri*
washing dishes	*atokatazuke*
cleaning house	*sōji*
washing clothes	*sen'taku*
taking care of pets	*petto no sewa*
what kind of thing?	*don'na koto*
what?	*nani*

*[VN] = Verbal Noun

Nouns (*e.g., Tenisu ga suki desu* "I like tennis"), function as verbs when followed by *(o) shimasu* and are called Verbal Nouns.

Examples

    Tenisu o shimasu.   "I play tennis."

    Sōji o shimasu.   "I do the cleaning."

Calligraphy
lesson

161

5. _____ o naratte imasu. _____ o oshiete imasu.

  Vocabulary: Things to study, to be taught by an instructor

Meaning	
Japanese (language)	Nihon-go
English	Ei-go
French	Furan'su-go
tea ceremony	ocha
Japanese flower arrangement	(o)hana, ikebana
calligraphy	sho
painting	e
Japanese painting	Nihon-ga
Japanese cooking	Nihon-ryōri
judo	jūdō
kendo	ken'dō
aikido	aikidō
karate	karate
dancing	dan'su
what kind of thing?	don'na koto
what?	nani

6. _____ ga arimasu.

  Vocabulary: Things you have to do, events you have to attend

Meaning	
work	shigoto
overtime work	zan'gyō
conference, meeting	kaigi
appointment	yakusoku, apoin'to
class, lesson	jugyō, ressun
Japanese lesson	Nihon-go no ressun
party	pātī
reception	resepushon
date	dēto
what kind of thing?	don'na koto
what?	nani

Drill 1 Substitute the underlined parts.

1. _Terebi_ o mimasu.

(1)	eiga	(2)	Nihon no eiga	(3)	nyūsu
(4)	sumō	(5)	yakyū	(6)	bideo

2. _On'gaku_ o kikimasu.

(1)	kurashikku	(2)	jazu	(3)	popyurā
(4)	Nihon no on'gaku	(5)	Nihon no uta	(6)	shizuka na on'gaku

3. *Hon o yomimasu.*

(1) zasshi (2) shin'bun (3) shorui
(4) shōsetsu (5) Nihon no shin'bun (6) Ei-go no zasshi

4. *Supōtsu o shimasu*

(1) ben'kyō (2) kaimono (3) sōji
(4) sukasshu (5) jogin'gu (6) suiei

5. *Nihon-go o naratte imasu.*

(1) ikebana (2) sumie (3) jūdō
(4) karate (5) Nihon-ryōri (6) dan'su

6. *Ei-go o oshiete imasu.*

(1) Furan'su-go (2) Doitsu-go (3) Furan'su-ryōri

7. *Kaigi ga arimasu.*

(1) pātī (2) shigoto (3) yakusoku
(4) resepushon (5) zan'gyō (6) Nihon-go no ressun

Drill 2 Complete the sentences by filling in the markers.

e.g., Gin'za, eiga, mimasu
⟶ *Gin'za de eiga o mimasu.*

(1) den'sha no naka, uōkuman "walkman," kikimasu
(2) den'sha no naka, hon, yomimasu
(3) Ei-go no gakkō, Ei-go, oshiete imasu
(4) Pegasasu Ran'gēji Sābisu, Nihon-go, naratte imasu
(5) Amerikan kurabu, ikebana, naratte imasu
(6) uchi, Nihon-go no ressun, arimasu
(7) sen'sei no uchi, ocha no ressun, arimasu

Drill 3 Substitute the underlined parts.
Change the verbs accordingly.

e.g., | A: *Terebi wa mimasu ka.*
         | B: *Ē, mimasu.*
         | A: *Don'na mono o mimasu ka.*
         | B: *Yakyū to sumō o mimasu.*

(1) eiga, akushon-eiga (2) terebi, nyūsu
(3) on'gaku, jazu (4) zasshi, Ei-go no zasshi

Drill 4 Answer the questions with **[Interrogative]** *mo* Verb (negative).

e.g., | A: *Do-yōbi wa nanika shimasu ka.*
         | B: *(Betsu ni) nani mo shimasen.*

(1) Shūmatsu wa nanika shimasu ka.
(2) Yoru wa itsumo nani o shimasu ka.
(3) Kinō nani o shimashita ka.
(4) Ashita nanika arimasu ka.
(5) Kinō nanika arimashita ka.
(6) Ashita dokoka e ikimasu ka.
(7) Kinō dokoka e ikimashita ka.

Drill 5   Complete the conversations.

> 📼 e.g.,   A: *Kinō (wa) nani o shimashita ka.*
> B: *Hon o yomimashita.*
> A: *Nani o yomimashita ka.*
> B: *Agasa Kurisutī o yomimashita.*
>   "Agatha Christie"

(1)   A: *Kinō (wa) nani o shimashita ka.*
B: *Eiga* _____ .
A: _____ .
B: *Sutā Uōzu* _____ .
     "Star Wars"

(2)   A: *Kinō (wa) nani o shimashita ka.*
B: *On'gaku* _____ .
A: _____ .
B: *Bahha* _____ .
     "A Bach concert"

(3)   A: *Kinō (wa) nani o shimashita ka.*
B: *Kaji* _____ .
A: _____ .
B: *Sōji to sen'taku* _____ .

(4)   A: *Kinō (wa) nani o shimashita ka.*
B: *Betsu ni nani mo* _____ .
A: *Sō desu ka. Watashi mo desu.*

📼 **Drill 6**   Substitute the underlined parts. Change the verb forms if necessary.

> *Yoru (wa)* <u>*itsumo*</u> *Nihon-go no ben'kyō o shimasu.*

(1)   *taitei*   (2)   *tokidoki*   (3)   *tamani*
(4)   *amari*   (5)   *mettani*   (6)   *zen'zen*

📼 **Drill 7**   Using Dialogue I as a model, take the part of the person in the picture first, then take the other person's role.

(1) Mr. Brown	
[a] usually	Tape: *Buraun-san, yoru wa itsumo nani o shimasu ka.*

[b]   always
    classical
    music
	You: [a] _____ .
	Tape: *Don'na on'gaku o kikimasu ka.*
	You: [b] _____ .
	Tae: *Kinō wa nani o kikimashita ka.*

[c] Mozart	You: [c] _____ . Tape: *Mōtsuaruto desu ka.*
[d] Ms. Inoue?	You: [d] _____ . Tape: *Ē, watashi mo tokidoki kikimasu.*

(2) Mr. Takahashi

[a] usually	Tape: *Takahashi-san, yoru wa itsumo nani o shimasu ka.*
	You: [a] _____ .
	Tape: *Don'na ban'gumi o mimasu ka.*
[b] often movies	You: [b] _____ .
	Tape: *Kinō wa nani o mimashita ka.*
[c] Seven Samurais	You: [c] _____ .
	Tape: *'Shichi-nin no Samurai' desu ka.*
[d] Mr. White?	You: [d] _____ .
	Tape: *Sō desu nē. Amari mimasen.*

Drill 8   Substitute the underlined parts.

1. *Kurashikku ga suki desu.*
   (1) *Nihon no eiga*   (2) *ikebana*   (3) *shigoto*

2. *Jazu wa amari suki ja arimasen*
   (1) *terebi*   (2) *sōji*   (3) *yakyū*

3. *Tanaka-san wa supōtsu wa suki desu ka.*
   (1) *jazu*   (2) *e*   (3) *eiga*

4. *Watashi mo Bahha ga suki desu.*
   (1) *sashimi*   (2) *Abe Kōbō*   (3) *Higashiyama Kaii*
        (raw fish dish)   (writer)   (painter)

5. *Don'na on'gaku ga suki desu ka.*
   (1) *supōtsu*   (2) *eiga*   (3) *hon*

6. *Sumisu-san wa Nihon-go ga jōzu desu nē.*
   (1) *tenisu*   (2) *uta*   (3) *e*

Drill 9   Make yes/no questions using **wa** for Contrast or Topic, and answer.

e.g., *Jazu ga suki desu.* ⟶ *Jazu wa suki desu ka.*

    (Yes) ⟶ *Ē, suki desu.*
    (No) ⟶ *Sō desu nē . . . , amari suki ja arimasen.*

   (1) *Sen'taku ga suki desu.*
   (2) *Sushi ga suki desu.*
   (3) *Nihon no tabemono ga suki desu.*
   (4) *Karaoke* ga suki desu.*
   (5) *Ryokō ga suki desu.*

   *Recorded background music to sing along with.

Drill 10   Complete the sentences by putting in the appropriate markers.

   e.g., *is-shūkan, ik-kai, tenisu, shimasu*
        ⟶   *Is-shūkan ni ik-kai tenisu o shimasu.*

   (1) *is'shūkan, ik-kai, ikebana, naratte imasu*
   (2) *is-shūkan, ni-kai, Nihon-go no ressun, arimasu*
   (3) *ik-kagetsu, ichi-ni-kai, gorufu, shimasu*
   (4) *ichi-nen, ik-kai, kuni, kaerimasu*
   (5) *ni-kagetsu, ik-kai gurai, toko-ya, ikimasu*
                    "barber"

Drill 11 Suppose this is your weekly schedule. Answer the questions.

Nichi-yōbi	Getsu-yōbi	Ka-yōbi	Sui-yōbi	Moku-yōbi	Kin-yōbi	Do-yōbi
church at Omotesando shopping in Hiro	8:30 ≀ 9:15 Japanese lesson at Pegasus Language Services in Otemachi overtime reading	overtime reading	8:30 ≀ 9:15 Japanese lesson at Pegasus Language Services in Otemachi reading	overtime reading	9:00 ≀ 9:45 Japanese lesson at Pegasus Language Services in Otemachi about 5:30 ≀ 6:00 squash reading	karate

(1) *Nihon-go wa naratte imasu ka.*
(2) *Doko de naratte imasu ka.*
(3) *Ressun wa is-shūkan ni nan-kai arimasu ka.*
(4) *Nan-ji kara nan-ji made desu ka.*

(5) *Hon wa suki desu ka.*
(6) *Don'na hon o yomimasu ka.*

(7) *Supōtsu wa suki desu ka.*
(8) *Nani o shimasu ka.*
(9) *Nan-yōbi ni shimasu ka.*
(10) *Zan'gyō wa arimasu ka.*
(11) *Is-shūkan ni nan-kai gurai arimasu ka.*
(12) *Nichi-yōbi wa nani o shimasu ka.*
(13) *Doko no kyōkai e ikimasu ka.*
(14) *Kaimono wa doko de shimasu ka.*

Drill 12 Make questions first, and then answer.

e.g., | A: *Nihon-go wa muzukashii desu ka.*
       | B: *Ē, tokuni kan'ji ga muzukashii desu.*

(1) *Furan'su-go, muzukashii, hatsuon* "pronunciation"
(2) *ano restoran, oishii, niku-ryōri* "meat dish"
(3) *Nihon no bukka, takai, yachin* "(house) rent"

Drill 13 Using Dialogue II as a model, take the part of the person in the picture first, and then take the other person's role.

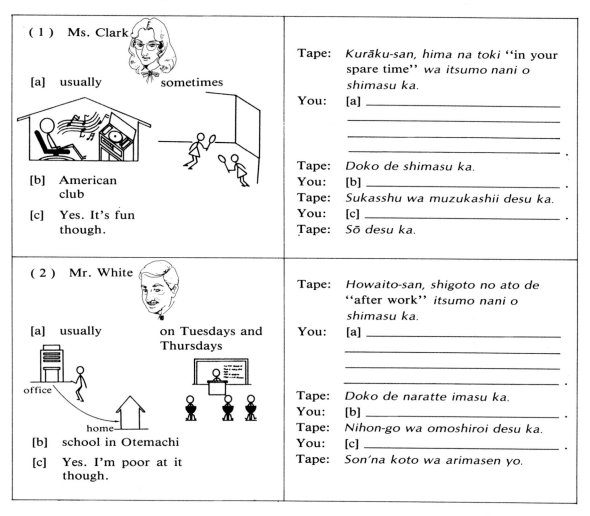

(1) Ms. Clark

[a] usually   sometimes

[b] American
     club

[c] Yes. It's fun
     though.

Tape: *Kurāku-san, hima na toki "in your spare time" wa itsumo nani o shimasu ka.*

You: [a] _____
      _____
      _____
      _____ .

Tape: *Doko de shimasu ka.*
You: [b] _____ .
Tape: *Sukasshu wa muzukashii desu ka.*
You: [c] _____ .
Tape: *Sō desu ka.*

(2) Mr. White

[a] usually   on Tuesdays and
                      Thursdays

office

home

[b] school in Otemachi

[c] Yes. I'm poor at it
     though.

Tape: *Howaito-san, shigoto no ato de "after work" itsumo nani o shimasu ka.*

You: [a] _____
      _____
      _____
      _____ .

Tape: *Doko de naratte imasu ka.*
You: [b] _____ .
Tape: *Nihon-go wa omoshiroi desu ka.*
You: [c] _____ .
Tape: *Son'na koto wa arimasen yo.*

Lesson 14

EATING, DRINKING AND SHOPPING

HIRU-GOHAN WA ITSUMO DOKO DE TABEMASU KA
"WHERE DO YOU USUALLY EAT LUNCH?"

📼 Dialogue I

Tanaka:	*Howaito-san, asa-gohan wa itsumo tabemasu ka.*
Howaito:	*Ē, tabemasu.*
Tanaka:	*Nani o tabemasu ka.*
Howaito:	*Kudamono to tōsuto to kōhī desu.*
	Tanaka-san wa.
Tanaka:	*Watashi wa mainichi gohan to misoshiru to*
	nori desu.
Howaito:	*Ten'keiteki na Nihon no asa-gohan*
	desu nē.

Mr. Tanaka:	Do you usually eat breakfast, Mr. White?
Mr. White:	Yes, I do.
Mr. Tanaka:	What do you eat (for breakfast)?
Mr. White:	I (usually) have some fruit, a piece of toast and coffee.
	How about you, Mr. Tanaka?
Mr. Tanaka:	I have rice, miso-soup and dried sea-weed (for breakfast) every day.
Mr. White:	Oh, that's a typical Japanese breakfast, isn't it?

Vocabulary

asa-gohan:	breakfast	*gohan:*	cooked rice
tabemasu ← taberu:	eat	*misoshiru:*	soy-bean paste soup
kudamono:	fruit	*nori:*	dried sea-weed (laver)
tōsuto:	toast	*ten'keiteki na:*	typical

▣ Dialogue II

Howaito:	*Hiru-gohan wa itsumo doko de tabemasu ka.*
Tanaka:	*Taitei shain shokudō desu.*
Howaito:	*Oishii desu ka.*
Tanaka:	*Sō desu nē. Māmā desu.*
	Howaito-san wa.
Howaito:	*Watashi wa yoku (kaisha no) chikaku no*
	mise de tabemasu.
Tanaka:	*Ii mise desu ka.*
Howaito:	*Ē. Kon'de imasu kedo, yasukute oishii*
	desu yo.

Mr. White:	Where do you usually eat lunch?
Mr. Tanaka:	Usually at the company cafeteria.
	[*Lit.* employee restaurant]
Mr. White:	(Is the food) good (there)?
Mr. Tanaka:	Well, (it's) so, so. (Where do you eat lunch,) Mr. White?
Mr. White:	I often eat lunch at a restaurant near my office.
Mr. Tanaka:	Do they have good food? [*Lit.* Is it a good store?]
Mr. White:	Yes. It's crowded, but it's not very expensive, and the food is good.

▣ Dialogue III

Howaito:	*Tabemono wa itsumo doko de kaimasu ka.*
Tanaka:	*Taitei chikaku no sūpā de kaimasu ga, sakana wa sakana-ya de kaimasu.*
Howaito:	*Sono sakana-ya wa doko desu ka.*
Tanaka:	*Ogikubo desu kedo, yasukute, shin'sen de ii desu yo.*
Howaito:	*Ā, sō desu ka.*
Tanaka:	*Howaito-san wa batā ya chīzu wa doko de kaimasu ka.*
Howaito:	*Ichiban Sutoa to iu mise de kaimasu.*

Mrs. White:	Where do you usually buy groceries?
Mrs. Tanaka:	I usually buy groceries at a neary-by store,
	but I sometimes buy fish at a fish shop.
Mrs. White:	Where is the fish shop?
Mrs. Tanaka:	It's in Ogikubo . . . ,
	the fish is not expensive, and it's good and fresh.
Mrs. White:	Oh, is that right?
Mrs. Tanaka:	Where do you usually buy butter, cheese and
	things like that?
Mrs. White:	I usually buy at a store called Ichiban Sutoa.

Vocabulary

hiru-gohan:	lunch	*tabemono:*	food
shain shokudō:	company cafeteria	*kaimasu ← kau:*	buy
oishii:	tasty, delicious	*sakana:*	fish
māmā:	so, so	*sakana-ya:*	fish shop
chikaku:	nearby, close, near	*shin'sen* [AN]:	fresh
mise:	store	*batā:*	butter
kon'de imasu:	is crowded	*chīzu:*	cheese
yasukute ← yasui:	cheap, less expensive		

I

田中　　：ホワイトさん、　あさごはんは　いつも　たべますか。

ホワイト：ええ、　たべます。

田中　　：なにを　たべますか。

ホワイト：くだものと　トーストと　コーヒーです。　田中さんは。

田中　　：わたしは　まいにち　ごはんと　みそしると　のりです。

ホワイト：てんけいてきな　日本の　あさごはんですねえ。

II

ホワイト：ひるごはんは　いつも　どこで　たべますか。

田中　　：たいてい　しゃいんしょくどうです。

ホワイト：おいしいですか。

田中　　：そうですねえ。　まあまあです。　ホワイトさんは。

ホワイト：わたしは　よく　（かいしゃの）　ちかくの　みせで　たべます。

田中　　：いい　みせですか。

ホワイト：ええ。　こんでいますけど、　やすくて　おいしいですよ。

III

ホワイト：たべものは　いつも　どこで　かいますか。

田中　　：たいてい　ちかくの　スーパーで　かいますが、
　　　　　　さかなは　さかなやで　かいます。

ホワイト：そのさかなやは　どこですか。

田中　　：荻窪ですけど、　やすくて　しんせんで　いいですよ。

ホワイト：ああ、　そうですか。

田中　　：ホワイトさんは　バターや　チーズは
　　　　　　どこで　かいますか。

ホワイト：いちばんストアという　みせで　かいます。

Grammar Note 1 — Verbs

New verbs in this lesson are the same type of verbs as in Lesson 13, which take the object marker *o* and the place marker **de**.

Meaning	
eat	*tabemasu*
drink	*nomimasu*
buy	*kaimasu*

Examples

Kissaten de asa-gohan o tabemasu.	"I eat breakfast in a coffee shop."
Bā de mizuwari o nomimashita.	"I drank whisky with water at a bar."
Tsukiji de sakana o kaimasu.	"I buy fish at Tsukiji."

Here are the vocabulary lists.   You do not need to memorize all of them.

1.   _____ *de* _____ *o tabemasu/nomimasu.*

Vocabulary: Places to eat or drink

Meaning	
home	*uchi*
outside	*soto*
company cafeteria	*shain shokudō*
restaurant	*resutoran*
coffee shop	*kissaten*
shop near the office	*(kaisha no) chikaku no mise*
what kind of place?	*don'na tokoro*
where?	*doko*

Vocabulary: Things to eat (*cf.* Lesson 6 – Restaurant)

Meaning	
meal	*gohan, shokuji**
breakfast	*asa-gohan, chō-shoku*
lunch	*hiru(-gohan), chū-shoku*
dinner	*ban-gohan, yū-shoku*
Japanese (style) food	*Nihon-ryōri, wa-shoku*
French (style) food	*Furan'su-ryōri*
Italian (style) food	*Itaria-ryōri*
Chinese (style) food	*Chūka-ryōri*
soba [brown, buckwheat] noodles	*soba*
udon [white] noodles	*udon*
Chinese noodles	*rāmen*
sandwiches	*san'doitchi*
what kind of food?	*don'na (tabe) mono*
what style of food?	*don'na ryōri*
what?	*nani*

*Shokuji o shimasu. **Shokuji** is not used with **tabemasu**.

Vocabulary: Things to drink

Meaning	
liquor	(o-)sake
Japanese rice wine	(o-)sake, Nihon-shu
whisky	uisukī
brandy	buran'dē
wine	wain, budōshu
beer	bīru
draft beer	nama-bīru
water	(o-)mizu
coffee	kōhī
tea	kōcha
green tea	ocha
soup**	sūpu
miso soup**	misoshiru
what kind of beverages?	don'na (nomi)mono
what?	nani

These usually go with the verb **nomimasu ''drink,'' not with **tabemasu** ''eat.''

2.   _____ **de** _____ **o kaimasu.**

Vocabulary: Places to make daily purchases

(a)   Famous discount shopping areas in Tokyo

Tsukiji [Tokyo central fish market area]
Akihabara [electric appliance area]
Ameyoko [food, clothing and imported goods area]
Shin'juku [cameras and watches area]

(b)   Shops

Meaning	
shop, store	mise
supermarket	sūpā
department store	depāto
meat shop	niku-ya
fish store	sakana-ya
vegetable store	yao-ya
fruit store	kudamono-ya
liquor store	saka-ya
flower shop	hana-ya
electric appliance shop	den'ki-ya
book store	hon-ya
drug store	kusuri-ya
shop near by	chikaku no mise
what kind of place?	don'na tokoro
what kind of store?	don'na mise
where?	doko

(c)   Merchandise

Meaning	
clothes	*fuku*
shoes	*kutsu*
furniture	*kagu*
electric appliances	*den'ki-seihin*
flowers	*hana*
medicine	*kusuri*
food	*tabemono*
meat	*niku*
fish	*sakana*
vegetables	*yasai*
fruit	*kudamono*
rice (uncooked)	*kome*
bread	*pan*
what kind of things?	*don'na mono*
what?	*nani*

Grammar Note 2 — Combining two or more nouns

(1)   **[Noun 1]** *to* **[Noun 2]**   **"N1 and N2"**
       kōhī   to   *tōsuto*   "coffee and toast"

(2)   **[Noun 1]** *ya* **[Noun 2]**   **"N1 and N2 and so on"**
       batā   ya   *chīzu*   "butter and cheese and so on"

(3)   **[Noun 1]** *ka* **[Noun 2]**   **"N1 or N2"**
       ocha   ka   *kōhī*   "tea or coffee"

In Lesson 5, you learned the first case, which is for "exhaustive listing" of things.

The second case indicates a mention of a few out of many from the same group of things.

Examples

Gorufu to tenisu o shimasu.	"I play golf and tennis."
Sashimi ya ten'pura ga suki desu.	"I like things like *sashimi* and *tempura* and so on."
Asa wa kōhī ka kōcha o nomimasu.	"I drink coffee or tea in the morning."

Grammar Note 3 — X *to iu* Y

Proper Noun		General Noun	
X	*to iu*	Y	
Ichiban Sutoa		*mise*	"a store called Ichiban Store"

When using a proper noun which you or the listener may not be familiar with, use this pattern.

Examples

Nagano	to iu	tokoro	"a place called Nagano"
Ogawaya	to iu	sūpā	"a supermarket called Ogawaya"
P.L.S.	to iu	gakkō	"a school called P.L.S."
Runoāru	to iu	resutoran	"a restaurant called Renoir"
Ogawa(-san)	to iu	hito	"a person called Ogawa"
nattō	to iu	mono	"a thing called natto"

Kinō Suehiro to iu resutoran e ikimashita.	"I went to a restaurant called Suehiro yesterday."
Ogawaya to iu sūpā de niku o kaimasu.	"I buy meat at a supermarket called Ogawaya."
San-ji goro Ogawa(-san) to iu hito ga kimashita.	"A person called Ogawa came at around three."

Grammar Note 4 — Making a few comments about something in one sentence

cf. Lesson 12

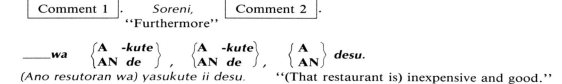

$$ \underline{\quad} wa \quad \begin{Bmatrix} \text{A} & \text{-kute} \\ \text{AN} & de \end{Bmatrix} , \quad \begin{Bmatrix} \text{A} & \text{-kute} \\ \text{AN} & de \end{Bmatrix} , \quad \begin{Bmatrix} \text{A} \\ \text{AN} \end{Bmatrix} desu. $$

(Ano resutoran wa) yasukute ii desu.   "(That restaurant is) inexpensive and good."

a.   When combining comments, use *-te/de* form of Adjectives and Adjectival Nouns.

With this pattern, you can add only positive comments to a positive comment, and only negative comments to a negative comment.

[Positive] *Yasui desu.*
[Positive] *Soreni, oishii desu.* } → *yasu-kute oishii desu.*   "It's inexpensive and delicious."

[Negative] *Takai desu.*
[Negative] *Soreni, mazui desu.* } → *Taka-kute mazui desu.*   "It's expensive and the taste is bad."

Positive Comment			Positive Comment
[A]	yasu-ku "cheap" taka-ku-naku* "not expensive"	-te	
[AN]	ben'ri "convenient" fuben-ja-naku* "not inconvenient"	-de -te	
Negative Comment			Negative Comment
[A]	taka-ku "expensive" yasu-ku-naku* "not cheap"	-te	
[AN]	fuben "inconvenient" ben'ri-ja-naku* "not convenient"	-de -te	

*You can make negative *-te/de* forms, but we do not use them in the drills and examples.

b. There are two nuances in this sequence:

(1) Simply adding up good or bad qualities

(2) Telling how one quality of a thing or place is due to the existence of the preceding quality (The reason comes first, the resulting comment comes last)

Examples

Ano resutoran wa yasui desu.
Soreni, oishii desu.
→ Ano resutoran wa yasukute oishii desu.
"That restaurant is cheap and [the food is] delicious."

Tōkyō wa kirei desu.
Soreni, an'zen desu.
→ Tōkyō wa kirei de an'zen desu.
"Tokyo is clean and safe."

Ano resutoran wa yasui desu.
{Dakara} ii desu.
{Soreni}
→ Ano resutoran wa yasukute ii desu.
"That restaurant is cheap and [therefore] I like it."

Tōkyō wa kirei desu.
Soreni an'zen desu.
{Dakara} ii tokoro desu.
{Soreni}
→ Tōkyō wa kirei de an'zen de ii tokoro desu.
"Tokyo is clean and safe, so it is a good place."

Drill 1 Substitute the underlined parts.

1. Taitei _uchi_ de _asa-gohan_ o tabemasu.
   (1) resutoran, hiru-gohan
   (2) uchi, ban-gohan
   (3) soto, gohan
   (4) soba-ya, soba ka udon

2. yoku _kissaten_ de _kōhī_ o nomimasu.
   (1) kissaten, ocha*
   (2) kaisha, kōhī
   (3) biyahōru "beer hall", namabīru
   *This **ocha** indicates non-alcholic beverages such as tea, coffee, juice, _etc._

3. _Sakana-ya_ de _sakana_ o kaimasu.
   (1) niku-ya, niku
   (2) pan-ya, pan ya miruku "milk"
   (3) hon-ya, hon ya zasshi
   (4) yao-ya, yasai ya kudamono
   (5) saka-ya, sake ya bīru
   (6) depāto, iroiro na "various" mono

4. _Ichiban_ to iu _sūpā_
   (1) Seibu, depāto
   (2) Fujiya, resutoran
   (3) Rairaiken, rāmen-ya
   (4) Maruzen, hon-ya
       "Chinese noodle shop"
   (5) Ameyoko, tokoro
   (6) Tanakaya, chikaku no mise

Drill 2   Change to yes/no questions and answer.

> e.g.,   *Mainichi "every day" asa-gohan o tabemasu.*
>
> ⟶   1.   *Mainichi asa-gohan o tabemasu ka.*
>
> ⟶   2.   *Asa-gohan wa mainichi tabemasu ka.*
>
> (yes) ⟶   *Ē, tabemasu.*
>
> (no) ⟶   *Iie, tabemasen.*

(1)   *Itsumo hiru-gohan o tabemasu.*   (2)   *Soto de ban-gohan o tabemasu.*

(3)   *Kaisha de kōhī o nomimasu.*   (4)   *Sūpā de batā ya chīzu o kaimasu.*

Drill 3   Give negative answers to the questions in Drill 2 using **wa**.

> e.g.,   not everyday ⟶   *Iie, mainichi wa tabemasen.*

(1)   not every morning   *maiasa*   (2)   not (eat) out

(3)   not in the office   (4)   not at a supermarket

Drill 4   Make a question asking about the underlined part.

> e.g.,   *Shichi-ji ni asa-gohan o tabemasu.*
>
> ⟶   1.   *Nan-ji ni asa-gohan o tabemasu ka.*
>
> ⟶   2.   *Asa-gohan wa nan-ji ni tabemasu ka.*

(1)   *Uchi de asa-gohan o tabemasu.*

(2)   *Shain shokudō de hirugohan o tabemasu.*

(3)   *Tanaka-san to sushi o tabemashita.*

(4)   *Tanaka-san to Akasaka de nomimashita.*

(5)   *Tanaka-san to Akasaka de nomimashita.*

(6)   *Chikaku no yao-ya-san de yasai o kaimasu.*

(7)   *Sūpā de niku ya yasai o kaimasu.*

Drill 5   Repeat the names of the breakfast foods shown.

gohan "rice"	misoshiru "miso-soup"	nattō "fermented soy beans"
tsukemono "salty pickles"	nori "sea laver"	(yude) tamago "(boiled) egg"
kōn'furēku "cold cereal"	ōtomīru "oatmeal"	bēkon-eggu "bacon and eggs"
tōsuto "toast"	jūsu "juice"	gurēpu-furūtsu "grapefruit"
kudamono "fruit"		

Drill 6   Replace the verbs with **desu.**

e.g.,   1.   *Tōsuto to bēkon-eggu o tabemasu.* ⟶ *Tōsuto to bēkon-eggu desu.*

2.   *Kōhi o nomimasu.*

Soshite, tōsuto to tamago o tabemasu. }⟶ *Kōhī to tōsuto to tamago desu.*

"and"

(1)   *Kudamono o tabemasu.*

(2)   *Kōn'furēku to tamago o tabemasu.*

(3)   *Gohan o tabemasu.*

Soshite, misoshiru o nomimasu.

(4)   *Kōhī o nomimaṣu.*

Soshite, tōsuto o tabemasu.

(5)   *Ōtomīru to bēkon-eggu to tōsuto o tabemasu.*

Soshite, kōcha o nomimasu.

(6)   *Gohan to nattō to nori to tsukemono o tabemasu.*

Soshite, misoshiru o nomimasu.

Drill 7   Using Dialogue I as a model, complete the following.

(1)	
	Tape: *Asa-gohan wa nanika tabemasu ka.*
[a] Yes.	You: [a]_____ .
	Tape: *Nani o tabemasu ka.*
[b] usually	You: [b]_____
	_____ .
[c] How about you?	[c]_____ .
	Tape: *Watashi wa gohan to misoshiru desu.*
[d] typical Japanese breakfast	You: [d]_____ .

(2)	
	Tape: *Asa-gohan wa itsumo tabemasu ka.*
[a] Yes, every day.	You: [a]_____ .
	Tape: *Nani o tabemasu ka.*
[b]	You: [b]_____
	_____ .
	Tape: *Nihon-teki* "Japanese style" *desu ne.*
[c] How about you?	You: [c]_____ .
	Tape: *Watashi wa ōtomīru to bēkon-eggu to tōsuto to kōcha desu.*
[d] typical British breakfast	You: [d]_____ .

(3)		Tape:	*Asa-gohan wa nani o tabemasu ka.*
[a] not at all		You:	[a]_____.
		Tape:	*Sō desu ka. Dōshite desu ka.*
[b] on a diet *daietto*		You:	[b]_____.
		Tape:	*Daietto desu ka.*
[c] How about you?		You:	[c]_____.
		Tape:	*Watashi wa kōcha dake desu.*
[d] Are you also on a diet?		You:	[d]_____.
		Tape:	*Ē.*

Drill 8 Answer the questions.

Itsumo doko de hiru-gohan o tabemasu ka.
  or
Hiru-gohan wa itsumo doko de tabemasu ka.

e.g., restaurant ⟶ *Taitei resutoran de tabemasu.*

(1) nearby restaurant
(2) hotel restaurant
(3) company cafeteria
(4) soba shop called *Yabu*
(5) *tonkatsu* restaurant called *Ton'ki*

Drill 9 Make *te/de* forms and add the meaning.

Meaning			Meaning		
expensive	*takai*	*taka-ku-te*	quiet	*shizuka*	*shizuka de*
	yasui		lively	*nigiyaka*	
	oishii		convenient	*ben'ri*	
	mazui		inconvenient	*fuben*	
	ii	*yo-ku-te*		*kirei*	
	chikai			*shin'sen*	
	tōi			*māmā*	
noisy	*urusai*		safe	*an'zen*	

Drill 10 Combine comments, using [A]-*kute.*

1. *e.g.,* *Yasui desu.*
       Soreni, oishii desu. } ⟶ *Yasukute oishii desu.*

(1) *Takai desu. Soreni, mazui desu.*
(2) *Yasui desu. Soreni, chikai desu.*
(3) *Takai desu. Soreni, tōi desu.*
(4) *Yasui desu. Soreni, kirei desu.*
(5) *Urusai desu. Soreni, kitanai* "dirty" *desu.*
(6) *Yasui desu. Soreni, oishii desu. Soreni, shizuka desu.*
(7) *Bukka ga takai desu. Soreni, hito ga ōi desu.*

2. *e.g.,*   Yasukatta desu.
           Soreni, oishikatta desu. } ⟶ *Yasukute oishikatta desu.*

   (1)   Takakatta desu. Soreni, mazukatta desu.
   (2)   Yasukatta desu. Soreni, chikakatta desu.
   (3)   Takakatta desu. Soreni, tōkatta desu.
   (4)   Yasukatta desu. Soreni, kirei deshita.
   (5)   Urusakatta desu. Soreni, kitanakatta desu.
   (6)   Yasukatta desu. Soreni, oishikatta desu. Soreni, shizuka deshita.
   (7)   Bukka ga takakatta desu. Soreni, hito ga ōkatta desu.

3. *e.g.,*   Yasui desu.
           Dakara/Soreni, ii desu. } ⟶ *yasukute ii desu.*

   (1)   Chikai desu. Dakara, ben'ri desu.
   (2)   Yasui desu. Dakara/Soreni, ii resutoran desu.
   (3)   Yasui desu. Soreni, oishii desu.
           Dakara/Soreni, ii resutoran desu.
   (4)   Isogashii "busy" desu. Dakara/Soreni, taihen "hard time" desu.
   (5)   Bukka ga takai desu. Soreni, hito ga ōi desu.
           Dakara, (watashi wa) iya desu.
   (6)   Omoshiroi hito ga ōi desu. Dakara, tanoshii desu.

Drill 11   Combine comments, using **[AN]** *de.*

1. *e.g.,*   Shizuka desu.
           Soreni kirei desu. } ⟶ *Shizuka de kirei desu.*

   (1)   An'zen desu. Soreni, kirei desu.
   (2)   Kirei desu. Soreni, takaku arimasen.
   (3)   Fukuzatsu desu. Soreni, nagai desu.
   (4)   Kan'tan desu. Soreni, mijikai desu.

2. *e.g.,*   Shizuka deshita.
           Soreni, kirei deshita. } ⟶ *Shizuka de kirei deshita.*

   (1)   An'zen deshita. Soreni, kirei deshita.
   (2)   Kirei deshita. Soreni, takaku arimasen deshita.
   (3)   Fukuzatsu deshita. Soreni, nagakatta desu.
   (4)   Kan'tan deshita. Soreni, mijikakatta desu.

3. *e.g.,*   Shizuka desu.
           Dakara/Soreni, ii desu. } ⟶ *Shizuka de ii desu.*

   (1)   An'zen desu. Soreni, kirei desu. Dakara/Soreni, ii tokoro desu.
   (2)   An'zen desu. Soreni, kirei desu. Dakara, (watashi wa) suki desu.
   (3)   Fukuzatsu desu. Dakara/Soreni, muzukashii desu.
   (4)   Kan'tan desu. Soreni, mijikai* desu. Dakara, yasashii desu.
   (5)   Shizuka desu. Dakara/Soreni, ii tokoro desu.
   (6)   Sakana ga shin'sen desu. Dakara, ii desu.
           * = A

Drill 12   Combine comments, using [A]-*kute* and [AN] *de*.

> e.g.,   Chiisai desu.
> Soreni, kan'tan desu.   } ⟶   *Chiisakute kan'tan de ben'ri desu.*
> Dakara/Soreni, ben'ri desu.

(1)   *Chikai desu. Soreni, shizuka desu. Dakara/Soreni, ii tokoro desu.*

(2)   *Yasui desu. Soreni, oishii desu. Soreni, kirei desu. Dakara, ii desu.*

(3)   *Takai desu. Soreni, fukuzatsu desu. Soreni, ōkii desu. Dakara, yoku arimasen.*

(4)   *Sakana ga yasui desu. Soreni, shin'sen desu. Soreni, oishii desu. Dakara, ii desu.*

Drill 13   Substitute the underlined parts. Change the form of Adjectives or Adjectival Nouns if necessary.

1. *Sono resutoran* wa *yasukute ii* desu yo.

(1)   *Shin'juku, yasui, ii*

(2)   *chikaku no mise, yasui, oishii*

(3)   *sono resutoran, chikai, ben'ri*

(4)   *Tsukiji no uogashi* "fish market", *yasui, ii*

(5)   *Akihabara, omoshiroi, yasui, ii*

2. *Setagaya-ku* wa *shizuka* de *ii* desu yo.

(1)   *Tōkyō, an'zen, ii*

(2)   *Shibuya, ben'ri, ii*

(3)   *Shin'juku, nigiyaka, omoshiroi*

(4)   *Kyōto, kirei, suki*

(5)   *Meiji Jin'gū, shizuka, kirei, suki*

3. *Ano mise wa* kon'de imasu "crowded" kedo, *yasukute ii* desu yo.

(1)   *chotto tōi desu, yasui, ii*

(2)   *kon'de imasu, chikai, ben'ri*

(3)   *chotto takai desu, sakana ga shin'sen, ii*

Drill 14   Using Dialogue II as a model, complete the following.

(1)	Tape: *Hiru-gohan wa itsumo doko de tabemasu ka.*
[a] usually restaurant nearby	You: [a] _____.
	Tape: *Oishii desu ka.*
[b] Yes. cheap and delicious	You: [b] _____.
[c] How about you?	You: [c] _____.
	Tape: *Watashi wa shain shokudō desu.*
[d] Is it good?	You: [d] _____.
	Tape: *Ē, māmā desu.*
(2) [Now you start first] [a] lunch?	You: [a] _____.
	Tape: *Taitei chikaku no mise de tabemasu.*

[b]	delicious?	You:	[b] _____ .
		Tape:	*Ē, chotto kon'de imasu kedo, oishii desu yo.*
			Anata wa doko de tabemasu ka.
[c]	often hotel restaurant	You:	[c] _____ .
		Tape:	*Hoteru no resutoran wa ii desu ·ka.*
[d]	a bit expensive, but quiet and nice	You:	[d] _____ .

(3)		Tape:	*Ban-gohan wa itsumo uchi de tabemasu ka.*
[a]	Yes, usually but sometimes eat out	You:	[a] _____ .
		Tape:	*Don'na tokoro e ikimasu ka.*
[b]	usually Akasaka	You:	[b] _____ .
		Tape:	*Oishii desu ka.*
[c]	a bit expensive, but delicious and nice	You:	[c] _____ _____ .

Drill 15   Answer the questions.

> *Itsumo doko de tabemono o kaimasu ka.*
>   *or*
> *Tabemono wa itsumo doko de kaimasu ka.*

e.g., *taitei, sūpā* ⟶ *Taitei sūpā de kaimasu kedo . . .*
     (o-)sake, saka-ya ⟶ *(O-)sake wa saka-ya de kaimasu.*

(1) *taitei, sūpā*
       pan, chikaku no pan-ya

(2) *taitei, chikaku no mise*
       sakana, Tsukiji

(3) *yoku, Yamadaya to iu mise*
       batā ya chīzu, sūpā

(4) *taitei, Ogawaya to iu sūpā*
       niku ya sakana, chikaku no mise

Drill 16   Using Dialogue III as a model, complete the following.

(1)		Tape:	*O-sake wa itsumo doko de kaimasu ka.*
[a]	usually, supermarket sometimes, shop called Meijiya	You:	[a] _____ .
		Tape:	*Sono mise wa doko desu ka.*
[b]	in Hiro, a good shop	You:	[b] _____ .
		Tape:	*Sō desu ka.*
[c]	butter, cheese and so on?	You:	[c] _____ .
		Tape:	*Sūpā de kaimasu.*
(2) [Now you start first]			
[a]	books?	You:	[a] _____ .
		Tape:	*Taitei chikaku no hon-ya de kaimasu ga, yōsho "foreign books" wa Maruzen to iu hon-ya de kaimasu.*
[b]	Is Maruzen a good book store?	You:	[b] _____ .
		Tape:	*Ē, chotto tōi desu kedo, hon ga ōkute ii desu yo.*

Lesson 15

DAILY ROUTINES

ASA WA ITSUMO NAN-JI NI OKIMASU KA
"WHAT TIME DO YOU USUALLY GET UP IN THE MORNING?"

📻 Dialogue

[It's seven thirty in the morning. Mr. Smith meets Mr. Yamashita in front of the office.]

Sumisu:	Ā, Yamashita-san ohayō gozaimasu. Kyō wa hayai desu nē.
Yamashita:	Ohayō gozaimasu. Sumisu-san mo hayai desu nē.
Sumisu:	Watashi wa itsumo shichi-ji han ni kimasu yo.
Yamashita:	Shichi-ji han desu ka.
	Asa wa itsumo nan-ji ni okimasu ka.
Sumisu:	Roku-ji han desu. Yamashita-san wa.
Yamashita:	Kyō wa roku-ji ni okimashita.
	Itsumo wa shichi-ji goro desu ga...
	kyō wa asa no kaigi ga arimasu kara...
Sumisu:	Jā, kinō wa hayaku nemashita ka.
Yamashita:	Ē, jū-ji han ni nemashita.
Sumisu:	Itsumo wa nan-ji goro desu ka.
Yamashita:	Sō desu nē, Jūni-ji goro desu.
Sumisu:	Osoi desu nē.
Yamashita:	Shigoto no ato de yoku nomi ni ikimasu kara...

Mr. Smith:	Good morning, Mr. Yamashita! You're early today, aren't you?
Mr. Yamashita:	Good morning. You're early, too, aren't you, Mr. Smith?
Mr. Smith:	I always come to the office at 7:30 a.m., you know.
Mr. Yamashita:	At 7:30 a.m.! (Then) what time do you usually get up in the morning?
Mr. Smith:	I usually get up at 6:30 a.m. How about you, Mr. Yamashita?
Mr. Yamashita:	I got up at six this morning.
	I usually get up at around 7:00 a.m., but (I got up earlier this morning) because I have a meeting (early) this morning.
Mr. Smith:	Then, did you go to bed earlier last night?
Mr. Yamashita:	Yes, I went to bed at 10:30 p.m.
Mr. Smith:	What time do you usually go to bed?
Mr. Yamashita:	Let me see, (I usually go to bed) around 12:00 midnight.
Mr. Smith:	Oh, that's late, isn't it?
Mr. Yamashita:	(Yes, it is) because I often go drinking after work.

Vocabulary

hayai: early, fast
okimasu ← okiru: get up
kaigi: meeting, conference
hayaku ← hayai: early

kara [Conjunction]: because, therefore
nemashita ← neru: went to bed
osoi: late, slow
nomi ni: for a drink

スミス：ああ、　山下さん　おはようございます。
　　　　きょうは　はやいですねえ。

山下　：おはようございます。　スミスさんも　はやいですねえ。

スミス：わたしは　いつも　7じはんにきますよ。

山下　：7じはんですか。　あさは　いつも　なんじに　おきますか。

スミス：6じはんです。　山下さんは。

山下　：きょうは　6じに　おきました。　いつもは　7じごろですが…
　　　　きょうは　あさの　かいぎが　ありますから…。

スミス：じゃあ、　きのうは　はやく　ねましたか。

山下　：ええ、　10じはんに　ねました。

スミス：いつもは　なんじごろですか。

山下　：そうですねえ、　12じごろです。

スミス：おそいですねえ。

山下　：しごとの　あとで　よく　のみに　いきますから…。

On the way to work — *Sarariman,* businessmen leaving Tokyo Station

183

Grammar Note 1 — Verbs

Verbs which do not have objects are introduced in this lesson.

Meaning	
get up	*okimasu*
go to bed	*nemasu*
begin	*hajimarimasu*
finish	*owarimasu*
leave	*demasu*
arrive	*tsukimasu*
be (stay)	*imasu*

Grammar Note 2 — Expressing "early" and "late"

Adverbs often used with these verbs are **hayaku** "early" and **osoku** "late."

[Adjective]			[Adverb]	
hayai	"early"	⟶	*haya**ku***	"early"
osoi	"late"	⟶	*oso**ku***	"late"

Examples

Kyō wa <u>hayai</u> desu nē.   "You're early today, aren't you?"
[Adjective]

Kyō wa <u>hayaku</u> kimashita nē.   "You've come early today, haven't you?"
[Adverb]

Kyō wa <u>osoi</u> desu nē.   "You're late today, aren't you?"
[Adjective]

Kyō wa <u>osoku</u> kimashita nē.   "You've come late today, haven't you?"
[Adverb]

Grammar Note 3 — Something starts/finishes

[Time] ø/ni [Thing/Event] ga $\begin{cases} \textit{hajimarimasu.} \\ \textit{owarimasu.} \end{cases}$

Jū-ji ni <u>kaigi</u> ga hajimarimasu.   "The conference starts at 10:00."

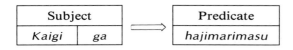

Subject		Predicate
Kaigi	*ga*	*hajimarimasu*

Hajimarimasu and **owarimasu** are verbs which take a thing or an event as their subject. They do not take a person as the subject.

Examples

Ku-ji ni gakkō ga hajimarimasu.   "School starts at 9:00."
Kyō wa shigoto ga hayaku owarimashita.   "I finished work early today."

A: *Kyō no kaigi wa nan-ji ni owarimasu ka.*   "What time will today's conference end?"

B: *San-ji goro owarimasu.*   "It will end around 3:00."

Grammar Note 4 — Place markers

So far, you have learned the following place markers:

e:	[Direction]	*e.g., Migi e onegai shimasu.*
kara:	[Starting Point]	*e.g., Amerika kara kimashita.*
made:	[Ending Point]	*e.g., Nikkō made ikura desu ka.*
de:	[Place of Action]	*e.g., Kissaten de kōhī o nomimasu.*

In this lesson, three more place markers are introduced:

a.   O   [Place to Leave Marker]

Place to Leave	
uchi	*o*

⟹ | Predicate |
|---|
| *demasu* |

"I leave my house . . ."

Examples

Mainichi shichi-ji han ni uchi o demasu.	"I leave my house at 7:30 every day."
A: *Kyō wa nan-ji ni Narita o demasu ka.*	"What time are you leaving Narita today?"
B: *Gogo san-ji desu.*	"At 3:00 p.m."

b.   Ni   [Place to Arrive Marker]

Place to Arrive	
kaisha	*ni*

⟹ | Predicate |
|---|
| *tsukimasu* |

"I arrive at my office . . ."

Examples

Mainichi hachi-ji han ni kaisha ni tsukimasu.	"I arrive at my office at 8:30 every day."
A: *Nan-ji ni Ōsaka ni tsukimashita ka.*	"What time did you arrive in Osaka?"
B: *Jūichi-ji ni tsukimashita.*	"I arrived at 11:00."

c.   Ni   [Location Marker]

Location	
uchi	*ni*

⟹ | Predicate |
|---|
| *imasu* |

"I stay home."

The verb *imasu* "to be" is used to express location or existence of a person.
The verb *desu* "to be" is used in different ways.

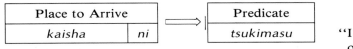

e.g.,	1.	*Tanaka desu.*	"I am Tanaka."
	2.	*Kirei desu nē.*	"It is pretty, isn't it!"
	3.	A: *Itsu Nihon e kimashita ka.*	"How long have you been here in Japan?"
		B: *Kyonen desu.*	"(I came to Japan) last year."

The verb *arimasu*, which is used to express location or existence of things, will be explained in Lesson 16.

Examples

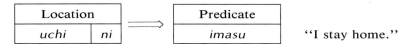

Do-yōbi wa uchi ni imasu.	"I stay at home on Saturday(s)."
A: *Tanaka-san wa doko ni imasu ka.*	"Where is Mr. Tanaka?"
B: *Kaisha desu.*	"At his office."

Grammar Note 5 — Expressing the action of going/coming/returning to do something

[Verb (Pre-*masu**)] ni** $\begin{cases} \textit{ikimasu.} \\ \textit{kimasu.} \\ \textit{kaerimasu.} \end{cases}$

*Verb (Pre-*masu*) means the verb from which preceeds *masu*.

Nomi ni ikimasu.   "I'm going drinking."

Some verbs can be combined with . . . *ni ikimasu/kimasu/kaerimasu* to indicate that you go/come/return in order to do something.

Examples

Soba-ya e ikimasu.
Hiru-gohan o tabemasu. ⟶ *Soba-ya e hiru-gohan o tabe ni ikimasu.*
"I go to a noodle restaurant."
"I eat lunch."
"I go to a noodle restaurant to eat lunch."

Kinō tomodachi to Roppon'gi e ikimashita.
Roppon'gi de nomimashita. ⟶ *Kinō tomodachi to Roppon'gi e nomi ni ikimashita.*
"I went to Roppongi with my friend yesterday."
"We drank in Roppongi."
"I went to Roppongi yesterday with my friend to drink."

Tokidoki settai de Gin'za e ikimasu.
Gin'za de nomimasu. ⟶ *Tokidoki settai de Gin'za e nomi ni ikimasu.*
"I sometimes go to Ginza to entertain clients."
"I drink in Ginza."
"I sometimes go drinking in Ginza to entertain clients."

Grammar Note 6 — Expressing the reasons for or results of something

[Reason] *kara*, [Result].
Kaigi ga arimasu kara, hayaku kimashita.   "I have a meeting, so I've come early."

a. *Kara* "so/therefore" appears at the end of a clause X which gives a reason to the main clause Y.
 X kara, Y can be translated into "X so Y" or "Because X, Y."

Examples

Kyō wa ressun ga arimasu kara, Ōtemachi e ikimasu.   "I have a lesson today, so I'll go to Otemachi."

Kinō nomi ni ikimashita kara, osoku kaerimashita.   "I went drinking yesterday, so I got home late."

Ano resutoran wa yasukute oishii desu kara, yoku ikimasu.   "That restaurant is inexpensive and [the food is] delicious, so I often go there."

b. You can change the order of the clauses:
[Result]. [Reason] *kara*.
Kyō wa hayaku kimashita. Kaigi ga arimasu kara.

c. **[Reason]** *kara* is often used as a response.

Examples

| A: *Kyō wa hayai desu nē.*   "You're early today, aren't you?"
| B: *Ē, kaigi ga arimasu kara.*   "Yes, because I have a meeting."

| A: *Dōshite* ano mise de kaimasu ka.*   "Why do you buy (it) at that store?"
| B: *Chikakute ben'ri desu kara.*   "Because it's close and convenient."

*Dōshite "Why" (*cf.* lesson 12, Grammar 3-c)

Drill 1   Substitute the underlined parts.

1. *Hachi-ji ni okimasu.*
   - (1) *shichi-ji ni*
   - (2) *roku-ji goro*
   - (3) *hayaku*
   - (4) *osoku*
   - (5) *asa hayaku*

2. *Jū-ji goro nemasu.*
   - (1) *jūni-ji ni*
   - (2) *hayaku*
   - (3) *yoru osoku*
   - (4) *yoru no jūni-ji sugi* "past" *ni*

3. *Ku-ji ni kaisha ga hajimarimasu.*
   - (1) *hachi-ji han ni, shigoto*
   - (2) *jū-ji ni, kaigi*
   - (3) *jūichi-ji ni, kyō no kaigi*
   - (4) *hachi-ji yonjūgo-fun ni, kodomo no gakkō*

4. *Go-ji han ni kaisha ga owarimasu.*
   - (1) *roku-ji ni, shigoto*
   - (2) *san-ji goro, gakkō*
   - (3) *yo-ji goro, kyō no kaigi*
   - (4) *ku-ji ni, Nihon-go no ressun*

5. *Itsumo shichi-ji ni uchi o demasu.*
   - (1) *go-ji ni, kaisha*
   - (2) *go-ji han ni, ofisu*
   - (3) *hachi-ji goro, kurabu*
   - (4) *asa hayaku, uchi*

6. *Mainichi hachi-ji goro kaisha ni tsukimasu.*
   - (1) *gogo roku-ji ni, uchi*
   - (2) *shichi-ji ni, eki*
   - (3) *shichi-ji han goro, kurabu*
   - (4) *yoru osoku, uchi*

7. *Ku-ji kara go-ji made kaisha ni imasu.*
   - (1) *shichi-ji goro, ku-ji goro, kurabu*
   - (2) *getsu-yōbi, sui-yōbi, Kyōto*
   - (3) *kin-yōbi no ban, nichi-yōbi no asa, Yamanakako* "Lake Yamanaka"

Drill 2   Expand the sentences.

    e.g., *okimasu*   ⟶ *Okimasu.*

           roku-ji ni ⟶ *Roku-ji ni okimasu.*

           mainichi ⟶ *Mainichi roku-ji ni okimasu.*

(1) *okimasu*   (2) *demasu*   (3) *tsukimasu*

       asa hayaku   *kaisha o*   *eki ni*

       itsumo   *go-ji ni*   *hachi-ji ni*

                             tamani   *taitei*

                                               watashi wa

(4) *owarimasu*   (5) *imasu*   (6) *imasu*

       hayaku   *kaisha ni*   *uchi ni*

       taitei   *zan'gyō de*   *ban made*

       kaisha no shigoto wa   *shichi-ji goro made*   *asa kara*

       kin-yōbi wa   *taitei*   *taitei*

                              ano hito wa   *nichi-yōbi wa*

Drill 3   Make questions which ask for the underlined parts, and then answer.

    e.g., <u>*Ku-ji*</u> *goro kaisha ni tsukimasu.* ⟶ { *Nan-ji goro kaisha ni tsukimasuka.*

                                                  { *Ku-ji goro desu.*

(1) <u>*Hachi-ji*</u> *ni uchi o demasu.*

(2) <u>*Jū-ji*</u> *ni kaigi ga hajimarimasu.*

(3) <u>*Go-ji*</u> *han ni kaisha ga owarimasu.*

(4) <u>*Hachi-ji*</u> *kara go-ji made ofisu ni imasu.*

(5) <u>*Shichi-ji*</u> *goro uchi ni tsukimasu.*

Drill 4   Substitute with verbs and the hours.

    e.g., *nemasu, 1:00, 10:30*

       A: *Kinō wa osoku* <u>*nemashita.*</u>

       B: *Nan-ji goro* <u>*nemashita*</u> *ka.*

       A: *Ichi-ji goro desu.*

       B: *Itsumo wa nan-ji goro* <u>*nemasu*</u> *ka.*

       A: *Jū-ji han goro desu.*

(1) *okimasu, 8:00, 6:00*   (2) *kaigi ga hajimarimasu, 10:00, 9:00*

(3) *uchi e kaerimasu, 11:00, 6:00*   (4) *ofisu o demasu, 8:00, 5:30*

Drill 5   Combine two sentences, using **Verb-*ni ikimasu/kimasu/kaerimasu.***

  1. e.g., *Ikimasu.*   } ⟶ *Tabe ni ikimasu.*

            Tabemasu. }

(1) *Ikimasu.*   (2) *Ikimashita.*

       Nomimasu.   *Mimashita.*

(3) *Kimasu.*   (4) *Ikimasu.*

       Asobimasu.   *Eiga o mimasu.*

(5) *Kimasu.*   (6) *Kaerimashita.*

       Ben'kyō o shimasu.   *Ban-gohan o tabemashita.*

2. *e.g.,* *Yokohama e ikimasu.*
        Yokohama de nomimasu. } ⟶ *Yokohama e nomi ni ikimasu.*

(1) *Ikebukuro e ikimasu.*
      Ikebukuro de kaimasu.

(2) *Tsukiji e ikimasu.*
      Tsukiji de sakana o kaimasu.

(3) *Hakone e ikimashita.*
      Hakone de doraibu shimashita.

(4) *Tomodachi ga Nihon e kimasu.*
      Nihon de asobimasu.

3. *e.g.,* *Ashita Meguro e ikimasu.*
        Ton'katsu o tabemasu. } ⟶ *Ashita Meguro e ton'katsu
                            o tabe ni ikimasu.*

(1) *Do-yōbi ni Asakusa e ikimasu.*
      Unagi o tabemasu.

(2) *Tomodachi to Aoyama e ikimashita.*
      Furan'su-ryōri o tabemashita.

(3) *Ashita kazoku to Amerikan Kurabu e ikimasu.*
      Shokuji o shimasu.

(4) *Watashi wa Nihon e kimashita.*
      Shigoto o shimasu.

(5) *Chikaku no sūpā e ikimasu.*
      Niku ya yasai o kaimasu.

(6) *Yoku settai* de o-kyaku-san to ikimasu.*
      Nomimasu.

(7) *Tokidoki shōtai* de ikimasu.*
      Gorufu o shimasu.

      *cf. Culture Note 8

         settai = entertaining clients

         shōtai = being invited/entertained as a client

Drill 6   Make short questions which ask for the underlined parts, and then answer.

    e.g., *Hachi-ji jūgo-fun ni eki ni tsukimasu.* ⟶ { *Doko ni tsukimasu ka.*
                                          { *Eki (ni) desu.*

(1) *Itsumo jū-ji goro nemasu.*

(2) *Hachi-ji jūgo-fun ni eki ni tsukimasu.*

(3) *Getsu-yōbi wa jū-ji ni kaigi ga hajimarimasu.*

(4) *Kaigi wa jū-ji kara jūichi-ji made desu.*

(5) *Do-yōbi ni kodomo ga yakyū ni ikimasu.*

(6) *Roppon'gi e nomi ni ikimashita.*

(7) *Tanaka-san to eiga o mi ni ikimashita.*

(8) *Zan'gyō de tokidoki osoku kaerimasu.*

Drill 7   Combine the two sentences into one, using *kara.*

    e.g., *Kyō wa sukasshu ni ikimasu.*
         Dakara, hayaku kaerimasu. } ⟶ *Kyō wa sukasshu ni ikimasu kara,
                               hayaku kaerimasu.*

(1) *Kyō wa asa no kaigi ga arimasu.*

Dakara, hayaku kimashita.

(2) *Ka-yōbi wa asa Nihon-go o naratte imasu.*

Dakara, shichi-ji ni uchi o demasu.

(3) *Shigoto no ato de yoku nomi ni ikimasu.*

Dakara, jūni-ji goro uchi ni tsukimasu.

(4) *Do-yōbi wa taitei pātī ni ikimasu.*

Dakara, Nihon-go no ben'kyō wa shimasen.

(5) *Watashi wa do-yōbi mo shigoto ga arimasu.*

Dakara, nichi-yōbi wa taitei uchi ni imasu.

Drill 8 Respond, using Drill 7.

e.g., *Kyō wa hayaku kaerimasu ka.*

⟶ *Ē, kyō wa sukasshu ni ikimasu kara.*

(1) *Kyō wa hayaku kimashita nē.*

(2) *Naze ka-yōbi wa shichi-ji ni uchi o demasu ka.*

(3) *Dōshite jūni-ji goro uchi ni tsukimasu ka.*

(4) *Do-yōbi wa Nihon-go no ben'kyō wa shimasu ka.*

(5) *Nichi-yōbi wa uchi ni imasu ka.*

Drill 9 Using the dialogue as a model, complete the following.

(1) —In the office. It's 7:30 a.m.—		
	Tape:	*Ohayō gozaimasu.*
		Kyō wa hayai desu nē.
[a] Good morning.	You:	[a] _____ .
You're early, too.	Tape:	*Watashi wa itsumo shichi-ji ni kimasu yo.*
[b: EL]	You:	[b] _____ .
[c] What time do you usually get up?	You:	[c] _____ .
	Tape:	*Go-ji han desu. Anata wa.*
[d] 6:00 today	You:	[d] _____
7:00 usually		_____ .
[e] Japanese lesson		[e] _____ .
	Tape:	*Jā, kinō wa hayaku nemashita ka.*
[f] Yes. 10:30	You:	[f] _____ .
	Tape:	*Itsumo wa nan-ji goro desu ka.*
[g] 12:00	You:	[g] _____ .
	Tape:	*Osoi desu nē.*
[h] often go to entertain clients	You:	[h] _____ .
	Tape:	*Taihen desu nē.* "That's tough, isn't it?"

(2) —Now you start the conversation. In the office, it's 7:50 a.m.—

[a]	Good morning. You're early today!	You:	[a] _____ .	
		Tape:	*Ē, anata mo hayai desu nē.*	
[b]	I usually come at 7:30.	You:	[b] _____ .	
		Tape:	*Shichi-ji han desu ka. Itsumo nan-ji ni okimasu ka.*	
[c]	6:00 And you?	You:	[c] _____ .	
		Tape:	*Watashi mo kyō wa roku-ji ni okimashita. Itsumo wa shichi-ji desu ga, kyō wa shigoto ga arimasu kara . . .*	
[d]	Then, did you go to bed early yesterday?	You:	[d] _____ .	
		Tape:	*Ē, sukoshi hayaku nemashita.*	
[e]	Usually?	You:	[e] _____ .	
		Tape:	*Jūni-ji sugi "past" desu.*	
[f:	EL]	You:	[f] _____ .	
		Tape:	*Itsumo zan'gyō de osoku kaerimasu kara . . .*	
[g:	EL "That's tough, isn't it?"]	You:	[g] _____ .	

Drill 10   Listen to what Mr. Tanaka usually does during the day and,

1. Look at the pictures below and fill in the blanks with the appropriate times.

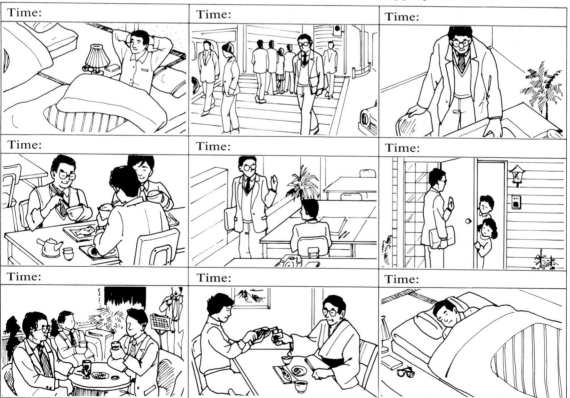

Time:	Time:	Time:
Time:	Time:	Time:
Time:	Time:	Time:

2. Answer the questions taking Mr. Tanaka's role.

(1) *Asa wa itsumo nan-ji ni okimasu ka.*

(2) *Asa-gohan wa tabemasu ka.*

(3) *Nani o tabemasu ka.*

(4) *Uchi wa nan-ji ni demasu ka.*

(5) *Kaisha e wa nan de ikimasu ka.*

(6) *Nan-ji goro kaisha ni tsukimasu ka.*

(7) *Hiru-gohan wa doko de tabemasu ka.*

(8) *Kaisha wa nan-ji kara nan-ji made desu ka.*

(9) *Zan'gyō wa arimasu ka.*

(10) *Taitei nan-ji goro kaisha o demasu ka.*

(11) *Futsū no hi "on regular days" wa nan-ji goro uchi ni tsukimasu ka.*

(12) *Shokuji no ato de nani o shimasu ka.*

(13) *Nan-ji goro nemasu ka.*

(14) *Shigoto no ato de nomi ni ikimasu ka.*

(15) *Is-shūkan ni nan-kai gurai desu ka.*

(16) *Nan de nomi ni ikimasu ka.*

(17) *Nan-ji goro uchi ni tsukimasu ka.*

3. Answer about yourself. Use the same questions in 2.

—Tape script—

(1) *Watashi wa itsumo roku-ji han ni okimasu.*

(2) *Sorekara asa-gohan o tabemasu. Taitei kōhī to tōsuto desu.*

(3) *Shichi-ji han ni uchi o demasu. Marunouchi-sen de kaisha e ikimasu.*

(4) *Hachi-ji han goro kaisha ni tsukimasu.*

(5) *Jūni-ji goro hiru-gohan o tabemasu.*

Taitei shain shokudō de tabemasu ga, tokidoki chikaku no mise e tabe ni ikimasu.

(6) *Kaisha wa hachi-ji yon'jūgo-fun kara go-ji han made desu.*

Demo yoku zan'gyō ga arimasu kara, shichi-ji goro kaerimasu.

(7) *Fūtsū no hi "on regular days" wa taitei hachi-ji goro uchi ni tsukimasu.*

(8) *Sorekara ban-gohan o tabemasu.*

(9) *Shokuji no ato de yoku terebi o mimasu.*

(10) *Jūichi-ji goro nemasu.*

(11) *Is-shūkan ni ni-san-kai shigoto no ato de nomi ni ikimasu.*

Settai* ya tsukiai* desu. Jūichi-ji ka jūni-ji goro uchi ni tsukimasu.

*cf. Culture Note 8

Drill 11 Listen to what Mrs. Tanaka usually does during the day, and

1. Look at the pictures below and fill in the blanks with the appropriate times.

2. Answer the questions, taking Mrs. Tanaka's role.

(1) *Asa wa itsumo nan-ji ni okimasu ka.*

(2) *Nan-ji goro asa-gohan o tabemasu ka.*

(3) *Go-shujin to okosan wa nan-ji goro uchi o demasu ka.*

(4) *Gozen'chū* "in the morning" *wa nani o shimasu ka.*

(5) *Hiru-gohan wa nan-ji goro tabemasu ka.*

(6) *Gogo wa uchi ni imasu ka.*

(7) *Gogo wa nani o shimasu ka.*

(8) *Okosan-tachi wa nan-ji goro gakkō kara kaerimasu ka.*

(9) *Kaimono wa itsumo doko e ikimasu ka.*

(10) *Nan-ji goro kara ban-gohan no shitaku o shimasu ka.*

(11) *Ban-gohan wa itsumo min'na de* "all together" *tabemasu ka.*

(12) *Yoru wa nan-ji ni nemasu ka.*

3. Answer about yourself. Use the same questions in 1.

—Tape Script—

(1) *Watashi wa itsumo roku-ji goro okimasu.*

(2) *Sorekara asa-gohan no shitaku o shimasu.*

(3) *Shichi-ji goro asa-gohan o tabemasu.*

(4) *Shujin wa shichi-ji han ni kaisha e ikimasu.*

(5)   *Kodomo-tachi wa hachi-ji ni gakkō e ikimasu.*

(6)   *Watashi wa sorekara atokatazuke* "tidying up" *to sōji to sen'taku o shimasu.*

(7)   *Jūni-ji goro hiru gohan o tabemasu.*

(8)   *Gogo wa,*

        Getsu-yōbi wa yoga "yoga exercise" *o shimasu.*

        Sui-yōbi wa sumie "Japanese ink painting" *o naratte imasu.*

        Tokidoki tenisu ni ikimasu.

(9)   *San-ji goro kodomo-tachi ga kaerimasu.*

(10)   *Taitei yo-ji goro chikaku no sūpā made kaimono ni ikimasu.*

(11)   *Go-ji han goro kara ban-gohan no shitaku o shimasu.*

(12)   *Shujin wa taitei osoku kaerimasu kara, kodomo-tachi to watashi dake de roku-ji han goro gohan o tabemasu.*

(13)   *Tamani shujin mo isshoni ban-gohan o tabemasu.*

(14)   *Taitei jūichi-ji goro nemasu.*

Drill 12   Listen to the conversation between Mr. White and Mr. Takahashi about what they usually do on the weekend and,

1. Answer the questions.

(1)   *Howaito-san wa yasumi no hi wa nani o shimasu ka.*

(2)   *Don'na tokoro e ikimasu ka.*

(3)   *Sen'shū wa doko e ikimashita ka.*

(4)   *Takahashi-san wa do-yōbi wa isogashii desu ka.*

(5)   *Nichi-yōbi wa hayaku okimasu ka.*

(6)   *Nichi-yōbi wa nani o shimasu ka.*

2. Answer about yourself using the questions in 1.

—Tape Script—

Takahashi:	*Howaito-san, yasumi no hi wa nani o shimasu ka.*
Howaito:	*Sō desu nē.*
	Yoku kazoku to doraibu ni ikimasu.
Takahashi:	*Don'na tokoro e ikimasu ka.*
Howaito:	*Chikai tokoro desu. Izu e yoku ikimasu.*
	Sen'shū wa Nikkō e ikimashita.
Takahashi:	*Ii desu nē.*
Howaito:	*Takahashi-san wa.*
Takahashi:	*Watashi wa do-yōbi mo taitei shigoto ga arimasu.*
Howaito:	*Do-yōbi mo shigoto desu ka. Taihen desu nē.*
Takahashi:	*Dakara, nichi-yōbi wa osoku okimasu.*
	Soshite taitei uchi ni imasu.
	Ik-kagetsu ni ik-kai gurai yama e ikimasu ga.
Howaito:	*Yama desu ka.*

Culture Note 8 — Salaryman's Life — Is it all *settai*, *shōtai* and *tsukiai*?

Settai and *shōtai* — these two words are very important in the world of business entertainment. They both mean "invitation" and the only difference between them of major importance is that *settai* means you pay and *shōtai* means the other guy pays. *Settai* also has the meaning of entertain, as to entertain clients.

You will often hear the phrase *settai de* or *shōtai de* mean by invitation as in "I played golf by invitation." If the phrase was *settai de* then that means you invited the other guys and you, as the inviter, were expected to pay. If the phrase was *shōtai de*, then you were invited and, as the invitee, were not expected to fork over anything. We often hear the phrase *shōtai-gorufu* meaning "invitation golf." Of course, if it's golf, it's the company rather than the person who pays.

But you must be careful with the word "invite." Whichever word you use carries built-in information indicating who will pay. This can hold true even for a casual drink after work. If you want the companionship and not the (double) bill, you must make your intentions clear from the start. You might otherwise end up with an uncomfortable moment at the cashier's desk.

Socializing in Japan oils the wheels of industry and even the office to a much greater extent than in the West and while none of it is ever compulsory, it is often as good as. Some appointments, like golf, would take the death of a spouse to avoid, and if you refuse to drink with your office colleagues you suffer in the promotion stakes. This kind of office and interoffice getting together is called *tsukiai*, and carries a slight nuance of reluctance. If you go drinking after work *tsukiai de*, then it means that you would probably prefer to go home. But if you refuse the group once too often, the group in the end will refuse you. And this can plunge your career right down the drain!

Socializing of the same kind is equally necessary between two companies. You meet, drink, size up the other fellow, and if you like the vibes, then you will eventually end up doing business. Without this, it is almost impossible to make necessary impressions and connections, to create the necessary milieu in which to work with one another.

So this means that the average "salaryman" works late and after that goes drinking. Even on week nights he can arrive home after midnight, because of *settai/shōtai* or *tsukiai*. Where do the wives fit in to all this? We might imagine them as long-suffering paragons of patience. What else could you be and still keep your marriage together? Not so. Many wives have their own lives planned meticulously and are more than happy not to have the husband home at all. Companionship is not a major reason for or expectation of a Japanese marriage. They have their household chores to do (even now, salarymen's wives more often don't work than work), and they have their own *tsukiai* during the day, as well as their children's welfare to look out for. Houses are so small that not many wives want what becomes an extra lump sitting around the place inconveniently demanding tea.

Wives play no part in their husbands' business lives (and likewise the husbands are equally remote from their wives' social lives). It is rare if not entirely unknown to entertain formally at home and informal occasions outside of the family are unusual. Things are beginning to change. More women are working in the younger generation, and younger men are taking different attitudes towards their family life. The words *nyū famiri* "new family" and *mai hōmu papa* "my home papa" can be heard now where they didn't exist ten years ago. And outside the salaryman world, self-employed men like farmers, shopkeepers, *etc.*, have a much more family oriented life because their workplace is the same as or close to their living place, and because they can arrange their own hours.

It paints a pretty dreary picture to Westerners perhaps, and certainly that is part of the price for the economic miracle, but now that necessity is not so dire, things show signs of changing. In ten years, who knows? People may have to look in a dictionary to find out the meanings of *settai* and *shōtai*.

After work — Businessmen *sarariman* at a *yakitori* stand

Review Quiz (Lesson 9 — Lesson 15)

I. Make six sentences using the information given below. Don't forget to use appropriate markers with them.

	1	2	3	4	5	6
General Time	yesterday		tomorrow			tomorrow
Specific Time		Sunday last week		Saturday	Friday next week	
Direction	Shinjuku	Totsuka Country Club	American Club	friend's house	Ginza	Osaka
Purpose						
Involvement	friend	customer	my wife/ husband & children	my wife/ husband	alone *hitoride*	
Means						
Cause						business trip

1.

2.

3.

4.

5.

6.

II. Complete the sentences using the words given by changing the forms accordingly.

1. | A: *Itsu Nihon e (   ) ka.*   [kimasu]
    | B: *Kyonen no go-gatsu ni (   ).*   [kimasu]

2. *Kon'do no yasumi ni dokoka e (   ) ka.*   [ikimasu]

3. | A: *Buraun-san wa Nihon ni imasu ka.*
    | B: *Iie, sen-getsu (   ).*   [kaerimasu]

4. | A: *Sen-shū no yasumi ni dokoka e (   ).*   [ikimasu]
    | B: *Ē, Izu e (   ).*   [ikimasu]
    | A: *Izu wa dō (   ) ka.*   [desu]
    | B: *(   ) desu yo.*   [omoshiroi]

5. |A: *Maiasa nan-ji ni (*   *) ka.*   [*okimasu*]
   |B: *Roku-ji han goro desu.*
        Demo kyō wa roku-ji ni (*).*   [*okimasu*]

6. |A: *Yoru wa itsumo nani o shimasu ka.*
   |B: *Taitei terebi o (*   *).*   [*mimasu*]
        Kinō eiga o (*).*   [*mimasu*]

III. Fill in the blanks with the words from below.

1. *Hiru-gohan wa itsumo doko (*   *) tabemasu ka.*
2. *Howaito-san wa asa nan-ji (*   *) okimasu ka.*
3. *Nikkō e wa kuruma (*   *) ikimasu ka.*
4. *Yoru wa taitei terebi (*   *) mimasu.*
5. *Raishū kazoku (*   *) Kyōto e ikimasu.*
    [*ni,   de,   to,   o,   de*]

IV. Fill in the blanks with the adverbs.

1. *(*   *) uchi o shichi-ji han ni demasu.*
    "always"
2. *Yoru wa (*   *) on'gaku o kikimasu.*
        "usually"
3. *Terebi wa (*   *) mimasen.*
      "not so often"
4. *(*   *) Shin'juku e nomi ni ikimasu.*
    "sometimes"
5. *Shūmatsu (*   *) gorufu o shimasu.*
       "often"

V. What Japanese expressions would you use in the following situations?

1. When someone says his Japanese is not good yet, or when someone says he is too old to study Japanese —
2. When you want to say that you won't go anywhere particularly —
3. When you meet somebody early in the morning, what would you say besides **Ohayō gozaimasu** —
4. When you meet somebody later than the usual time in the evening —
5. When using a store or restaurant name which you or the listener may not be familiar with, for instance, "I went to Sakura restaurant yesterday." —
6. When expressing agreement to what others have said —
7. When you hear somebody has had a nice time or had a nice experience —
8. When you hear somebody missed something which that person had been looking forward to —
9. When you hear someone's exciting plan for a trip, vacation, *etc,* meaning "That's great!" in English —

VI. Express in Japanese.

1. Is the Japanese language interesting?
2. What do you usually do after work?
3. I have Japanese lessons twice a week.
4. I sometimes go drinking in Ginza to entertain clients.
5. I have a meeting, so I've come early.
6. I often eat lunch at a restaurant near my office.
7. I buy meat at a supermarket called Ogawaya.
8. That restaurant is cheap and [the food is] delicious.
9. How do you like Japan?
10. I don't like raw fish so much.

Unit V

Location

SCOPE OF UNIT V

The main function of Unit V is GIVING DIRECTIONS TO LOCATIONS.

Lesson 16   practices the expressions needed to ask for and give directions on the street.

Lesson 17   deals with locating specific items or places, using sections of a department store and a client's office as examples. It will also introduce you to the extremely polite speech style which is normally used by people in the service industry.

Lesson 18   covers location of both people and things in an office and extends to a store where you may need to describe exact locations in a display or a showcase.

Lesson 16
ASKING FOR AND GIVING LOCATIONS
— ON THE STREET —

SUMIMASEN, KUYAKUSHO E IKITAI'N DESU GA . . .
"EXCUSE ME, I'D LIKE TO GO TO THE WARD OFFICE . . ."

Dialogue I

[At a police box]

Ton'puson:	Sumimasen, kuyakusho e ikitai-n desu ga . . .
Omawari-san:	Kuyakusho wa ano shin'gō no saki desu.
Ton'puson:	Ano shin'gō no saki desu ne.
Omawari-san:	Ē, sō desu.
Ton'puson:	Dōmo arigatō gozaimashita.
Omawari-san:	Hai.

Ms. Thompson:	Excuse me, I'd like to go to the ward office . . .
Policeman:	It's beyond that traffic light.
Ms. Thompson:	Oh, beyond that traffic light.
Policeman:	That's right.
Ms. Thompson:	Thank you very much.
Policeman:	You're welcome.

Vocabulary

kuyakusho: ward office

ikitai-n desu ga: I'd like to go . . .

Dialogue II

[On the street]

Ton'puson: Sumimasen. Mikimoto Pāru wa doko deshō ka.

Nihon-jin: Ēto ... Wakō wa wakarimasu ka.

Ton'puson: Ē, wakarimasu. ←—→

Nihon-jin: Mikimoto wa Wakō no
narabi desu yo.

Ton'puson: Wakō no narabi desu ne.
Dōmo arigatō gozaimashita.

Nihon-jin: Iie.

Ton'puson: Chotto ... wakarimasen
ga ...

Nihon-jin: Sore jā, kono michi o
massugu itte kudasai.
Sōsuruto kōsaten no
kado ni Wakō to iu
depāto ga arimasu.

Ton'puson: Hai.

Nihon-jin: Mikimoto wa Wakō no
narabi desu.

Ton'puson: Massugu itte, kōsaten no
kado no Wakō no narabi
desu ne.

Nihon-jin: Ē, sō desu.

Ton'puson: Dōmo arigatō
gozaimashita.

Nihon-jin: Iie.

Wako Dept.
Mikimoto Pearl

Ms. Thompson: Excuse me, I wonder where the Mikimoto Pearl (shop) is?

Japanese: Let me see, do you know where Wako is?

Ms. Thompson: Yes, I do. ←—→

Japanese: Mikimoto is on the same side of the street.

Ms. Thompson: Oh, the same side of the street as Wako.
Thank you very much.

Japanese: You're welcome. [Lit. Yes.]

Ms. Thompson: Well, I'm not sure.
[Lit. I don't understand a little.]

Japanese: Then, walk straight ahead on this street, and you'll see the Wako store at the corner of the intersection.

Ms. Thompson: O.K.

Japanese: Mikimoto is on the same side as the department store.

Ms. Thompson: I go straight and I'll see Wako at the corner of the intersection. (Mikimoto) is on the same side as Wako, (right?)

Japanese: That's right.

Ms. Thompson: Thank you very much.

Japanese: You're welcome.

Vocabulary

Mikimoto Pāru: famous pearl shop in Ginza
Wakō: first rate department store in Ginza
wakarimasu ←wakaru: understand
narabi: a row, the same side, a line

michi: street
sōsuruto: then, when you've done that
arimasu ← aru: exist, be (there)

⊟Dialogue III ─────────────────

[On the street]

Ton'puson:	*Sumimasen.*
Nihon-jin:	*Hai.*
Ton'puson:	*Anō . . . kono hen ni posuto wa arimasen ka.*
Nihon-jin:	*Posuto desu ka. Eki no mae ni arimasu yo.*
Ton'puson:	*Eki no mae desu ne.*
Nihon-jin:	*Ē.*
Ton'puson:	*Arigatō gozaimashita.*
Nihon-jin:	*Iie.*

Ms. Thompson:	Excuse me.
Japanese:	Yes.
Ms. Thompson:	Well . . ., is there [*Lit.* isn't there] a mail box around here?
Japanese:	Mail box . . ., [*Lit.* Is it a mail box?] There is one in front of the station.
Ms. Thompson:	Oh, in front of the station, (right?)
Japanese:	That's right.
Ms. Thompson:	Thank you very much.
Japanese:	Not at all. [*Lit.* No.]

I

トンプソン　　：すみません、　くやくしょへ　いきたいんですが…。

おまわりさん：くやくしょは　あの　しんごうの　さきです。

トンプソン　　：あの　しんごうの　さきですね。

おまわりさん：ええ、　そうです。

トンプソン　　：どうも　ありがとうございました。

おまわりさん：はい。

Vocabulary ─────────────────

anō: well, hello

kono hen ni: around this area, in this vicinity

posuto: mail box

arimasen ← aru: isn't there, doesn't exist there

mae: in front of

II

トンプソン：すみません。　ミキモトパールは　どこでしょうか。

日本人　　：ええと…　和光は　わかりますか。

トンプソン：ええ、　わかります。　←→　トンプソン：ちょっと…

日本人　　：ミキモトは　和光の　　　　　　　　　　わかりませんが…。

　　　　　　ならびですよ。　　　　日本人　　：それじゃあ　このみちを

トンプソン：和光の　ならびですね。　　　　　　　　まっすぐ

　　　　　　どうも　　　　　　　　　　　　　　　いってください。

　　　　　　ありがとうございました。　　　　　　そうすると

日本人　　：いいえ。　　　　　　　　　　　　　　こうさてんの　かどに

　　　　　　　　　　　　　　　　　　　　　　　　和光という

　　　　　　　　　　　　　　　　　　　　　　　　デパートが　あります。

　　　　　　　　　　　　　　トンプソン：はい。

　　　　　　　　　　　　　　日本人　　：ミキモトは　和光の

　　　　　　　　　　　　　　　　　　　　ならびです。

　　　　　　　　　　　　　　トンプソン：まっすぐ　いって、

　　　　　　　　　　　　　　　　　　　　こうさてんの　かどの

　　　　　　　　　　　　　　　　　　　　和光の　ならびですね。

　　　　　　　　　　　　　　日本人　　：ええ、　そうです。

　　　　　　　　　　　　　　トンプソン：どうも

　　　　　　　　　　　　　　　　　　　　ありがとうございました。

　　　　　　　　　　　　　　日本人　　：いいえ。

III

トンプソン：すみません。

日本人　　：はい。

トンプソン：あのう…、　このへんに　ポストはありませんか。

日本人　　：ポストですか。　えきの　まえに　ありますよ。

トンプソン：えきの　まえですね。

日本人　　：ええ。

トンプソン：ありがとうございました。

日本人　　：いいえ。

Grammar Note 1 — Asking for directions I

a.   **Sumimasen, [Place you want to go] wa doko** $\begin{cases} \textbf{\textit{desu ka}} \nearrow. \\ \textbf{\textit{deshō ka}} \searrow. \end{cases}$

Sumimasen, <u>kuyakusho</u> wa doko deshō ka ↘.   "Excuse me, where is the ward office?"

X wa doko desu ka ↗**/deshō ka** ↘ is the simplest way to ask where something specific is located. **Deshō ka** ↘ sounds more polite than **desu ka** ↗.

b.   **Sumimasen, [Place you want to go] e ikitai-n desu ga**...

Sumimasen, <u>kuyakusho</u> e ikitai-n desu ga...   "Excuse me, I'd like to go to the ward office..."

This is a more indirect way to ask directions.

Grammar Note 2 — Giving directions I

When giving someone directions to a location in reference to the place where you are at the time, use the following patterns:

a.   **[The destination] wa [Direction/Location] desu.**

<u>Kuyakusho</u> wa <u>atchi</u> desu.   "The ward office is in that direction."

Topic	
Destination	
kuyakusho	wa

⇩

Predicate	
atchi	desu

Vocabulary: Location words I

Meaning	
here	koko
there	soko*
over there [away from both the listener and the speaker]	asoko
right there	sugu soko
where?	doko

*Soko "there" has two meanings: 1)   "there" near the listener
2)   "there" closer than **asoko** "over there"

Meaning	
here, this direction	kotchi, kochira
there, that direction	sotchi, sochira
over there, that direction	atchi, achira
where?, which direction?	dotchi, dochira

Kochira, sochira, etc., are polite equivalents of **kotchi, sotchi**, etc.

b. [The destination] *wa* **[Point of reference]** *no* **[Position]** *desu.*

Kuyakusho wa ano shin'gō no saki desu.   ''The ward office is beyond that traffic light.''

Topic	
Destination	
kuyakusho	wa

Predicate			
Location			
Point of Reference		Position	
ano shin'gō	no	saki	desu

Vocabulary

Meaning	
the first (in the sequence)	hitotsu-me no
the second (in the sequence)	futatsu-me no
the third (in the sequence)	mittsu-me no
traffic light	shin'gō
crossing	kōsaten
street	tōri
corner	kado

Vocabulary   Position — Location words II

Meaning	
the right side	migi-gawa
the left side	hidari-gawa
this side	kotchi-gawa
that side	atchi-gawa
before	temae
after, beyond	saki

Examples

kono tōri no migi-gawa	''the right side of this street''
ano kōsaten no saki	''beyond that intersection''
futatsu-me no shin'gō no kado	''the corner at the second traffic light''
kono saki	''a little further on (from here)''
San'kei Biru wa kono saki desu.	''The Sankei Building is a little further on from here.''

Grammar Note 3 — Giving directions II — Mentioning a landmark

When giving a location using a landmark as a point of reference, use the following sequence of patterns:

a.   First, ask if the person knows the landmark.
[Landmark] *wa wakarimasu ka.*

Wakō wa wakarimasu ka.   ''Do you know where Wako is?''

b. If the person knows the suggested landmark, give the location using the following pattern.

[Place you want to go] *wa* **[Landmark]** *no* **[Position]** *desu.*

<u>Mikimoto</u> *wa* <u>Wakō</u> *no* <u>narabi</u> *desu.*   "Mikimoto is on the same side of (the street as) Wako (is)."

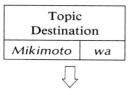

Topic Destination	
Mikimoto	*wa*

Predicate			
Location			
Suggested Landmark		Position	
Wakō	*no*	*narabi*	*desu*

Vocabulary: Position — Location words III

Meaning	
very close	*soba*
close	*chikaku*
next (door) to	*tonari*
side	*yoko*
in front of	*mae*
in back of, behind	*ushiro*
across the street	*mukai-gawa*
on the same side	*narabi*
inside	*naka*

Examples

A:	*Y wa wakarimasu ka.*	"Do you know Y?"
B:	*Ē, wakarimasu.*	"Yes, I do."
A:	*Kuyakusho wa Y no soba desu yo.*	"The ward office is very close to Y."

c. If the person does not know the landmark, he/she might answer:
Chotto wakarimasen ga . . .   "Well, I'm not sure . . ."

d. Then, give him/her directions to the landmark.
Sore jā, kono michi o massugu itte kudasai.   "Well, go straight ahead on this street."

e. Then, tell him/her where the landmark is.
Sōsuruto, [Location] *ni* **[Landmark]** *ga arimasu.*
Sōsuruto, <u>kōsaten no kado</u> *ni* <u>Wakō to iu depāto</u> *ga arimasu.*

"Then, you'll see [*Lit.* there is] (a department store called) Wako at the corner of the intersection."

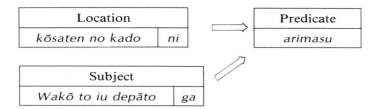

Arimasu in this lesson means "there is." In Lesson 13 arimasu is used as "have."

Ni   [Location Marker]
    Ni is used with the verb **arimasu** "there is" which indicates existence and location of a thing.

f.   Then, give him/her the location using the landmark — **Wakō** — as a point of reference. Use the same pattern as in Grammar Note 3-b.

Examples

A:	X wa doko deshō ka.	"Where is X?"
B:	Y wa wakarimasu ka. → (cf. **a.**)	"Do you know Y?"
A:	Chotto . . ., wakarimasen ga . . . → (cf. **c.**)	"Well . . ., I don't know."
B:	Sore jā, kono michi o massugu itte kudasai. → (cf. **d.**)	"Then, go straight along this street."
	Sōsuruto migi-gawa ni Y ga arimasu. → (cf. **e.**)	"Then, you'll see Y on your right."
	X wa Y no saki desu. → (cf. **b,f.**)	"X is beyond Y."

▐ Grammar Note 4 ▌ — Asking for directions II

Sumimasen, [Place] ni [Something] wa arimasen ka.
Sumimasen, kono hen ni posuto wa arimasen* ka.
    "Excuse me, is there [*Lit.* isn't*there] a post office around here?"

When you want to find a mail box, telephone booth, gas station, hospital, *etc.*, use this form.

    *The negative form is simply a form of politeness and does not imply any expectations as it does in English. You can also use **arimasu ka**.

▐ Grammar Note 5 ▌ — Giving directions II

Here is another way of giving locations. Use **ni arimasu** instead of **desu**.

([What you are looking for] wa) [Place] ni arimasu.
(Posuto wa) eki no mae ni arimasu.   "(Mail box is) in front of the station."

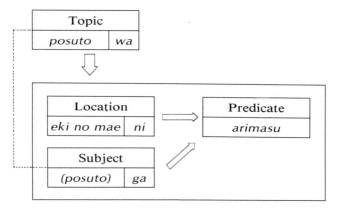

Example

A: *Kono hen ni den'wa wa arimasen ka.*   "Is there a telephone around here?"

B: *Eki no yoko ni arimasu yo.*   "There's one at the side of the station."

Grammar Note 6 — Summing up and confirming

Here we show how to sum up and confirm directions.

⌜**V-*te*** *kudasai.*
⎸ *Sōsuruto,* [**Location**] *ni* [**Y**] *ga arimasu.*
⌞ *X wa* [**Y**] *no* [**Position**] *desu.*

→ **V-*te*,** [**Location**] *no* [**Y**] *no* [**Position**] *desu ne.*

Example

⌜*Massugu itte kudasai.*
⎸ *Sōsuruto, kōsaten no kado ni Wakō ga arimasu.*
⌞ *Mikimoto wa Wakō no narabi desu.*

→ *Massugu itte, kōsaten no kado no Wakō no [narabi] desu ne.*

⌜"Go straight.
⎸ Then you'll see Wako on the corner of the intersection.
⌞ Mikimoto is on the same side as Wako."

→ "I go straight and I'll see Wako on the corner of the intersection. Mikomoto is on the same side, (right?)"

Giving directions at Ginza Subway Station

地下鉄 銀座駅
(*chi-ka-tetsu Gin-za-eki*)

Drill 1   Substitute the underlined parts.

1. *Sumimasen, <u>kuyakusho</u> wa doko deshō ka.*

　　(1)　*Tōkyō Eki*　　　　(2)　*Japan Taimuzu no biru* "*The Japan Times* Building"

　　(3)　*Tōkyū Depāto*

2. *Sumimasen ga, <u>kuyakusho</u> e ikitai-n desu ga…*

　　(1)　*chikatetsu no Gin'za Eki*　　　　(2)　*Nakameguro Eki*

　　(3)　*Seiroka Byōin* "St. Luke's Hospital"　　(4)　*Sakura to iu resutoran*

Drill 2   Complete the dialogues, following the example. Look at the pictures.

e.g.	A: *Sumimasen, Sankei Biru e ikitai-n desu ga…* B: *Kotchi desu.* A: *Sotchi desu ne.* B: *Ē, sō desu.* A: *Dōmo.* B: *Hai.*	
(1)	You: _____ . Tape: *Kotchi desu.* You: _____ . Tape: *Ē, sō desu.* You: _____ . Tape: *Iie.*	*Sonī Biru*
(2)	You: _____ . Tape: *Sotchi desu.* You: _____ . Tape: *Ē, sō desu.* You: _____ . Tape: *Hai.*	*chikatetsu no Gin'za Eki*
(3)	You: _____ . Tape: *Atchi desu.* You: _____ . Tape: *Ē, sō desu.* You: _____ . Tape: *Iie.*	*Matsuya Depāto*

▦Drill 3   Substitute the underlined parts.

1. *Ano shin'gō no <u>saki</u> desu.*

    (1)   *temae*   (2)   *sugu saki*   (3)   *hyaku-mētoru* "100 meters" *saki*

2. *Ano shin'gō no <u>saki</u> desu.*

    (1)   *ano kōsaten*   (2)   *futatsu-me no shin'gō*   (3)   *mittsu-me no kōsaten*

3. *Kono tōri no <u>migi-gawa</u> desu.*

    (1)   *hidari-gawa*   (2)   *gojū-mētoru saki no migi-gawa*

Drill 4   Choose the points (A, B, C . . .) which match the sentences given.

      e.g., Hitotsu-me no kōsaten no temae desu.   ⟶   A, B

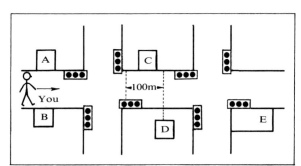

(1)   *Kono tōri no migi-gawa desu.*

(2)   *Kono tōri no hidari-gawa desu.*

(3)   *Hitotsu-me no kōsaten no saki desu.*

(4)   *Hitotsu-me no kōsaten no hyaku-mētoru saki desu.*

(5)   *Sugu soko desu.*

(6)   *Futatsu-me no shin'gō no temae desu.*

(7)   *Futatsu-me no shingō no kado desu.*

▦Drill 5   Using Dialogue I as a model, complete the following.

(1)	You:	_____.	Kabukiza
	Tape:	*Ano shin'gō no saki desu.*	
	You:	_____.	
	Tape:	*Ē, sō desu.*	
	You:	_____.	
	Tape:	*Hai.*	
(2) Hibiya Cinema Street	You:	_____.	Hibiya no eigagai
	Tape:	*Kono saki desu.*	
	You:	_____.	
	Tape:	*Ē, sō desu.*	
	You:	_____.	
	Tape:	*Iie.*	
(3) Matsuzakaya Dept. Store	You:	_____.	Matsuzakaya Depāto
	Tape:	*Futatsu-me no shin'gō no kado desu.*	
	You:	_____.	
	Tape:	*Ē, sō desu.*	
	You:	_____.	
	Tape:	*Hai.*	

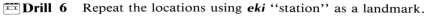

Drill 6   Repeat the locations using **eki** "station" as a landmark.

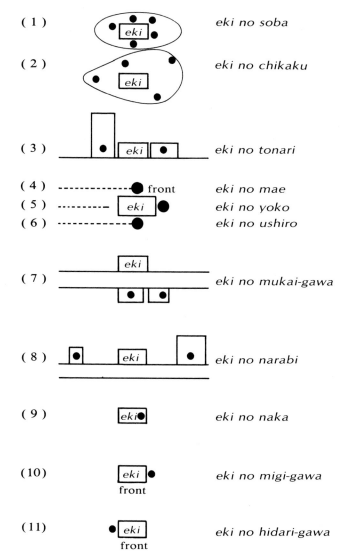

(1)   eki no soba

(2)   eki no chikaku

(3)   eki no tonari

(4)   front   eki no mae
(5)   eki no yoko
(6)   eki no ushiro

(7)   eki no mukai-gawa

(8)   eki no narabi

(9)   eki no naka

(10)   eki no migi-gawa
     front

(11)   eki no hidari-gawa
     front

Drill 7   Give the location, using F as a landmark.

e.g.,   B wa F no mukai-gawa desu.

A	B	C	D

(1)   E wa F no _____ desu.

(2)   E to G wa F no _____ desu.

front   I

(3)   H wa F no _____ desu.

E	F	K	G	H

(4)   C wa F no _____ desu.

(5)   I wa F no _____ desu.

(6)   J wa F no _____ desu.

J

(7)   K wa F no _____ desu.

(8)   A to B to C to D wa F no _____ desu.

(9)   A to B to C to D to E to G to H to I to J wa F no _____ desu.

Drill 8   Using Dialogue II as a model, complete the following.

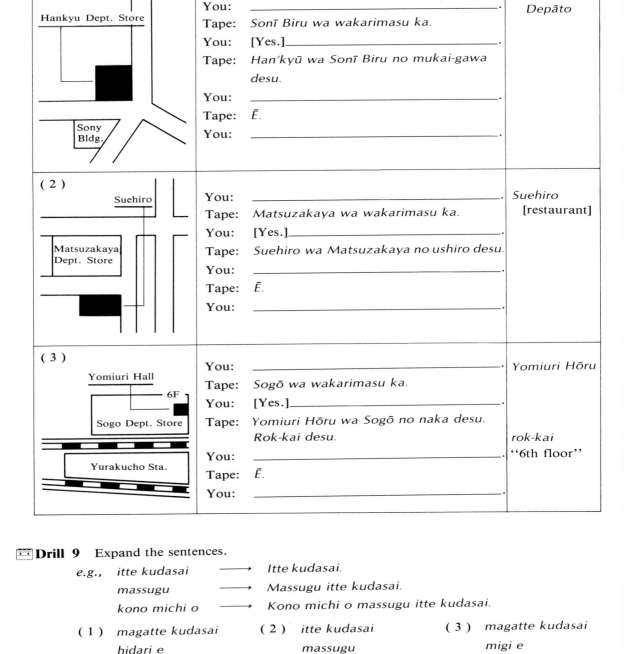

(1) Hankyu Dept. Store / Sony Bldg.	You: _____. Tape: *Sonī Biru wa wakarimasu ka.* You: [Yes.]_____. Tape: *Han'kyū wa Sonī Biru no mukai-gawa desu.* You: _____. Tape: *Ē.* You: _____	*Han'kyū Depāto*
(2) Suehiro / Matsuzakaya Dept. Store	You: _____. Tape: *Matsuzakaya wa wakarimasu ka.* You: [Yes.]_____. Tape: *Suehiro wa Matsuzakaya no ushiro desu.* You: _____. Tape: *Ē.* You: _____	*Suehiro [restaurant]*
(3) Yomiuri Hall / 6F / Sogo Dept. Store / Yurakucho Sta.	You: _____. Tape: *Sogō wa wakarimasu ka.* You: [Yes.]_____. Tape: *Yomiuri Hōru wa Sogō no naka desu. Rok-kai desu.* You: _____. Tape: *Ē.* You: _____	*Yomiuri Hōru* *rok-kai* "6th floor"

Drill 9   Expand the sentences.

e.g.,   *itte kudasai* ⟶ *Itte kudasai.*
        massugu ⟶ *Massugu itte kudasai.*
        kono michi o ⟶ *Kono michi o massugu itte kudasai.*

(1)   *magatte kudasai*   (2)   *itte kudasai*   (3)   *magatte kudasai*
        hidari e   *massugu*   *migi e*
        sono kōsaten o   *depāto no mae o*   *shingō o*
                                                                     futatsu-me no

Drill 10

1.   Substitute the underlined parts.

   Sōsuruto, <u>migi-gawa</u> ni <u>depāto</u> ga arimasu.

   (1)   *hidari-gawa, sūpā*

   (2)   *migi-gawa, eki*

(3) *shin'gō no kado, kōban* "police box"

(4) *kōsaten no temae, kissaten* "coffee shop"

(5) *shin'gō no saki, chūshajō* "parking lot"

2. Give the name of each point (A, B . . .) using 1.

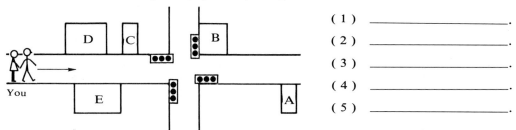

(1) ————————————————.

(2) ————————————————.

(3) ————————————————.

(4) ————————————————.

(5) ————————————————.

Drill 11 Confirm the underlined parts.

1. *e.g.,*   *Kono michi o <u>massugu</u> itte kudasai.*   ⟶   *Massugu desu ne.*

(1) *Asoko o <u>migi</u> e magatte kudasai.*

(2) *Sono kado o <u>hidari</u> e magatte kudasai.*

(3) *<u>Futatsu-me no shin'gō</u> o <u>migi</u> e itte kudasai.*

(4) *<u>Massugu itte</u> kudasai.*

    Sorekara, <u>hitotsu-me no kado o</u> <u>hidari</u> e itte kudasai.

2. *e.g.,*   *Sōsuruto, <u>migi-gawa ni</u> <u>sūpā</u> ga arimasu.*   ⟶   *Migi-gawa ni sūpā desu ne.*

(1) *Sōsuruto, <u>hidari-gawa ni</u> <u>kuroi biru</u> ga arimasu.*

(2) *Sōsuruto, <u>hitotsu-me no kado ni</u> <u>hon-ya</u> ga arimasu.*

(3) *Sōsuruto, <u>mukai-gawa ni</u> <u>chūshajō</u> ga arimasu.*

(4) *Sōsuruto, <u>migi-gawa ni</u> <u>Ichiban to iu sūpā</u> ga arimasu.*

3. *e.g.,*   *X wa sono <u>sūpā no saki</u> desu.*   ⟶   *Sūpā no saki desu ne.*

(1) *X wa sono <u>biru no chika</u>* "basement" *desu.*

(2) *X wa sono <u>hon-ya no saki</u> desu.*

(3) *X wa sono <u>chūshajō no soba</u> desu.*

(4) *X wa sono <u>sūpā no ushiro</u> desu.*

Drill 12   Sum up and confirm the underlined parts.

    e.g.,   *Kono michi o <u>massugu itte</u> kudasai.*

        Sōsuruto, <u>migi-gawa ni</u> <u>depāto</u> ga arimasu.

        X wa sono <u>depāto no ushiro</u> desu.

        ⟶   *Massugu itte, migi-gawa no depāto no ushiro desu ne.*

(1) *Kono michi o <u>massugu itte</u> kudasai.*

    Sōsuruto, <u>hidari-gawa ni</u> <u>ōkii sūpā</u> ga arimasu.

    X wa sono. <u>sūpā no saki</u> desu.

(2) *<u>Futatsu-me no shin'gō</u> o <u>migi</u> e <u>magatte</u> kudasai.*

    Soshite <u>nihyaku-mētoru gurai itte</u> kudasai.

    Sōsuruto, <u>migi-gawa ni</u> <u>kuroi biru</u> ga arimasu.

    X wa sono <u>biru no chika</u> desu.

Drill 13   Using Dialogue II as a model, complete the following.

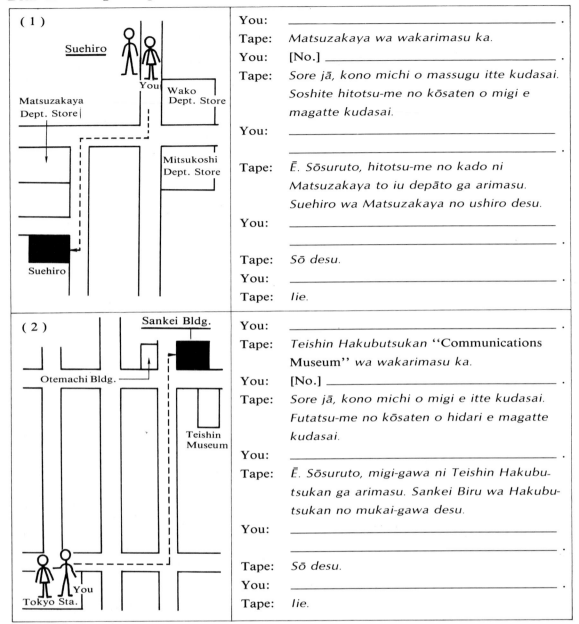

(1)

You: _____ .
Tape: *Matsuzakaya wa wakarimasu ka.*
You: [No.] _____ .
Tape: *Sore jā, kono michi o massugu itte kudasai. Soshite hitotsu-me no kōsaten o migi e magatte kudasai.*
You: _____
_____ .
Tape: *Ē. Sōsuruto, hitotsu-me no kado ni Matsuzakaya to iu depāto ga arimasu. Suehiro wa Matsuzakaya no ushiro desu.*
You: _____
_____ .
Tape: *Sō desu.*
You: _____ .
Tape: *Iie.*

(2)

You: _____ .
Tape: *Teishin Hakubutsukan "Communications Museum" wa wakarimasu ka.*
You: [No.] _____ .
Tape: *Sore jā, kono michi o migi e itte kudasai. Futatsu-me no kōsaten o hidari e magatte kudasai.*
You: _____ .
Tape: *Ē. Sōsuruto, migi-gawa ni Teishin Hakubutsukan ga arimasu. Sankei Biru wa Hakubutsukan no mukai-gawa desu.*
You: _____
_____ .
Tape: *Sō desu.*
You: _____ .
Tape: *Iie.*

Now, change the starting point and make dialogues as you like.

Drill 14   Repeat and memorize the things/places you may look for.

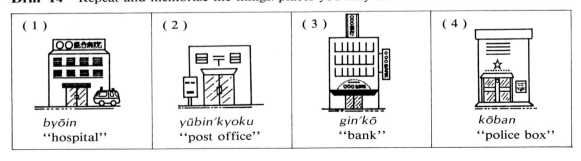

(1)	(2)	(3)	(4)
byōin "hospital"	*yūbin'kyoku* "post office"	*gin'kō* "bank"	*kōban* "police box"

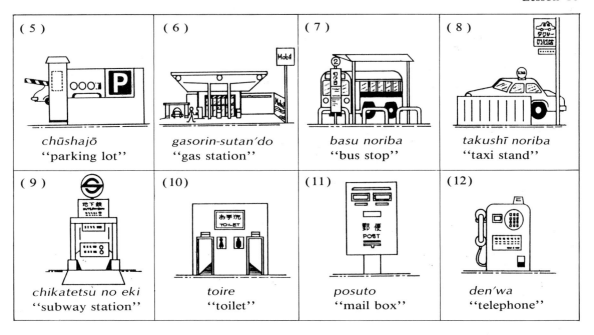

(5)
chūshajō
"parking lot"

(6)
gasorin-sutan'do
"gas station"

(7)
basu noriba
"bus stop"

(8)
takushī noriba
"taxi stand"

(9)
chikatetsu no eki
"subway station"

(10)
toire
"toilet"

(11)
posuto
"mail box"

(12)
den'wa
"telephone"

Telephone corner

電話

(den-wa)

Post office and mail box

郵便局

(yū-bin-kyoku)

Drill 15   Make questions and answers.

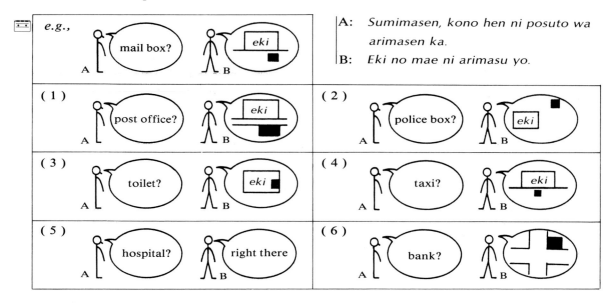

A: *Sumimasen, kono hen ni posuto wa arimasen ka.*

B: *Eki no mae ni arimasu yo.*

Drill 16   Translate into Japanese.

      e.g.,   Mail box; go straight ahead and you'll see it on your left.

          ⟶   *Posuto wa, massugu itte, hidari-gawa $\begin{Bmatrix} ni\ arimaru \\ desu \end{Bmatrix}$ yo.*

(1)   Bus stop; you'll see it behind the station.

(2)   Taxi; you'll see it in front of the station.

(3)   Gas station; go straight ahead and you'll see it on your right.

(4)   Parking lot; go straight ahead and you'll see it beyond the crossing.

(5)   Hospital; go straight ahead, turn right at the first traffic light and you'll see it on your left.

Drill 17   Using Dialogue III as a model, complete the following.

(1)   telephone (booth)

             station

    You

You: _____ .

Tape: *Hai.*

You: _____ .

Tape: *Den'wa desu ka.*

           Eki no yoko ni arimasu yo.

You: _____ .

Tape: *Ē.*

You: _____ .

Tape: *Iie.*

(2)

gas station	

You: _____ .
Tape: *Hai.*
You: _____ .
Tape: *Gasorin sutan'do desu ka.*
Kono michi o massugu itte kudasai.
Sōsuruto gasorin sutan'do wa migi-gawa no
kado ni arimasu.
You: _____ .
Tape: *Ē, sō desu.*
You: _____ .
Tape: *Iie.*

(3)

parking lot

20m

super-market

You

You: _____ .
Tape: *Hai.*
You: _____ .
Tape: *Sō desu nē. . . Kono michi o massugu itte*
kudasai. Sōsuruto, migi-gawa ni sūpā ga
arimasu.
Sūpā no saki o migi e magatte kudasai.
Chūshajō wa nijū-mētoru gurai saki ni
arimasu yo.
You: _____
_____ .
Tape: *Sō desu.*
You: _____ .
Tape: *Iie.*

(4)

florist

super-market

You

You: _____ .
Tape: *Hai.*
You: _____ .
Tape: *Hana-ya-san desu ka. Asoko ni sūpā ga*
arimasu nē. Ano kado o hidari e magatte
kudasai. Sōsuruto, hana-ya-san wa migi-
gawa ni arimasu yo.
You: _____ .
Tape: *Ē.*
You: _____ .
Tape: *Iie.*

Now, change the starting point and make dialogues as you like.

Drill 18

1. Using the map, set the starting point as you like and give directions to the following questions.

(1)   *Sumimasen, eki wa dotchi deshō ka.*

(2)   *Sumimasen ga, Nishi Yūbin'kyoku wa doko deshō ka.*

(3)   *Anō ... Z to iu kissaten e ikitai-n desu ga ...*

(4)   *Anō ... kono hen ni kusuri-ya-san wa arimasen ka.*

2. Choose any point and make a dialogue.

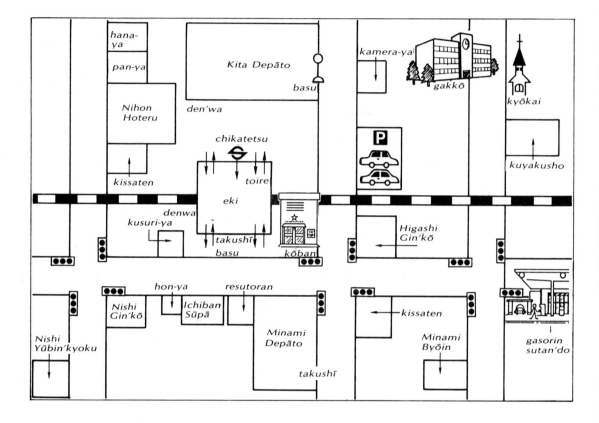

Lesson 17

FINDING WHERE TO BUY THINGS IN A STORE; FINDING THE WAY TO A CLIENT'S OFFICE

SHOKKI URIBA WA NAN-GAI DESHŌ KA
"WHICH FLOOR IS THE CHINA DEPARTMENT ON?"

▣ Dialogue I

[At the information counter at a department store]

Howaito:	Sumimasen.
An'naigakari:	Hai, irasshaimase.
Howaito:	Shokki uriba wa nan-gai deshō ka.
An'naigakari:	Nana-kai de gozaimasu.*1
Howaito:	Dōmo.
An'naigakari:	[Bows politely]

*   *   *

[On the seventh floor]

Howaito:	Sumimasen, shokki uriba wa doko deshō ka.
Ten'in:	Hai. Kochira o hidari e oide kudasai.*2
	Sōshimasuto, shōmen ni gozaimasu.*3
Howaito:	Soko o hidari e itte, shōmen desu ne.
Ten'in:	Hai, sayō de gozaimasu.*4
Howaito:	Dōmo.
Ten'in:	[Bows politely]

Mrs. White:	Excuse me.
Clerk:	Yes, may I help you? [*Lit.* Welcome (to the store).]
Mrs. White:	Which floor is the china and pottery [*Lit.* dishes and plates] department on?
Clerk:	It's on the seventh floor.
Mrs. White:	Thank you very much.

*   *   *

Mrs. White:	Excuse me, where is the china department (on this floor)?
Salesclerk:	Go this way to your left. Then you'll find the china and pottery department in front of you.
Mrs. White:	I go this way to my left and I'll see the china department right ahead of me.
Salesclerk:	That's right.
Mrs. White:	Thank you very much.

Level 2 Expressions

*1 Nana-kai desu.
*2 Hai. Koko o hidari e itte kudasai.
*3 Sōsuruto, shōmen ni arimasu.
*4 Hai, sō desu.

Vocabulary

an'naigakari: information clerk
irasshaimase: May I help you? [*Lit.* Welcome.]
shokki uriba: china [including pottery] department
nan-gai: which floor
. . . de gozaimasu: (it) is . . .
kochira: this way [Level 3]

oide kudasai: go/come, please [Level 3]
sōshimasuto: When you have done that, then . . . [Level 3]
shōmen: front
sayō de gozaimasu: that's right

219

📻 Dialogue II

[At the receptionist's desk in a company]

Shuwarutsu:	*Shitsurei shimasu.*
Uketsuke:	*Hai, irasshaimase.*
Shuwarutsu:	*Kikaku-bu no Howaito-san ni ome ni kakaritai-n desu ga . . .*
Uketsuke:	*Hai, o-yakusoku de irasshaimasu ka.*[*1]
Shuwarutsu:	*Hai, Tōkyō Gin'kō no Shuwarutsu to mōshimasu.*
Uketsuke:	*Shōshō omachi kudasai.*[*2]

*   *   *

[The receptionist calls Mr. White's secretary and tells her that Mr. Schwartz has arrived]

Uketsuke:	*Omatase itashimashita.*
	Howaito no heya wa jūik-kai de gozaimasu.[*3]
	Erebētā o oori ni natte migi-gawa de gozaimasu.[*4]
Shuwarutsu:	*Jūik-kai de erebētā o orite migi-gawa desu ne.*
Uketsuke:	*Hai, sayō de gozaimasu.*[*5]
Shuwarutsu:	*Dōmo arigatō gozaimashita.*
Uketsuke:	[Bows politely]

Mr. Schwartz:	Excuse me.
Receptionist:	Yes, sir. May I help you?
Mr. Schwartz:	I'd like to see Mr. White of the Planning Department.
Receptionist:	Yes, do you have an appointment, sir?
Mr. Schwartz:	Yes, my name is Schwartz [*Lit.* I'm called Schwartz] from the Bank of Tokyo.
Receptionist:	Could you wait a moment?

*   *   *

Receptionist:	Sorry to have kept you waiting. Mr. White's office is on the 11th floor. When you get off on the 11th floor, you'll see Mr. White's office on your right.
Mr. Schwartz:	I get off the elevator on the 11th floor and his office is to my right?
Receptionist:	Yes, sir.
Mr. Schwartz:	Thank you very much.

Vocabulary

kikaku-bu: planning department

ome ni kakaritai: I'd like to see . . . [Level 3]

yakusoku: appointment

. . . de irasshaimasu ka: do you have . . .? [*Lit.* Is it . . .?] [Level 3]

shōshō: for a while, a little (moment) [Level 3]

omatase itashimashita: (sorry) to have kept you waiting [Level 3]

heya: room

oori ni natte ⟵ *orite:* having got off [Level 3]

*   *   *

[On the eleventh floor]

Shuwarutsu:	*Shitsurei itashimasu, Howaito-san ni ome ni kakaritai-n desu ga . . .*
Nihon-jin:	*Kochira no tsukiatari de gozaimasu.*[6]
Shuwarutsu:	*Sochira no tsukiatari desu ne.*
Nihon-jin:	*Hai.*
Shuwarutsu:	*Dōmo arigatō gozaimashita.*
Nihon-jin:	[Bows politely]

*   *   *

Mr. Schwartz:	Excuse me. I'd like to see Mr. White . . .
Japanese:	His office is at the end of this hallway.
Mr. Schwartz:	Oh, at the end of this hallway.
Japanese:	Yes.
Mr. Schwartz:	Thank you very much.

Level 2   Expressions

*1 *Yakusoku desu ka.*
*2 *Chotto matte kudasai.*
*3 *Howaito no heya wa jūik-kai desu.*
*4 *Erebētā o orite migi-gawa desu.*
*5 *Hai, sō desu.*
*6 *Kotchi no tsukiatari desu.*

I

ホワイト　：すみません。

案内係
あんないがかり　：はい、　いらっしゃいませ。

ホワイト　：しょっき　うりばは　なんがいでしょうか。

案内係　：7かいでございます。

ホワイト　：どうも。

*   *   *

ホワイト：すみません、　しょっき　うりばは　どこでしょうか。

てんいん：はい。　こちらを　ひだりへ　おいでください。

　　　　　そうしますと、　しょうめんに　ございます。

ホワイト：そこを　ひだりへ　いって、　しょうめんですね。

てんいん：はい、　さようでございます。

ホワイト：どうも。

Vocabulary _____

tsukiatari:　dead end, end of the hallway or street　　*sochira:*　that direction, that way

II

シュワルツ：しつれいします。

受付　　　：はい、　いらっしゃいませ。

シュワルツ：きかくぶの　ホワイトさんに　おめにかかりたいんですが…。

受付　　　：はい、　おやくそくでいらっしゃいますか。

シュワルツ：はい、　東京銀行の　シュワルツと　もうします。

受付　　　：しょうしょう　おまちください。

＊　　＊　　＊

受付　　　：おまたせいたしました。

　　　　　　ホワイトの　へやは　11かいでございます。

　　　　　　エレベーターを　おおりになって　みぎがわで　ございます。

シュワルツ：11かいで　エレベーターを　おりて　みぎがわですね。

受付　　　：はい、　さようでございます。

シュワルツ：どうも　ありがとうございました。

＊　　＊　　＊

シュワルツ：しつれいします、

　　　　　　ホワイトさんに　おめにかかりたいんですが…。

日本人　　：こちらの　つきあたりでございます。

シュワルツ：そちらの　つきあたりですね。

日本人　　：はい。

シュワルツ：どうも　ありがとうございました。

Grammar Note 1 — Asking for location in a store or office building

Sumimasen, [Item] (no) uriba wa nan-gai/doko $\begin{cases} \textit{desu ka} \nearrow. \\ \textit{deshō ka} \searrow. \end{cases}$

Sumimasen, kimono no uriba wa nan-gai deshō ka.　　　"Excuse me, which floor is the
　　　　　　　　　　　　　　　　　　　　　　　　　　kimono department on?"

　Uriba means the place or the department where they sell goods. ***-kai*** or ***-gai*** is the counter for the floors.

Example

A:	*Omocha (no) uriba wa nan-gai desu ka.*	"Which floor is the toy department on?"
B:	*Go-kai de gozaimasu.*	"It's on the fifth floor."

Vocabulary: Floors

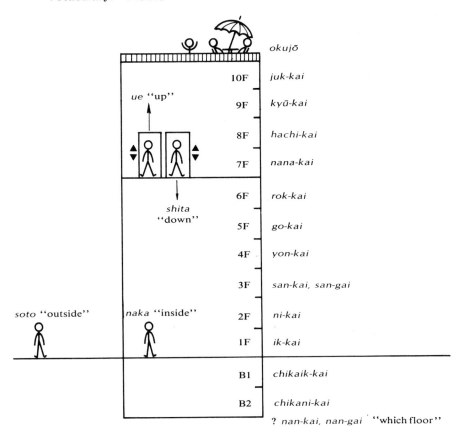

		okujō
	10F	*juk-kai*
ue "up"	9F	*kyū-kai*
	8F	*hachi-kai*
	7F	*nana-kai*
	6F	*rok-kai*
shita "down"	5F	*go-kai*
	4F	*yon-kai*
	3F	*san-kai, san-gai*
soto "outside" *naka* "inside"	2F	*ni-kai*
	1F	*ik-kai*
	B1	*chikaik-kai*
	B2	*chikani-kai*

? *nan-kai, nan-gai* "which floor"

Grammar Note 2 — Giving locations in a store or office building

a. When giving location, use the same patterns you learned in Lesson 16. Here is some more vocabulary for giving directions inside a building.

Vocabulary

Meaning	
facing you right in front of $\}$	*shōmen*
dead end	*tsukiatari*
far end	*oku*
place where Y is	*Y no tokoro*
place/counter where Y is sold $\}$	*Y no uriba*

Examples

X wa Y no uriba no saki desu. — "X is further than the Y counter."

Massugu itte kudasai. — "Go straight ahead."

Sōsuruto, (X wa) migi-gawa ni arimasu. — "Then you'll see X on your right."

Y no tokoro o hidari e itte kudasai. — "Turn left at (the place where) Y (is)."

Sōsuruto, (X wa) oku ni arimasu. — "Then you'll see X at the far end."

b.

V-*te*, [Place] { *ni arimasu.*
                 { *desu.*

Erebētā o orite, shōmen ni arimasu.   ''Get off the elevator, and you'll see it right in front of you. [*Lit.* It'll be facing you.]''

You used this pattern when summing up directions in Lesson 16.
Orimasu is the verb meaning to get off something; *i.e.*, a train, bus, elevator, taxi, *etc*. It takes the marker *o* or ***kara***.
Norimasu means to get on. It takes the marker ***ni***.

Examples

Esukarētā ni norimasu. ⎫ ⟶ *Esukarētā ni notte,*
San-gai made ikimasu.   ⎭   *san-gai made ikimasu.*
Erebētā o orimasu. ⎫ ⟶ *Erebētā o orite,*
Shōmen ni arimasu. ⎭   *shōmen ni arimasu.*

Grammar Note 3 — Giving location in Level 3 speech

It is very often a problem for students because salesclerks or people at information counters use a lot of respectful or formal vocabulary (Level 3), which is unfamiliar.

Here are some typical words and expressions for recognition, not for memorization.

Meaning	Level 2	Level 3
It's [Noun].	[Noun] *desu.*	[Noun] *de gozaimasu.*
It's over there.	*Atchi desu.*	*Achira de gozaimasu.*
(It's) on the 7th floor. ⎫ (This is) the 7th floor. ⎭	*Nana-kai desu.*	*Nana-kai de gozaimasu.*
That's right.	*Sō desu.*	*Sayō de gozaimasu.*
(It's) in/on/at [Noun].	[Noun] *ni arimasu.*	[Noun] *ni gozaimasu.*
(It's) on the 5th floor.	*Go-kai ni arimasu.*	*Go-kai ni gozaimasu.*
(It's) on the right.	*Migi-gawa ni arimasu.*	*Migi-gawa ni gozaimasu.*
Please go.	*Itte kudasai.*	{ *Irashite/irasshatte kudasai.* { *Oide kudasai.*
Please get on.	*Notte kudasai.*	*Onori ni natte kudasai.*
Please get off.	*Orite kudasai.*	*Oori ni natte kudasai.*
if you do so ...	*sōsuruto*	*sōshimasuto*

Grammar Note 4 — Going to a client's office

Here are some Level 3 expressions you need when making a formal visit to someone's office.

a. **[Department]** *no* **[Person]**-*san ni ome ni kakari tai-n desu ga* ...
Kikaku-bu no Howaito-san ni ome ni   ''I'd like to see Mr. White of the
kakari tai-n desu ga ...   Planning Department.''

b. { *O-yakusoku de irasshaimasu ka.*   [Level 3] } ''Do you have an appointment?''
      { *Yakusoku desu ka.*   [Level 2] }

c. *(Watashi wa)* **[Person]**-*san to yakusoku ga arimasu.*   ''I have an appointment with Mr./Ms._____ .''

Drill 1   Repeat the general names of the items you can buy at a department store.

(1)	(2)	(3)
fujin-fuku "women's clothes"	*shin'shi-fuku* "men's clothes"	*kodomo-fuku* "children's clothes"
(4)	(5)	(6)
tōki, shokki "china"	*omocha* "toys"	*bun'bōgu* "stationery"
(7)	(8)	(9)
shokuryōhin "food"	*kagu* "furniture"	*supōtsu-yōhin* "sports goods"
(10)	(11)	(12)
den'ki-seihin "electric appliances"	*shitagi* "underwear"	*kimono* "Japanese *kimono*"
(13)	(14)	(15)
kaban "bags"	*saifu* "wallets, purses"	*megane* "eye glasses"

Drill 2 Make short dialogues using the pictures.

e.g., | A: *Sumimasen, omocha uriba wa nan-gai deshō ka.*
| B: *Go-kai de gozaimasu.*

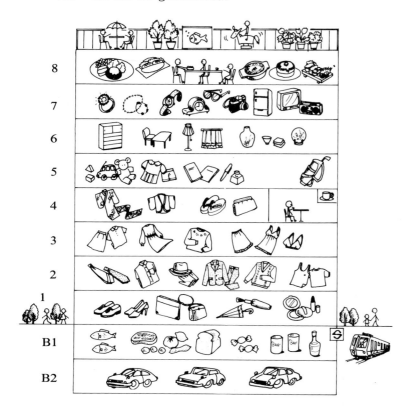

Drill 3

1. Repeat the things/places you may look for in a department store.
2. Ask where things/places are, using _____ **wa doko deshō ka.**

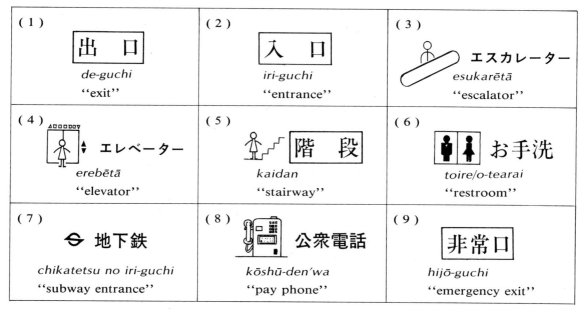

(1)
出 口
de-guchi
"exit"

(2)
入 口
iri-guchi
"entrance"

(3)
エスカレーター
esukarētā
"escalator"

(4)
エレベーター
erebētā
"elevator"

(5)
階 段
kaidan
"stairway"

(6)
お手洗
toire/o-tearai
"restroom"

(7)
地下鉄
chikatetsu no iri-guchi
"subway entrance"

(8)
公衆電話
kōshū-den'wa
"pay phone"

(9)
非常口
hijō-guchi
"emergency exit"

Drill 4

1. Repeat the names of the things you can buy at a supermarket.

2. Ask where you can buy something, using _____ *wa doko* { *ni arimasu* / *desu* } *ka.*

(1)	(2)	(3)
yasai "vegetable"	*niku* "meat"	*sakana* "fish"
(4)	(5)	(9)
o-kashi "sweets, candy"	*kan'zume* "canned food"	*reitō-shokuhin* "frozen food"
(7)	(8)	(9)
tōfu "soy bean curd"	*shōyu* "soy sauce"	*sen'zai* "detergents"

Drill 5 Sum up and confirm the directions.

1. *e.g.,* ⎰ *Kochira o migi e oide kudasai.*
   ⎱ *Sōshimasuto, shōmen ni gozaimasu.*
   ⟶ *Migi e itte, shōmen desu ne.*

(1) *Kochira o hidari e oide kudasai.*
Sōshimasuto, oku ni gozaimasu.

(2) *Sochira e oide kudasai.*
Sōshimasuto, tokei uriba no saki ni gozaimasu.

(3) *Achira no kado o migi e oide kudasai.*
Sōshimasuto, den'wa wa kaidan no tokoro ni gozaimasu.

2. *e.g.,* ⎧ *Kochira o migi e irashite/irasshatte kudasai.*
   ⎨ *Esukarētā ga gozaimasu.*
   ⎩ *Kamera (no uriba) wa esukarētā no saki de gozaimasu.*
   ⟶ *Migi e itte, esukarētā no saki desu ne.*

(1)   *Kochira o hidari e irashite/irasshatte kudasai.*

Omocha uriba ga gozaimasu.

Pen (no uriba) wa omocha uriba no yoko ni gozaimasu.

(2)   *Kochira e oide kudasai.*

Kodomo-fuku uriba ga gozaimasu.

Kodomo-fuku no tokoro o hidari e oide kudasai.

O-tearai wa oku ni gozaimasu.

Drill 6   The pictures show a department store and a supermarket. Suppose you are standing at point X, make short dialogues.

1. *Depāto*

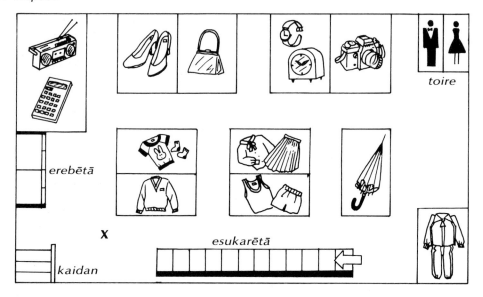

2. *Sūpā*

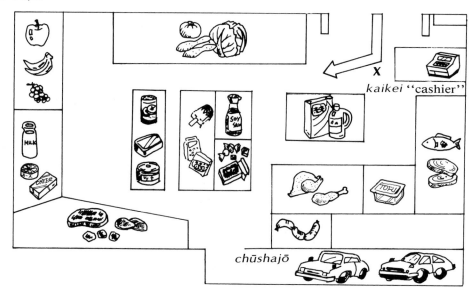

Drill 7   Using Dialogue I as a model, complete the following.

(1)   — At the information counter —

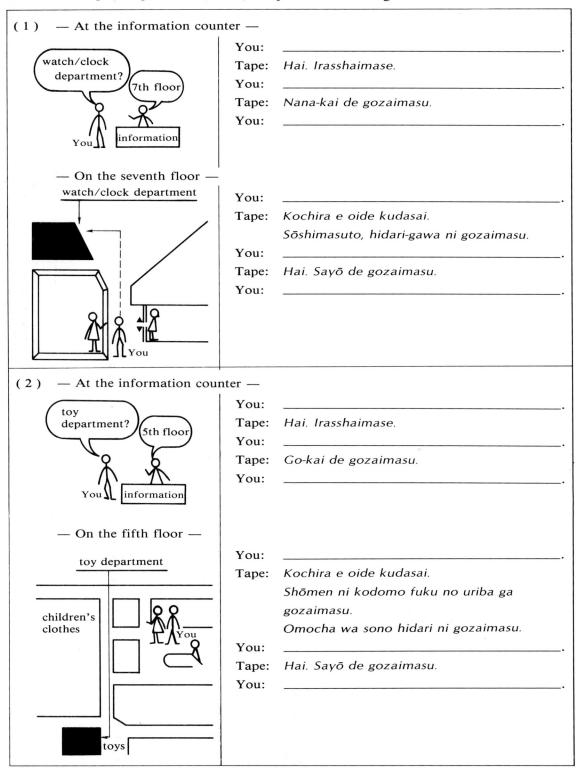

You: _____.
Tape: *Hai. Irasshaimase.*
You: _____.
Tape: *Nana-kai de gozaimasu.*
You: _____.

— On the seventh floor —
watch/clock department

You: _____.
Tape: *Kochira e oide kudasai.*
      Sōshimasuto, hidari-gawa ni gozaimasu.
You: _____.
Tape: *Hai. Sayō de gozaimasu.*
You: _____.

(2)   — At the information counter —

You: _____.
Tape: *Hai. Irasshaimase.*
You: _____.
Tape: *Go-kai de gozaimasu.*
You: _____.

— On the fifth floor —

toy department

You: _____.
Tape: *Kochira e oide kudasai.*
      Shōmen ni kodomo fuku no uriba ga
      gozaimasu.
      Omocha wa sono hidari ni gozaimasu.
You: _____.
Tape: *Hai. Sayō de gozaimasu.*
You: _____.

(3)

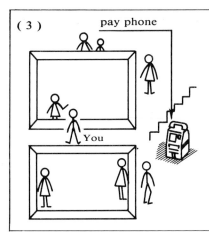

You: _____ .

Tape: *Hai.*

You: _____ .

Tape: *Sochira e oide kudasai.*

Sōshimasuto, kaidan ga gozaimasu.

Kōshū-den'wa wa kaidan no tokoro ni

gozaimasu.

You: _____ .

Tape: *Hai.*

You: _____ .

Information clerks at a department store

China section in a department store

Drill 8   Look at this plan of an office building and substitute the floors and the names of the departments.

📻 *e.g.,* 1. *Ik-kai ni uketsuke ga arimasu.*

   e.g., 2. | A: *Jin'ji-bu wa nangai ni arimasu ka.*
            | B: *Nana-kai desu.*

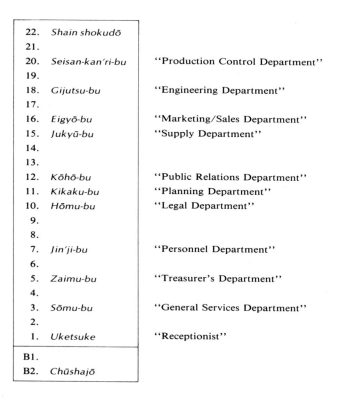

22.	*Shain shokudō*	
21.		
20.	*Seisan-kan'ri-bu*	"Production Control Department"
19.		
18.	*Gijutsu-bu*	"Engineering Department"
17.		
16.	*Eigyō-bu*	"Marketing/Sales Department"
15.	*Jukyū-bu*	"Supply Department"
14.		
13.		
12.	*Kōhō-bu*	"Public Relations Department"
11.	*Kikaku-bu*	"Planning Department"
10.	*Hōmu-bu*	"Legal Department"
9.		
8.		
7.	*Jin'ji-bu*	"Personnel Department"
6.		
5.	*Zaimu-bu*	"Treasurer's Department"
4.		
3.	*Sōmu-bu*	"General Services Department"
2.		
1.	*Uketsuke*	"Receptionist"
B1.		
B2.	*Chūshajō*	

Drill 9   Subsitute the underlined parts.

📻 *e.g.,*   Planning, Mr. White

⟶   1. *Kikaku-bu no Howaito-san ni ome ni kakaritai-n desu ga* ...
   2. *Kikaku-bu no Howaito-san to yakusoku ga arimasu.*

(1)   Legal, Mr. Johnson   (2)   Treasurer's, Mr. Suzuki
(3)   Public Relations, Ms. Okada   (4)   Marketing/Sales, Mr. Uno

Drill 10   Using Dialogue II as a model, complete the following.   —

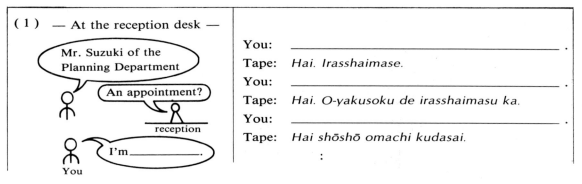

(1)   — At the reception desk —

Mr. Suzuki of the Planning Department

An appointment?

reception

I'm _____.

You

You: _____ .
Tape: *Hai. Irasshaimase.*
You: _____ .
Tape: *Hai. O-yakusoku de irasshaimasu ka.*
You: _____ .
Tape: *Hai shōshō omachi kudasai.*
          :

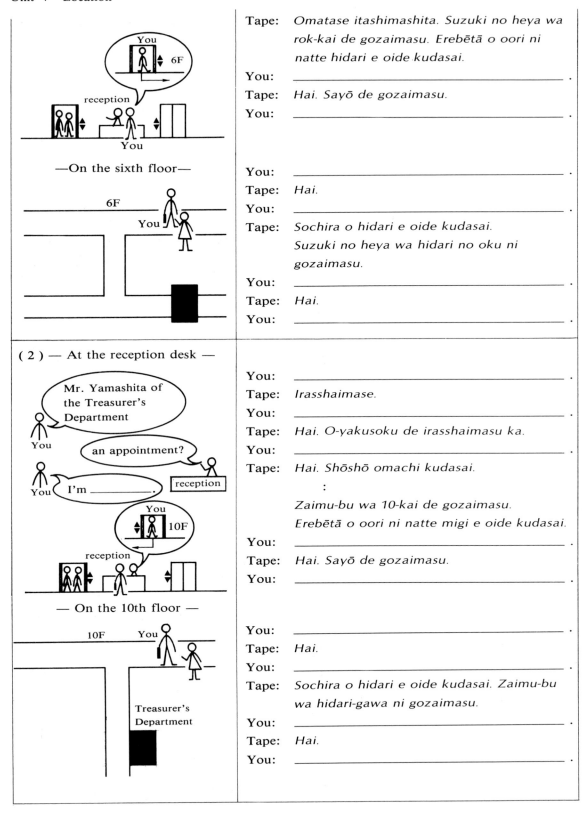

—On the sixth floor—

6F

You

(2) — At the reception desk —

Mr. Yamashita of the Treasurer's Department

You

an appointment?

You I'm _____.

reception

You 10F

reception

— On the 10th floor —

10F You

Treasurer's Department

Tape: *Omatase itashimashita. Suzuki no heya wa rok-kai de gozaimasu. Erebētā o oori ni natte hidari e oide kudasai.*

You: _____ .

Tape: *Hai. Sayō de gozaimasu.*

You: _____ .

You: _____ .

Tape: *Hai.*

You: _____ .

Tape: *Sochira o hidari e oide kudasai. Suzuki no heya wa hidari no oku ni gozaimasu.*

You: _____ .

Tape: *Hai.*

You: _____ .

You: _____ .

Tape: *Irasshaimase.*

You: _____ .

Tape: *Hai. O-yakusoku de irasshaimasu ka.*

You: _____ .

Tape: *Hai. Shōshō omachi kudasai.*

    :

 Zaimu-bu wa 10-kai de gozaimasu. Erebētā o oori ni natte migi e oide kudasai.

You: _____ .

Tape: *Hai. Sayō de gozaimasu.*

You: _____ .

You: _____ .

Tape: *Hai.*

You: _____ .

Tape: *Sochira o hidari e oide kudasai. Zaimu-bu wa hidari-gawa ni gozaimasu.*

You: _____ .

Tape: *Hai.*

You: _____ .

Lesson 18

LOOKING FOR SOMEONE/SOMETHING
— IN A ROOM —

SUMIMASEN, JISHO SHIRIMASEN KA
"EXCUSE ME, DO YOU KNOW WHERE THE DICTIONARY IS?"

Dialogue I

[At the office]

Tanaka: *Sumimasen, jisho shirimasen ka.*
Ōno: *E, eiwa-jiten desu ka.*
Tanaka: *Ē.*
Ōno: *Ano tsukue no ue desu yo.*
Tanaka: *A, dōmo . . .*
       *   *   *
Howaito: *Tanaka-san wa doko deshō ka.*
Ōno: *Kon'pyūtā no tokoro ni imashita yo.*
Howaito: *Demo ima wa imasen ga . . .*
Ōno: *Jā, tabun kaigi-shitsu deshō.*
Howaito: *A, sō desu ka. Dōmo . . .*

Mr. Tanaka: Do you know [*Lit.* Don't you know] where the dictionary is?
Ms. Ono: Excuse me, is it the English-Japanese dictionary (you are looking for)?
Mr. Tanaka: Yes, it is.
Ms. Ono: It's on the desk over there.
Mr. Tanaka: Oh, thanks.
      *   *   *
Mr. White: (I wonder if you know) where Mr. Tanaka is?
Ms. Ono: He was at the computer.
Mr. White: But he's not there...
Ms. Ono: Well then, he's probably in the conference room.
Mr. White: Oh, I see. Thank you.

Vocabulary

jisho: dictionary
shirimasen ← shiru: don't know
eiwa-jiten: English-Japanese dictionary
tsukue: desk
ue: on

kon'pyūtā: computer
imashita ← iru: exist, be [animate]
ima: now
kaigi-shitsu: conference room

🎧 Dialogue II ━━━━━━━━━━━━━━━━━━━━━━━━━━━━━━━━━━━━

[At a delicatessen]

Ten'in: *Irasshaimase.*

Kyaku: *Sumimasen. Kore futa-tsu kudasai.*

Ten'in: *Dore deshō ka.*

Kyaku: *Ichiban shita no hidari kara
san-ban-me no desu.*

Ten'in: *Kore desu ka.*

Kyaku: *Ie, sono migi no desu.*

Ten'in: *Kore desu ne.*

Kyaku: *Ē.*

Ten'in: *Sen-en desu.*

Salesclerk: May I help you? [*Lit.* Welcome.]
Mrs. White: Excuse me, give me two of these,
            please.
Salesclerk: Which one, ma'am?
Mrs. White: I'd like to have the bottom-most one,
            the third from the left.
Salesclerk: Is this the one?
Mrs. White: No, (it's) the next one to the right.
Salesclerk: This is it, isn't it?
Mrs. White: That's right.
Salesclerk: That'll be 1000 yen.

I

田中：すみません、　じしょ　しりませんか。
たなか

大野：えっ、　えいわじてんですか。
おおの

田中：ええ。

大野：あの　つくえの　うえですよ。

田中：あ、　どうも…。

　　　　　　　＊　　　＊　　　＊

ホワイト：田中さんは　どこでしょうか。
　　　　　たなか

大野　　：コンピューターの　ところに　いましたよ。
おおの

ホワイト：でも　いまは　いませんが…。

大野　　：じゃあ、　たぶん　かいぎしつでしょう。

ホワイト：あ、　そうですか。　どうも…。

Vocabulary ━━━━━━━━━━━━━━━━━━━━━━━━━━━━━━━━━━━━

ichiban shita: bottom-most

hidari kara: from the left

san-ban-me: the third (one)

II

てんいん：いらっしゃいませ。

きゃく　：すみません。　これ　2つ　ください。

てんいん：どれでしょうか。

きゃく　：1ばん　したの　ひだりから　3ばんめのです。

てんいん：これですか。

きゃく　：いえ、　そのみぎのです。

てんいん：これですね。

きゃく　：ええ。

てんいん：1,000えんです。

Grammar Note 1 — Asking where things/people are — Inside a room

You have learned:

X *wa doko* $\begin{cases} desu\ ka. \\ deshō\ ka. \end{cases}$ "Where is X?"

Now we introduce another way:

[Item/Person] *(o/wa) shirimasen ka.*

<u>Jisho</u> *shirimasen ka.* "Do you know [*Lit.* Don't you know] where the dictionary is?"

a. ***Shirimasen ka.*** "Do you know? [*Lit.* Don't you know?]"
Use this when asking a colleague, friend, *etc.*, about something.
Shirimasen "do not know" is a negative form. As you have seen in ***arimasen ka*** "is there [*Lit.* isn't there]," the negative form does not imply nuance as in English.

b. Answers to these questions would be:
[Place] *ni arimasu (yo).* "It's over there."
or
[Place] *ni imasu* (yo).* "He/She's over there."
* This will be discussed in Grammar Note 2 below.

Grammar Note 2 — Telling where things/people are — Inside a room

Compare:

[Thing] *wa* [Place] *ni **arimasu**.*
[Person/Animal, Birds, *etc.*] *wa* [Place] *ni **imasu**.*

a. ***Arimasu*** *vs.* ***Imasu*** "There is"
Arimasu "there is" is for inanimate things including trees and flowers, *etc.*
Imasu "there is" is for animate things excluding trees and flowers, *etc.*, and including cars with drivers, *etc.*

b.   Observe how you use the location words:

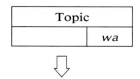

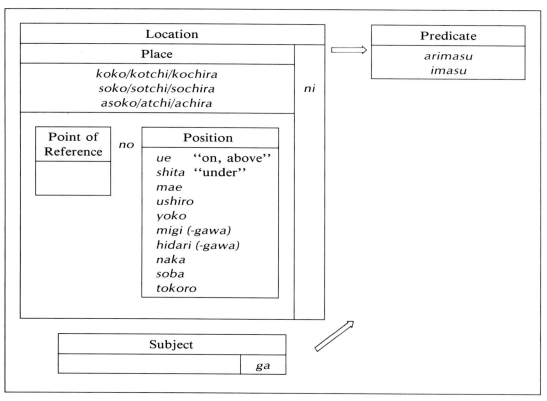

Examples

Asoko ni Tanaka-san ga imasu yo.	"Look, Mr. Tanaka is over there."
Erebētā no mae ni Ōno-san ga imasu yo.	"Look, Ms. Ono is in front of the elevator."
Doa no tokoro ni Sumisu-san ga imasu.	"Mr. Smith is at the door."

A: *Sumisu-san shirimasen ka.*   "Do you know where Mr. Smith is?"

B: *Doa no tokoro* { *ni imasu* / *desu.* } *yo.*   "He is at the door."

A: *Kyō no shin'bun shirimasen ka.*   "Do you know where today's paper is?"

B: *Ano tēburu no ue* { *ni arimasu* / *desu.* } *yo.*   "It's on that table."

Kinō wa tsukue no soba ni arimashita ga ima wa arimasen.   "It was by the desk yesterday but it's not there today."

Sumisu-san wa sakki kaigi-shitsu ni imashita.   "Mr. Smith was in the conference room just a little while ago."

Grammar Note 3 — Describing exact locations in a display or showcase

When you have to describe locations precisely, use combinations of the following patterns:

a. (X *wa*) [Starting Point] *kara* [Number]-*ban-me no desu*.

(X *wa*) <u>hidari</u> *kara* <u>ni</u>-*ban-me no desu*.   "X is the second one from the left."

Examples

ue	*kara*	ichi	-*ban-me no*	"the first one from the top"
shita		ni		"the second one from the bottom"
migi		san		"the third one from the right"
hidari		yon		"the fourth one from the left"
temae		go		"the fifth one from here/me"
oku		roku		"the sixth one from the other end"

Ue kara ni-ban-me no hon desu.   "It's the second book from the top."

Shita kara san-ban-me no desu.   "It's the third one from the bottom."

Hidari kara yon-ban-me no o onegaishimasu.   "I'd like to have the fourth one from the left."

Ue kara ni-ban-me no hidari kara yon-ban-me no o kudasai.   "I'd like the one which is the second from the top and the fourth from the left."

b. (X *wa*) *ichi-ban* [Position] *no desu*.

(X *wa*) *ichi-ban* <u>shita</u> *no desu*.   "X is the one at the bottom."

Examples

ichi-ban	ue	*no*	"the topmost one"
	shita		"the bottom-most one"
	migi		"the extreme right one"
	hidari		"the extreme left one"
	temae		"the closest one"
	oku		"the one in back"

Ichi-ban ue no pan desu.   "It's the loaf/rolls on the top."

Ichi-ban shita no ichi-ban migi no o kudasai.   "I'd like to have the one on the bottom, to the far right."

c. (X *wa*) *man'naka no desu*.   "X is the middle one."

Grammar Note 4 — Expressing probability

***Tabun* [Noun] *deshō*.**

Tabun <u>kaigi-shitsu</u> *deshō*.   "Probably (he is) in the conference room."

We introduced ***deshō*** as an indirect equivalent of ***desu***. Here, we add one more meaning to ***deshō*** — indicating probability. Even without the word ***tabun*** "probably", **[Noun]** + ***deshō*** only can indicate probability.

Examples

A: *Ōno-san wa doko ni imasu ka.*   "Where is Ms. Ono?"
B: *Go-kai deshō.*   "She is probably on the fifth floor."

A: *Jisho wa doko ni arimasu ka.*   "Where is the dictionary?"
B: *Tabun ano kyabinetto no naka deshō.* "It's probably in that cabinet."

Drill 1

1. Look at this floor map of an office building and memorize the names of the rooms.

2. Suppose you are explaining the floor map to someone. Point to the room/place and say:

> *Koko ni _____ ga arimasu.*

3. Make short dialogues.

> *e.g.,* | A: *Ichi-ban no kaigi-shitsu wa doko desu ka.*
> | B: [Pointing] *koko desu.*

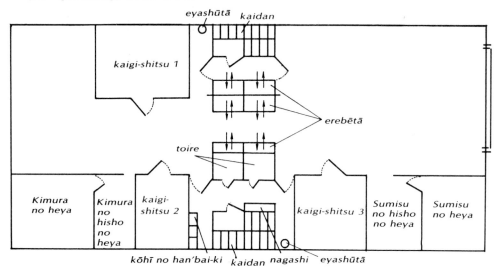

X no heya	"X's room"
X no hisho no heya	"X's secretary's room"
eyashūtā	"air shooter"
nagashi	"sink"
kōhī no han'bai-ki	"coffee vending machine"

Drill 2   Repeat the locations using ***tsukue*** "desk" as a point of reference.

(1)

 tsukue no ue

(2)

 *tsukue no shita*

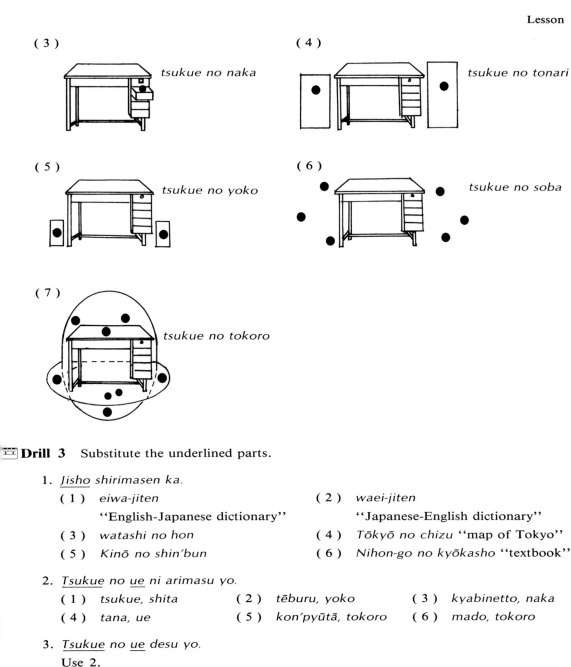

(3) tsukue no naka

(4) tsukue no tonari

(5) tsukue no yoko

(6) tsukue no soba

(7) tsukue no tokoro

Drill 3   Substitute the underlined parts.

1. *Jisho shirimasen ka.*
   - (1) eiwa-jiten
     "English-Japanese dictionary"
   - (2) waei-jiten
     "Japanese-English dictionary"
   - (3) watashi no hon
   - (4) Tōkyō no chizu "map of Tokyo"
   - (5) Kinō no shin'bun
   - (6) Nihon-go no kyōkasho "textbook"

2. *Tsukue no ue ni arimasu yo.*
   - (1) tsukue, shita
   - (2) tēburu, yoko
   - (3) kyabinetto, naka
   - (4) tana, ue
   - (5) kon'pyūtā, tokoro
   - (6) mado, tokoro

3. *Tsukue no ue desu yo.*
   Use 2.

4. *Tabun tsukue no ue deshō.*
   Use 2.

5. *Mae wa mado no tokoro ni arimashita ga, ima wa arimasen.*
   - (1) kinō, kyō
   - (2) chotto mae, ima
   - (3) sen'shū, kon'shū
   - (4) ichi-jikan mae, ima

Drill 4

1. Look at and learn the names of things in an office/room.
2. Suppose you are explaining where things are in this office.
   Point to the thing and say:

   Koko ni _____ ga arimasu.

3. Make short dialogues.

   e.g., A: *Den'wa wa doko ni arimasu ka.*

   B: *Tsukue no ue ni arimasu.*

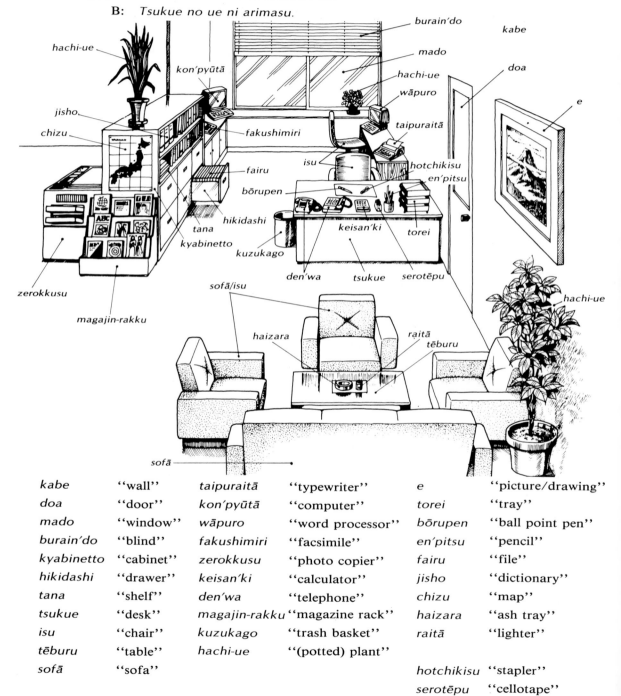

kabe	"wall"	taipuraitā	"typewriter"	e	"picture/drawing"
doa	"door"	kon'pyūtā	"computer"	torei	"tray"
mado	"window"	wāpuro	"word processor"	bōrupen	"ball point pen"
burain'do	"blind"	fakushimiri	"facsimile"	en'pitsu	"pencil"
kyabinetto	"cabinet"	zerokkusu	"photo copier"	fairu	"file"
hikidashi	"drawer"	keisan'ki	"calculator"	jisho	"dictionary"
tana	"shelf"	den'wa	"telephone"	chizu	"map"
tsukue	"desk"	magajin-rakku	"magazine rack"	haizara	"ash tray"
isu	"chair"	kuzukago	"trash basket"	raitā	"lighter"
tēburu	"table"	hachi-ue	"(potted) plant"		
sofā	"sofa"			hotchikisu	"stapler"
				serotēpu	"cellotape"

Drill 5 Using the first of Dialogue I as a model, complete the following.

---

(1)

today's paper?

You

You: _____ .
Tape: *E? Japan Taimuzu desu ka.*
You: _____ .
Tape: *Ano tēburu no ue desu yo.*
You: _____ .

---

(2)

dictionary?

You

No, English-Japanese dictionary.

You: _____ .
Tape: *E? Waei-jiten desu ka.*
You: _____ .
Tape: *Ā, eiwa-jiten wa taipuraitā no tokoro ni arimasu yo.*
You: _____ .

---

(3) [Now you answer]

this week's?

Mr. Tanaka's room

You

Tape: *Taimu "Time Magazine" shirimasen ka.*
You: _____ .
Tape: *Iie, sen'shū no desu.*
You: _____ .
Tape: *A, dōmo arigatō.*

---

(4)

map of Tokyo?

You

top (drawer) of the cabinet

Tape: *Chizu shirimasén ka.*
You: _____ .
Tape: *Iie, Yokohama no desu kedo...*
You: _____ .
Tape: *A, sō desu ka. Dōmo.*

Drill 6   Look at these and learn how to use the position words when answering the question
Tanaka-san wa doko ni imasu ka "Where is Mr. Tanaka?"

(1)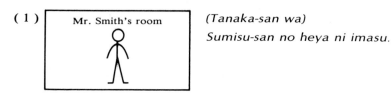

(Tanaka-san wa)
Sumisu-san no heya ni imasu.

(2)

Kaigi-shitsu ni imasu.

(3)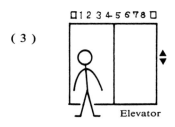

Erebētā no $\left\{\begin{array}{l} tokoro \\ mae \end{array}\right\}$ ni imasu.

(4)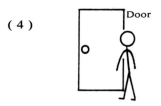

Doa no $\left\{\begin{array}{l} tokoro \\ soba \\ mae \\ yoko \end{array}\right\}$ ni imasu.

(5)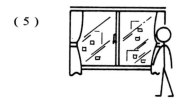

Mado no $\left\{\begin{array}{l} tokoro \\ soba \\ mae \\ yoko \end{array}\right\}$ ni imasu.

(6)

Kon'pyūtā no $\left\{\begin{array}{l} tokoro \\ soba \\ mae \end{array}\right\}$ ni imasu.

(7)

$\left\{\begin{array}{l} Tsukue\ no\ tokoro \\ Seki\ \text{"seat"} \end{array}\right\}$ ni imasu.

Drill 7 Answer the questions.

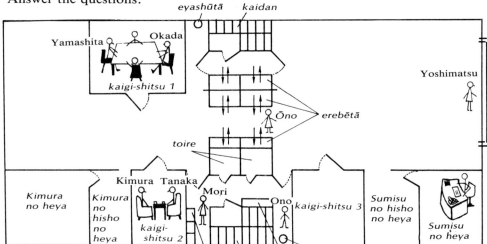

(1) *Sumisu-san wa doko ni imasu ka.*

(2) *Yamashita-san wa doko desu ka.*

(3) *Okada-san wa doko deshō ka.*

(4) *Kimura-san mo ichi-ban no kaigi-shitsu ni imasu ka.*

(5) *Dare ga ni-ban no kaigi-shitsu ni imasu ka.*

(6) *Ōno-san wa doko ni imasu ka.*

(7) *Ono-san mo erebētā no tokoro desu ka.*

(8) *Mori-san wa kaigi-shitsu ni imasu ka.*

(9) *Dare ga mado no tokoro ni imasu ka.*

Drill 8 Answer the questions.

(1) *Kono heya ni hachiue wa arimasu ka.*

(2) *Doko ni arimasu ka.*

(3) *On'na no hito "woman" ga imasu ne. Doko ni imasu ka.*

(4) *Tēburu no ue ni nani ga arimasu ka.*

(5) *Neko "cat" wa doko ni imasu ka.*

(6) *Inu "dog" wa doko ni imasu ka.*

(7) *Kōhī kappu wa doko desu ka.*

Drill 9   Use the second half of Dialogue I as a model, complete the following.

(1)

Mr. Tanaka?

You

You: _____.
Tape: *Seki ni imasu yo.*
You: _____.

(2)

Ms. Ono?

You

But she's not there now.

You: _____.
Tape: *Nana-kai no kaigi-shitsu ni imashita yo.*
You: _____.
Tape: *Jā, tabun go-kai no zerokkusu no tokoro deshō.*
You: _____.

(3)   [Now you answer]

?

Mr. Smith

You

over there

Tape: *Sumisu-san wa doko deshō ka.*
You: _____.
Tape: *Ā, sō desu ne. Dōmo.*

(4)

?

You

Ms. Inoue

Tape: *Inoue-san wa doko deshō ka.*
You: _____.
Tape: *A, sō desu ka. Dōmo.*

(5)

Mr. Oka

He was at his desk just a little while ago.

Mr. White's room

Probably in Mr. White's room.

Mr.Oka

Tape: *Oka-san wa doko ni imasu ka.*
You: _____.
Tape: *Ima wa imasen ga . . .*
You: _____.
Tape: *A, sō desu ka. Dōmo.*

▣ Drill 10

1. Repeat the locations in the displays, looking at the pictures.
2. Make short dialogues.

> e.g., (1) ⟶ | A: *Kore kudasai.*
> | B: *Dore deshō ka.*
> | A: *Ichiban ue no desu.*

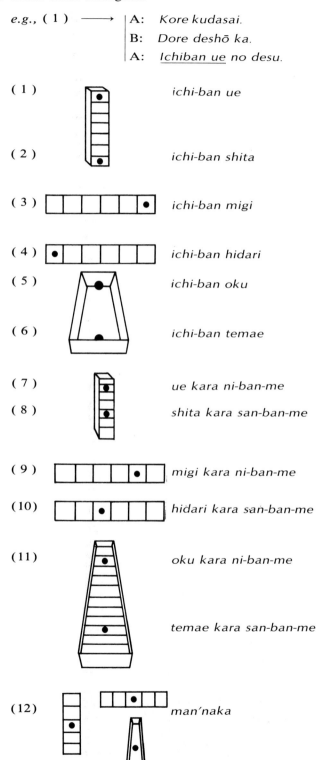

(1) *ichi-ban ue*

(2) *ichi-ban shita*

(3) *ichi-ban migi*

(4) *ichi-ban hidari*

(5) *ichi-ban oku*

(6) *ichi-ban temae*

(7) *ue kara ni-ban-me*

(8) *shita kara san-ban-me*

(9) *migi kara ni-ban-me*

(10) *hidari kara san-ban-me*

(11) *oku kara ni-ban-me*

temae kara san-ban-me

(12) *man'naka*

Drill 11 Describe the location of the thing you would like to buy.

e.g., 1 ⟶ *Ichi-ban ue no (ichi-ban) hidari no desu.*

Drill 12 Use the picture for Drill 11.

e.g., 1. ☐1, Two, please.

⟶ *Ichi-ban ue no (ichi-ban) hidari no (o) futa-tsu onegai shimasu.*

2. ☐1, How much?

⟶ *Ichi-ban ue no (ichi-ban) hidari no wa ikura desu ka.*

(1) ☐2, Three, please.   (2) ☐4, Four hundred grams, please.

(3) ☐5, How much?   (4) ☐6, Two, please.

(5) ☐10, How much?

Drill 13 Substitute the underlined parts.

1. *Kore (o) futa-tsu kudasai.*

  (1) *mit-tsu*   (2) *nihyaku-guramu* "grams"   (3) *ichi-kiro* "kilograms"

2. *Iie, sono migi no desu.*

  (1) *hidari*   (2) *tonari*   (3) *ue*

  (4) *shita*   (5) *temae*   (6) *futa-tsu ue*

Living-dining room
in a Japanese apartment

Drill 14   Using Dialogue II as a model, complete the following.

(1)

[a]

two of this

[b]

this one?

You

[c]   No. the one on the right

[d]   Yes.

Tape:	*Irasshaimase.*
You:	[a]_____.
Tape:	*Dore deshō ka.*
You:	[b]_____.
Tape:	*Kore desu ka.*
You:	[c]_____.
Tape:	*Kore desu ne.*
You:	[d]_____.
Tape:	*Happyaku-en desu.*

(2)

[a]

three of that

[b]

You

[c]   No. the one closer

[d]   Yes.

Tape:	*Irasshaimase.*
You:	[a]_____.
Tape:	*Dore deshō ka.*
You:	[b]_____.
Tape:	*Kore desu ka.*
You:	[c]_____.
Tape:	*Kore desu ne.*
You:	[d]_____.
Tape:	*Sen'gohyaku-en desu.*

(3)

You

[a]   how much?

[b]   How much is the next one?

[c]   No. the one on the left

[d]   Could you show me that one?

[e]   I'll take three of these.

Tape:	*Irasshaimase.*
You:	[a]_____.
Tape:	*San'zen-en de gozaimasu.*
You:	[b]_____.
Tape:	*Kochira* de gozaimasu ka.*
You:	[c]_____.
Tape:	*Kochira* de gozaimasu ne. Nisen-*
	gohyaku-en de gozaimasu ga . . .
You:	[d]_____.
Tape:	*Hai. Dōzo . . .*
You:	[e]_____.
Tape:	*Hai. Arigatō gozaimasu.*

*kochira = polite equivalent of *kore*

247

Drill 15 Additional — Here is a floor plan of a house. You can talk about houses in Japan with your instructor.

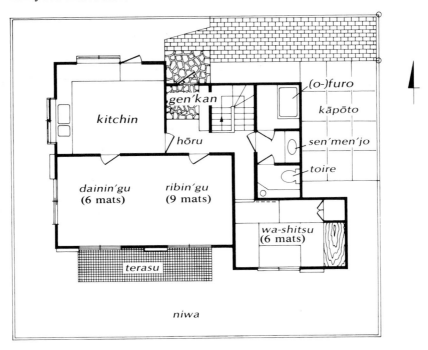

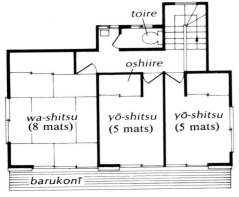

ribin'gu (-rūmu)	} "living room"	gen'kan	"entry way"
ima		hōru	"hall"
dainin'gu (-rūmu)	"dining room"	pōchi	"porch"
beddo (-rūmu)	"bedroom"	kāpōto	"car port"
kitchin	"kitchen"	terasu	"terrace"
(o-)furo, yoku-shitsu	"bath room"	barukonī	"balcony"
sen'men'jo	"Lit. washing hands/face place"	oshiire	"closet"
toire	"toilet"	wa-shitsu	"Japanese style room"
		yō-shitsu	"western style room"
		niwa	"garden"

Katakana is strongly associated with clarity in Japanese. Hence emphasis is expressed in *katakana*, telegrams are written in *katakana* and words with obscure *kanji*, like the names of some birds or trees, are written in *katakana*. (This is to show the reader that while the writer may have forgotten it and the reader may not be able to remember it, he or she at least acknowledges that the *kanji* exists. If the words were written in *hiragana* the reader would be pardoned for thinking the writer uneducated.)

And, as has already been discussed, *katakana* clarifies foreign words. We looked at ways to render English in *katakana* so by now you should, by a process of back-tracking, be able to figure out the following:

>   *nisu   rimokon   hotto   amefuto   patokā   bea*

Clarity? Not to us at any rate. But abbreviation is one obstacle (of the many) to correctly interpreting *katakana* words. As you have surely noticed, English words become terribly expanded when made into syllables, and the Japanese are no different from anyone in wanting to save themselves trouble. So they abbreviate:

>   *nisu/bānisu* — varnish
>   *rimokon/rimōto-kon'torōru* — remote control
>   *hotto/hotto-kōhī* — hot coffee
>   *amefuto/amerikan-futtobōru* — American football
>   *patokā/patorōru kā* — patrol car
>   *bea/bēsu-appu* — base up

So now you know. But what about this "base up" affair? Sure, the words are English but what do they mean? Let's introduce you to another barrier (hilarious, if frustrating) to comprehension — Japlish (*cf.* Franglais, Chinglish), a term defined as English-derived words that have a Japanese meaning, which are moreover thought by the Japanese to have that meaning in English. Therefore they are sometimes transliterated back to "English" much to the mystification of anyone who thought they could speak that language. "Base up" means the raising of the basic rate of pay of employees, negotiated in spring each year.

Other examples are:

>   *chīkudansu* — "cheek dance," a waltz or other close dancing
>   *fanshīkēsu* — "fancy case," a vinyl, zippered clothes closet
>   *dekorēshon kēki* — "decoration cake," a decorated cake
>   *chāmu pointo* — "charm point," the feature a girl considers her most charming

Next on the list are hybrids. These words are half English and half Japanese in structure, and all Japanese in meaning:

>   *nin'gen-dokku* — "human" dock, going in for a full physical exam at the hospital
>   *chūka baikingu* — "Chinese" viking, Chinese food buffet style
>   *saboru* — from *sabotāju suru*, or "do" sabotage, but means play hookey
>   *naui* — "now," an adjective meaning fashionable, modern or up-to-date

Then there are the words that are really far out. These words are narrower than, or broader than, or just different from, the English derivative:

>   *sutōbu* — "stove," a heater or heating appliance
>   *sābisu* — "service," a small extra, like knocking the three yen off your bill
>   *gādo* — "guard," any overhead bridge
>   *waishatsu* — "white shirt," a business or dress shirt of any color

han'doru — "handle," the steering wheel of your car

pointo — "point," the motif on the breast of your sweater

Last but not least, are the words that pose as English but are really taken from other languages, like German, which is most used for medical and scientific terms:

enerugī — energy (Energie)

arerugī — allergy (Allergie)

There is the occasional French:

hire — fillet (filet)

an'kēto — questionnaire (enquête)

And there is the occasional faux pas:

shū kurīmu — chou á la créme, those custard-filled pastries, which are often mistakenly billed as "shoe cream!"

So now you should be prepared to tackle anything. Cut your teeth on the following if you feel you need practice before going out into the real world (and collecting your own list):

1. shō-ene	*2. bakku-mirā*	*3. en-suto*
4. pan'ku-suru	*5. toran'su*	*6. mēdē*
7. eroguro	*8. sākasu*	*9. arakaruto*
10. katto-ban	*11. an'shin'jiraburu*	*12. manē jōhō*

ANSWERS

1. *shōenerugī* — saving energy (*shō* = to conserve)
2. "back mirror" — rear-view mirror
3. *enjin sutoppu* — "engine stop," said whenever a train is delayed, for whatever reason, engine failure or not.
4. to get a puncture, a flat
5. short for transformer (of electricity)
6. "May Day" doesn't mean SOS. It is May 1 when the labor unions start protesting
     on the streets for higher wages.
7. "grotesque erotica," speaks for itself
8. circus
9. á la carte
10. "cut bandage" meaning band aids
11. very slangy, unbelievable (*shin'jiru* means to believe)
12. "money information," that is, financial investment information

Unit VI

Transportation

SCOPE OF UNIT VI

The main function of Unit VI is USING TRANSPORTATION.

Lesson 19 deals with asking and telling how long it takes to get from one place to another.

Lesson 20 gives you expressions useful in planning a bus or train trip. It also gives you more practice in making requests.

Lesson 21 covers the expressions related to finding the right train track and bus number and asking how much further it is to your destination.

251

Lesson 19

ASKING/TELLING HOW LONG IT TAKES TO GET TO A PLACE

SHIN'ŌSAKA MADE DONO GURAI KAKARU DESHŌ KA
"HOW LONG DOES IT TAKE TO GET TO SHIN'OSAKA?"

Dialogue I

[At the station, Mr. Smith asks a station employee questions.]

Sumisu:	Sumimasen.
Ekiin:	Hai.
Sumisu:	Shin'ōsaka made dono gurai kakaru deshō ka.
Ekiin:	Hikari de wa san-jikan hap-pun de, Kodama de wa yo-jikan go-fun desu.
Sumisu:	Sumimasen, mō ichido onegai shimasu. Hikari de wa dono gurai desu ka.
Ekiin:	San-jikan hap-pun desu.
Sumisu:	Ā, sō desu ka. Dōmo arigatō gozaimashita.
Ekiin:	Hai.

Mr. Smith:	Excuse me.
Station Employee:	Yes. (May I help you?)
Mr. Smith:	How long does it take to get to Shin'osaka (Station)?
Station Employee:	(It takes) three hours and eight minutes by Hikari, or four hours and five minutes by Kodama (to get to Shin'osaka Station).
Mr. Smith:	Sorry, can you repeat that again, please? How long does it take by Hikari?
Station Employee:	Three hours and eight minutes.
Mr. Smith:	Oh, I see. Thank you very much.
Station Employee:	You're welcome.

Bullet train
shinkansen

Vocabulary

Shin'ōsaka: New Osaka (Sta.)
dono gurai: how long
kakaru deshō ka: does it take?
Hikari: Super express bullet train
     [*Lit.* lightning]

Kodama: Limited express bullet train
     [*Lit.* echo]
mō ichido: once again

Dialogue II

[Mr. White interrupts Ms. Ono while she is working at her desk to ask a few questions.]

Howaito: *Ōno-san, chotto ii desuka.*

Ōno: *Ē, dōzo.*

Howaito: *Kon'do Nikkō made ikitai-n desu ga,*
den'sha de wa dono gurai kakaru deshō ka.

Ōno: *Asakusa kara Tōbu tokkyū de ni-jikan gurai*
desu yo.

Howaito: *Ni-jikan desu ka. Kuruma de wa dono gurai*
deshō ka.

Ōno: *Heijitsu wa yo-jikan gurai desu kedo...*

Howaito: *Yasumi no hi wa...*

Ōno: *Yasumi no hi wa jikan ga kakarimasu yo.*
Sō desu nē. Roku-jikan kara hachi-jikan gurai
kakaru deshō.

Howaito: *Sō desu kā...* ⟷ Howaito: *Demo yappari kuruma de*
jā, den'sha de ikimasu.   *ikimasu.*
Dōmo arigatō.   *Dōmo arigatō.*

Ōno: *Iie.*

Mr. White:	May I interrupt for a moment, Ms. Ono?
	[*Lit.* Ms. Ono, is it all right for a moment?]
Ms. Ono:	Sure, go ahead.
Mr. White:	I'd like to go to Nikko in the near future, but how long does it take (to get there) by train?
Ms. Ono:	It will probably take about two hours by Tobu limited express from Asakusa.
Mr. White:	Oh (it takes) two hours! How long does it take by car?
Ms. Ono:	It takes four hours on weekdays, but...
Mr. White:	(What about) on the weekend(?)
Ms. Ono:	On the weekend it'll take more time (to get there). Well, let me see...it'll probably take six to eight hours.

Mr. White: Is that so? ⟷ Mr. White: Well, then I'll go by
Well, then I'll take   car just as I planned.
the train. Thank you   Thank you very much.
very much.

Ms. Ono: Not at all.

Vocabulary

tokkyū: limited express train

heijitsu: week day

jikan ga kakarimasu yo: it'll take time

yappari: just as I planned, or thought

I

スミス　：すみません。

えきいん：はい。

スミス　：新大阪まで　どのぐらい　かかるでしょうか。
　　　　　しん おお さか

えきいん：ひかりでは　3じかん　8ぷんで、　こだまでは　4じかん

　　　　　　　5ふんです。

スミス　：すみません、　もういちど　おねがいします。

　　　　　ひかりでは　どのぐらいですか。

えきいん：3じかん　8ぷんです。

スミス　：ああ、　そうですか。　どうも　ありがとうございました。

えきいん：はい。

II

ホワイト：大野さん、　ちょっと　いいですか。
　　　　　おお の

大野　　：ええ、　どうぞ。

ホワイト：こんど　日光まで　いきたいんですが、
　　　　　　　　にっこう

　　　　　でんしゃでは　どのぐらい　かかるでしょうか。

大野　　：浅草から　東武特急で　2じかんぐらいですよ。
　　　　　あさくさ　　とう ぶ とっきゅう

ホワイト：2じかんですか。　くるまでは　どのぐらいでしょうか。

大野　　：へいじつは　4じかんぐらいですけど……。

ホワイト：やすみのひは…。

大野　　：やすみのひは　じかんが　かかりますよ。

　　　　　そうですねえ。　6じかんから　8じかんぐらい　かかるでしょう。

ホワイト：そうですか…。　　　　　　　　　⟵　ホワイト：でも　やっぱり

　　　　　じゃあ、　でんしゃで　いきます。　　　　　くるまで

　　　　　どうも　ありがとう。　　　　　　　　　　いきます。

大野　　：いいえ。　　　　　　　　　　　　　　　　どうも

　　　　　　　　　　　　　　　　　　　　　　　　ありがとう。

Grammar Note 1 — Asking how long it takes to go somewhere

[Starting point] *kara* [Destination] *made* [Means] *de dono gurai* $\begin{cases} \textit{kakarimasu ka} \nearrow. \\ \textit{kakaru deshō ka} \searrow. \end{cases}$

Tōkyō kara <u>Nikkō</u> *made* <u>kuruma</u> *de dono gurai* $\begin{cases} \textit{kakarimasu ka.} \\ \textit{kakaru deshō ka.} \end{cases}$

　　"How long $\begin{cases} \text{does it take} \\ \text{do you think it will take} \end{cases}$ from Tokyo to Nikko by car?"

Starting Point	
Tōkyō	kara

Predicate	Final
kakarimasu	ka ↗
kakaru deshō	ka ↘

Ending Point	
Nikkō	made

Means	
kuruma	de

Amount of Time
dono gurai

a. **Kakari masu ka ↗.**   "Does it take?"
   Kakaru deshō ka ↘.   "Does it take?, do you think it'll take?"

   Kakaru deshō ka is more indirect or uncertain therefore a more polite sounding way than **kakarimasu ka** just as you have seen in **deshō ka** and **desu ka**.
   The verb form **kakaru deshō** is new but the grammar is not explained here because of its complexity.

b. Replacing **kakari masu** with **desu**
   kakaru deshō with **deshō**

   If what the verb means is clear from the context, you get:

   Dono gurai {*kakarimasu* / ↓ / *desu*} *ka.*   "How long does it take?"

   and

   Dono gurai {*kakaru deshō* / ↓ / *deshō*} *ka.*   "How long does it take?"
                                                          "How long do you think it'll take?"

   Examples

   Koko kara dono gurai {*kakarimasu* / ↓ / *desu*} *ka.*   "How long does it take from here?

   Sen'dai made dono gurai {*kakaru deshō* / ↓ / *deshō*} *ka.* "How long do you think it'll take to Sendai?"

Grammar Note 2 — Answering about how long it takes to go somewhere

a. **[Amount of Time]** *(gurai)* {**kakarimasu.** / **kakaru deshō.**}

   Ichi-jikan gurai {*kakarimasu.* / *kakaru deshō.*}   "It takes about an hour."
                                                             "It think it'll take about an hour."

   You can replace the verb with **desu** or **deshō**.

b. ***Ni-san-jikan***   "two to three hours"

In Lesson 13, you learned ***ni-san-kai***   "two or three times"   (Grammar Note 3–b).
This time, add ***-jikan*** "hours" or ***-pun*** "minutes," *etc.*, instead of ***-kai*** "times."

Meaning	
1 to 2 hours	*ichi-ni-jikan*
2 to 3 hours	*ni-san-jikan*
3 to 4 hours	*san-yo*-jikan*
4 to 5 hours	*shi*-go-jikan*
5 to 6 hours	*go-roku-jikan*
:	
:	
1 to 2 minutes	*ichi-ni-fun*
2 to 3 minutes	*ni-san-pun*
3 to 4 minutes	*san-yon-pun**
4 to 5 minutes	*shi*-go-fun*
5 to 6 minutes	*go-rop-pun*
:	
:	
20 to 30 minutes	*ni-san-jup-pun*
30 to 40 minutes	*san-yon*-jup-pun*
40 to 50 minutes	*shi*-go-jup-pun*
50 to 60 minutes	*go-roku-jup-pun*
:	

* Be careful of the pronunciation

c.   **[Minimum Number]** *kara* **[Maximum Number]**

Ichi-ji kan han kara *ni-jikan*   "from 1½ to 2 hours"

Meaning	
from 3 to 5 hours	*san-jikan kara go-jikan*
from 1 hour 15 minutes to 1½ hours	*ichi-jikan jūgo-fun kara ichi-jikan han*
from 10 to 15 minutes	*jup-pun kara jūgo-fun*

Examples

A: *Sen'dai made hikōki de dono gurai kakarimasu ka.*   "How long does it take to Sendai by plane?"
B: *Ichi-jikan gurai desu yo.*   "About an hour."

A: *Hiroshima made dono gurai kakaru deshō ka.*   "How long do you think it'll take to Hiroshima?"
B: *Go-roku-jikan deshō.*   "Maybe five or six hours."

A: *Roppon'gi made dono gurai deshō ka.*   "How long do you think it'll take to Roppongi?"
B: *Jūgo-fun kara nijup-pun gurai deshō.*   "Maybe about fifteen to twenty minutes."

Grammar Note 3 — Expressions to show that it takes time to do something

Here we introduce two expressions without using the amount of time:

a. **Jikan ga kakarimasu.**   "It takes (a lot of) time."

Subject			Predicate
Jikan	*ga*	⟹	*kakarimasu*

b. **(Michi ga) komimasu.**   "(The street/road) gets congested."

These expressions are often preceded by ———— *wa.*

Examples

Rasshu-awā wa jikan ga kakarimasu yo.	"It takes time during rush hour."
Yasumi no hi wa komimasu yo.	"It gets crowded on holidays."
Kuruma wa jikan ga kakarimasu.	"It takes time by car."

This diagram shows all the markers for this lesson.

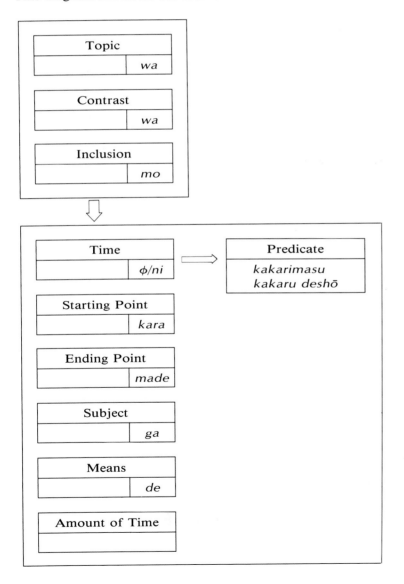

Grammar Note 4 — Asking if you can interrupt someone for a moment

X-san, chotto ii desu ka.   "May I interrupt you for a moment, Mr./Ms. X?"

You have seen a lot of ***ii desu*** in different meanings. (*cf.* Lesson 24, Grammar Note 12)
Ii desu ka is used in asking for someone's permission. It can mean:

May I interrupt you?
May I borrow your dictionary?
May I come in?
May I use the phone?

and so on.

Observe how variations of ***ii desu ka*** is used after ***sumimasen***, which you learned in Lesson 5.

	Attract attention	Asking for permission to interrupt	Response	Meaning
L.1	[Name]＋*san* ↗	*Chotto ii* ↗	*Un, ii yo* ↗ [m] *Ē, ii wa yo* ↗ [f]	Is it OK to interrupt for a moment?...Sure.
L.2	[Name]＋*san* ↗ *Sumimasen* *Shitsurei shimasu*	*Chotto ii desu ka* ↗ *Chotto yoroshii desu ka* ↗	*Ē, dōzo* *Hai*	Excuse me. May I interrupt you for a moment?
L.3	*Shitsurei itashimasu*	*Yoroshii deshō ka* ↘	*Hai*	...Yes, you may.

The responses in Level-1 show expressions used by men [m] and women [f].

Grammar Note 5 — Stating a decision after thinking it over

Sorejā "Well, then"	(*yappari**)	⟹	How you have decided to go
Demo "In spite of that"			

*Yappari means "After thinking it over or just as I'd planned or thought ..."

Examples

Sorejā, yappari den'sha de ikimasu.   "Well, then, I'll take the train,
                                               just as I'd planned."

Demo, yappari ashita ikimasu.   "In spite of that, I'll go
                                        tomorrow, just as I'd planned."

Drill 1   Substitue the underlined parts.

Tōkyō kara Kyōto made shin'kan'sen de dono gurai { kakarimasu ka.
                                                  { kakaru deshō ka.

(1)   Tōkyō, Hokkaidō, hikōki   (2)   Ōsaka, Kyōto, kuruma
(3)   Nihon, Hawai, fune   (4)   Shibuya, Gin'za, chikatetsu
(5)   koko, Kōkyo "Imperial Palace", aruite

Drill 2   Translate and substitute the underlined parts.

1.   e.g.,   1½ hours ⟶   Ichi-jikan han { kakarimasu.
                                           { kakaru deshō.

(1)   1 hour   (2)   about 3 hours   (3)   about 15 minutes

2.   e.g.,   1 or 2 hours ⟶   Ichi-ni-jikan { kakarimasu.
                                              { kakaru deshō.

(1)   2 or 3 hours   (2)   4 or 5 minutes   (3)   20 or 30 minutes

3.   e.g.,   from 1½ hours to 2 hours ⟶   Ichi-jikan han kara ni-jikan { kakarimasu.
                                                                         { kakaru deshō.

(1)   from 3 to 5 hours   (2)   from 10 to 15 minutes
(3)   from 45 minutes to 1 hour

Drill 3   Replace the underlined part with **desu** or **deshō**.

e.g.,   Nikkō made dono gurai kakarimasu ka.
   ⟶   Nikkō made dono gurai desu ka.

(1)   Aomori made kuruma de dono gurai kakarimasu ka.
(2)   Itō made kyūkō de dono gurai kakaru deshō ka.
(3)   Shin'ōsaka made san-jikan han gurai kakarimasu.
(4)   Yokohama kara ichi-jikan gurai kakaru deshō.

Drill 4   Complete the conversation following the example.

e.g.,

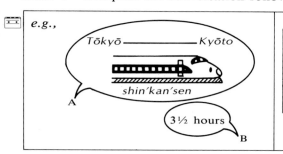

A: Tōkyō kara Kyōto made shin'kan'sen de dono gurai kakaru deshō ka.
B: San-jikan han desu.
A: San-jikan han desu ka.
B: Ē.

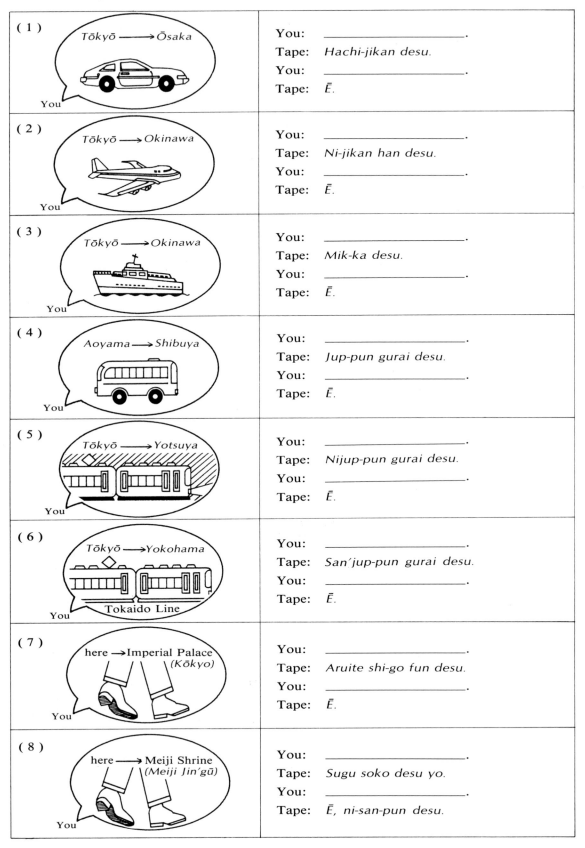

(1)   *Tōkyō* ⟶ *Ōsaka*

You
You: _____.
Tape: *Hachi-jikan desu.*
You: _____.
Tape: *Ē.*

(2)   *Tōkyō* ⟶ *Okinawa*

You
You: _____.
Tape: *Ni-jikan han desu.*
You: _____.
Tape: *Ē.*

(3)   *Tōkyō* ⟶ *Okinawa*

You
You: _____.
Tape: *Mik-ka desu.*
You: _____.
Tape: *Ē.*

(4)   *Aoyama* ⟶ *Shibuya*

You
You: _____.
Tape: *Jup-pun gurai desu.*
You: _____.
Tape: *Ē.*

(5)   *Tōkyō* ⟶ *Yotsuya*

You
You: _____.
Tape: *Nijup-pun gurai desu.*
You: _____.
Tape: *Ē.*

(6)   *Tōkyō* ⟶ *Yokohama*
Tokaido Line

You
You: _____.
Tape: *San'jup-pun gurai desu.*
You: _____.
Tape: *Ē.*

(7)   here ⟶ Imperial Palace
(*Kōkyo*)

You
You: _____.
Tape: *Aruite shi-go fun desu.*
You: _____.
Tape: *Ē.*

(8)   here ⟶ Meiji Shrine
(*Meiji Jin'gū*)

You
You: _____.
Tape: *Sugu soko desu yo.*
You: _____.
Tape: *Ē, ni-san-pun desu.*

Drill 5   Make questions, using **wa** for contrast.

> *e.g.,*   *shin'kan'sen, kuruma.*
>
> ⟶ ⎰ *Shin'kan'sen de wa dono gurai kakaru deshō ka.*
> ⎱ *Kuruma de wa dono gurai deshō ka.*

(1)   *chikatetsu, kuruma*   (2)   *den'sha, hikōki*

(3)   *basu, takushī*   (4)   *kyūkō* "express", *tokkyū* "special express"

(5)   *Hikari, Kodama*

Drill 6   Combine the two sentences.

> *e.g.,* ⎰ *Den'sha de wa sanjup-pun desu.*
> ⎱ *Kuruma de wa gojup-pun desu.*
>
> ⟶   *Den'sha de wa sanjup-pun de, kuruma de wa gojup-pun desu.*

(1)   *Kyūkō de wa ni-jikan han desu.*
　　　　Tokkyū de wa ni-jikan desu.

(2)   *Chikatetsu de wa jūni-san-pun desu.*
　　　　Kuruma de wa ni-san-jup-pun desu.

(3)   *Basu de wa jūgo-fun kara nijup-pun deshō.*
　　　　Takushī de wa jup-pun gurai deshō.

Drill 7   Look at the cues and make dialogues.

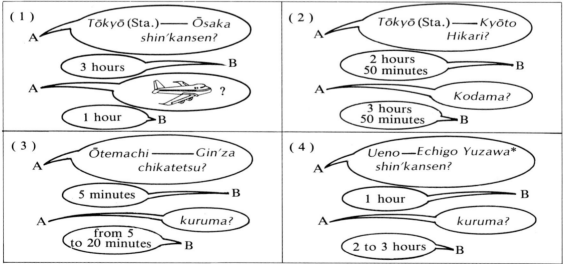

e.g.

Tōkyō (Sta.) ── Ōsaka shin'kansen?　A

3½ hours ── B

A　🚗 ?

8 hours ── B

A:　*Tōkyō kara Ōsaka made shin'kan'sen de wa dono gurai kakaru deshō ka.*
B:　*San-jikan han gurai desu.*
A:　*Kuruma de wa dono gurai deshō ka.*
B:　*Kuruma de wa hachi-jikan gurai deshō.*

(1)   Tōkyō (Sta.) ── Ōsaka shin'kansen?   A
3 hours ── B
A　✈ ?
1 hour ── B

(2)   Tōkyō (Sta.) ── Kyōto Hikari?   A
2 hours 50 minutes ── B
A　Kodama?
3 hours 50 minutes ── B

(3)   Ōtemachi ── Gin'za chikatetsu?   A
5 minutes ── B
A　kuruma?
from 5 to 20 minutes ── B

(4)   Ueno ── Echigo Yuzawa* shin'kansen?   A
1 hour ── B
A　kuruma?
2 to 3 hours ── B

*ski resort

Drill 8   Using Dialogue I, complete the following. Write down how long it takes in the bubble of the cue.

(1) — You are on the platform of the Tohoku Shinkansen at Ueno Station. There are two types of bullet trains: *Yamabiko* and *Aoba*—

You: _____ .
Tape: *Hai.*
You: _____ .
Tape: *Yamabiko wa ni-jikan san-pun de, Aoba wa ni-jikan san'jūni-fun desu.*
You: _____ .
Tape: *Ni-jikan san-pun desu.*
You: _____ .
Tape: *Hai.*

(2) — You want to get on the Joetsu Shinkansen. There are two types of bullet trains: *Asahi* and *Toki*—

You: _____ .
Tape: *Hai.*
You: _____ .
Tape: *Tsugi no Asahi wa ni-jikan nana-fun de, (tsugi no) Toki wa ni-jikan nijup-pun desu.*
You: _____ .
Tape: *Ni-jikan nana-fun desu.*
You: _____ .
Tape: *Hai.*

Drill 9   Substitute the underlined parts.

1. <u>Asa</u> *wa jikan ga kakarimasu yo.*
2. <u>Asa</u> *wa komimasu yo.*

(1)   *hiru goro*
(2)   *ku-ji goro made*
(3)   *hachi-ji goro kara ku-ji goro made*
(4)   *rasshu-awā* "rush hour"
(5)   *kono jikan* "this hour (of the day)"
(6)   *ame no hi* "rainy days"
(7)   *yasumi no hi* "holidays (including Sundays)"
(8)   *heijitsu* "weekdays"
(9)   *shūmatsu* "weekend"
(10)   *kōsoku* "expressway" *no iri-guchi*

Drill 10 Look at the cues and make dialogues.

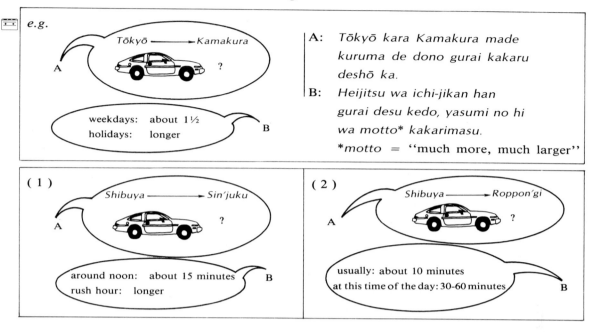

e.g.

Tōkyō ——→ Kamakura

weekdays: about 1½
holidays: longer

A: Tōkyō kara Kamakura made
    kuruma de dono gurai kakaru
    deshō ka.
B: Heijitsu wa ichi-jikan han
    gurai desu kedo, yasumi no hi
    wa motto* kakarimasu.
    *motto = "much more, much larger"

(1)

Shibuya ——→ Sin'juku

around noon: about 15 minutes
rush hour: longer

(2)

Shibuya ——→ Roppon'gi

usually: about 10 minutes
at this time of the day: 30-60 minutes

Drill 11 Using Dialogue II as a model, complete the following.

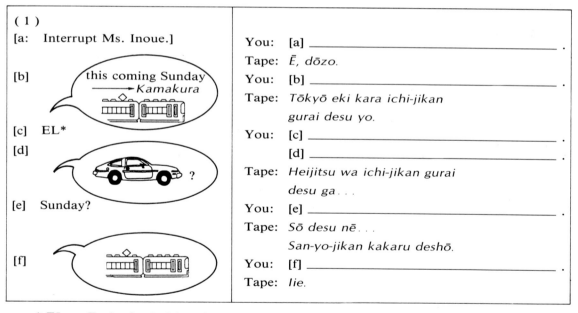

(1)
[a: Interrupt Ms. Inoue.]

[b] this coming Sunday
     ——→ Kamakura

[c] EL*
[d]

[e] Sunday?

[f]

You: [a] _____ .
Tape: Ē, dōzo.
You: [b] _____ .
Tape: Tōkyō eki kara ichi-jikan
       gurai desu yo.
You: [c] _____ .
      [d] _____ .
Tape: Heijitsu wa ichi-jikan gurai
       desu ga. . .
You: [e] _____ .
Tape: Sō desu nē. . .
       San-yo-jikan kakaru deshō.
You: [f] _____ .
Tape: Iie.

* EL = Enthusiastic Listening

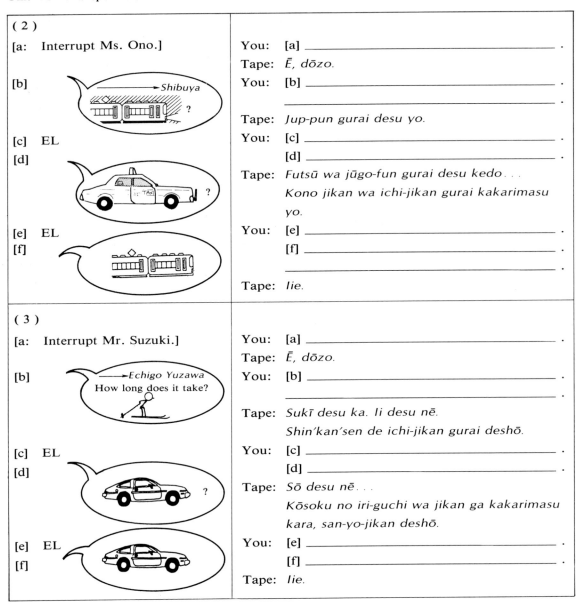

(2)

[a: Interrupt Ms. Ono.]

You: [a] _____ .

Tape: *Ē, dōzo.*

You: [b] _____ .
_____ .

[b]   → Shibuya

Tape: *Jup-pun gurai desu yo.*

[c]   EL

You: [c] _____ .

[d]

[d] _____ .

Tape: *Futsū wa jūgo-fun gurai desu kedo...*
*Kono jikan wa ichi-jikan gurai kakarimasu
yo.*

[e]   EL

You: [e] _____ .

[f]

[f] _____ .
_____ .

Tape: *Iie.*

(3)

[a: Interrupt Mr. Suzuki.]

You: [a] _____ .

Tape: *Ē, dōzo.*

[b]   → Echigo Yuzawa
How long does it take?

You: [b] _____ .
_____ .

Tape: *Sukī desu ka. Ii desu nē.*
Shin'kan'sen de ichi-jikan gurai deshō.

[c]   EL

You: [c] _____ .

[d]

[d] _____ .

Tape: *Sō desu nē...*
*Kōsoku no iri-guchi wa jikan ga kakarimasu
kara, san-yo-jikan deshō.*

[e]   EL

You: [e] _____ .

[f]

[f] _____ .

Tape: *Iie.*

Lesson 20

ASKING/TELLING HOW TO GET TO A PLACE

SHIN'JUKU KARA CHŪŌ-SEN DE MATSUMOTO MADE ITTE KUDASAI
"TAKE THE CHUO LINE FROM SHINJUKU TO MATSUMOTO."

Dialogue

Howaito:	Tanaka-san, chotto oshiete kuremasen ka.
Tanaka:	Hai, nan deshō ka.
Howaito:	Kon'do Kamikōchi e ikitai-n desu ga, dō ittara ii deshō ka.
Tanaka:	Sō desu nē, Kamikōchi wa Matsumoto kara Shin'shimashima e itte basu desu ga, Matsumoto made wa wakarimasu ka.
Howaito:	Chotto wakarimasen ga...
Tanaka:	Otaku wa Minami Azabu deshita yo ne. [Unfolding the map]
Tanaka:	Sorejā, mazu Shin'juku made itte...
Howaito:	Hai.
Tanaka:	Shin'juku kara Chūōhon-sen de Matsumoto made itte kudasai.
Howaito:	Hai.
Tanaka:	Sorekara Matsumoto de Matsumoto Den'tetsu ni norikaete Shin'shimashima made itte kudasai.
Howaito:	Shin'shimashima desu ka.
Tanaka:	Ē. Shin'shimashima de Kamikōchi-yuki no basu ni notte shūten de orimasu.
Howaito:	Sumimasen ga, rōma-ji de kaite kuremasen ka.
Tanaka:	Ii desu yo.

Vocabulary

oshiete ← oshieru: teach, inform
Nan deshō ka: What can I do for you?
  [*Lit.* I wonder what it is?]
Dō ittara ii deshō ka: How could I get to...?
mazu: first (of all)
Kamikōchi: place name in Nagano Pref.
Chūōhon-sen: the main Chuo Line
  [long distance train]
norikaete ← norikaeru: transfer, change
Matsumoto: place name in Nagano Pref.

Shin'shimashima: place name in Nagano Pref.
Matsumoto Den'tetsu: Matsumoto Railway (Co.)
Kamikōchi-yuki: bound for Kamikochi
notte ← noru: get on, take
shūten: the last stop, station
orimasu ← oriru: get off
rōma-ji: Romanization, Roman letters
kaite ← kaku: write

[Looking at the directions written in Romanized letters]

Howaito: *Shin'juku kara Chūōhon-sen de Matsumoto made itte,*
              Matsumoto Den'tetsu ni norikaete Shin'shimashima made
              itte Kamikōchi-yuki no basu de shūten desu ne.

Tanaka: *Ē, sō desu.*

Howaito: *Zen'bu de dono gurai kakaru deshō ka.*

Tanaka: *Sō desu nē..., go-jikan gurai deshō.*

Howaito: *Dōmo iroiro arigatō.*

Tanaka: *Iie, itsu demo dōzo.*

Mr. White:	Mr. Tanaka, could you please tell me something?
Mr. Tanaka:	Yes, what can I do for you?
Mr. White:	I'd like to go to Kamikochi one of these days..., how can I get there?
Mr. Tanaka:	Let's see..., to get to Kamikochi you go to Shinshimashima from Matsumoto by bus, but do you know how to get to Matsumoto?
Mr. White:	I'm not sure.
Mr. Tanaka:	(As I recall, you said that) you lived in Minami Azabu, right?

Mr. Tanaka: Well, then. Go to Shinjuku first...
Mr. White: Yes, (go on).
Mr. Tanaka: Take the main Chuo Line from Shinjuku to Matsumoto.
Mr. White: O.K.
Mr. Tanaka: Then, transfer to Matsumoto Railway at Matsumoto and go to Shinshimashima.
Mr. White: That's Shinshimashima?
Mr. Tanaka: That's right. Get on the bus bound for Kamikochi at Shinshimashima and get off at the last stop.
Mr. White: Sorry (to bother you), but could you write it down for me in Roman letters?
Mr. Tanaka: Oh, O.K.

Mr. White: I take the main Chuo Line from Shinjuku to Matsumoto and transfer there to the Matsumoto Railway and go to Shinshimashima. Then, I get on the bus there bound for Kamikochi and get off at the last stop, right?
Mr. Tanaka: Very good, that's right.
Mr. White: How long would it take altogether to get there?
Mr. Tanaka: Well, it'll probably take five hours.
Mr. White: Thanks for everything.
Mr. Tanaka: Not at all, any time (it's my pleasure).

Vocabulary

zen'bu de: totally, all together

iroiro arigatō: thanks (for everything)

itsu demo dōzo: Any time (it's) my pleasure. [*Lit.* Please.]

ホワイト：田中さん、　ちょっと　おしえてくれませんか。

田中　　：はい、　なんでしょうか。

ホワイト：こんど　上高地へ　いきたいんですが、
　　　　　どう　いったら　いいでしょうか。

田中　　：そうですねえ、　上高地は　松本から　新島々へ　いって
　　　　　バスですが、　松本までは　わかりますか。

ホワイト：ちょっと　わかりませんが…。

田中　　：おたくは　南麻布でしたよね。

田中　　：それじゃあ、　まず　新宿まで　いって…。

ホワイト：はい。

田中　　：新宿から　中央本線で　松本まで　いってください。

ホワイト：はい。

田中　　：それから　松本で　松本電鉄に　のりかえて、
　　　　　新島々まで　いってください。

ホワイト：新島々ですか。

田中　　：ええ。　新島々で上高地ゆきの　バスに　のって
　　　　　しゅうてんで　おります。

ホワイト：すみませんが、　ローマじで　かいてくれませんか。

田中　　：いいですよ。

ホワイト：新宿から　中央本線で　松本まで　いって、
　　　　　松本電鉄に　のりかえて　新島々まで　いって
　　　　　上高地ゆきの　バスで　しゅうてんですね。

田中　　：ええ、　そうです。

ホワイト：ぜんぶで　どのぐらい　かかるでしょうか。

田中　　：そうですねえ…、　5じかんぐらいでしょう。

ホワイト：どうも　いろいろ　ありがとう。

田中　　：いいえ、　いつでも　どうぞ。

Grammar Note 1 — Asking how to get to a certain place

a.   [X] *made/e (ikitai-n desu ga,)*
    dō ittara ii deshō ka.   "(I'd like to go) to X . . . , how can I get there?"

Use this pattern when you are planning to go or actually going somewhere.
Ittara is a conditional form of the verb ***ikimasu*** but how to make this form is not discussed here.

Examples: Variations

Takao e wa dō ittara ii deshō ka.	"How can I get to Takao?"
Izu e wa den'sha de wa dō ittara ii deshō ka.	"How can I get to Izu by train?"
Ashinoko e iki-tai-n desu ga dō ittara ii deshō ka.	"I'd like to go to Ashinoko, how can I get there?"

b.   [X] *made/e **dōyatte ikimasu ka** ↗.*   "How do you get to X?"

You learned ***dōyatte*** "how" in Lesson 11. This pattern is used to ask how another person gets to the office and so on, as a matter of conversation.

Example

Sumisu-san wa kaisha made dōyatte ikimasu ka.	"How do you get to your office, Mr. Smith?" *or* "How does Mr. Smith get to his office?"

Grammar Note 2 — Verbs for transportation

The following verbs are introduced in this lesson:

norimasu	"get on (take)"
orimasu	"get off'
norikaemasu	"change (trains, *etc.*)"

a.   **[Place]** *de* **[Train/Line,** *etc.***]** *ni* **norimasu.**
Ebisu de Yamanote-sen ni norimasu.   "I/you get on (take) the Yamanote Line at Ebisu (Station)."

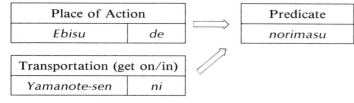

b.   **[Place]** *de* **[Train/Line,** *etc.***]** *o* **orimasu.**
Mitaka de den'sha o orimasu.   "I/you get off the train at Mitaka (Station)."

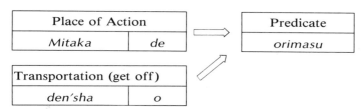

O is a marker to indicate that you are alighting from *or* getting off a train, bus, taxi, elevator, *etc.*

c. **[Place]** *de* **[Train/Line,** *etc.***]** *o* **[Train/Line,** *etc.***]** *ni norikaemasu.*

<u>Shin'juku</u> de <u>Yamanote-sen</u> o   "I/you change from the Yamanote Line to the
<u>Chūō-sen</u> ni norikaemasu.   Chuo Line at Shinjuku (Station).''

Place of Action	
Shin'juku	*de*

⟹

Predicate
norikaemasu

Transportation (get on)	
Yamanote-sen	*o*

Transportation (get off)	
Chūō-sen	*ni*

d.   **[Place to Leave]** *kara demasu.*

<u>Minami-guchi</u> kara demasu.   "I/you go out the south exit."

You learned **[Place]** *o demasu* in Lesson 15. You can use either *kara* or *o* to indicate the place you are leaving but *kara* has a stronger meaning of "starting point."

Grammar Note 3 — Telling how you get to a place

a.   **. . . Verb-***te*, **(. . . Verb-***te*,**) . . . Verb-***masu*∗.

Chūō-hon'sen ni notte, Matsumoto   "I/you get on (take) the Chuo Main
  de orimasu.   Line, and get off at Matsumoto."

  ∗**Verb-***masu/masen*. The **verb-***masu/masen* has been introduced having the following meanings:
       Lesson 10:   What you will *or* will not do.
       Lesson 13:   What you generally or habitually do *or* do not do.
  Now we add one more meaning which is:
       To give directions while explaining.

b. *Te* form **[Verb-***te***]**
You have learned the following verb forms in the previous lessons. (*cf.* Lessons 7, 8, 13, and 16)

Te forms	*Masu* forms	Meaning
itte	*ikimasu*	go
magatte	*magarimasu*	turn
tomatte	*tomarimasu*	stop
tōtte	*tōrimasu*	go through
misete	*misemasu*	show
naratte	*naraimasu*	learn
oshiete	*oshiemasu*	teach

As you can see, the verbs end with *-te* or *-tte*. This is called the *Te* form of the verb. (Sometimes this ending is pronounced *-de*. You will see later which verbs take which variation.)

The following are the *Te* forms of the new verbs used for expressing how to get to a place.

Te forms	*Masu* forms	Meaning
notte	norimasu	get on
norikaete	norikaemasu	transfer
orite	orimasu	get off
dete	demasu	get out

c.   Combining sentences using Verb-*te*.
Two or more sentences become one using the **Te** form.
(*cf.* Lesson 16, Grammar Note 6)

Examples

Shibuya de Yamanote-sen ni norikaemasu.	"I/you change to the Yamanote Line at Shibuya."
Yamanote-sen de Shin'juku made ikimasu.	"I/you take the Yamanote Line to Shinjuku."
Shibuya de Yamanote-sen ni norikaete, Shin'juku made ikimasu.	"I/you change to the Yamanote Line at Shibuya and go to Shinjuku."
Shibuya de Yamanote-sen ni norikaete kudasai.	"Please change to the Yamanote Line at Shibuya."
Yamanote-sen de Shin'juku made itte kudasai.	"Please take the Yamanote Line to Shinjuku."
Shibuya de Yamanote-sen ni norikaete, Shin'juku made itte kudasai.	"Please change to the Yamanote Line at Shibuya and go to Shinjuku."
Shibuya de Yamanote-sen ni norikaemashita.	"I/you/he changed to the Yamanote Line at Shibuya."
Yamanote-sen de Shin'juku made ikimashita.	"I/you/he went to Shinjuku on the Yamanote Line."
Shibuya de Yamanote-sen ni norikaete, Shin'juku made ikimashita.	"I/you/he changed to the Yamanote Line at Shibuya and went to Shinjuku."

Grammar Note 4 — Requesting using Verb-*te*

. . .[Verb-te] kuremasen ka.
Chotto oshiete kuremasen ka.   "May I ask you something?"
[*Lit.* Could you give me some information, please?]

a.   Verb-*te* plus **kuremasen ka** "Could you. . .for me? [*Lit.* Could you give me. . .]" or **kudasai** "Please. . .for me. [*Lit.* Please give me.]" forms a request, as you learned in Lesson 8.

b.   **oshiete**
Oshiete is the **Te** form of the verb **oshiemasu**, which means "teach, inform, guide, *etc.*"

c.   Answers to these requests would be:
Ē, ii desu yo ↗.   "Sure. [*Lit.* That's fine.]"
Hai, nan deshō ka ↘.   "Yes. What can I do for you?" [*Lit.* What will it be?]

| **Troublesome factor** | **wa chotto. . .** | "Well. . ., | | is a little bit (troublesome). . ." |

Examples

A: Kan'ji to kana de kaite kuremasen ka.	"Could you write it in kanji and kana, please?"
B: Ē, ii desu yo.	"Sure."

270

A: *Chizu o kaite kuremasen ka.*   "Could you draw a map, please?"

B: *Hai, ii desu yo.*   "Sure."

A: *Sumimasen, chotto oshiete kuremasen ka.*   "May I ask you something?"
B: *Hai, nan deshō ka.*   "Yes, what can I do for you?"

A: *Ashita san-ji ni kite kuremasen ka.* "Could you come at 3:00 tomorrow, please?"

B: *San-ji wa chotto...*   "Well, 3:00 is a little bit..."

Grammar Note 5 — More about the *Te* form of a verb

a. The following is a list, although not exclusive, of some of the Functions/Notions in which the *Te* form of the verb is used:

Requesting :	Taking a taxi [Lesson 7]	*Tsugi o migi e **magatte** kudasai.* "Turn to the right at the next [intersection], please."
	Shopping [Lesson 8]	*Sono kuroi sētā o **misete** kuremasen ka.* "Could you show me that black sweater?"
Routines:	Habitual actions [Lesson 13]	PLS *de Nihon-go o **naratte** imasu.* "I'm taking Japanese (lessons) at PLS."
Giving directions:	Location [Lesson 16]	*Kono michi o massugu **itte** kudasai.* "Go straight along this street."
	Confirming [Lesson 17]	*Soko o hidari e **itte**, shōmen desu ne.* "I go this way to my left and I'll see it right ahead of me, right?"
Telling the way to get somewhere, giving directions:	Transportation A sequence of actions [Lesson 20]	*Matsumoto de Matsumoto Den'tetsu ni **norikaete**, Shin'shimashima made **itte** kudasai.* "Transfer to the Matsumoto Railway Line at Matsumoto, and go to Shin-shimashima."

b. Now, let's look at how *Te* forms are made using the *Masu* forms.
It is helpful to divide all the verbs into the following three groups in explaining the rules of making *Te* forms.

Group A	There are only two verbs: *kimasu* "come" and *shimasu* "do."
Group B	This group includes all verbs which end with -*emasu*. There are also a few which end in -*imasu*. *e.g.,* ***misemasu*** "show" ***mimasu*** "see"
Group C	All the verbs end in -*imasu*. *e.g.,* ***nomimasu*** "drink" ***kikimasu*** "listen"

The following is a list of rules for making **Te** forms:

Rule I :   Replace **-masu** of Group A and B verbs with **-te.**

Rule II: (All the verbs of Group C can be further divided into four groups for **Te** forms.)

       −1   Replace **-shimasu** ending with **-shite.**

       −2   Replace **-kimasu** and **-gimasu** endings with **-ite** and **-ide** respectively.

       −3   Replace **-mimasu, -nimasu** and **-bimasu** endings with **-ide.**

       −4   Replace **-chimasu, -rimasu** and **-imasu** endings with **-tte.**

	Masu forms	**Te** forms	Meaning
Group A [Rule I]	*kimasu* *shimasu*	*kite* *shite*	come do
Group B [Rule I]	*misemasu* *mimasu*	*misete* *mite*	show see, look
Group C [Rule II] −1	*hanashimasu*	*hanashite*	talk, speak
−2	*kikimasu* *isogimasu* *ikimasu*	*kiite* *isoide* *itte**	listen, hear hurry go
−3	*yomimasu* *shinimasu* *asobimasu*	*yon'de* *shin'de* *ason'de*	read die play, have fun
−4	*tachimasu* *magarimasu* *kaimasu*	*tatte* *magatte* *katte*	stand turn buy

* **Iki-masu** in Group C-2 is an exception and becomes **itte.**

Consequently, when you come across a new verb, you can figure out what the **Te** form will be by checking the group of the verb and its **Masu** form.

Grammar Note 6 — Confirming old information

[Information — Past Tense] *yo ne* ↗.

<u>*O-taku wa Aoyama deshita yo ne.*</u>   "(As I recall, you said that) you lived in Aoyama, right?"

When confirming information that you remember from some time ago, use the past tense of the predicate plus the markers **yo ne** with rising intonation.

The final marker **yo ne** is used when you are fairly certain, and **yo nē** is used when you are not sure.

Examples

Sumisu-san, otaku wa Hiroo deshita yo ne.   "Mr. Smith, (you said) you lived in Hiro, right?"

Tanaka-san, o-shigoto wa Mōbiru Sekiyu deshita yo ne.   "Mr. Tanaka (you said) you worked for Mobil Oil."

Sumisu-san wa Nihon-go o naratte imashita yo ne.   "(Someone said) Mr. Smith was taking Japanese lessons, wasn't he?"

Grammar Note 7 — Asking/giving destinations, routes

[Destination]-*yuki*

Shin'ōsaka-yuki "Train/bus, *etc.*, bound for Shin'osaka"

Examples

Shin'ōsaka-yuki no Hikari	"The Hikari (bound) for Shin'osaka"
Shibuya-yuki no basu	"Bus (bound) for Shibuya"
Shibuya-yuki ni norimasu.	"I get on the bus/train (bound) for Shibuya."
Shibuya-yuki wa doko deshō ka.	"Where is the bus/train (bound) for Shibuya?"

Drill 1 Substitute the underlined parts.

1. *Ebisu de Yamanote-sen ni norimasu.*
   - (1) *Shin'juku, Odakyū-sen*
   - (2) *Shibuya, Gin'za-sen*
   - (3) *Mitaka, Jin'daiji-yuki no basu*

2. *Shibuya de orimasu.*
   - (1) *Harajuku*
   - (2) *Aoyama it-chōme*
   - (3) *Shin'juku san-chōme*

3. *Shin'juku Eki de Chūō-sen ni norikaemasu.*
   - (1) *Takadanobaba, Tōzai-sen*
   - (2) *Kasumigaseki, Hibiya-sen*
   - (3) *Hamamatsuchō, monorēru*

4. *Minami-guchi kara demasu.*
   - (1) *kita-guchi* (2) *nishi-guchi* (3) *higashi-guchi* (4) *chūō-guchi*

Sign in Shinjuku Station
西口   東口
(nishi-guchi) (higashi-guchi)

Drill 2 Combine the sentences using *-te.*

{ *Hiroo Eki made aruite ikimasu.*
{ *Hiroo Eki de Hibiya-sen ni norimasu.*

 ⟶ *Hiroo Eki made aruite itte, Hibiya-sen ni norimasu.*

- (1) *Hibiya-sen de Kasumigaseki made ikimasu.*
  Kasumigaseki de Marunouchi-sen ni norikaemasu.
- (2) *Basu de Ogikubo made ikimasu.*
  Ogikubo de Tōzai-sen ni norimasu.
- (3) *Kasumigaseki de Marunouchi-sen ni norikaemasu.*
  Marunouchi-sen de Ōtemachi made ikimasu.
- (4) *Aoyama it-chōme de orimasu.*
  Aoyama it-chōme kara taishikan made aruite ikimasu.

(5)   *Chūō-hon'sen de Matsumoto made ikimasu.*
Matsumoto de Matsumoto Den'tetsu ni norikaemasu.
Matsumoto Den'tetsu de Shin'shimashima made ikimasu.
Shin'shimashima de basu ni norimasu.
Shūten de orimasu.

Drill 3   Do you remember the drills for introducing people in Unit I? Confirm the information you have gotten from Drill 9 of Lesson 3. (A summary of the information is given below.)

e.g.,   *Inoue-san wa uchi wa Den'en'chōfu desu.*
Sasaki-san wa Kamakura desu.
⟶ *Inoue-san wa o-taku wa Den'en'chōfu deshita yo ne.*
Sasaki-san wa Kamakura deshita yo ne.

(1)   *Howaito-san wa kuni wa Amerika desu.*
Sumisu-san mo Amerika desu.
Howaito-san wa shigoto wa Mōbiru ni tsutomete imasu.
Sumisu-san wa Esso desu.

(2)   *Rūsu-san wa uchi wa Aoyama desu.*
Maririn-san mo Aoyama desu.
Rūsu-san wa shufu desu.
Maririn-san wa Ei-go no kyōshi desu.

Drill 4   Take the part of Mr. White, Ms. Thompson and other people.

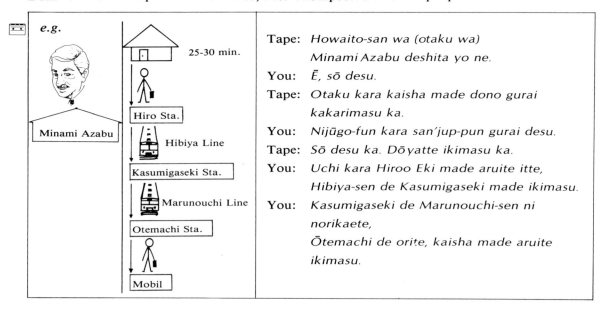

e.g.

25-30 min.

Hiro Sta.

Minami Azabu

Hibiya Line

Kasumigaseki Sta.

Marunouchi Line

Otemachi Sta.

Mobil

Tape: *Howaito-san wa (otaku wa)*
Minami Azabu deshita yo ne.
You: *Ē, sō desu.*
Tape: *Otaku kara kaisha made dono gurai*
kakarimasu ka.
You: *Nijūgo-fun kara san'jup-pun gurai desu.*
Tape: *Sō desu ka. Dōyatte ikimasu ka.*
You: *Uchi kara Hiroo Eki made aruite itte,*
Hibiya-sen de Kasumigaseki made ikimasu.
You: *Kasumigaseki de Marunouchi-sen ni*
norikaete,
Ōtemachi de orite, kaisha made aruite
ikimasu.

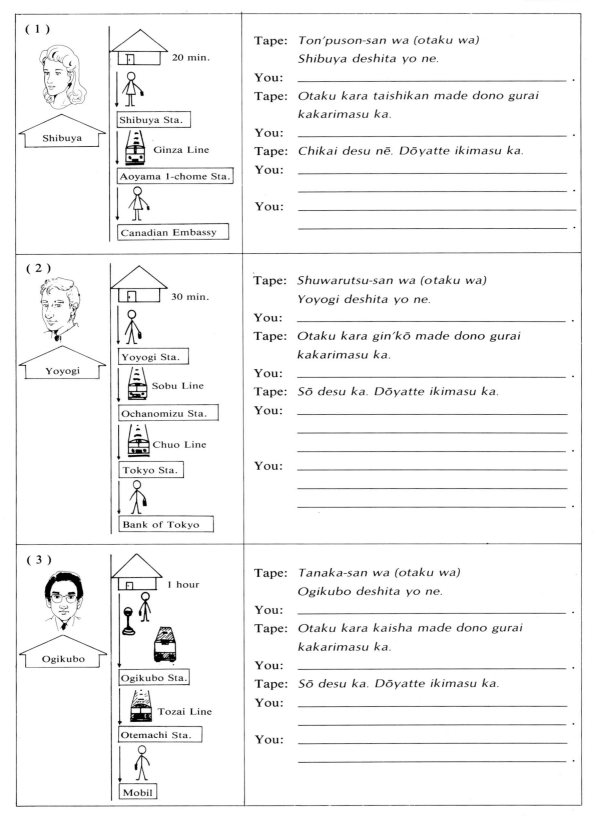

(1)

20 min.

Shibuya Sta.

Ginza Line

Aoyama 1-chome Sta.

Canadian Embassy

Shibuya

Tape: *Ton'puson-san wa (otaku wa) Shibuya deshita yo ne.*

You: _____.

Tape: *Otaku kara taishikan made dono gurai kakarimasu ka.*

You: _____.

Tape: *Chikai desu nē. Dōyatte ikimasu ka.*

You: _____
_____.

You: _____
_____.

(2)

30 min.

Yoyogi Sta.

Sobu Line

Ochanomizu Sta.

Chuo Line

Tokyo Sta.

Bank of Tokyo

Yoyogi

Tape: *Shuwarutsu-san wa (otaku wa) Yoyogi deshita yo ne.*

You: _____.

Tape: *Otaku kara gin'kō made dono gurai kakarimasu ka.*

You: _____.

Tape: *Sō desu ka. Dōyatte ikimasu ka.*

You: _____
_____
_____
_____.

You: _____
_____
_____.

(3)

1 hour

Ogikubo Sta.

Tozai Line

Otemachi Sta.

Mobil

Ogikubo

Tape: *Tanaka-san wa (otaku wa) Ogikubo deshita yo ne.*

You: _____.

Tape: *Otaku kara kaisha made dono gurai kakarimasu ka.*

You: _____.

Tape: *Sō desu ka. Dōyatte ikimasu ka.*

You: _____
_____.

You: _____
_____.

Drill 5   Fill in the blanks.

	Meaning	-masu		-te
1	come	ki	-masu	kite
		shi	-masu	
2		de	-masu	
		i	-masu	
		mi	-masu	
		mise	-masu	
		ne	-masu	
		norikae	-masu	
		oki	-masu	
		oshie	-masu	
		tabe	-masu	
3		kaki	-masu	
		kiki	-masu	
		iki	-masu	
	speak	hanashi	-masu	hanashite
		nomi	-masu	
		yomi	-masu	
		kaeri	-masu	
		magari	-masu	
		nori	-masu	
		tomari	-masu	
		tōri	-masu	
		machi	-masu	
		kai	-masu	
		narai	-masu	
	say	ii	-masu	itte

Drill 6   Make request forms.

    e.g.,   *Kan'ji o oshiemasu.*   ⟶   *Kan'ji o oshiete* { *kudasai.*
                                                              kuremasen ka.

1. (1)   *Kotchi e kimasu.*
   (2)   *San-ji goro kimasu.*
   (3)   *Sōji o shimasu.*
   (4)   *Taipu "typing" o shimasu.*
   (5)   *Kore o taipu shimasu.*
   (6)   *Ashita no yakusoku o kyan'seru "cancel" shimasu.*

2. (1) *Koko ni imasu.*

(2) *Sore o misemasu.*

(3) *Hayaku okimasu.*

(4) *Tsugi de orimasu.*

(5) *Kore o tabemasu.*

(6) *Issho ni terebi o mimasu.*

(7) *Higashi-guchi kara demasu.*

(8) *Den'wa bangō* "telephone number" *o oshiemasu.*

3. (1) *Rōmaji de kakimasu.*

(2) *Issho ni on'gaku o kikimasu.*

(3) *Kono wain o nomimasu.*

(4) *Tsugi o hidari e magarimasu.*

(5) *Kono hen de tomarimasu.*

(6) *Meiji Dōri o tōrimasu.*

(7) *Amerikan Kurabu made ikimasu.*

(8) *Atarashii kutsu o kaimasu.*

(9) *Kono hon o yomimasu.*

(10) *Eki no namae o hiragana de kakimasu.*

(11) *Kyō wa hayaku kaerimasu.*

(12) *Yukkuri* "slowly" *ikimasu.*

(13) *Yukkuri iimasu.*

(14) *Ei-go de hanashimasu.*

(15) *Chotto machimasu.*

Drill 7   Make short dialogues.

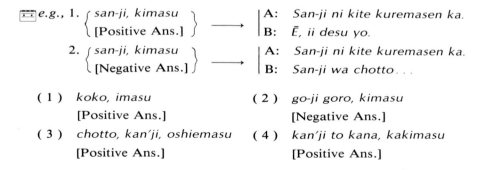

e.g., 1. { *san-ji, kimasu* / [Positive Ans.] } ⟶ | A: *San-ji ni kite kuremasen ka.*
| B: *Ē, ii desu yo.*

2. { *san-ji, kimasu* / [Negative Ans.] } ⟶ | A: *San-ji ni kite kuremasen ka.*
| B: *San-ji wa chotto...*

(1) *koko, imasu*
[Positive Ans.]

(2) *go-ji goro, kimasu*
[Negative Ans.]

(3) *chotto, kan'ji, oshiemasu*
[Positive Ans.]

(4) *kan'ji to kana, kakimasu*
[Positive Ans.]

Drill 8   Substitute the underlined parts. (Ask how to get to the places given.)

e.g.,   next time, *Tsukiji* [fish market area]
⟶   *Kon'do Tsukiji e iki-tai-n desu ga, dō ittara ii deshō ka.*

(1) the coming holiday, *Ashinoko* [a lake]

(2) this weekend, *Jin'daiji* [a temple]

(3) this coming Sunday, *San'keien* [a spacious Japanese style garden with old houses]

277

Drill 9   Tell how to get to the places shown.

e.g.,   Tsukiji ←———[bus]——— Shin'bashi

———→ Tsukiji wa Shin'bashi kara basu desu.

(1)   Tōshōgū ←———[bus]——— Nikkō Eki

(2)   Hakone Yumoto ←———[train]——— Shin'juku
Odakyu Line

(3)   Ashinoko ←———[bus]———Hakone Yumoto

(4)   Hida Takayama ←———[train]———
Nagoya Takayama Honsen Line

Drill 10   Translate into Japanese.

(1)   Please stop here.
(2)   Please speak slowly.
(3)   Could you say it once more?
(4)   Please study.   (mō ichido)
(5)   Could you show me that book?
(6)   Could you write it in Roman letters?
(7)   Could you cancel the appointment?
(8)   Could you come at 8:00 tomorrow?
(9)   Wait a moment, please.
(10)   May I ask you something? [*Lit.* Could you inform me a little...?]

Drill 11   Take the parts of the people in the cue and ask Mr. Tanaka, your colleague, how to
get to the place indicated. Use the dialogue as a model.

(1)

Ms. Thompson [Shibuya]

next time
Tsukiji (fish market)

Yamanote Line

Shinbashi Sta.

east exit

Bus Terminal

bound for
Tsukiji
Chuoichiba

Tsukiji Chuoichiba

You: ————————————————————— .
Tape: *Hai, nan deshō ka.*
You:
————————————————————— .
Tape: *Sō desu nē... Tsukiji wa shin'bashi kara
basu desu kedo, Shin'bashi made
wa wakarimasu ka.*
You: ————————————————————— .
Tape: *Ton'puson-san wa Shibuya deshita yo ne.*
You: ————————————————————— .
Tape: *Sore jā, Yamanote-sen de Shin'bashi made
itte...*
You: [C*] ————————————————————— .
Tape: *Shin'bashi de wa higahi-guchi kara dete,
Tsukiji Chūōichiba-yuki no basu ni notte,
shūten made ikimasu.*

Roman letters?	You: _____ _____ . Tape: *Ii desu yo.* You: [C] _____ _____ . Tape: *Ē, sō desu.*
How long does it take from Shinbashi to Tsukiji?	You: _____ _____ . Tape: *Jup-pun ka jūgo-fun gurai desu.* You: _____ . Tape: *Iie.*

(2)

Mr. Schwartz
Yoyogi

this coming holiday
Lake Ashinoko

Shinjuku Sta.

Odakyu Line

Hakone-Yumoto Sta.

bound for
Motohakone

Motohakone

You: _____ .
Tape: *Hai, nan deshō ka.*
You: _____
_____ .
Tape: *Sō desu nē. . . Ashinoko wa Odakyū-sen no Hakone-Yumoto kara basu desu ga, Hakone-Yumoto made wa wakarimasu ka.*
You: _____ .
Tape: *Shuwarutsu-san wa Yoyogi deshita yo ne.*
You: _____ .
Tape: *Sore jā, mazu Shin'juku made itte, Odakyū-sen de shūten no Hakone-Yumoto made itte kudasai.*
You: [C] _____
_____ .
Tape: *Ē. Hakone-Yumoto de Motohakone-yuki no basu ni notte shūten de orite kudasai.*

kanji and kana?

You: _____
_____ .
Tape: *Ē, ii desu yo.*
You: [C] _____
_____ .
Tape: *Ē, sō desu.*

How long does it take altogether?

You: _____ .
Tape: *Sō desu nē. . .*
Ni-jikan kara ni-jikan han gurai deshō.
You: _____ .

[C*] = Confirm the direction

Lesson 21

TAKING THE TRAIN/BUS

SHŪTEN MADE ATO DONO GURAI DESHŌ KA
"HOW MUCH FURTHER IS IT TO THE LAST STOP?"

Dialogue I

[Mr. and Mrs. White are at Shinjuku Station. They are on the way to Kamikochi. Mrs. White is speaking to a station employee.]

Howaito:	*Sumimasen, tokkyū Azusa ichi-gō wa nan-ban-sen deshō ka.*
Ekiin:	*Ichi-ban-sen desu.*
Howaito:	*Dōmo...*
	[Station employee nods]

      *   *   *

[Mr. White is speaking to a waiting passenger while pointing to a train standing at the platform.]

Howaito: *Sumimasen, kore wa Azusa ichi-gō desu ka.*

Nihon-jin:	*Hai, sō desu.*	⟵⟶	Nihon-jin:	*Iie, Azusa ichi-gō wa kono*
Howaito:	*Dōmo...*			*tsugi desu. Roku-ji gojup-pun ni kimasu.*
			Howaito:	*Ā, sō desu ka. Dōmo...*

Mrs. White:	Excuse me, which track does the Azusa No. 1 leave from?
Station Employee:	Track one.
Mrs. White:	Thank you.

      *   *   *

Mr. White:	Excuse me, is this the Azusa No. 1 (train)?
Japanese:	Yes, that's right.
Mr. White:	Thank you.

Japanese:	No, it's the next train. It'll arrive at 6:50 a.m.
Mr. White:	Oh, I see. Thank you.

Vocabulary

ato dono gurai:	how much further	*nan-ban-sen:*	which track
tokkyū:	limited express train	*ekiin:*	station employee
Azusa ichi-gō:	limited express, Azusa No. 1	*ichi-ban-sen:*	track No. 1

🔲 Dialogue II

[At Matsumoto Station]

Howaito: *Sumimasen, kore wa Shin'shimashima e ikimasu ka.*

Ekiin: *Hai, ikimasu.* ⟷ Ekiin: *Shin'shimashima-yuki no hōmu*

Howaito: *Dōmo arigatō.* *wa atchi desu yo.*

Howaito: *A, sō desu ka. Dōmo...*

*   *   *

[At the bus terminal in front of Shinshimashima Station]

Howaito: *Sumimasen, Kamikōchi-yuki no basu wa dore deshō ka.*

Nihon-jin: *Are desu yo.*

Howaito: *Dōmo arigatō.*

Nihon-jin: *Iie.*

Mr. White:	Excuse me, does this (train) go to Shinshimashima Station?		
Station Employee:	Yes, it does. ⟷	Station Employee:	The train bound for Shinshimashima leaves from that platform over there.
Mr. White:	Thank you.		
		Mr. White:	Oh, O.K. Thank you.

*   *   *

Mrs. White: Excuse me, (I wonder) which bus goes to Kamikochi?

Japanese: That's the one over there.

Mrs. White: Thank you very much.

Japanese: Not at all.

🔲 Dialogue III

[On the bus to Kamikochi]

Howaito: *Sumimasen, shūten made ato dono gurai deshō ka.*

Nihon-jin: *Sō desu nē..., ato jup-pun gurai deshō.*

Howaito: *A, dōmo.*

[Looking around at the scenery through the window]

Howaito: *Kono hen wa kirei desu nē.*

Nihon-jin: *Ē... o-kuni wa dochira desu ka.*

Howaito: *Amerika desu.*

Nihon-jin: *Ā, Amerika desu ka.*

Howaito: *Anō, dokoka de shokuji o shitai-n desu kedo, doko ga ii deshō ka.*

Nihon-jin: *Kappa-bashi no chikaku wa dō desu ka. Resutoran ga takusan arimasu kara.*

Howaito: *Kappa-bashi (??)*

Nihon-jin: *Ē. Shūten kara aruite go-rop-pun desu yo.*

Howaito: *Ā, sō desu ka.*

Vocabulary

hōmu: platform

Kappa-bashi: a bridge over the Azusa river in Kamikochi

Kappa is a legendary animal which is believed to live in the water.

chikaku ← *chikai:* nearby

takusan: many, a lot

Mrs. White: Excuse me, I wonder how much further it is to the last stop?
Japanese: Let's see..., it will probably be ten minutes.
Mrs. White: Thank you.

Mr. White: The scenery is very beautiful around here, isn't it?
Japanese: Yes, it is. Where are you from?
Mr. White: (I'm from the United States of) America.
Japanese: Oh, from the States!
Mrs. White: Excuse me, I'd like to have lunch [*Lit.* meal] somewhere (in Kamikochi),
                but do you know a good place to eat? [*Lit.* What place would be good?]
Japanese: How about near the Kappa-bashi area?
                (For) there are many restaurants around there.
Mrs. White: Oh, Kappa-bashi?
Japanese: Yes, it's just a five or six minute walk from the bus terminal.
Mrs. White: Oh, I see.

I

ホワイト：すみません、　特急あずさ1号は　なんばんせんでしょうか。

えきいん：1ばんせんです。

ホワイト：どうも…。

　　　　　　　　　＊　　＊　　＊

ホワイト：すみません、　これは　あずさ1号ですか。

日本人　：はい、　そうです。⟵⟶　日本人　：いいえ、　あずさ1号は

ホワイト：どうも…。　　　　　　　　　　このつぎです。

　　　　　　　　　　　　　　　　　　　6じ　50ぷんに

　　　　　　　　　　　　　　　　　　　きます。

　　　　　　　　　　　　　　ホワイト：ああ、　そうですか。

　　　　　　　　　　　　　　　　　　　どうも…。

II

ホワイト：すみません、　これは　新島々へ　いきますか。

えきいん：はい、　いきます。⟵⟶　えきいん：新島々ゆきの　ホームは

ホワイト：どうも　ありがとう。　　　　　　あっちですよ。

　　　　　　　　　　　　　　ホワイト：ああ、　そうですか。

　　　　　　　　　　　　　　　　　　　どうも…。

　　　　　　　　＊　　＊　　＊

ホワイト：すみません、　上高地ゆきの　バスは　どれでしょうか。

日本人　：あれですよ。

ホワイト：どうも　ありがとう。

日本人　：いいえ。

III

ホワイト ：すみません、 しゅうてんまで あと どのぐらいでしょうか。

日本人 　：そうですねえ…、 あと 10ぷんぐらいでしょう。

ホワイト ：あっ、 どうも。

ホワイト ：このへんは きれいですねえ。

日本人 　：ええ。 おくには どちらですか。

ホワイト ：アメリカです。

日本人 　：ああ、 アメリカですか。

ホワイト ：あのう、 どこかで しょくじを したいんですけど、
　　　　　　どこが いいでしょうか。

日本人 　：河童橋の ちかくは どうですか。
　　　　　　レストランが たくさん ありますから。

ホワイト ：河童橋。

日本人 　：ええ。 しゅうてんから あるいて 5、6ぷんですよ。

ホワイト ：ああ、 そうですか。

Grammar Note 1 — Finding the right train/bus/track

To ask where to get/take the right train or bus, use the following expressions.

a.

[Train name] [Your destination]-*yuki* "bound for" [Number]-*ban no basu*	*wa*	*doko* *nan-ban-sen* "which track" *nan-ban-noriba*	*desu ka* ↗ *deshō ka* ↘

X-*ban-sen* indicates the track number (of the train):

ichi-ban-sen	"track No. 1"
ni-ban-sen	"track No. 2"
san-ban-sen	"track No. 3"
:	
:	
nan-ban-sen	"which track?"

X-*ban-noriba* indicates the place to get on (the bus):

ichi-ban-noriba	"bus stop No. 1"
ni-ban-noriba	"bus stop No. 2"
san-ban-noriba	"bus stop No. 3"
:	
:	
nan-ban-noriba	"which bus stop?"

X-*ban no basu* indicates the bus line/route numbers:

    ichi-ban no basu   "bus No. 1"

    nijū-ban no basu   "bus No. 20"

       :

       :

    nan-ban no basu   "which number bus?"

Examples

Hikari ichi-gō* wa nan-ban-sen desu ka.	"From which track does the Hikari No. 1 leave?"
Shinagawa-yuki wa nan-ban-noriba desu ka.	"From which place does the bus for Shinagawa leave?"
Go-ban no basu wa doko deshō ka.	"Where do I get/take bus No. 5?"

*-*gō* is the counter for scheduled train runs.

—Variation—

A:	*Kore wa Hikari ichi-gō desu ka.*	"Is this the Hikari No. 1?"
B:	*Iie. Hikari ichi-gō wa kono tsugi desu.*	"No. The Hikari No. 1 is the next one."

b. ***X wa* [Your destination] *e ikimasu ka.***

    Kore wa Atami e ikimasu ka.   "Does this (train) go to Atami?"

c. ***X wa* [Your destination] *ni tomarimasu ka.***

    Kore wa Atami ni tomarimasu ka.   "Does this (train) stop at Atami?"

Place to Stop			Predicate	Final
Atami	*ni*	⟹	*tomarimasu*	*ka* ↗

Examples

A:	*Sumimasen, kore wa Akihabara e ikimasu ka.*	"Excuse me, does this (train) go to Akihabara?"
B:	*Ē, ikimasu yo.*	"Yes, it does."

A:	*Sumimasen, kore wa Kichijōji ni tomarimasu ka.*	"Excuse me, does this (train) stop at Kichijoji?"
B:	*Iie, tomarimasen yo.*	"No, it doesn't."
	Kichijōji wa yon-ban-sen desu.	"Trains stopping at Kichijoji leave from track No. 4."

Grammar Note 2 — Expressing how much further it is to the destination

a. **[Your destination] *made ato dono gurai*** $\begin{cases} \textbf{\textit{desu ka}} ↗. \\ \textbf{\textit{deshō ka}} ↘. \end{cases}$ "How much further is it to [Destination]?"

b. Answers to the question would be:

Ato	**[Amount of time]** **[Distance]** **[Number of stations]** *etc.*	*desu* *deshō*

Examples

Ato jup-pun desu.	"It takes ten more minutes."
Ato go-kiro gurai deshō.	"It's about five more kilometers."
Ato mit-tsu desu.	"(It's) After (stopping at) three more stations."
Mō sugu desu.	"Very soon."

Grammar Note 3 — Asking for suggestions/recommendations when going somewhere

X wa $\begin{cases} doko \\ itsu \\ nani \end{cases}$ *ga ii deshō ka* ↘.
  etc.

Shokuji wa doko ga ii deshō ka.	"Where would you recommend/suggest having a meal? [*Lit.* Which place would be good?]"

Examples

O-miyage wa nani ga ii deshō ka.	"As for (buying) a souvenir, what would be good?"
Sakura wa doko ga ii deshō ka.	"As for (viewing) cherry blossoms, where would you recommend?"
Sukī wa doko ga·ii deshō ka.	"As for skiing, where would you recommend?"
Kōyō wa itsu ga ii deshō ka.	"As for autumn leaves, when would you recommend (to go)?"

Grammar Note 4 — Expressing what you would like to do

[Verb (Pre-*masu*)] *-tai-n desu ga/kedo* . . .
Shokuji o shi-tai-n desu ga . . . "I'd like to have a meal . . ."

a. **[Verb (Pre-*masu*)]** *-tai*   "want to [Verb]"
Take away *-masu* from a verb and put *-tai* in its place and you will get "want to do so-and-so." **Verb-*tai*** is used like a verb but it is really an adjective.

This form, like other adjectives expressing emotion, feeling or desire is basically used to express only the speaker's desire (and the listener's also).

Observe how you make this form:

iki-masu	⟶	*iki-tai*	"want to go"
kaeri-masu	⟶	*kaeri-tai*	"want to go, return home"
mi-masu	⟶	*mi-tai*	"want to see, watch"
tabe-masu	⟶	*tabe-tai*	"want to eat"
nomi-masu	⟶	*nomi-tai*	"want to drink"
kai-masu	⟶	*kai-tai*	"want to buy"
shi-masu	⟶	*shi-tai*	"want to do"

b. *-n desu ga/kedo* . . .
-n desu is the form used to explain the situation or circumstances, and it does not have an English equivalent. With the sentence marker *ga* or *kedo* of [Hesitation], *-n desu ga/kedo* . . . expresses the humble explanation of the speaker's situation.

Thus, ***Mikimoto e iki-tai-n desu ga*** . . . "I'd like to go to Mikimoto . . . ," (in Lesson 16) or ***Dokoka de shokuji o shi-tai-n desu ga*** . . . "I'd like to have a meal some place . . . ," (this lesson) give the speaker's situation in a humble way, which implies asking for a recommendation/suggestion.

Examples

Kon'do Nikkō e iki-tai-n desu ga . . .	"I'd like to go to Nikko soon . . ."
O-miyage o kai-tai-n desu ga . . .	"I'd like to buy a souvenir . . ."
Sakura o mi ni iki-tai-n desu ga . . .	"I'd like to go to see cherry blossoms . . ."

c. Using the following, you can express what you would like to do more specifically than ***X wa*** in Grammer Note 3.

Examples

Hokkaidō e iki-tai-n desu ga, itsu ga ii deshō ka.	"I'd like to go to Hokkaido, when would you recommend (to go)?"
Kamakura no matsuri ni iki-tai-n desu ga, dō ittara ii deshō ka.	"I'd like to go to the festival in Kamakura, how should I go?"
Sakura o mi ni iki-tai-n desu ga, doko ga ii deshō ka.	"I'd like to go to see cherry blossoms, where would you recommend?"
Haha ni miyage o kai-tai-n desu ga, nani ga ii deshō ka.	"I'd like to buy a souvenir for my mother, what would you recommend?"

Grammar Note 5 — Offering a suggestion/recommendation in going somewhere

Here, we introduce patterns for suggestions/recommendations:
   a)   is very straightforward.
   b)   is rather indirect.

a. **[Topic] *wa* [Recommended place/time/thing] *ga ii desu yo* ↗.**
   Kōyō wa Nikkō ga ii desu yo.   "As for (viewing) autumn leaves, I recommend Nikko." [*Lit.* Nikko is good.]

b. **[Topic] *wa* [Recommended place/time/thing] *wa dō desu ka* ↗.**
   Kōyō wa Nikkō wa dō desu ka.   "As for (viewing) autumn leaves, how about Nikko?"

c. Adding the reason for the suggestion/recommendation

In Lesson 15, you learned:
[Result]. [Reason] *kara.*

Here we introduce:

[Suggestion/Recommendation].	**[Reason] *kara.***
Kōyō wa Nikkō ga ii desu yo.	*Momiji no ki ga takusan* arimasu kara.*
"I recommend Nikko for autumn leaves."	"There are a lot of maple trees, so . . ."

*takusan = a lot of. (*cf.* Lesson 24, quantity words)

Examples

Sushi wa Tsukiji ga ii desu yo.
Yasukute oishii desu kara.

"As for sushi, I recommend Tsukiji."
"It's inexpensive and good, so . . ."

Kamera wa Shin'juku ga ii
desu yo.
Yasui mise ga takusan arimasu
kara.

"As for cameras, I recommend
Shinjuku."
"There are a lot of cheap stores,
so . . ."

Drill 1   Substitute the underlined parts.

1. *Azusa ichi-gō* wa nan-ban-sen deshō ka.
   (1)   Hikari hyaku-san-gō   (2)   Takao-yuki

2. *Asakusa-yuki* wa dore deshō ka.
   (1)   Shibuya-yuki, doko   (2)   Ueno-yuki, nan-ban no basu

3. *Kore* wa *Akihabara* e ikimasu ka.
   (1)   kono den'sha, Kan'da   (2)   ichi-ban-sen no den'sha, Izu

4. *Kore* wa *Akihabara* ni tomarimasu ka.
   (1)   kore, Yoyogi   (2)   tsugi no Hikari, Yokohama

5. *Atami* made ato dono gurai deshō ka.
   (1)   shūten "final stop"   (2)   tsugi no eki

Drill 2   Answer with yes and no.

   e.g.,   Kore wa Yokohama ni tomarimasu ka.
   ⟶ ⎰Ē, tomarimasu.
       ⎱Iie, (Yokohama ni wa) tomarimasen.

   (1)   Kono den'sha wa Yoyogi ni tomarimasu ka.
   (2)   Kore wa Amerikan Kurabu no tokoro e ikimasu ka.
   (3)   Tokkyū wa Matsumoto ni tomarimasu ka.
   (4)   Ichi-ban-sen no den'sha wa Izu e ikimasu ka.

Drill 3   Answer the question by translating and substituting the underlined part.

   Shūten made ato dono gurai deshō ka.
   e.g.,   10 minutes   ⟶   Ato *jup-pun* desu yo.

   (1)   20 minutes   (2)   about an hour   (3)   about 3 kilometers
   (4)   five more stops   (5)   5 or 6 kilometers   (6)   very soon (*mō sugu*)

Drill 4 Using Dialogues I, II and III as a model, complete the following.

(1) You are going to Tsukiji [fish market]

[1] —At the wicket of Shibuya Station—

Shin'bashi?

You

You: _____ .
Tape: *Ni-ban-sen desu.*
You: _____ .

[2] —On the Platform—

Shin'bashi?

You

You: _____ .
Tape: *Ē, ikimasu yo.*
You: _____ .

[3] —At the bus terminal—

Tsukiji?

You

You: _____ .
Tape: *Ichi-ban noriba kara desu yo.*
You: _____ .

[4] —At the No. 1 bus stop—

Tsukiji?

You

You: _____ .
Tape: *Ikimasu yo.*
You: _____ .

[5] —On the bus—

Fish Market

You

You

You: _____ .
Tape: *Mō sugu desu yo.*
You: _____ .

(2)   You are going to Lake Ashinoko

[1] —At the wicket of Odakyu Shinjuku Station—

Hakone-Yumoto?

You: _____ .
Tape: *Ni-ban-sen desu.*
You: _____ .

[2] —On the platform—

Hakone-Yumoto?

You: _____ .
Tape: *Ē, ikimasu yo.*
You: _____ .

[3] —On the train—

You

? Hakone Yumoto Sta.

You: _____ .
Tape: *Sakki Odawara deshita kara, ato jup-pun gurai desu yo.*
You: _____ .

[4] —At the bus terminal—

Lake Ashinoko?

You: _____ .
Tape: *Ano basu desu yo.*
You: _____ .

[5] —At the bus stop—

Ashinoko?

You: _____
_____ .
Tape: *Ē, ikimasu.*
You: _____ .

[6] —On the bus—

Hakonemachi Ashinoko
You

?

You: _____ .
Tape: *Tsugi wa Hakonemachi desu kara, ato go-rop-pun desu yo.*
You: [EL] _____ .
Tape: *Iie.*

⊟ Drill 5   Make sentences using **[Verb]-*tai-n desu ga/kedo*...**

　　　e.g.,   *Ikimasu* ⟶ *ikitai-n desu ga/kedo*...

　　(1)   *tabemasu*　　(2)   *nomimasu*　　(3)   *mimasu*
　　(4)   *kikimasu*　　(5)   *kaimasu*　　(6)   *shimasu*
　　(7)   *naraimasu*　　(8)   *oshiemasu*　　(9)   *norimasu*
　　(10)   *orimasu*　　(11)   *norikaemasu*　　(12)   *demasu*

Drill 6   Make sentences using **[Object] *o* [Verb]-*tai-n desu ga/kedo*...**

　1.　e.g.,   *(o-)miyage* "souvenir" ⟶ *(O-)miyage o kaitai-n desu ga*...

　　(1)   *Imari-yaki* "Imari pottery"
　　(2)   *ōkii saizu* "size" *no kutsu*
　　(3)   *an'tīku no* "antique" *tan'su* "chest of drawers"
　　(4)   *yukata* "summer cotton kimono"

　2.　e.g.,   *karate* ⟶ *Karate o narai-tai-n desu ga*...

　　(1)   *aikidō*　　　　　　　　(2)   *sumie* "Japanese ink painting"
　　(3)   *Nihon-ryōri*　　　　　　(4)   *ikebana*

　3.　e.g.,   *oishii ten'pura* ⟶ *Oishii ten'pura o tabetai-n desu ga*...

　　(1)   *kaiseki-ryōri* "very formal Japanese style meal"
　　(2)   *shōjin-ryōri* "Japanese style vegetarian meal"
　　(3)   *shabushabu* "Japanese style hot pot"

　4.　e.g.,   *kabuki*
　　　　　　　⟶ *Kabuki o mitai-n desu ga*...

　　(1)   *sakura* "cherry blossoms"
　　(2)   *ume* "plum blossoms"
　　(3)   *shōbu* "irises"
　　(4)   *kiku-nin'gyō*
　　　　　　"doll made of chrysanthemums"
　　(5)   *kōyō* "autumn leaves"
　　(6)   *bon'odori*
　　　　　　"Buddhist all-souls dance festival"
　　(7)   *hanabi* "fireworks"

Iris garden — Meiji Shrine

　5.　e.g.,   *kabuki* ⟶ *Kabuki ni iki-tai-n desu ga*...

　　(1)   *bon'odori*
　　(3)   *Daruma-ichi* "Daruma doll market — festival"
　　(5)   *Kyōto no Gion Matsuri*
　　(2)   *(o-)matsuri* "festival"
　　(4)   *Asagao-ichi* "Morning glory market — festival"

Drill 7   Make sentences using **[Object] *o* [Verb] *ni iki-tai-n desu ga/kedo*...**

　　　e.g.,   *Kabuki, mimasu* ⟶ *Kabuki o mi ni iki-tai-n desu ga*...

　　(1)   *kōyō, mimasu*　　　　　(2)   *Imari-yaki, kaimasu*
　　(3)   *kaiseki-ryōri, tabemasu*　　(4)   *bon'odori, mimasu*

Drill 8 Translate and substitute the underlined part.

e.g., _ where ⟶ *Doko ga ii deshō ka.*

(1) what   (2) when   (3) around when
(4) around what time (5) who   (6) which line

Drill 9 Make suggestions using _____*wa* _____ *ga ii desu yo.*

e.g., *Sakura desu ka.*
       Ueno wa dō desu ka. } ⟶ *Sakura wa Ueno ga ii desu yo.*

(1) *Kōyō desu ka.*
       Nikkō wa dō desu ka.

(2) *Imari-yaki desu ka.*
       Aoyama wa dō desu ka.

(3) *Kaiseki-ryōri desu ka.*
       Aoi to iu mise wa dō desu ka.

(4) *Ōkii saizu no kutsu desu ka.*
       Gin'za no Daiana wa dō desu ka.

(5) *Karate desu ka.*
       Watashi no sen'sei wa dō desu ka.

(6) *Shokuji desu ka.*
       Shabushabu wa dō desu ka.

(7) *O-miyage desu ka.*
       Sen'su "folding fan" wa dō desu ka.

Drill 10 Substitute the underlined parts.

San-gatsu no hajime "beginning" goro ga ii desu yo.

(1) *shi-gatsu, hajime*   (2) *go-gatsu, naka "middle"*
(3) *jū-gatsu, owari "end"*   (4) *roku-gatsu, tō-ka*
(5) *haru "spring", hajime*   (6) *natsu "summer", naka*
(7) *aki "autumn", owari*   (8) *fuyu "winter", hajime*

Drill 11 Make short dialogues.

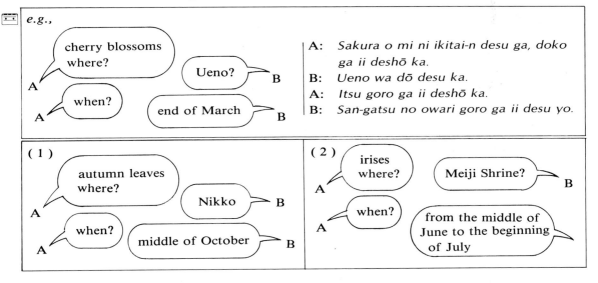

Drill 12   Substitute the underlined parts. Offer a suggestion and the reason.

> *Roppon'gi wa dō desu ka.*
> *Ii resutoran ga takusan arimasu kara.*

(1)   *Tsukiji, oishii sushi-ya*
(2)   *Kan'da, ii furuhon-ya* "used book store"
(3)   *Akihabara, yasui den'ki-ya*
(4)   *Aoyama, ii kobijutsu* "antique" *no mise*
(5)   *Kyōto, furui* "old" *otera* "temples"

Drill 13   Suppose you are talking to a Japanese on a local bus/train. Using the second part of Dialogue III as a model, complete the following.

(1)	
[a] Mountains are beautiful in this area.	You: [a] _____ Tape: *Ē. O-kuni wa dochira desu ka.* You: _____ .
[b] What should I buy for a souvenir?	You: [b] _____ . Tape: *Sō desu nē . . .* *Yosegi-zaiku* "wood mosaic" *wa dō desu ka.* *Shūten no chikaku ni o-miyage-ya ga* *takusan arimasu kara.* You: _____ . Tape: *Iie.*
(2)	
[a] Cold, isn't it?	You: [a] _____ . Tape: *Ē. Dochira kara irasshaimashita ka.* "Where do [*Lit.* did] you come from?" You: _____ .
[b] I'd like to have a good fish dinner. Where should I go?	You: [b] _____ . Tape: *Sakana ryōri wa* *Tsuruya to iu ryokan* "Japanese style inn" *ga ii desu yo.* *Yasukute oishii desu kara.* You: _____ . Tape: *Iie.*

Culture Note 10 — *Iie!*

The Japanese, as we have already seen, have a great predilection for the word "yes." They have a corresponding distaste for the word "no." How then, do we recognize a refusal in Japanese? Furthermore, how do we ourselves refuse in Japanese? And what do we make of *iie* when we do hear it?

To begin with, demurral is a very typical way of refusal. If you are in a shop and the assistant offers you something you'd prefer not to have, to say *Iie, irimasen* "No, I don't want it" is very abrupt and will make you no friends. Say instead the demurring (and untranslatable) *Sō desu nē. . .* in an unenthusiastic manner and everyone will understand and no hard feelings. What is unstated should be left unstated. This is the usual and not-at-all strange response for such a situation.

When the people in your office invite you out for a drink *Sō desu nē. . . .* prepares the listener for a refusal but it is not a refusal in itself. To say *Iie, kyō wa dame desu* "No, today's no good" will ensure you will never get a repeated invitation, and more, the atmosphere in the office could well turn frosty, permanently. You have rejected the overtures of friendship quite strongly. Better to say *Kyō wa chotto. . .* "Today's a bit. . .," and again leave the actual bad news unstated. *Chotto* says it all, and your listeners infer that you can't go today (for whatever reason) but would love to be invited for, say, tomorrow. This inference is a second, very typical, way of refusing.

In an objective situation, where nobody's feelings are at stake, it is quite possible to say *iie*. But even here, there is a strong inclination to soften it with something. For example in answer to a wrong telephone call, "Is this the Tanaka residence?" to say *Iie, chigaimasu.* "No, it isn't" is a little pitiless, even if it is a stranger on the other end. *Iie, chigaimasu kedo. . .* with the inevitable unstated statement hanging in the air is more polite and more natural.

But there is a situation where an unqualified, positive "no" is called for. When you are praised, you should never thank the other person. This is quite unJapanese. You should instead instantly disclaim any implied superiority over the other and state quite clearly that no, your new shoes are not at all nice, they're really only cheap things you picked up the other day. (Meanwhile, Gucci dies.) Equally when you are thanked, you should, as in English, reply *Iie* "Not at all."

Despite it's initial strangeness this reply to praise is really quite understandable in terms of Japanese society. To be or appear superior to others is not conducive to harmonious relationships. Therefore, anything which strengthens the sense of the group, of solidarity and cooperation is fostered, and anything which does not is avoided. So while it feels a little odd to downplay the excruciating cost of your Gucci shoes, by the same token, if you deprecate yourself or your qualities, the others will instantly chorus "No, you're not stupid at all." And for all its mawkishness, its gives you a nice feeling inside to know you have friends!

Review Quiz (Lesson 16 — Lesson 21)

I. Look at the picture and ask for the location:

a. Using _____ **wa doko desu ka.**

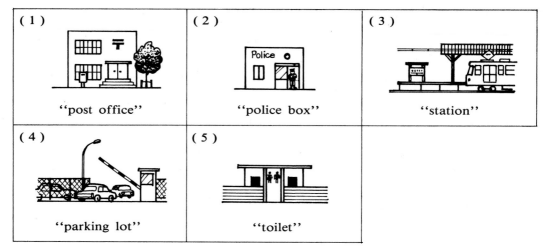

(1) "post office" (2) "police box" (3) "station"

(4) "parking lot" (5) "toilet"

b. Using _____ **uriba wa nan-gai deshō ka.**

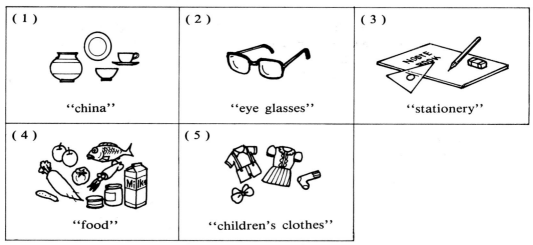

(1) "china" (2) "eye glasses" (3) "stationery"

(4) "food" (5) "children's clothes"

II. Match up the pictures with the phrases below.

(1)

(2)

(3)

(4)

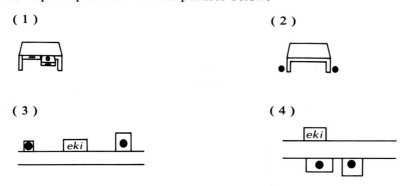

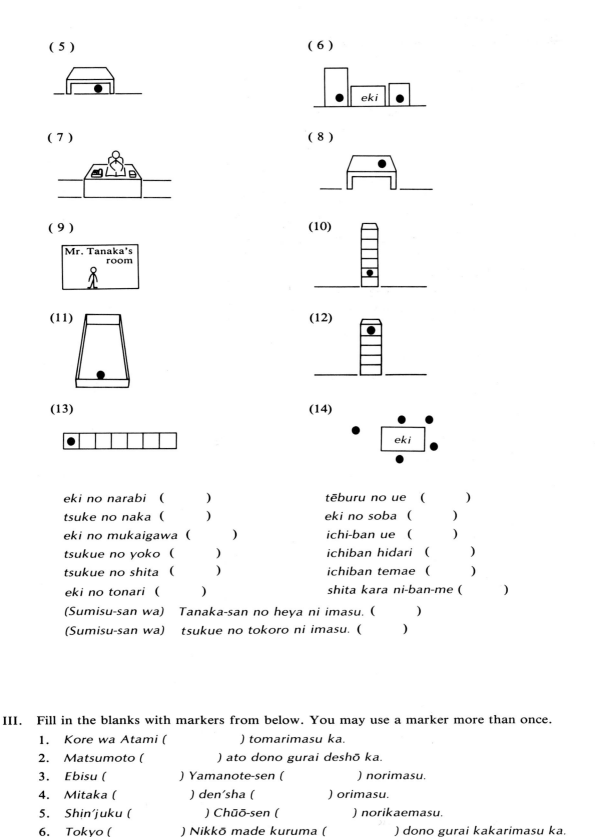

(5)

(6)

eki

(7)

(8)

(9)

Mr. Tanaka's room

(10)

(11)

(12)

(13)

(14)

eki

eki no narabi   (   )

tsuke no naka (   )

eki no mukaigawa (   )

tsukue no yoko (   )

tsukue no shita (   )

eki no tonari (   )

(Sumisu-san wa)   Tanaka-san no heya ni imasu. (   )

(Sumisu-san wa)   tsukue no tokoro ni imasu. (   )

tēburu no ue   (   )

eki no soba (   )

ichi-ban ue (   )

ichiban hidari (   )

ichiban temae (   )

shita kara ni-ban-me (   )

III.   Fill in the blanks with markers from below. You may use a marker more than once.

1.   Kore wa Atami (   ) tomarimasu ka.

2.   Matsumoto (   ) ato dono gurai deshō ka.

3.   Ebisu (   ) Yamanote-sen (   ) norimasu.

4.   Mitaka (   ) den'sha (   ) orimasu.

5.   Shin'juku (   ) Chūō-sen (   ) norikaemasu.

6.   Tokyo (   ) Nikkō made kuruma (   ) dono gurai kakarimasu ka.

   [de, ni, kara, o, made]

IV. Fill in the blanks with appropriate verbs from below.

1. *Erebētā no tokoro ni Aoki-san ga (   ).*

2. *Tsukue no tokoro ni hachiue ga (   ).*

3. *Tanaka-san wa doko ni (   ) ka.*

4. *Den'wa wa tsukue no ue ni (   ).*

5. *Taipuraitā no tonari ni wāpuro ga (   ).*

[*arimasu, imasu*]

V. What Japanese expressions would you use in the following situations?

1. When you ask for directions to the ward office . . .

2. When you mention a station as a landmark in giving directions . . .

3. When you stop a passer-by on the street and ask for directions . . .

4. When making a formal visit to Mr. White's office, at the receptionist's desk . . .

5. When asking a colleague or a friend where the Japan Times newspaper is . . .

6. When you tell someone that Mr. Tanaka is in a meeting indicating probability . . .

7. When you express that it takes time to do something . . .

8. When you want to interrupt your colleague for a moment . . .

9. When you ask which track the train bound for Kamikochi leaves from . . .

10. When you offer a suggestion (to go to) Nikko to see autumn leaves . . .

VI. Express in Japanese.

1. Sorry, can you repeat that again, please?

2. Mr. Tanaka, could you please tell me something?

3. Sorry (to bother you), but could you write it down for me in Roman letters?

4. Thanks for everything.

5. Excuse me, does this (train) go to Matsumoto (Station)?

6. Mr. Tanaka was at the computer.

7. I'd like to have the second one from the left.

8. Which floor is the china and pottery [Lit. dishes and plates] department on?

9. I go this way to my left and (I'll see the china department) right in front of me.

10. The ward office is beyond that traffic light, isn't it?

Unit VII

Inviting Someone, Making a Visit

SCOPE OF UNIT VII

The main function of Unit VII is INVITATIONS in various situations and VISITS to people's homes.

Lesson 22 deals with inviting someone to join in activities and how to accept or decline invitations. The language involved includes setting dates, expressing preferences, indicating times and places and making suggestions.

Lesson 23 concerns inviting someone to your home. Useful terms for giving directions to drivers are also given. The lesson is then expanded to include ways of asking permission.

Lesson 24 focuses on offers in the context of a visit to someone's home. Asking for and giving one's preferences regarding food and drink are covered as well as customs and expressions used by a guest and a host in a Japanese home.

Lesson 22

INVITING SOMEONE TO JOIN IN ACTIVITIES

HIRU-GOHAN NI IKIMASEN KA
"WHY DON'T WE GO FOR LUNCH?"

Dialogue I

[Mr. Smith invites Mr. Yamashita, his colleague, to join him for lunch.]

Sumisu: Mō jūni-ji desu yo.

Yamashita: A, sō desu nē.

Sumisu: Hiru-gohan ni ikimasen ka.

Yamashita: Ē, ikimashō. ⟷	*Yamashita:* Mada chotto...
Doko e ikimashō ka.	Dōzo osakini.
Sumisu: Ton'katsu wa dō	*Sumisu:* Sore jā, osakini.
desu ka.	
Yamashita: Ii desu nē. ⟵	*Yamashita:* Ton'katsu wa chotto...
Sumisu: Sore jā, ikimashō.	*Sumisu:* Sore jā, sushi wa dō deshō ka.
	Yamashita: Ii desu nē.
	Sumisu: Sore jā, ikimashō.
	Yamashita: Ē.

Mr. Smith:	It's noon already.
Mr. Yamashita:	Oh, so it is.
Mr. Smith:	Why don't we go for lunch?
Mr. Yamashita:	Yes, let's go. ⟷	Mr. Yamashita: Well, not yet.../
	Where shall we go?	Go ahead, please (without me).
Mr. Smith:	How about a pork	Mr. Smith: O.K. See you later.
	cutlet (restaurant)?	[*Lit.* Before you.]
Mr. Yamashita:	That sounds good. ⟷	Mr. Yamashita: Well...really, I don't feel like eating pork cutlet...so...
Mr. Smith:	Then, let's go (to	Mr. Smith: Then, how about sushi?
	a pork cutlet restaurant).	Mr. Yamashita: That sounds good.
		Mr. Smith: Then, let's go (to a sushi shop).
		Mr. Yamashita: O.K.

Vocabulary

mō: already

ikimasen ka: Why don't we go?
   [*Lit.* Don't you/we go?]

ikimashō: let's go

ikimashō ka: Shall we go?

ton'katsu: pork cutlet

mada: not yet

dōzo osaki ni: go ahead, please after you

sore jā, osaki ni: then, (I'll go) before you

📼 Dialogue II

[Mr. Brown is inviting Ms. Inoue to go to a movie.]

Buraun: Inoue-san, kon'do no do-yōbi (wa)
yotei (wa) arimasu ka.

Inoue: Iie, betsu ni arimasen kedo... ⟵⟶

Buraun: Jā, eiga o mi ni ikimasen ka.

Inoue: Ii desu nē.

Buraun: 'Kaze to Tomo ni Sarinu' wa dō
desu ka.

Inoue: A, ii desu nē.

Buraun: Jā, doko de aimashō ka.

Inoue: Doko demo ii desu kedo...

Buraun: Sonī Biru no mae wa dō
desu ka.

Inoue: Ē, ii desu.

Buraun: Jikan wa ni-ji goro wa dō
desu ka.

Inoue: Ē.

Buraun: Sorejā, kon'do no do-yōbi no
ni-ji ni Sonī Biru no mae de.

A *Inoue:* Ē, chotto...

Buraun: Jā, nichi-yōbi wa.

Inoue: Nichi-yōbi wa betsu ni
yotei wa arimasen
kedo...

B *Inoue:* Ē, chotto yotei ga
arimasu kedo.

Buraun: Sō desu ka. Zan'nen
desu nē. Jā, mata
kon'do.

Inoue: Ē, mata kon'do.

Vocabulary

yotei: plan

betsu ni...(arimasen): have (nothing) special

mi ni ikimasen ka: Why don't we go to
see...?

aimashō ka: Shall we meet...?

doko demo: anywhere (is fine)

mata kon'do: next time
[*Lit.* Again, next time.]

Mr. Brown: Do you have any (special) plan this coming Saturday, Ms. Inoue?

Ms. Inoue: No, (I have) nothing special...   ⟶   A Ms. Inoue: Well...Yes, I have... so...

Mr. Brown: Then, why don't we go to see a movie?   Mr. Brown: Then, how about Sunday?

Ms. Inoue: That sounds good.   Ms. Inoue: Oh, (I don't) have anything special on Sunday...

Mr. Brown: How about the movie 'Gone With the Wind'?

Ms. Inoue: That sounds good.

Mr. Brown: Then, where shall we meet?   B Ms. Inoue: Well...Yes, I have a plan (already)...so it's a bit...

Ms. Inoue: Any place is all right (with me).

Mr. Brown: How about meeting in front of the Sony Building (in Ginza)?   Mr. Brown: Oh, that's too bad. Then, next time.

Ms. Inoue: That's fine.   Ms. Inoue: Yes, next time.

Mr. Brown: [*Lit.* As for meeting time] How does 2 o'clock sound to you?

Ms. Inoue: That sounds great.

Mr. Brown: All right, (let's meet) in front of the Sony Building at 2:00 this coming Saturday.

Ms. Inoue: O.K. Fine.

I

スミス：もう　12じですよ。

山下　：あっ、　そうですねえ。
やました

スミス：ひるごはんに　いきませんか。

山下　：ええ、　いきましょう。　⟵⟶　山下　：まだ　ちょっと…。
　　　　どこへ　いきましょうか。　　　　　どうぞ　おさきに。

　　　　　　　　　　　　　　　　　　　スミス：それじゃあ、　おさきに。

スミス：とんかつは　どうですか。

山下　：いいですねえ。　　⟵⟶　山下　：とんかつは　ちょっと…。

スミス：それじゃあ、　いきましょう。　スミス：それじゃあ、　すしは
　　　　　　　　　　　　　　　　　　　　　　　どうでしょうか。

　　　　　　　　　　　　　　　　　　　山下　：いいですねえ。

　　　　　　　　　　　　　　　　　　　スミス：それじゃあ、
　　　　　　　　　　　　　　　　　　　　　　　いきましょう。

　　　　　　　　　　　　　　　　　　　山下　：ええ。

II

ブラウン：井上さん、　こんどの
　　　　　どようび（は）　よてい（は）
　　　　　ありますか。

井上　　：いいえ、　べつに　　　←──────→　A　井上　　　：ええ、　ちょっと…。
　　　　　ありませんけど…。　　　　　　　　　　ブラウン：じゃあ、
ブラウン：じゃあ、　えいがを　　　　　　　　　　　　　　　にちようびは
　　　　　みにいきませんか。　　　　　　　　　井上　　　：にちようびは　べつに
井上　　：いいですねえ。　　　　　　　　　　　　　　　　　よていは
ブラウン：「風と　ともに　去りぬ」は　　　　　　　　　　ありませんけど。
　　　　　どうですか。
井上　　：あ、　いいですねえ。　　　B　井上　　　：ええ、
ブラウン：じゃあ、　どこで　　　　　　　　　　　　　　ちょっと　よていが
　　　　　あいましょうか。　　　　　　　　　　　　　　ありますけど…。
井上　　：どこでも　いいですけど…。　　　　ブラウン：そうですか。
ブラウン：ソニービルの　まえは　　　　　　　　　　　ざんねんですねえ。
　　　　　どうですか。　　　　　　　　　　　　　　　じゃあ、　また　こんど。
井上　　：ええ、　いいです。　　　　　　　井上　　　：ええ、　また　こんど。
ブラウン：じかんは　2じごろは
　　　　　どうですか。
井上　　：ええ。
ブラウン：それじゃあ、　こんどの　どようびの
　　　　　2じに　ソニービルの　まえで。

Grammar Note 1 — Inviting someone to join in activities

a. Here are the verb patterns for invitations:

Verb [Pre-*masu*]	-*mashō* ↘	"Let's [Verb]"
	-*mashō ka* ↘	"Shall we [Verb]?"
	-*masen ka* ↗	"Why don't we [Verb]?" *or* "Would you like to [Verb]?"

Examples

Ikimashō.	"Let's go."
Ikimashō ka.	"Shall we go?"
Ikimasen ka.	"Why don't we go?"
	or
	"Would you like to go?"
Tenisu o shimashō.	"Let's play tennis."
Tenisu o shimashō ka.	"Shall we play tennis?"
Tenisu o shimasen ka.	"Why don't we play tennis?"
	or
	"Would you like to play tennis?"

b.   **[Activity,** *etc.***] *ni*** ⎧ ***iki-mashō*** ↘**.**
⎨   ***-mashō ka*** ↘**.**
⎩   ***-masen ka*** ↗**.**

Hiru-gohan ni ikimasen ka.   "Why don't we go for lunch?"

Purpose		⟹	Predicate	Final
hiru-gohan	*ni*		*ikimasen*	*ka* ↗

Examples

Kabuki ni ikimasen ka.	"Why don't we go to Kabuki?"
Kon'do issho ni gorufu ni ikimasen ka.	"Would you like to go play golf together soon?"
Shokuji ni ikimashō ka.	"Shall we go for dinner?"
Doraibu ni ikimashō.	"Let's go for a drive."
Ashita Tsukiji e ikimasu kedo, *issho ni ikimasen ka.*	"Tomorrow I'm going to Tsukiji, (but) would you like to come with me?"

c.   **[Thing]** *o* **[Verb (Pre-*masu*)]** *ni* ⎧ ***iki-mashō*** ↘**.**
⎨   ***-mashō ka*** ↘**.**
⎩   ***-masen ka*** ↗**.**

Sushi o tabe ni ikimasen ka.   "Why don't we go to eat sushi?"

(*cf.* Lesson 15, Grammar Note 5)

Purpose		⟹	Predicate	Final
sushi o tabe	*ni*		*ikimasen*	*ka* ↗

Examples

Eiga o mi ni ikimasen ka.	"Why don't we go to see a movie?"
O-miyage o kai ni ikimasen ka.	"Why don't we go to buy a souvenir?"

d.   Indirectly inviting someone to join
***Mō* [Time]** *desu yo* ↗**.**
Mō jūni-ji desu yo.   "It's noon already."
        Meaning: Let's go for lunch.

Stating the time is one way to invite someone indirectly.

Examples

A, mō go-ji desu yo.	"Oh, it's five o'clock already."
	Meaning: It's time to stop work.
Mō jikan desu yo.	"It's that time already!"
	Meaning: The time has come. [*Lit.* Time is up!]

Grammar Note 2 — Accepting an invitation

a. *Ē, [Verb (Pre-masu)]-mashō* ↘.
   Ē, ikimashō.　　　"Yes, let's go."

b. *Ii desu nē* ↘.　　　"That sounds good." [*Lit.* That's good, isn't it?]

c. *Ii desu yo* ↗.　　　"All right."

Grammar Note 3 — Declining an invitation

a. *Sō desu nē...*　　　"Well, let's see..."
   [In a negative tone]

b. **[Inconvenient factor]** *wa chotto...*
   Ima wa chotto...　　　"Well..., now, it's not very..."

   As you have seen all through this textbook, Japanese usually do not say "no" clearly, (*cf.* Culture Note 10) especially when they are offered something or an invitation. They mumble something in a low tone, and it is very often preceded by a sharp intake of breath (usually men). You can guess that this usually means non-acceptance.

c. **[Inconvenient factor]** *wa tsugō ga warui-n desu ga...*
   Ima wa tsugō ga warui-n desu ga...　　　"It's inconvenient now..."
   [*Lit.* As for now, convenience is bad...]

   This non-acceptance is less indirect than a) or b).

   Examples

   | A: | *Shokuji ni ikimasen ka.* | "Why don't we go for dinner?" |
   | B: | *Ima wa chotto...* | "Now, it's a bit..." |

   | A: | *Kon'ban nomi ni ikimasen ka.* | "Why don't we go for a drink tonight?" |
   | B: | *Sō desu nē..., kon'ban wa chotto... tsugō ga warui-n desu ga...* | "Let me see..., this evening; well, it's not very convenient..." |

Grammar Note 4 — Invitation to join in making a decision

a. **[*Doko/Nan-ji/Nani, etc.*]** + **[Marker]** + **[Verb (Pre-masu)]-*mashō ka* ↘.**
   Doko de aimashō ka.　　　"Where shall we meet?"

   Examples

Itsu φ*	*ikimashō ka.*	"When shall we go?"
Nan-ji ni	*aimashō ka.*	"What time shall we meet?"
Doko e	*ikimashō ka.*	"Where shall we go?"
Doko de	*kaimashō ka.*	"Where shall we buy it?"
Nani o	*tabemashō ka.*	"What shall we eat?"

   *φ=No marker is needed.

b. **[*Doko/Nan-ji/Nani, etc.*]** *ga ii desu ka* ↗.
   Doko ga ii desu ka.　　　"Where would you like?"
   [*Lit.* Which place is good?]

   When asking what the other person would like to do, use this pattern.
   (In Lesson 21, Grammar Note 3, *...ga ii deshō ka* ↘ was introduced.)

Grammar Note 5 — Leaving the decision up to the conversation partner

When you do not want to initiate the decision, offer a free choice using the following:
[*Doko/Itsu/Nan, etc.*] *demo ii desu (ga/kedo. . .)*
Doko demo ii desu kedo. . .   "Any place is all right..."

Interrogative Noun plus **demo** means "no matter _____ it is" or "any _____ at all," *etc.*

The sentence particle *yo* of [Emphasis] or **kedo/ga** of [Hesitation] is often added after **desu.**

Vocabulary

Meaning	
any time (general)	*itsu demo*
any time (hour)	*nan-ji demo*
any day	*nan-nichi demo*
any day of the week	*nan-yōbi demo*
anywhere	*doko demo*
anything	*nan demo*
anybody	*dare demo*

Examples

A: *Nan-ji ga ii desu ka.*   "What time would you like?"
B: *Nan-ji demo ii desu kedo. . .*   "Any time is all right..."

A: *Doko e ikimashō ka.*   "Where shall we go?"
B: *Doko demo ii desu yo.*   "Anywhere is all right."

Grammar Note 6 — Suggesting/Accepting a specific plan

a.   **[Suggested place/time/thing]** *wa dō desu ka* ↗.
Ton'katsu wa dō desu ka.   "How about having pork cutlet?"

This pattern is the same as Lesson 21, Grammar Note 5-b.

b.   The responses would be:
[Agreement]:   *Ē,* {*ii* / *kekkō*} *desu.*   "Yes, that's fine."

[Disagreement]:   Same as Grammar Note 3 – Declining an invitation

Grammar Note 7 — Reiterating the accepted plan

[Signal for breaking off] [Time] [Place] ([Verb]).
Sore jā, ni-ji ni eki de (aimashō).   "All right, then let's meet at the station at two."

The verb is often omitted.

≈≈≈≈≈≈≈≈≈≈≈≈≈≈≈≈≈≈≈≈≈≈≈≈≈≈≈≈

Drill 1   Substitute the underlined parts.

1. *A, mō jūni-ji desu yo.*
   (1) *go-ji*   (2) *o-hiru*   (3) *jikan*

2. *Hiru-gohan ni ikimasen ka.*
   (1) *shokuji*   (2) *san'po* "go for a walk"

3. *Hiru-gohan o tabe ni ikimasen ka.*

(1) *kōhī, nomi*　　(2) *eiga, mi*

4. *Doko e ikimashō ka.*

(1) *nan-ji ni*　　(2) *itsu*　　(3) *nan-yōbi ni*　　(4) *dōyatte*

5. *Ton'katsu-ya wa dō desu ka.*

(1) *unagi*　　(2) *jūni-ji goro*　　(3) *do-yōbi*

6. *Ton'katsu wa chotto . . .*

(1) *soba*　　(2) *ano mise*　　(3) *ima*

7. *Jā, ton'katsu-ya e ikimashō.*

(1) *sushi-ya*　　(2) *kissaten*　　(3) *chikaku no mise*

Drill 2　Suppose you are in your office. Complete the following using Dialogue I as a model.

(1)		
[a]		You:　[a]_____.
		Tape:　*A, sō desu nē.*
[b]　lunch?		You:　[b]_____.
		Tape:　*Ē, ikimashō. Doko e ikimashō ka.*
[c]　*soba* shop?		You:　[c]_____.
		Tape:　*Ii desu nē.*
[d:　Review the plan.]		You:　[d]_____.
(2)		
[a]		You:　[a]_____.
		Tape:　*A, sō desu nē.*
[b]　lunch?		You:　[b]_____.
		Tape:　*Ima wa chotto . . .*
[c]　*Lit.* I'm going/leaving before you.		You:　[c]_____.
(3)		
[a]		You:　[a]_____.
		Tape:　*A, sō desu nē.*
[b]　meal?		You:　[b]_____.
		Tape:　*Ē, ikimashō. Nani o tabemashō ka.*
[c]　*ton'katsu?*		You:　[c]_____.
		Tape:　*Sō desu nē. . . Ton'katsu wa chotto. . .*
[d]　*sushi?*		You:　[d]_____.
		Tape:　*Ii desu nē.*
[e:　Review the plan.]		You:　[e]_____.
		Tape:　*Ē, ikimashō.*

(4) [Now you answer]	Tape:	A, mō jūni-ji han desu yo.
[a] So it is.	You:	[a]_____.
	Tape:	O-hiru ni ikimashō ka.
[b] Yes.	You:	[b]_____.
where?	Tape:	Unagi-ya wa dō desu ka.
[c] No.	You:	[c]_____.
	Tape:	Jā, rāmen wa dō desu ka.
[d] Yes.	You:	[d]_____.
	Tape:	Jā, Rairaiken e ikimashō ka.
[e] Yes, let's go.	You:	[e]_____.

Drill 3   Fill in the blanks.

Meaning	Verb	Let's...	Shall we...?	Why don't we...?
go	ikimasu	ikimashō	ikimashō ka	ikimasen ka
come				
	kaerimasu			
		shimashō		
			tabemashō ka	
rest	yasumimasu			
meet		aimashō		

Drill 4   Expand the sentences.

e.g., nomimasen ka ⟶ Nomimasen ka.
       kōhī o   ⟶ Kōhī o nomimasen ka.
       issho ni   ⟶ Issho ni kōhī o nomimasen ka.

(1) ikimasen ka
       shokuji ni
       kon'ban

(2) ikimashō ka
       kon'sāto ni
       kin-yōbi ni
       raishū no

(3) shimasen ka
       tenisu o
       issho ni
       kon'do

(4) aimashō
       eki no kaisatsu-guchi de
              "wicket gate"
       roku-ji ni
       ashita no

(5) kaerimasen ka
       sorosoro
       "soon" [Lit. slowly, gradually]
       Tanaka-san

(6) owarimashō
       sorosoro
       sore jā

⊞**Drill 5**   Make questions which ask for the underlined parts.

  e.g.,   <u>Ton'katsu-ya</u> e ikimashō.   ⟶   Doko e ikimashō ka.

  (1)   <u>Tanaka-san</u> to ikimashō.
  (2)   <u>Den'sha</u> de ikimashō.
  (3)   <u>Go-ji han</u> ni aimashō.
  (4)   <u>Nihon-ryōri</u> o tabemashō.
  (5)   <u>Tsukiji</u> de sushi o tabemashō.
  (6)   <u>Roku-ji</u> ni <u>robī</u> de aimashō.
  (7)   <u>Do-yōbi no gogo</u> ikimashō.
  (8)   <u>Ano basu</u> ni norimashō.
  (9)   <u>Hibiya-sen</u> ni norikaemashō.
  (10)   <u>Tsugi</u> de orimashō.

Drill 6   Respond to the invitation/suggestion.

  ⊞e.g.,   Ashita ikimasen ka.
      (Yes) ⟶   Ii desu nē. Ikimashō.
      (No) ⟶   Ashita wa chotto (tsugō ga warui-n desu ga . . .)

  (1)   Kon'ban nomi ni ikimashō.
  (2)   Go-ji han ni aimashō ka.
  (3)   Shin'juku Eki kara ikimashō ka.
  (4)   Chūō-sen ni norimashō.

Drill 7   Substitute the underlined parts.
  1. <u>Kon'do no do-yōbi</u> wa <u>yotei</u> arimasu ka.
      (1)   kon'do no yasumi, yakusoku
      (2)   ashita no ban, yotei
      (3)   raishū no sui-yōbi, nanika
  2. <u>Doko</u> ga ii desu ka.
      (1)   itsu   (2)   nani   (3)   nan-yōbi
      (4)   nan-ji   (5)   dare   (6)   dore
  3. <u>Doko</u> demo ii desu kedo . . .
      (1)   itsu   (2)   nan   (3)   nan-yōbi
      (4)   nan-ji   (5)   dare   (6)   dore

Drill 8   Put the appropriate words in the blanks.

  e.g.,   Kon'do [no] do-yōbi [ni] kabuki [o] mi [ni] ikimasu kedo,
      issho ni ikimasen ka.

  (1)   Ashita tomodachi ☐ bon'odori ☐ mi ☐ ikimasu kedo, issho
      ni ikimasen ka.
  (2)   Watashi ☐ kon'do Hakone ☐ kōyō ☐ mi ☐ ikimasu
      kedo, issho ni ikimasen ka.
  (3)   Ashita ☐ ban Amerikan kurabu ☐ shibai "play" ☐ arimasu
      kedo, issho ni ikimasen ka.
  (4)   Kon'do ☐ shūmatsu Yokohama ☐ tenisu ☐ shimasu kedo,
      issho ni shimasen ka.

Drill 9   Using Dialogue II as a model, complete the following.

(1)	
[a] next Saturday?	You: [a]_____.
	Tape: *Betsu ni arimasen kedo...*
[b] to Ueno to a *shakuhachi* "bamboo flute" concert?	You: [b]_____.
	Tape: *Ii desu nē.*
[c] Where shall we meet?	You: [c]_____.
	Tape: *Doko demo ii desu kedo...*
[d] koen-guchi of Ueno Station?	You: [d]_____.
	Tape: *Ē, ii desu.*
[e] around 6:30?	You: [e]_____.
	Tape: *Ē, ii desu.*
[f: Review the plan.]	You: [f]_____.
	Tape: *Ē.*
(2)	
[a] next Sunday?	You: [a]_____.
	Tape: *Betsu ni arimasen kedo...*
[b] Hakone to see autumn leaves?	You: [b]_____.
	Tape: *Ii desu nē. Iki-tai desu.*
[c] Where shall we meet?	You: [c]_____.
[d] wicket gate *(kaisatsu-guchi)* of the Odakyu Line at Shinjuku Station?	Tape: *Doko demo ii desu kedo...*
	You: [d]_____.
	Tape: *Ē, ii desu.*
[e] around 8:00?	You: [e]_____.
	Tape: *Hachi-ji wa chotto... hayai desu nē.*
[f] around 9:00?	You: [f]_____.
	Tape: *Ē, daijōbu desu. Den'sha wa nan-ji desu ka.*
[g] 9:15 train	You: [g]_____.
	Tape: *Sō desu ka.*
[h: Review the plan.]	You: [h]_____.
	_____.
	Tape: *Ē, sore jā.*

(3)   [Now you are invited to join]

	Tape:	Kon'do no do-yōbi wa yotei arimasu ka.
[a] not especially	You:	[a]_____.
	Tape:	Jā, Mashiko e tōki "pottery" o mi ni ikimasen ka.
[b] Yes, I'd love to.	You:	[b]_____.
	Tape:	Doko de aimashō ka.
[c] any place	You:	[c]_____.
	Tape:	Ueno Eki no roku-ban-sen no hōmu wa dō desu ka.
[d] fine	You:	[d]_____.
	Tape:	Jikan wa shichi-ji han wa dō desu ka.
[e] Well. . . That's early.	You:	[e]_____.
[f] fine	Tape:	Jā hachi-ji han wa dō desu ka.
	You:	[f]_____.
	Tape:	Jā, kon'do no do-yōbi no hachi-ji han ni Ueno Eki no roku-ban-sen no hōmu de.
[g] O.K.	You:	[g]_____.

Downtown Ginza

Lesson 23

INVITING SOMEONE TO YOUR HOME

UCHI E SHOKUJI NI KIMASEN KA
"WOULD YOU LIKE TO COME TO MY HOUSE FOR DINNER?"

Dialogue I

Tanaka:	Sumisu-san, raishū no do-yōbi o-hima deshitara uchi e shokuji ni kimasen ka.
Sumisu:	Dōmo arigatō gozaimasu. Demo raishū no do-yōbi wa chotto tsugō ga warui-n desu ga...
Tanaka:	Sore jā, nichi-yōbi wa dō desu ka.
Sumisu:	Nichi-yōbi deshitara daijōbu desu. Nan-ji goro desu ka.
Tanaka:	Go-ji goro wa dō desu ka.
Sumisu:	Ē, kekkō desu. Anō, kanai mo itte mo ii desu ka.
Tanaka:	Ē, mochiron. Okosan mo dōzo.
Sumisu:	Kodomo wa bebīshittā ga imasu kara...
Tanaka:	Ā, sō desu ka.

Mr. Tanaka:	Mr. Smith, if you're free, would you like to come to my home for dinner next Saturday?
Mr. Smith:	Thank you very much. But next Saturday is a bit inconvenient...
Mr. Tanaka:	Then, how about Sunday?
Mr. Smith:	If it's Sunday, all right with me. What time (shall I come)?
Mr. Tanaka:	How does 5 o'clock sound to you?
Mr. Smith:	That'll be fine. Well, may I bring my wife?
Mr. Tanaka:	Of course. Bring your children, too.
Mr. Smith:	The children can stay home with a babysitter, (so don't worry about them).
Mr. Tanaka:	Oh, O.K.

Vocabulary

o-hima deshitara: if you are free
tsugō: convenience
daijōbu: no problem, all right

Itte mo ii desu ka: May I come/go?
mochiron: of course
bebīshittā: babysitter

Dialogue II

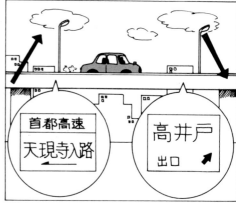

Tanaka:	Kore wa watashi no jūsho to den'wa ban'gō desu. Chizu o kakimashō ka.
Sumisu:	Ē, onegai shimasu.
Tanaka:	Sumisu-san wa Hiroo deshita yo ne. Kuruma de kimasu ka.
Sumisu:	Ē.
Tanaka:	Sore jā, ētto, Ten'gen'ji Intā kara Shuto Kōsoku ni notte, Takaido In'tā de orite kudasai.
Sumisu:	Ten'gen'ji kara Takaido desu ne. [Looking at the map...,]
Tanaka:	Sorekara Kan'pachi ni haitte, Takaido Eki no mae o tōrimasu. Makudonarudo no kado o migi e magatte, Itsukaichi Kaidō ni haitte kudasai.
Sumisu:	Kan'pachi kara Itsukaichi Kaidō desu ne.
Tanaka:	Ē, uchi wa hitotsu-me no kōsaten o hidari e magatte san'jū-mētoru gurai saki no migi-gawa no shiroi uchi desu.
Sumisu:	Hai, wakarimashita. Dono gurai kakarimasu ka.
Tanaka:	Shi-gojup-pun deshō.
Sumisu:	Sō desu ka.
Tanaka:	Sore jā, raishū no nichi-yōbi no go-ji goro.
Sumisu:	Jā. Dōmo.

Mr. Tanaka:	Here are my address and telephone number. Shall I draw a map for you?
Mr. Smith:	Yes, please.
Mr. Tanaka:	Mr. Smith, (as I recall you said that) you lived in Hiro, right? Are you going to come by car?
Mr. Smith:	Yes, I will.
Mr. Tanaka:	Then, let's see... get on the Metropolitan Expressway at the Tengenji interchange and get off at the Takaido interchange.
Mr. Smith:	(I get on) at Tengenji interchange and get off at the Takaido exit, right?
Mr. Tanaka:	Then, go into Loop road No.8 and keep going past the front of Takaido Station. Turn to the right at the corner where you'll see a McDonald's and go into Itsukaichi Kaido (road).

Vocabulary

jūsho: address
den'wa ban'gō: telephone number
chizu: map
ētto: let me see
Ten'gen'ji: place name in Tokyo
in'tā: interchange
Shuto Kōsoku: (Tokyo) Metropolitan Expressway

Kan'pachi [Kan'jo hachi-gō-sen]: Loop road No. 8
haitte ← hairu: enter
Makudonarudo: McDonalds' Hamburger Shop
Itsukaichi Kaidō: Itsukaichi Route
Takaido: place name in Tokyo

Mr. Smith: From Loop road No. 8 to Itsukaichi Kaido (road), right?
Mr. Tanaka: Right. Turn to the left at the first intersection and (you'll see) a white house about 30 meters to your right. That's my house.
Mr. Smith: O.K. I've got it. How long does it take to get there?
Mr. Tanaka: It'll probably take forty to fifty minutes.
Mr. Smith: Oh, O.K.
Mr. Tanaka: Then, (I'll see you) at around five o'clock next Sunday.
Mr. Smith: O.K. Good.

I

田中　：スミスさん、　らいしゅうの　どようび　おひまでしたら
　　　　うちへ　しょくじに　きませんか。

スミス：どうも　ありがとうございます。　でも　らいしゅうの　どようびは
　　　　ちょっと　つごうが　わるいんですが…。

田中　：それじゃあ、　にちようびは　どうですか。

スミス：にちようびでしたら　だいじょうぶです。　なんじごろですか。

田中　：5じごろは　どうですか。

スミス：ええ、　けっこうです。
　　　　あのう、　かないも　いっても　いいですか。

田中　：ええ、　もちろん。　おこさんも　どうぞ。

スミス：こどもは　ベビーシッターが　いますから…。

田中　：ああ、　そうですか。

II

田中　：これは　わたしの　じゅうしょと　でんわばんごうです。
　　　　ちずを　かきましょうか。

スミス：ええ、　おねがいします。

田中　：スミスさんは　広尾でしたよね。　くるまで　きますか。

スミス：ええ。

田中　：それじゃあ、　ええっと、　天現寺インターから
　　　　首都高速に　のって、　高井戸インターで　おりてください。

スミス：天現寺から　高井戸ですね。

田中　：それから　環八に　はいって、　高井戸駅の　まえを　とおります。
　　　　マクドナルドの　かどを　みぎへ　まがって、　五日市街道に
　　　　はいってください。

スミス：環八から　五日市街道ですね。

スミス：環八から　五日市街道ですね。

田中　：ええ、　うちは　1つめの　こうさてんを　ひだりへ　まがって
　　　　　30メートルぐらいさきの　みぎがわの　しろい　うちです。

スミス：はい、　わかりました。　どのぐらい　かかりますか。

田中　：4、50ぷんでしょう。

スミス：そうですか。

田中　：それじゃあ、　らいしゅうの　にちようびの　5じごろ。

スミス：じゃあ。　どうも。

Grammar Note 1 — Inviting someone to your home

[Time], _o-hima deshitara_, [Activity, _etc._] _ni kimasen ka_ ↗.

Do-yōbi (ni), o-hima deshitara,　　　"If you're free on Saturday, would you like to come (to
　shokuji ni ki-masen ka.　　　　　　　my house) for dinner?"

a.　_O-hima deshitara_　　"If you're free"
　　This phrase is derived from **_hima desu_** "I/You/He do/does not have things to do."
　　Deshitara is the conditional form of **_desu_**.

b.　_Ki-masen ka_ ↗.　　"Why don't you come over (to my house)?"
　　　　　　　　　　　　　"Would you like to come over (to my house)?"
　　Irasshai-masen ka is used as an honorific equivalent of **_ki-masen ka_** in Level-3 speech.

　　Examples
　　　　Ashita shokuji ni kimasen ka.　　　　"Why don't you come over for din-
　　　　　　　　　　　　　　　　　　　　　　ner tomorrow?"
　　　　Kon'do no nichi-yōbi, o-hima deshitara　"Next Sunday, if you're free, would
　　　　　uchi e asobi ni kimasen ka.　　　　you like to come over to my house
　　　　　　　　　　　　　　　　　　　　　　(for a visit)?"

Grammar Note 2 — Accepting/Declining an invitation

a.　When accepting:
　　Dōmo arigatō gozaimasu.　　"Thank you very much.
　　Yorokon'de (ukagaimasu).　　I'd love to visit you."

　　Yorokon'de "happily, with pleasure" is derived from **_yorokobimasu_** "rejoice, be
　　pleased." **_Ukagaimasu_** is a humble way of saying "visit."

b.　When declining:
　　Dōmo arigatō gozaimasu.　　"Thank you very much, but . . ."
　　Demo . . . [Same as Lesson 22, Grammar Note 3-b,c]

　　Say thank you first, and then use the expressions for declining an invitation.

　　Examples
　　　　Dōmo arigatō gozaimasu.　　　　"Thank you very much."
　　　　　Demo do-yōbi wa chotto...　　　　"But Saturday is a bit..."
　　　　　Demo go-ji wa chotto tsugō　　　　"But five o'clock is a bit
　　　　　　ga warui-n desu ga...　　　　　inconvenient..."

Grammar Note 3 — Offering to do something for somebody

[Verb (Pre-*masu*)]-*mashō ka* ↗.
Chizu o kaki-mashō ka.   "Shall I draw a map for you?"

> **[Verb]-*mashō ka*** was introduced as "Shall we . . .?" in Lesson 22.
> This form is also used as "Shall I. . .?"

> **Examples**
> *Kore, taipu shimashō ka.*   "Shall I type this (for you)?"
> *Uchi made no chizu o kakimashō ka.*   "Shall I draw a map to show the way to my house (for you)?"

Grammar Note 4 — Accepting/Declining an offer

a.   When accepting:
Sumimasen.   "Thank you very much."
Ē, onegai shimasu.   "Yes, please."
Ē, [Verb]-*te kudasai.*   "Yes, please [Verb]."

b.   When declining:
(Iie,) ii desu.   ⎫   [*Lit.* (I'm) fine.]
(Iie,) kekkō desu.   ⎬ "No, thank you."   [*Lit.* (I would be) fine.]
(Iie,) daijōbu desu.   ⎭   [*Lit.* I can manage.]

> **Examples**
> A: *Chizu o kakimashō ka.*   "Shall I draw a map (for you)?"
> B: *Ē, onegai shimasu.*   "Yes, please."
>
> A: *Kore, taipu shimashō ka.* "Shall I type this?"
> B: *Iie, ima wa ii desu.*   "No, thank you, not right now."

Grammar Note 5 — Coming and going

> The usage of *ikimasu* "go" and *kimasu* "come" is different from English.
> *Ikimasu* is used to express motion away from the speaker's home base or present location.
> *Kimasu* is used to express motion towards the speaker's home base or present location.

> Observe the following and notice the difference:
> A: *Issho ni shokuji ni ikimasen ka.*   "Why don't we go for dinner together?"
> B: *Ē, ikimashō.*   "Yes, let's go."
>
> A: *Uchi e shokuji ni kimasen ka.*   "Why don't you come to my house for dinner?"
> B: *Dōmo. Nan-ji ni ikimashō ka.*   "Thank you. What time shall I come*?"

> * For B, he is going **away** from his home base. Therefore, B says *ikimashō ka.*

Study the following:

I.

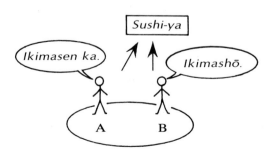

A: Why don't we go?
B: Let's go.

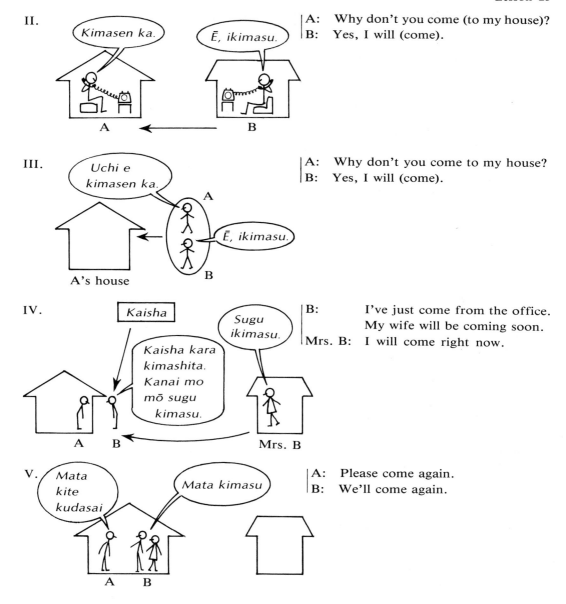

II.
A: Why don't you come (to my house)?
B: Yes, I will (come).

Kimasen ka.

Ē, ikimasu.

III.
A: Why don't you come to my house?
B: Yes, I will (come).

Uchi e kimasen ka.

Ē, ikimasu.

A's house

IV.
B: I've just come from the office. My wife will be coming soon.
Mrs. B: I will come right now.

Kaisha

Sugu ikimasu.

Kaisha kara kimashita. Kanai mo mō sugu kimasu.

Mrs. B

V.
A: Please come again.
B: We'll come again.

Mata kite kudasai

Mata kimasu

Grammar Note 6 — Expressing when/where/what is all right with you

[Noun] *deshitara daijōbu desu.*
Gogo *deshitara daijōbu desu.*　　　"If it's in the afternoon, that's fine."

Examples

A: *Do-yōbi wa dō desu ka.*　　　"How about Saturday?"
B: *Do-yōbi wa chotto...*　　　"Saturday is a bit..."
A: *Jā, nichi-yōbi wa dō desu ka.*　　　"Then, how about Sunday?"
B: *Nichi-yōbi deshitara daijōbu desu.*　　　"If it's on Sunday, fine."

A: *Sashimi wa dō desu ka.*　　　"How about *sashimi*?"
B: *Sō desu nē... Chotto...*　　　"Let's see . . . Well . . ."
A: *Jā, shabushabu wa.*　　　"Then, how about *shabushabu*?"
B: *Ā, shabushabu deshitara daijōbu desu.*　　　"Oh, if it's *shabushabu*, fine."

315

Grammar Note 7 — Asking for permission

In Lesson 19 (Grammar Note 4), you learned to ask if you can interrupt someone:
X-san, chotto ii desu ka.   ''Mr. X, may I interrupt you for a moment?''

a. Now we introduce a more specific way to ask for someone's permission:

[Verb]-*te mo ii* $\begin{cases} \textit{\textbf{desu ka}} \nearrow. \\ \textit{\textbf{deshō ka}} \searrow. \end{cases}$

<u>*Chotto kiite*</u> *mo ii desu ka.*   ''May I ask you something?''

This form literally means ''Is it all right (even) if I do so and so?''

b. Here are some new verbs for asking for permission:

Meaning	-*masu*	-*te*
borrow	*kari-masu*	*karite*
stop	*tome-masu*	*tomete*
enter	*hairi-masu*	*haitte*
sit down	*suwari-masu*	*suwatte*
take (a picture)	*tori-masu*	*totte*
use	*tsukai-masu*	*tsukatte*
smoke	*sui-masu*	*sutte*

Three verbs (from above) take the place marker **ni**.

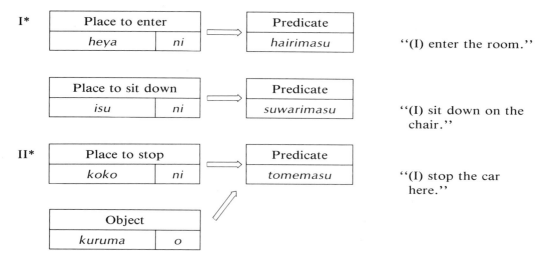

I*

Place to enter	
heya	*ni*

Predicate
hairimasu

''(I) enter the room.''

Place to sit down	
isu	*ni*

Predicate
suwarimasu

''(I) sit down on the chair.''

II*

Place to stop	
koko	*ni*

Predicate
tomemasu

''(I) stop the car here.''

Object	
kuruma	*o*

* I = Verb which does not take an object
* II = Verb which takes an object

Examples

Den'wa o tsukatte mo ii desu ka.	''May I use the telephone?''
Den'wa o karite mo ii desu ka.	''May I borrow (use) the telephone?''
Shashin o totte mo ii desu ka.	''May I take a picture?''
Koko ni suwatte mo ii desu ka.	''May I sit here?''
Koko ni tomete mo ii desu ka.	''May I stop/park (the car) here?''
Kono heya ni haitte mo ii desu ka.	''May I enter this room?''
Koko de tabako o sutte mo ii *desu ka.*	''May I smoke here?''

Grammar Note 8 — Giving/Not giving permission

Responses to the question (asking for permission) would be:

a. Positive

Ē, dōzo.	"Yes, go ahead."
Ē, ii desu yo.	"Yes, that's all right."
Ē, mochiron.	"Yes, of course."
Ē, [Verb]-te mo ii desu (yo).	"Yes, you may [Verb]."

b. Negative

Sō desu nē . . .	"Let me see . . ."
Chotto . . .	"It's a bit . . ."
Chotto komarimasu.	"It's a bit troublesome . . ."
Iie, dame desu.	"No, you can't."
	[*Lit.* It's no good.]

There are some verb forms to say "No, you may/can/must not."
They are not introduced in this textbook because expressing prohibition explicitly in Japanese is limited to certain situations.

Examples

A: *Den'wa o tsukatte mo ii desu ka.* "May I use your telephone?"
B: *Ē, dōzo.* "Yes, go ahead."

A: *Tabako o sutte mo ii desu ka.* "Do you mind if I smoke?"
B: *Chotto . . .* "Well, I do." [*Lit.* It's a bit . . .]
A: *A, dōmo sumimasen.* "Oh, I'm sorry."
B: *Iie, kochira koso.* "I'm sorry, too."

A: *Koko ni tomete mo ii deshō ka.* "Is it all right to park here?"
B: *Chotto komarimasu.* "Well, you shouldn't."
[*Lit.* It's a bit troublesome.]

Drill 1 Substitute the underlined parts.

1. <u>Kon'do no do-yōbi</u>, o-hima deshitara,
   (1) *raishū no kin-yōbi*　　(2) *kon'do no yasumi*
   (3) *ashita no gogo*　　　　(4) *kon'ban shichi-ji kara*

2. Uchi e <u>shokuji</u> ni kimasen ka.
   (1) *hiru-gohan*　　　　(2) *asobi*
   (3) *rekōdo o kiki*　　(4) *ocha o nomi*

3. <u>Nichi-yōbi</u> deshitara daijōbu desu.
   (1) *getsu-yōbi*　　　　　　(2) *rai-getsu no mik-ka*
   (3) *Tōkyō Eki no soba*　(4) *chikaku no mise*

4. <u>Kanai</u> mo itte mo ii deshō ka.
   (1) *kazoku*　　(2) *kodomo*　　(3) *tomodachi*

5. _Kon'do_ uchi de _pātī_ o shimasu kedo, kimasen ka.

(1)   raishū no do-yōbi, Nakamura-san no sōbetsu-kai "farewell party"

(2)   ku-gatsu. jūyok-ka, tan'jō pātī "birthday party"

Drill 2   Respond with "yes."

e.g.,   1.   (Issho ni) shokuji ni ikimasen ka.

⟶   Ē, ikimashō.

2.   (Uchi e) shokuji ni kimasen ka.

⟶   Dōmo. Yorokon'de (ukagaimasu).

(1)   (Issho ni) nomi ni ikimasen ka.

(2)   (Issho ni) bīru o nomimasen ka.

(3)   (Uchi e) nomi ni kimasen ka.

(4)   (Uchi e) asobi ni kimasen ka.

(5)   (Issho ni) asobi ni ikimasen ka.

Drill 3   Put appropriate verbs in the blanks using the appropriate forms.

e.g., right now	
A ← B	A: Sugu `kite` kudasai. B: Ima `iki`-masu.
(1) B → `eki` 9:00	A: Ku-ji ni eki e ☐ kudasai. B: Hai, ☐-masu.
(2) tomorrow A ← B	A: Ashita ☐-masen ka. B: Ē, ☐-masu.
(3) A Saturday A's house B	A: Do-yōbi ni ☐-masen ka. B: Ē, ☐-masu.
(4) together ☐ A—B	A: Issho ni ☐-masen ka. B: Ē, ☐-mashō.
(5) A B C	A: C-san wa ☐-masu ka. B: Ē, ☐-masu.

(6)	A: Kuruma de ⬚-masu ka.
	B: Ē, kuruma de ⬚-masu.

(7)	A: Nan de ⬚-mashita ka.
	B: Kuruma de ⬚-mashita.

(8)	B: Uchi e ⬚-masu.

(9)	A: Mata ⬚ kudasai.
	B: Dōmo. Mata ⬚-masu.

Drill 4   Make questions asking for permission.

e.g.,   Kore o karimasu. ⟶ Kore o karite mo ii ⎰ desuka.
⎱ deshō ka.

1. (1) Den'wa o shimasu.
    (2) Ressun o kyan'seru shimasu.
    (3) Ashita osoku kimasu.

2. (1) Koko ni imasu.
    (2) Go-ji kara terebi o mimasu.
    (3) Chotto den'wa o karimasu.
    (4) Koko ni kuruma o tomemasu.

3. (1) Rōmaji de kakimasu.
    (2) Chotto kikimasu "ask".
    (3) Ima shin'bun o yomimasu.
    (4) Kazoku to issho ni ikimasu.
    (5) Kyō wa hayaku kaerimasu.
    (6) Chotto den'wa o tsukaimasu.
    (7) Koko de tabako o suimasu.
    (8) Koko ni suwarimasu.
    (9) Ei-go de hanashimasu.
    (10) Ima shashin "picture, photograph" o torimasu.

Drill 5   Make short dialogues.

e.g.,   1. ⎰ den'wa, karimasu ⎱   A: Anō, den'wa (o) karitemo ii deshō ka.
        ⎱ "Yes, go ahead." ⎰ ⟶   B: Ē, dōzo.
        2. ⎰ den'wa, karimasu ⎱   A: Anō, den'wa (o) karite mo ii deshō ka.
        ⎱ "Now, it's a bit..." ⎰ ⟶   B: Ima wa chotto...

(1)   *kono jisho, tsukaimasu*
         "Yes, go ahead."
(2)   *koko, tabako, suimasu*
         "Cigarette, it's a bit. . ."
(3)   *koko, suwarimasu*
         "Yes, of course."
(4)   *kono hen, kuruma, tomemasu*
         "Well, it's a bit troublesome . . ."
(5)   *kono hon, karimasu*
         "That book, it's a bit. . ."
(6)   *Rōmaji, kakimasu*
         "Yes, you may write in Roman letters."

Drill 6   Change the sentences.

e.g.,   *Kyō wa hayaku kaette mo ii deshō ka.*
         ⟶   *Kyō wa hayaku kaeri-tai-n desu ga/kedo, ii deshō ka.*

(1)   *Kono zasshi o yon'de mo ii deshō ka.*
(2)   *Koko ni kuruma o tomete mo ii desu ka.*
(3)   *Ashita wa chotto osoku kite mo ii deshō ka.*
(4)   *Yo-ji han kara kon'pyūtā o tsukatte mo ii desu ka.*
(5)   *Gakkō no hon o karite mo ii desu ka.*
(6)   *Kin-yōbi no ressun o kyan'seru shite mo ii deshō ka.*

Drill 7   Substitute the underlined parts.

1.   *Kodomo wa, gakkō ga arimasu kara . . .*
     (1)   *kanai, hoka no yakusoku*
     (3)   *kodomo, juku* "a cram school"
     (2)   *shujin, shigoto*

2.   *Kodomo wa, bebīshittā ga imasu kara, daijōbu desu.*
     (1)   *mēdo-san* "maid", *uchi ni imasu*
     (2)   *kyōdai* "brothers and sisters", *uchi de asobimasu*

Drill 8   .Using Dialogue I as a model, complete the following.

(1)		
	Tape:	*Raishū no do-yōbi, o-hima deshitara uchi e shokuji ni kimasen ka.*
[a] It's a bit incovenient.	You:	[a]_____ .
	Tape:	*Jā, kin-yōbi no ban wa dō desu ka.*
[b] fine	You:	[b]_____ .
[c] what time?	You:	[c]_____ .
	Tape:	*Shichi-ji goro wa dō deshō ka.*
[d] fine	You:	[d]_____ .
[e] my wife, too?		[e]_____ .
	Tape:	*Ē, mochiron. Okosan mo dōzo.*
[f] We have a baby-sitter for the children.	You:	[f]_____ _____ .
	Tape:	*A, sō desu ka.*

(2)		
	Tape:	Rai-getsu no mik-ka, shujin no tan'jō pātī o shimasu kedo, kimasen ka.
[a] I'm sorry but I have an appointment.	You:	[a]_____ .
	Tape:	Sō desu ka. Sore wa zan'nen desu ne. Jā mata kon'do.
[b] next time	You:	[b]_____ .

(3) [You invite the other person this time.]		
[a] next Saturday, dinner	You:	[a]_____ .
	Tape:	Dōmo arigatō gozaimasu. Yorokon'de ukagaimasu. Nan'ji goro desu ka.
[b] around 5:00	You:	[b]_____ .
	Tape:	Sō desu ne. . . Go-ji wa chotto tsugō ga warui-n desu ga . . .
[c] around 6:30	You:	[c]_____ .
	Tape:	Roku-ji han deshitara daijōbu desu. Anō, shujin mo ii desu ka.
[d] of course your children, too	You:	[d]_____ .
	Tape:	Kodomo wa juku ga arimasu kara . . .
	You:	[EL]_____ .

(4)		
[a] Friday next week small party	You:	[a]_____ .
	Tape:	Dōmo arigatō gozaimasu. Demo, zan'nen desu ga, raishū no kin-yōbi wa chotto tsugō ga warui-n desu ga . . .
[b] That's too bad. next time, then	You:	[b]_____ .
	Tape:	Ē, mata kon'do. Dōmo sumimasen.

Drill 9 Make short dialogues.

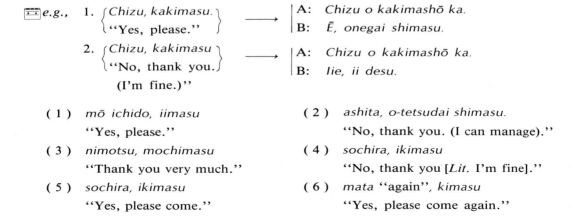

e.g., 1. { Chizu, kakimasu. } ⟶ A: Chizu o kakimashō ka.
        { "Yes, please." }   B: Ē, onegai shimasu.

      2. { Chizu, kakimasu } ⟶ A: Chizu o kakimashō ka.
        { "No, thank you.   B: Iie, ii desu.
          (I'm fine.)" }

(1) mō ichido, iimasu
    "Yes, please."

(2) ashita, o-tetsudai shimasu
    "No, thank you. (I can manage)."

(3) nimotsu, mochimasu
    "Thank you very much."

(4) sochira, ikimasu
    "No, thank you [Lit. I'm fine]."

(5) sochira, ikimasu
    "Yes, please come."

(6) mata "again", kimasu
    "Yes, please come again."

321

Drill 10   Give directions.

 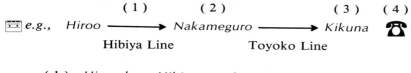

(1)   (2)   (3)   (4)

e.g.,   Hiroo ———→ Nakameguro ———→ Kikuna ☎

　　　　　Hibiya Line　　　　Toyoko Line

(1)   *Hiroo* kara *Hibiya-sen* de *Nakameguro* made itte,
(2)   *Tōyoko-sen* ni norikaete,
(3)   *Kikuna* de orite kudasai.
(4)   Eki kara den'wa shite kudasai.

(1)   (2)   (3)   (4)

1.   Roppon'gi ———→ Nakameguro ———→ Jiyūgaoka ☎

　　　　Hibiya Line　　　　Toyoko Line

(1)   (2)   (3)   (4)

2.   Harajuku ———→ Takadanobaba ———→ Tanashi ☎

　　　Yamanote Line　　　Seibu Shinjuku Line

(1)   (2)   (3)

3.   Tōkyo ———→ Kichijōji ☎ ———→ Sekimachi

　　　Chuo Line　　　　Bus No. 63 or 64

Drill 11   Repeat and practice the pronunciation of the vocabulary for giving directions to
　　　　　　drivers (in the Tokyo area).

1.   [＿＿＿] *kōsoku (dōro)*　　　"expressway"
　　e.g.,   Shuto Kōsoku　　　　"Shuto (Metropolitan) Expressway"
　　　　　　Chūō Kōsoku　　　　　"Chuo (Central) Expressway"

2.   [＿＿＿] *kaidō*　　　　　　"road, route, highway"
　　e.g.,   Ōme Kaidō　　　　　"Ome highway"
　　　　　　Kōshū Kaidō　　　　　"Koshu highway"

3.   [＿＿＿] *dōri*　　　　　　"street, avenue"
　　e.g.,   Meiji Dōri　　　　　"Meiji Street"
　　　　　　Aoyama Dōri　　　　"Aoyama Street"

4.   Kan'jō [＿＿＿] -gō-sen　　　"Loop road No. ＿＿"
　　e.g.,   Kan'jō hachi-gō-sen　　"Loop road No. 8"
　　　　　　(*or* Kan' pachi)
　　　　　　Kan'jō nana-gō-sen　　"Loop road No. 7"
　　　　　　(*or* Kan' nana)

5. *(Kokudō)* ☐ *-gō-sen*   "National Highway No.___"

     e.g.,   *Kokudō nihyaku-yon'jū-roku-gō-sen*   "National Highway No. 246"

         (or 246) nī yon roku

         Kokudō jū-nana-gō-sen   "National Highway No. 17"

6. ☐ *in'tā (chen'ji)*   "interchange (exit/entrance)"

     e.g.,   *Kasumigaseki Intā*   "Kasumigaseki Interchange"

         Goten'ba Intā   "Gotemba Interchange"

7. ☐ *hōmen*   "for/toward/in the direction of..."

     e.g.,   *Yokohama hōmen*   "for Yokohama"

         Hachiōji hōmen   "for Hachioji"

8. ☐ *-ban no de-guchi*   "exit No.___"

     e.g.,   *ichi-ban no de-guchi*   "exit No. 1"

         ni-ban no de-guchi   "exit No. 2"

9.   *iri-guchi*   "entrance"

10.   *ryōkin'jo*   "toll gate"

Drill 12   Give directions looking at the illustrations.

1.   *e.g.,*   I.C. ──────────→ I.C.
         Ten'gen'ji   *Shuto Kō(soku)*   *Takaido*

         Ten'gen'ji In'tā kara Shuto Kō(soku) ni notte Takaido In'tā de orimasu.

   (1)   I.C. ──────────→ I.C.
         Kasumigaseki   *Shuto Kō(soku)*   *Hakozaki*

   (2)   I.C. ──────────→ I.C.
         Shibakōen   *Shuto Kō(soku)*   *Haneda*

2.   *e.g.,*   *Yōga* ──→ _____ *Tōmei Kōsoku* _____

         Yōga kara Tōmei Kōsoku ni hairimasu.

   (1)   *Takaido* ──→ _____ *Chūō Kōsoku* _____

   (2)   *Iriya* ──→ _____ *Nikkō Kaidō* _____

▦3.   *e.g.,*   toward *Shibuya*

⟶ *Shibuya* hōmen e ikimasu.

(1)   toward *Shin'juku*
(2)   toward *Gin'za*

▦4.   *e.g.,*   ⟶ Ogikubo
Kan'pachi

Kan'pachi o tōtte *Ogikubo* made ikimasu.

(1)   ⟶ Nakameguro
Yamate Dōri

(2)   ⟶ Tamagawa "Tama River"
Nakahara Kaidō

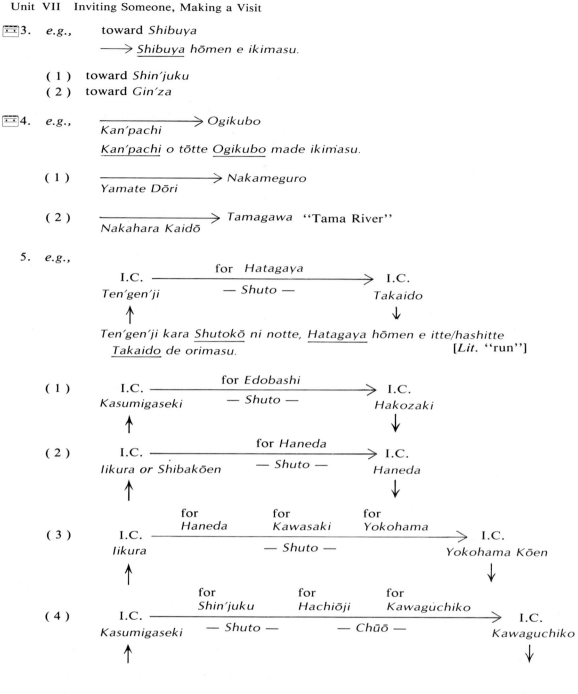

5.   *e.g.,*

I.C. ———— for *Hatagaya* ————→ I.C.
Ten'gen'ji   — Shuto —   *Takaido*

Ten'gen'ji kara Shutokō *ni notte,* Hatagaya *hōmen e itte/hashitte*
Takaido *de orimasu.*   [*Lit.* "run"]

(1)   I.C. ———— for *Edobashi* ————→ I.C.
Kasumigaseki   — Shuto —   *Hakozaki*

(2)   I.C. ———— for *Haneda* ————→ I.C.
Iikura or Shibakōen   — Shuto —   *Haneda*

(3)   I.C. ——— for   for   for ———→ I.C.
Iikura   *Haneda* *Kawasaki* *Yokohama* *Yokohama Kōen*
                — Shuto —

(4)   I.C. ——— for   for   for ———→ I.C.
Kasumigaseki *Shin'juku* *Hachiōji* *Kawaguchiko* *Kawaguchiko*
               — Shuto —   — Chūō —

Drill 13   Make short dialogues.

e.g.,   *Tsukiji*   │ A: *Tsukiji wa doko de orimasu ka.*
          Gin'za (Intā) ⟶ │ B: *Gin'za (Intā) desu.*

(1)   *Ueno no dōbutsuen* "zoo"
        Ueno (Intā)
(2)   *Yokohama no Chūka-gai* "China Town"
        Yokohama Kōen (Intā)
(3)   *Nikkō*
        Tōhoku Jidōsha-dō no Utsunomiya (Intā)

Drill 14 Using Dialogue II as a model, complete the following.

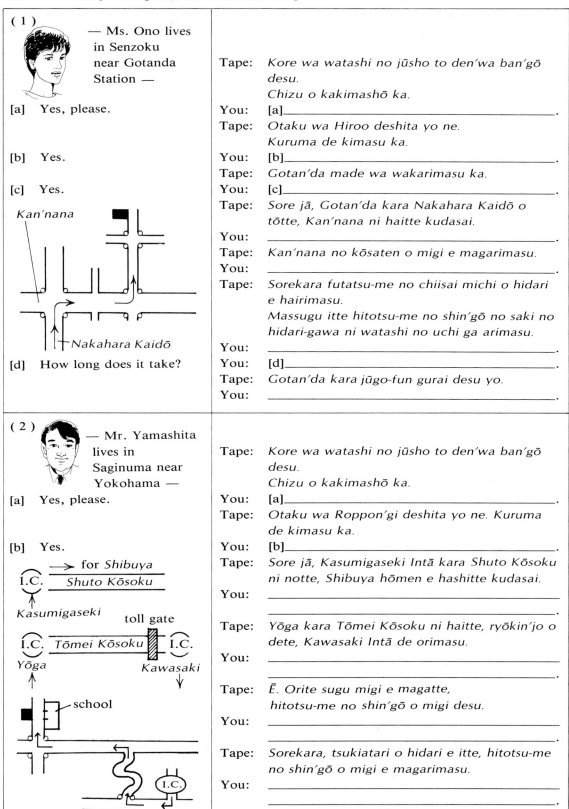

(1)
— Ms. Ono lives in Senzoku near Gotanda Station —

[a] Yes, please.

[b] Yes.

[c] Yes.

Kan'nana

Nakahara Kaidō

[d] How long does it take?

Tape: *Kore wa watashi no jūsho to den'wa ban'gō desu.*
Chizu o kakimashō ka.
You: [a]_____.
Tape: *Otaku wa Hiroo deshita yo ne.*
Kuruma de kimasu ka.
You: [b]_____.
Tape: *Gotan'da made wa wakarimasu ka.*
You: [c]_____.
Tape: *Sore jā, Gotan'da kara Nakahara Kaidō o tōtte, Kan'nana ni haitte kudasai.*
You: _____.
Tape: *Kan'nana no kōsaten o migi e magarimasu.*
You: _____.
Tape: *Sorekara futatsu-me no chiisai michi o hidari e hairimasu.*
Massugu itte hitotsu-me no shin'gō no saki no hidari-gawa ni watashi no uchi ga arimasu.
You: _____.
You: [d]_____.
Tape: *Gotan'da kara jūgo-fun gurai desu yo.*
You: _____.

(2)
— Mr. Yamashita lives in Saginuma near Yokohama —

[a] Yes, please.

[b] Yes.

→ for *Shibuya*
I.C. *Shuto Kōsoku*

Kasumigaseki
toll gate
I.C. *Tōmei Kōsoku* I.C.
Yōga *Kawasaki*

school

I.C.

Tape: *Kore wa watashi no jūsho to den'wa ban'gō desu.*
Chizu o kakimashō ka.
You: [a]_____.
Tape: *Otaku wa Roppon'gi deshita yo ne. Kuruma de kimasu ka.*
You: [b]_____.
Tape: *Sore jā, Kasumigaseki Intā kara Shuto Kōsoku ni notte, Shibuya hōmen e hashitte kudasai.*
You: _____.
Tape: *Yōga kara Tōmei Kōsoku ni haitte, ryōkin'jo o dete, Kawasaki Intā de orimasu.*
You: _____.
Tape: *Ē. Orite sugu migi e magatte, hitotsu-me no shin'gō o migi desu.*
You: _____.
Tape: *Sorekara, tsukiatari o hidari e itte, hitotsu-me no shin'gō o migi e magarimasu.*
You: _____.

	Tape:	*Sōsuruto, migi-gawa ni gakkō ga arimasu. Watashi no uchi wa gakkō no mon "gate" no mae desu.*
	You:	_____.
[c] How long does it take?	You:	[c]_____.
	Tape:	*Ichi-jikan gurai deshō.*

(3) — Mr. Takahashi lives in Kichijoji. —

[a]   Yes, please.

[b]   Yes.

Shibuya━━━━━━Kichijoji
↑ Inokashira Line ↓

Kita-guchi

←━━━━━━━━

Kichijoji Eki

eki

[c]   How long does it take from the station?

Tape:	*Kore wa watashi no jūsho to den'wa ban'gō desu.*
	Chizu o kakimashō ka.
You:	[a]_____.
Tape:	*Den'sha de kimasu ka.*
You:	[b]_____.
Tape:	*Otaku wa Yoyogi deshita yo ne.*
	Jā, Shibuya kara Inokashira-sen ni notte shūten no Kichijōji de orite kudasai.
You:	_____.
Tape:	*Ē. Kita-guchi kara dete, hidari e massugu kite kudasai.*
You:	_____.
Tape:	*Sorekara, futatsu-me no shin'gō o migi e magatte kudasai.*
	Uchi wa san'jū-mētā gurai saki no migi-gawa no Musashino Haitsu to iu man'shon desu.
You:	_____.
Tape:	*Ē. Heya wa san-gai no 305 desu.*
You:	[c]_____.
Tape:	*Shichi-hap-pun desu yo.*
	Wakaranakattara "If you get lost [Lit. If you don't understand]" den'wa shite kudasai.
You:	_____.

Drill 15   Supposing you are inviting friends to your house. Draw a map and give directions.

Shuto Expressway

326

Lesson 24

MAKING A VISIT TO A FRIEND'S HOUSE

SUMISU-SAN, IRASSHAI
"WELCOME (TO MY HOUSE), MR SMITH!"

Dialogue I

[Mr. Smith is at the front door of the Tanaka's. He rings the door bell.]

—Pin'pon—

Tanaka: Hāi, donata desu ka.

Sumisu: Sumisu desu ga . . .

Tanaka: A, Sumisu-san, chotto omachi kudasai.

[Mrs. Tanaka opens the door.]

Tanaka: Sumisu-san irasshai.

Sumisu: Kon'ban'wa. Anō, asoko ni kuruma o tomete mo ii desu ka.

Tanaka: Ē, dōzo.

[Mr. Smith goes back and parks the car.]

    *   *   *

Tanaka: Dōzo ohairi kudasai.

Sumisu: Ojama shimasu. [Mr. and Mrs. Smith go into the house.]

Tanaka: Uchi wa sugu wakarimashita ka.

Sumisu: Ē. [They leave their shoes and step inside.]

Tanaka: Dōzo kochira e.

Mrs. Tanaka:	Yes, who is it, please?
Mr. Smith:	(It's) (John) Smith.
Mrs. Tanaka:	Oh, Mr. Smith, just a moment please.
Mrs. Tanaka:	Hello, Mr. Smith. [*Lit.* Welcome to my home.]
Mr. Smith:	Good evening. Well, may I park the car over there?
Mr. Tanaka:	Yes, you can.
	* * *
Mr. & Mrs. Tanaka: }	Please come in.
Mr. & Mrs. Smith: }	Thank you. [*Lit.* We're going to interrupt.]
Mr. Tanaka:	Was it easy to find my house?
Mr. Smith:	Yes. It was quite easy.
Mrs. Tanaka:	Please come this way.

Vocabulary

omachi kudasai
  ← matte kudasai: Could you please wait?

irasshai: welcome [to my house]

ohairi kudasai ← haitte kudasai: Please come in.

ojama shimasu: excuse me (for entering), thank you [*Lit.* I'll interrupt]

wakarimashita: was easy to find

▭ Dialogue II ——————————————————————

[In the living room]

Tanaka: *Dōzo okake kudasai.*

Sumisu: *Anō, kore . . .* [She presents a little gift.]

Tanaka: *A, dōmo sumimasen nē.*

             [He accepts the gift.]

[They sit down on the sofa.]

Tanaka: *Nomimono wa ikaga desu ka.*

Sumisu: *Dōmo. Itadakimasu.*

Tanaka: *Wain to bīru to uisukī ga arimasu*
           kedo . . .
           Dore ga ii desu ka.

Sumisu: *Jā, wain onegai dekimasu ka.*

Tanaka: *Hai. Okusan wa nani ga ii desu ka.*

Sumisu: *Watashi mo wain o onegai shimasu.*

Tanaka: *Hai.*

        **   *   **

Tanaka: *O-shokuji (o) dōzo.*

Tanaka: *Dōzo kochira e.* [He shows them to the table.]

Tanaka: *Nani mo arimasen ga, dōzo . . .*

Sumisu: *Itadakimasu.*

Mr. Tanaka:	Please, have a seat.
Mrs. Smith:	Here's (a little, small something for you).
Mr. Tanaka:	Oh, thank you very much. You shouldn't have done this. [*Lit.* I'm sorry.]
Mr. Tanaka:	Would you like to have something to drink?
Mr. Smith:	Yes, we will. Thank you.
Mr. Tanaka:	We have wine, beer and whisky, what would you like? [*Lit.* Which one is good?]
Mr. Smith:	Then, could I have wine, please?
Mr. Tanaka:	Sure, how about you, Mrs. Smith?
Mrs. Smith:	I'll have wine, too.
Mr. Tanaka:	O.K.

                *   *   *

Mrs. Tanaka:	Dinner is ready. [*Lit.* Please, have dinner.]
Mr. Tanaka:	Come this way, please.
Mrs. Tanaka:	We have nothing special, but please go ahead.
Mr. & Mrs. Smith:	Oh, Thank you (let's eat).

Vocabulary ——————————————————————

okake kudasai ← kakete kudasai: please sit down

nomimono: beverages

dore: which one (of more than three things)

nani mo arimasen ga . . . :   [*Lit.* There is nothing, but . . .]

📼 Dialogue III

[After dinner]

Sumisu: Gochisōsama deshita. Totemo oishikatta desu.

Sumisu: Okusan wa (o)-ryōri ga (o)-jōzu desu nē.

Tanaka: Iie, osomatsusama deshita.

          *   *   *

Tanaka: Kōhī ka kōcha demo ikaga desu ka.

Sumisu: Dōmo sumimasen. Sore jā, kōhī

             onegai dekimasu ka.

Tanaka: Kōhī wa dō shimasu ka.

Sumisu: Burakku onegai shimasu.

Tanaka: Hai. Okusan wa.

Sumisu: Remon-tī onegai dekimasu ka.

          *   *   *

Tanaka: Okusan, mō ippai ikaga desu ka.

Sumisu: Dōmo. Mō kekkō desu.

Tanaka: Sumisu-san wa.

Sumisu: Jā, onegai shimasu.

Tanaka: Sumisu-san wa kōhī ga suki desu nē.

Sumisu: Ē, ichi-nichi ni go-hai gurai nomimasu.

Mr. Smith:	It was delicious. I enjoyed it very much.
Mrs. Smith:	You are a very good cook, Mrs. Tanaka.
Mrs. Tanaka:	Oh, no (I'm not). It was a humble (meal).
	* * *
Mrs. Tanaka:	Would you like to have coffee, tea or something?
Mr. Smith:	Thank you. Could I have some coffee, please?
Mrs. Tanaka:	How would like your coffee?
Mr. Smith:	(I'll have it) black, please.
Mrs. Tanaka:	Sure. How about you, Mrs. Smith?
Mrs. Smith:	Could I have some lemon tea, please?
	* * *
Mrs. Tanaka:	Mrs. Smith, would you like to have another cup of tea?
Mrs. Smith:	Thank you. I've already had enough.
Mr. Tanaka:	How about you, Mr. Smith?
Mr. Smith:	I'll have another, please.
Mr. Tanaka:	Mr. Smith, you like coffee, don't you?
Mr. Smith:	Yes. I (usually) drink about five cups (of coffee) a day.

Vocabulary

gochisōsama deshita: thank you for the meal

osomatsusama deshita: (it) was a humble
                          meal

[Noun] *ka* [Noun]:   (something) or
                (something)

demo: and the like

. . . wa dō shimasu ka: how would you like
                        to have . . .

burakku: black (coffee)

mō ippai: one more cup of . . .

📼 ▶Dialogue IV

[Mr. Smith looks at the clock.]

Sumisu: *Sorosoro shitsurei shimasu.*

Tanaka: *Mada ii ja arimasen ka.*

Sumisu: *Demo mō osoi desu kara . . .*

Tanaka: *Sō desu ka . . . Sore jā . . .*

　　　　　*   *   *

[They go back to the entrance.]

Sumisu: *Kyō wa gochisōsama deshita.*

Tanaka: *Iie.*

Sumisu: *Hon'tō ni tanoshikatta desu. Dōmo arigatō.*

Tanaka: *Kochira koso. Dōmo arigatō gozaimashita.*

Tanaka: *Zehi mata kite kudasai.*

Sumisu: *Ē. Uchi e mo asobi ni kite kudasai.*

Tanaka: *Dōmo.*

Sumisu: *Jā, ojama shimashita.*

Sumisu: *Oyasuminasai.*

Tanaka: *Oyasuminasai, ki o tsukete.*

Mr. Smith:	We must be leaving now. [*Lit.* I'm leaving soon/slowly.]
Mr. Tanaka:	It's not so late. [*Lit.* It's still all right].
Mr. Smith:	Well, it's rather late, so...
Mr. Tanaka:	Do you think so? If you say so... [*Lit.* Then...]

　　　　　*   *   *

Mr. Smith:	Thank you for inviting us today. It was a very good dinner.
Mrs. Tanaka:	Not at all.
Mr. Smith:	We really enjoyed it. Thank you.
Mr. Tanaka:	You're welcome. Thank you very much for coming.
Mrs. Tanaka:	Please come back again.
Mr. Smith:	We will. Please come and see us sometime, too.
Mr. & Mrs. Tanaka:	Thank you.
Mr. Smith:	Well, thank you. [*Lit:* we interrupted you.]
Mr. & Mrs. Smith:	Good night.
Mr. & Mrs. Tanaka:	Good night. Take care.

Ｉ

　　　　　　　　　　　　　　　—ピンポン—

田中（おくさん）：はあい、　どなたですか。
た なか

スミス　　　　　：スミスですが…。

田中（おくさん）：あ、　スミスさん、　ちょっと　おまちください。

　　　　　　　　　スミスさん、　いらっしゃい。

Vocabulary

sorosoro: almost, gradually, slowly

mada: still

gochisōsama: a feast

hon'tō ni: really, truthfully

tanoshikatta ← tanoshii: enjoyable

zehi: by all means

ki o tsukete: be careful, take care

スミス　　　　　：こんばんは。　あのう、　あそこに　くるまを
　　　　　　　　　とめても　いいですか。

田中　　　　　：ええ、　どうぞ。
　たなか

　　　　　　　　　　＊　　　＊　　　＊

田中
田中（おくさん）｝：どうぞ　おはいりください。

スミス
スミス（おくさん）｝：おじゃまします。

田中　　　　　：うちは　すぐ　わかりましたか。

スミス　　　　　：ええ。

田中（おくさん）：どうぞ　こちらへ。

II

田中　　　　　：どうぞ　おかけください。
　たなか
スミス（おくさん）：あのう、　これ…

田中　　　　　：あ、　どうも　すみませんねえ。

田中　　　　　：のみものは　いかがですか。

スミス　　　　　：どうも。　いただきます。

田中　　　　　：ワインと　ビールと　ウイスキーが　ありますけど…。
　　　　　　　　　どれが　いいですか。

スミス　　　　　：じゃあ、　ワイン　おねがいできますか。

田中　　　　　：はい。　おくさんは　なにが　いいですか。

スミス（おくさん）：わたしも　ワインを　おねがいします。

田中　　　　　：はい。

　　　　　　　　　　＊　　　＊　　　＊

田中（おくさん）：おしょくじ（を）　どうぞ。
　たなか
田中　　　　　：どうぞ　こちらへ。

田中（おくさん）：なにも　ありませんが、　どうぞ…。

スミス
スミス（おくさん）｝：いただきます。

III

スミス	：ごちそうさまでした。　とても　おいしかったです。
スミス（おくさん）	：おくさんは　（お）りょうりが
	（お）じょうずですねえ。
田中（おくさん）	：いいえ、　おそまつさまでした。

　　　　　　　　　＊　　　＊　　　＊

田中（おくさん）	：コーヒーか　こうちゃでも　いかがですか。
スミス	：どうも　すみません。
	それじゃあ、　コーヒー　おねがいできますか。
田中（おくさん）	：コーヒーは　どうしますか。
スミス	：ブラック　おねがいします。
田中（おくさん）	：はい。　おくさんは。
スミス（おくさん）	：レモンティー　おねがいできますか。

　　　　　　　　　＊　　　＊　　　＊

田中（おくさん）	：おくさん、　もう1ぱい　いかがですか。
スミス（おくさん）	：どうも。　もう　けっこうです。
田中	：スミスさんは。
スミス	：じゃあ、　おねがいします。
田中	：スミスさんは　コーヒーが　すきですねえ。
スミス	：ええ、　1にちに　5はいぐらい　のみます。

IV

スミス	：そろそろ　しつれいします。
田中	：まだ　いいじゃありませんか。
スミス	：でも　もう　おそいですから…。
田中	：そうですか…。　それじゃあ…。

　　　　　　　　　＊　　　＊　　　＊

スミス	：きょうは　ごちそうさまでした。
田中（おくさん）	：いいえ。
スミス	：ほんとうに　たのしかったです。
	どうも　ありがとう。
田中	：こちらこそ。　どうも　ありがとうございました。
田中（おくさん）	：ぜひ　また　きてください。

スミス　　　　　　　：ええ。　うちへも　あそびに　きてください。

田中
田中（おくさん）}：どうも。

スミス　　　　　　　：じゃあ、　おじゃましました。

スミス
スミス（おくさん）}：おやすみなさい。

田中
田中（おくさん）}：おやすみなさい、　きをつけて。

In Japan, when visiting people, ordinarily you are offered something to drink or food without being asked. You decline the offer, but eventually end up drinking or eating what has been offered anyway.

That's the basic rule (*cf.* Culture Note 11 — *En'ryo*). So, you do not need any sentence patterns such as asking for/telling your preference, if you follow the traditional Japanese way.

However, as we know that the students would really like to know how to offer/accept/decline/ask and tell preferences, we introduce the following patterns, which are sufficiently polite.

Grammar Note 1 — Offering food, beverages, *etc.*

[Thing to be offered] *wa/demo ikaga desu ka* ↗.
<u>*Nomimono*</u> *wa ikaga desu ka.*　　"Would you like a drink?"

a.　*Ikaga, Dō*　　"How"
　　Ikaga is a humble equivalent of *dō*.
　　Ikaga desu ka literally means "How about it?"
　　In this lesson, this sentence is used for offering, "Would you like . . .?"

　　Let's review how we have used *dō/ikaga desu ka.*
　　　　Lesson 8　*Kore wa ikaga de gozaimasu ka.*　　[Recommending]
　　　　　　　　　"How about this one?"　　　　　　　　(by a sales clerk)
　　　　Lesson 10　*Nihon wa dō/ikaga desu ka.*　　[Asking for comments]
　　　　　　　　　"How do you like Japan?"　　　　　on Japan
　　　　Lesson 12　*Yasumi wa dō/ikaga deshita ka.*　[Asking generally how
　　　　　　　　　"How was your holiday?"　　　　　the holiday went]
　　　　Lesson 21　*Nikkō wa dō/ikaga desu ka.*　　[Giving suggestions
　　　　　　　　　"How about (going to) Nikko?"　　or recommendations]

b.　*Demo*　[Sample Listing Marker]　　". . . or something"
　　Compare the following:
　　　　Kōhī wa ikaga desu ka.　　"Would you like coffee?"
　　　　Kōhī demo ikaga desu ka.　　"Would you like coffee or something?"

　　Examples
　　　　Wain demo ikaga desu ka.　　　　　　"Would you like wine or
　　　　　　　　　　　　　　　　　　　　　　something?"

　　　　Kōhī ka kōcha demo ikaga desu ka.　　"Would you like coffee, tea or
　　　　　　　　　　　　　　　　　　　　　　something?"

Grammar Note 2 — Offering/Inviting someone to/for food, beverages, *etc.*

Nanika* [Verb (Pre-*masu*)]-*masen ka* ↗.

Nanika <u>*nomi*</u>*masen ka.*   "Would you like to drink something?"
      **Nanika = cf.* Lesson 13, Grammar Note 2-b

Remember that **[Verb (Pre-*masu*)]-*masen ka*** can mean "Why don't we?" or "Would you like to . . .?" (Lesson 22)

Examples

Nanika yomimasen ka.   "Would you like to read something?"
Nanika tabemasen ka.   "Would you like to eat something?"

Grammar Note 3 — Accepting/Declining an offer

a.   When accepting:

Dōmo arigatō gozaimasu. { **Itadakimasu.**   "I'll have some."
                           Onegai shimasu.   "Please."

b.   When declining:

Dōmo arigatō gozaimasu. **Demo ima wa kekkō desu.**   "(But) I'm fine for now."

c.   When refusing for politeness sake:

Dōzo okamai naku.   "Please don't bother."   (*cf.* Culture Note 11)

Grammar Note 4 — Telling what you have and asking for a preference

a.   **[X *to* Y] *ga arimasu kedo*,**   "We/I have X and Y,
       <u>*dotchi*</u> *ga ii desu ka* ↗.   but <u>which</u> (of the two) would you like?"

b.   **[X *to* Y *to* Z] *ga arimasu kedo*,**   "We/I have X, Y and Z,
       <u>*dore*</u> *ga ii de su ka* ↗.   but <u>which</u> (of the three or more) would you like?"

Subject		
dotchi/dochira *dore/dochira*	*ga*	

⟹

Predicate	Final
ii desu	*ka* ↗

Compare:

Dore/Dochira   "Which of the many [three or more]"
Nani   "What"

The most Japanese-like answer would be:

Dotchi demo ⎫
Dore demo   ⎬ *ii/kekkō desu.*   "Whichever is fine."
Nan demo   ⎭   "Whichever is fine."
                                         "Whatever is fine."

Examples

| A: | *Kōhī to kōcha ga arimasu kedo, dotchi ga ii desu ka. .* | "I have coffee and tea. . ., which would you like?" |
| B: | *Jā, kōcha onegai shimasu.* | "Then, tea, please." |

| A: | *Wain to bīru to uisukī ga arimasu kedo, dore ga ii desu ka.* | "We have wine, beer and whisky, which would you like?" |
| B: | *Jā, bīru onegai dekimasu ka.* | "Then, I'll have beer, please." |

A: *Nomimono wa nani ga ii desu ka.*   "What would you like to drink?"
B: *Oren'ji jūsu onegai shimasu.*   "Orange juice, please."

Grammar Note 5 — Asking/Telling how you like the beverages/food served

a.   **[Beverage/Food] *wa dō shimasu ka* ↗.**
    Uisukī wa dō shimasu ka.   "How would you like your whisky?"
                      [*Lit.* As for your whisky, what do you do (with it)?]

Examples

A: *Uisukī wa dō shimasu ka.*   "How would you like your whisky?"
B: *On'zarokku onegai shimasu.*   "On the rocks, please."

A: *Kōhī wa dō shimasu ka.*   "How would you like your coffee?"
B: *Burakku onegai shimasu.*   "Black, please."

A: *Kōcha wa dō shimasu ka.*   "How would you like your tea?"
B: *Miruku dake onegai shimasu.*   "Milk only, please."

A: *Sutēki wa dō shimasu ka.*   "How would you like your steak?"
B: *Midiamu onegai shimasu.*   "Medium, please."

b.   **[Milk/Sugar, *etc.*] *wa iremasu ka* ↗.**
    Satō wa iremasu ka.   "Do you put (take) sugar?"

Examples

A: *Kōhī wa satō wa iremasu ka.*   "Do you put (take) sugar in your coffee?"
B: *Ē, hitotsu onegai shimasu.*   "Yes, one, please."
    or   *or*
    Iie, (Satō wa) kekkō desu.   "No, thank you,"

A: *Satō to miruku wa iremasu ka.*   "Do you put (use) sugar and milk?"
B: *Satō mo miruku mo kekkō desu.*   "Neither sugar nor milk, please."

Grammar Note 6 — Offering/Declining another cup

Mō [Amount] *ikaga desu ka* ↗.
Mō ip-pai ikaga desu ka.   "Would you like one more cup?"

Examples

mō sukoshi   "a little more"
mō hitotsu   "one more"
mō ip-pai   "one more cup/glass"
mō ip-pon   "one more bottle"

Kēki, mō hitotsu ikaga desu ka.   "Would you like another piece of cake?"

Declining the offer is:
    Mō* kekko desu.   "I've already had enough."
                      [*Lit.* Already fine.]

∗ This **mō** means "already," and is different from the **mō** in **mō sukoshi** "a little more."

Grammar Note 7 — Suggesting/Offering for somebody to do something politely

Dōzo o-[Verb (pre-masu)] kudasai.

Dōzo ohairi kudasai.   "Would you come in, please?"

Compare:

Dōzo.	"Please (go ahead)."
Dōzo haitte kudasai.	"Come in, please."
Dōzo ohairi kudasai.	"Would you come in, please?"

O-[Verb (Pre-*masu*)] *kudasai* is one of the Level 3 suggesting/offering forms. However, you can't apply this form to every verb. Let us limit it to the verbs listed below which are used in a visiting situation. Very often, ***dōzo*** . . . is just enough and polite for suggesting/offering for someone to go ahead and do something.

Dōzo {	ohairi oagari okake osuwari otori	} *kudasai*	"Would you {	come in come in sit down sit down take it	} , please?"

hairimasu	"enter the room/house"
agarimasu	"come in(to) the room/house (stepping up)"
kakemasu	"sit down on a chair/sofa"
suwarimasu	"sit down on the floor or chair/sofa"
torimasu	"take"

Grammar Note 8 — Quantity words

There are two types of quantity words:
a) adverbs of quantity
b) numbers with counters — adverbial phrases

a. Adverbs of quantity

	Meaning	
I.	many, much a fair amount a few, a little	*takusan* *kanari* *sukoshi, chotto*
II.	not so many/much not at all	*amari* *zen'zen*
	how many, how long, far?	*dono gurai**

I . . . used with affirmative form of the verb.
II . . . used with negative form of the verb.

Dono gurai is a useful interrogative indicating quantity.
Its exact meaning will be determined by the verb.

b. Numbers with counters
Here are some new counters:

OBJECT	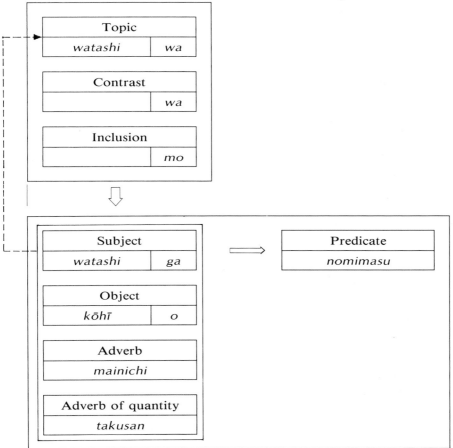		
	-hai	-satsu	-hako
1	ip-pai	is-satsu	hito-hako
2	ni-hai	ni-satsu	futa-hako
3	san-bai	san-satsu	mi-hako
4	yon-hai	yon-satsu	yo(n)-hako
5	go-hai	go-satsu	go-hako
6	rop-pai	roku-satsu	rop-pako
7	nana-hai	nana-satsu	nana-hako
8	hap-pai	has-satsu	hap-pako
9	kyū-hai	kyū-satsu	kyū-hako
10	jup-pai	jus-satsu	jup-pako
?	nan-bai	nan-satsu	nan-hako

Grammar Note 9 — Expressing quantity in a sentence

a. [Other element] [Object] *o* [Quantity] [Verb]

Watashi wa mainichi kōhī o takusan nomimasu   ''I drink a lot of coffee every day.''

Topic	
watashi	wa

Contrast	
	wa

Inclusion	
	mo

⇩

Subject	
watashi	ga

⟹

Predicate
nomimasu

Object	
kōhī	o

Adverb
mainichi

Adverb of quantity
takusan

Verbs which take *o* [Object Marker] fit in this diagram.

337

Examples

Watashi wa kōhī o sukoshi nomimasu.	"I drink a little coffee."
Ichi-nichi ni ip-pai gurai nomimasu.	"I drink about a cup a day."

A: *Kōhī wa dono gurai nomimasu ka.*　　"How much coffee do you drink?"
B: *Ichi-nichi ni ni-san-bai desu.*　　"Two or three cups a day."

a.   [Place] *ni wa* **[Subject]** *ga* **[Quantity]** *arimasu/imasu.*

　　Kono hen ni wa resutoran ga takusan arimasu.　　"There are a lot of restaurants in this area."

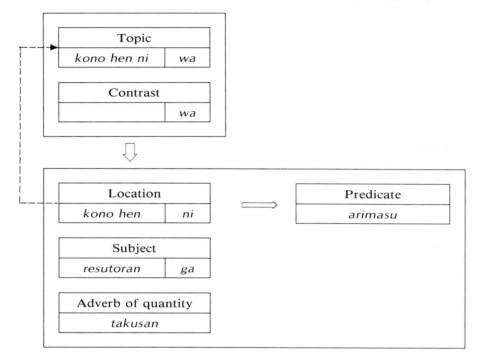

Examples

Kyōto ni wa o-tera ga takusan arimasu.	"There are a lot of temples in Kyoto."
Koko ni wa resutoran ga san-gen arimasu.	"There are three restaurants here."
Watashi no kurasu ni wa seito ga san-nin imasu.	"There are three students in my class."

A: *Seito wa nan-nin imasu ka.*　　"How many students are there?"
B: *San-nin desu.*　　"Three."

Grammar Note 10 — Ritual expressions for visiting

There are some ritual expressions to use when you are visiting people. Study the following:

[At the door]

Guest Host

Guest: *Kon'nichiwa. or Kon'ban'wa.*　　"Good afternoon/evening."
Host: *Irasshai (mase).*　　"Hello." [*Lit.* Welcome.]

| Host: | Dōzo ohairi or oagari kudasai... | "Would you come in, please?" |
| Guest: | Ojama shimasu. or
Shitsurei shimasu. | "Excuse me (for entering).
[*Lit.* I'll bother you.]" |

| Guest: | Anō, kore, tsumaranai mono
desu ga... | "Err... this is just a small
something..." |
| Host: | Dōmo sumimasen.
or
Dōzo go-shin pai naku... | "Oh, thank you."
or
"You shouldn't have done
that.
[*Lit.* Do not worry.]" |

| Host: | Dōzo okake/osuwari
kudasai. | "Would you sit down, please?" |
| Guest: | Shitsurei shimasu. | "Excuse me (for sitting down)." |

[Before the meal]

| Host: | Nani mo arimasen ga, dōzo... | "We don't have anything special
to offer, but please..." |
| Guest: | Itadakimasu. | "Thank you. I'll have some." |

[After the meal]

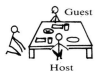

| Guest: | Dōmo gochisōsama deshita. | "Thank you for the delicious
meal." |
| Host: | Iie, osomatsusama deshita. | "Not at all. I hope you liked it.
[*Lit.* It must have been
terrible.]" |

| Guest: | Sorosoro shitsurei shimasu. | "I must be leaving now.
[*Lit.* I'm leaving
soon/slowly.]" |
| Host: | Mada ii ja arimasen ka. | "It's not so late.
[*Lit.* It's still all right.]" |

Guest:	Kyō wa dōmo arigatō gozaimashita.	"Thank you very much for today."
Host:	Iie, kochira koso.	"Thank you for coming. [*Lit.* Me too.]"
Guest:	Ojama shimashita.	"Thank you for all your trouble. [*Lit.* I've bothered you.]"
Host:	Dōzo mata kite kudasai.	"Please come again."
Guest:	Shitsurei shimasu. or Oyasumi nasai. or Sayonara.	"Good-bye. [*Lit.* Excuse me for leaving.]" or "Good night." or "Good-bye."
Host:	Jā, ki o tsukete...	"Well, take care (on the way home)."

Grammar Note 11 — Small talk

a. Here, we introduce one more usage of the verb **Te** form. (*cf.* Lesson 20, Grammar Note 5)

Reason		Resulting
Verb-*te*	**,**	comment

*Midori ga takusan **atte***, ii tokoro desu nē.   "There is a lot of greenery so/and it's a nice place, isn't it?"

   ***Atte** is derived from the verb **arimasu**.

This idea of connecting sentences was shown in Lesson 14, Grammar Note 4.

   A-kute   ...   A ⎫
   AN de ,   AN ⎬ *desu.*

      Yasukute, ii desu.   "Cheap, so/and good."

b. **[Adjective]**–*ku narimashita nē.*

   Samu-ku narimashita nē.   "It has gotten cold, hasn't it?"

Remove the final **-i** from the Adjective and add **-ku narimashita.**
Narimashita is from **narimasu** "become."

Expressions for small talk:

I.   Commenting on the weather

Atatakaku narimashita nē.	"It's gotten warm, hasn't it?"
Atsuku narimashita nē.	"It's gotten hot, hasn't it?"
Suzushiku narimashita nē.	"It's gotten cool, hasn't it?"
Samuku narimashita nē.	"It's gotten cold, hasn't it?"
Hi ga nagaku narimashita nē.	"The days have gotten longer, haven't they?"
Hi ga mijikaku narimashita nē.	"The days have gotten shorter, haven't they?"

II.   Offering praise

Kono hen wa shizuka de, ii tokoro desu nē.	"This neighborhood is nice and quiet, isn't it?"
Kono hen wa eki kara chikakute, ii desu nē.	"This neighborhood is close to the station so/and that's good, isn't it?"
Kono hen wa midori ga takusan atte, ii desu nē.	"This neighborhood has a lot of trees so/and that's nice, isn't it?"
Okusan wa ryōri go (o-)jōzu desu nē.	"You are good at cooking, (Mrs. Tanaka)!"
Kono ikebana wa kirei desu nē.	"This flower arrangement is pretty!"
Are wa Imari-yaki desu ne.	"That's a piece of Imari chinaware, isn't it?"

Grammar Note 12 — Review of *ii/kekkō desu*

You may have been aware of different usage and meaning of *ii/kekkō desu* throughout the textbook. The basic meaning of *ii desu* is "it's fine," and *kekkō desu* is a humble equivalent of *ii desu.*

Now let's see how we have used *ii/kekkō desu*:

Lessons

"fine, nice, good"	*Ii ten'ki desu nē.*	"Fine weather, isn't it?"	2
	Nihon wa ii kuni desu nē.	"Japan is a nice country, isn't it?"	10
"(It's) nice and I like it."	*Ā, ii desu nē.*	"Oh, I like it!" —Shopping	8
	Kyōto wa yokatta desu yo.	"Kyoto was nice."	12
	Ano resutoran wa yasukute ii desu yo.	"That restaurant is inexpensive and/so I like it."	14
	Doko ga ii desu ka.	"Where would you like (to go)?"—Inviting	22
Enthusiastic Listening sign	*Ii desu nē.*	"That's great!"	11
	Yokatta desu nē.	"That's great!"	12
	Ii desu nē.	"That's a good idea!" —Inviting	22
Asking for *or* giving permission/ agreement/ suggestion/ preference	*Kono hen de ii desu.*	"Just here will be fine. [Stop here, please.]"—Taxi	7
	Chotto ii desu ka.	"May I interrupt for a moment?"	19
	Ii desu yo.	"(Yes,) it's O.K."	19,22,23
	Dō ittara ii deshō ka.	"How can I get there?"	20
	Doko ga ii deshō ka.	"Do you know a good place (to go)?"	21
	Nikkō ga ii desu yo.	"I recommend (visiting) Nikko."	21
	Doko ga ii desu ka.	"Where would you like (to go)?"	22
	Doko demo ii desu kedo...	"Any place is all right..."	22
	Haitte mo ii desu ka.	"May I come in?"	23
	Dore ga ii desu ka.	"Which would you like?"	24
Accepting/ declining an offer	*Ē, kekō desu.*	"Yes, that's fine."	23
	Iie, kekkō desu.	"No, I'm fine. [No, thank you.]"	23
	Ima wa kekkō desu.	"I'm all right for now, thank you. [No, thank you.]"	24
	Mō kekkō desu.	"I've already had enough, thank you. [No, thank you.]"	24

Drill 1   Substitute the underlined parts.

1. _Kōhī_ wa ikaga desu ka.
   (1)   kōcha   (2)   kukkī "cookies"   (3)   nomimono

2. _Kōhī_ demo ikaga desu ka.
   (1)   o-sake   (2)   tsumetai mono "something cold"
   (3)   kōhī ka kōcha

3. _Nanika_ nomimasen ka.
   (1)   kōhī o   (2)   o-cha demo   (3)   wain ka bīru demo

4. _Nanika_ tabemasen ka.
   (1)   kukkī o   (2)   kēki demo   (3)   amai mono demo

Drill 2   Make short dialogues.

e.g., 1.   Wine?
           Yes, please.   ⟶   A: Wain wa ikaga desu ka.
                              B: Dōmo (arigatō gozaimasu).
                                   Itadakimasu.

   2.   Coffee or something?
        No, thank you, not now.   ⟶   A: Kōhī demo ikaga desu ka.
                                      B: Dōmo (arigatō gozaimasu).
                                           Demo, ima wa kekkō desu.

   3.   Something to drink?
        Please don't bother.   ⟶   A: Nomimono demo ikaga desu ka.
                                    B: Dōzo okamai naku.

   (1)   Japanese tea?   (2)   Something cold?
           No, thank you, not now.   Yes, please.
   (3)   Wine or something?   (4)   Coffee or something?
           No, thank you, not now.   Please don't bother.

Drill 3   Using the example as a model, complete the dialogues.

Example — Mr. Brown is visiting Mr. Takahashi's house —

I. | Takahashi: Kōhī demo ikaga desu ka.
[A] | Buraun: Dōmo.   ⟷   [B]   Buraun: Dōmo. Demo, ima
     | Ja... itadakimasu.   wa kekkō desu.
     | [Mr. Takahashi puts   Takahashi: Sore jā, atode dōzo.
     | the coffee on the table]   Buraun:.   Dōmo arigato.
     | Takahashi: Dōzo
     | Buraun: Dōmo.

II. |*Takahashi*: *Mō ippai ikaga desu ka.*

[A] |*Buraun*: *Dōmo. Jā...* ←——→ [B] *Buraun*: *Dōmo.*

onegai shimasu. *Demo, mō kekkō desu.*

More?

Yes, please.

No, thank you.

(1) — You are the guest —	Tape: *Bīru demo ikaga desu ka.*
[a] Yes, please.	You: [a] _____ .
	Tape: *Dōzo...*
	You: _____ .
	⋮
	Tape: *Mō ip-pai ikaga desu ka.*
[b] I've had enough.	You: [b] _____ .
(2) —You are the guest—	Tape: *Tsumetai mono demo ikaga desu ka.*
[a] No, thank you, not now.	You: [a] _____ .
	Tape: *Jā, ato de dōzo.*
	You: _____ .
(3) — You are the guest, acting like a Japanese —	
	Tape: *Chotto omachi kudasai. Ima nomimono o...*
	"Would you please wait a while. I'll bring something to drink..."
[a] Please don't bother.	You: [a] _____ .
	⋮
	[The hostess brings in coffee.]
	Tape: *Dōzo...*
[b] Thank you.	You: [b] _____ .
(4) — You are the host/hostess this time—	
[a]	You: [a] _____ .
	Tape: *Dōmo. Jā itadakimasu.*
	⋮
[b] Here you are.	You: [b] _____ .
	Tape: *A, dōmo sumimasen.*
	⋮
[c] More?	You: [c] _____ .
	Tape: *Jā, mō ip-pai dake onegai shimasu.*

(5)

[a]   Cookies?

[b]   Here you are.

[c]   More?

You: [a] _____ .
Tape: *Dōmo arigatō gozaimasu. Itadakimasu.*
You: [b] _____ .
Tape: *Dōmo.*

⋮

You: [c] _____ .
Tape: *Mō kekkō desu. Totemo oishikatta desu.*

Drill 4   Make questions using **dotchi** or **dore**.

e.g.,   1.   *bīru, uisukī* ⟶ *Bīru to uisukī ga arimasu kedo, dotchi ga ii desu ka.*

2.   *bīru, uisukī, wain* ⟶ *Bīru, to uisukī to wain ga arimasu kedo,*
dore ga ii desu ka.

(1)   *kōhī, kōcha*
(2)   *miruku, jūsu, kōra*
(3)   *mikan* "tangerine orange", *rin'go* "apple"
(4)   *Nihon'shu* "Japanese sake", *aka-wain, nama-bīru* "draft beer"

Drill 5   Repeat and learn the names of the beverages and what you would add to them.

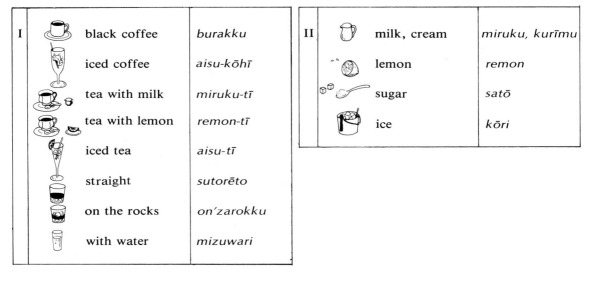

I		black coffee	*burakku*
		iced coffee	*aisu-kōhī*
		tea with milk	*miruku-tī*
		tea with lemon	*remon-tī*
		iced tea	*aisu-tī*
		straight	*sutorēto*
		on the rocks	*on'zarokku*
		with water	*mizuwari*

II		milk, cream	*miruku, kurīmu*
		lemon	*remon*
		sugar	*satō*
		ice	*kōri*

Drill 6   Express how you like your beverage/food served.

1.   *Kōhī wa dō shimasu ka.*

e.g.,   1.   (black) ⟶ *Burakku (o) onegai* { *shimasu.*
{ *dekimasu ka.*

2.   (put a little sugar) ⟶ *Satō (o) sukoshi irete* { *kudasai.*
{ *kuremasen ka.*

(1)   *Kōcha wa dō shimasu ka.*   (tea with lemon, please)
(2)   *Kōhī wa dō shimasu ka.*   (milk and a little sugar, please)
(3)   *Uisukī wa dō shimasu ka.*   (with water, please)

(4)   *Uisukī wa dō shimasu ka.*   (on the rocks, please)
(5)   *Sutēki wa dō shimasu ka.*   (medium rare *midiamurea*, please)
(6)   *Doresshin'gu wa dō shimasuka.*   (French *Furen'chi*, please)

2.   *Kōhī wa, satō wa iremasu ka.*

e.g.,   1.   (Yes, one.)   ⟶   *Ē, hitotsu onegai shimasu.*
              (No, thank you.)   ⟶   *Iie, satō wa kekkō desu.*

(1)   *Kōcha wa, satō wa iremasu ka.*   (Yes, two.)
(2)   *Kōhī wa, miruku wa iremasu ka.*   (Yes, a little.)
(3)   *Jūsu wa, kōri wa iremasu ka.*   (No, thank you.)

Drill 7   Using the example as a model complete the dialogues.

Example

— At Mr. Smith's house —

Sumisu:	*Nanika nomimasen ka.*
Itō:	*Dōmo arigatō gozaimasu.*
	Itadakimasu.
Sumisu:	*Uisukī to jin to bīru ga arimasu kedo,*
	dore ga ii desu ka.
Itō:	*Jā, uisukī onegai shimasu.*
Sumisu:	*Hai. Uisukī wa dō shimasu ka.*
Itō:	*On'zarokku onegai dekimasu ka.*
Sumisu:	*Hai, wakarimashita.*

(1) — You are the guest —	
	Tape: *Nanika nomimasen ka.*
[a] Yes, please.	You: [a] _____ .
	Tape: *Uisukī to wain to bīru ga arimasu kedo,*
	dore ga ii desu ka.
[b] whisky	You: [b] _____ .
	Tape: *Uisukī wa dō shimasu ka.*
[c] straight	You: [c] _____ .
	Tape: *Hai, wakarimashita.*
(2)	
	Tape: *Nomimono demo ikaga desu ka.*
[a] Yes, please.	You: [a] _____ .
	Tape: *Kōhī to kōcha to jūsu ga arimasu kedo,*
	dore ga ii desu ka.
[b] tea	You: [b] _____ .
	Tape: *Kōcha wa dō shimasu ka.*
[c] a little milk, please	You: [c] _____ .
	Tape: *Hai, wakarimashita.*

(3) — Now you are the host/hostess —

[a]   Something to drink?

You: [a] _____ .

Tape: *Dōmo arigatō gozaimasu. Itadakimasu.*

[b]   ?

You: [b] _____ .

_____ .

Tape: *Jā, uisukī onegai shimasu.*

[c]   How?

You: [c] _____ .

Tape: *On'zarokku onegai dekimasu ka.*

You: _____ .

(4)

[a]   Something to drink?

You: [a] _____ .

Tape: *Sumimasen. Jā itadakimasu.*

[b]   ?

You: [b] _____ .

_____ .

Tape: *Jā, kōcha onegai shimasu.*

[c]   Cream or milk?

You: [c] _____ .

Tape: *Kekkō desu.*

[d]   Sugar?

You: [d] _____ .

Tape: *Satō mo kekkō desu.*

You: _____ .

Drill 8   Change the verb forms.

e.g.,   1.   *hairimasu* ⟶ *Dōzo ohairi kudasai.*

2.   *hairimasu* ⟶ *Dōzo haitte kudasai.*

(1)   *agarimasu*

(2)   *kakimasu*

(3)   *suwarimasu*

(4)   *torimasu*

(5)   *Koko ni hairimasu.*

(6)   *Kono isu ni kakemasu.*

(7)   *Koko ni suwarimasu.*

(8)   *Ryōri o torimasu.*

Drill 9   Substitute the underlined parts.

1.   *Kōhī o ichi-nichi ni ip-pai nomimasu.*

(1)   *kōcha, ichi-nichi, ni-san-bai*

(2)   *(o-)sake, ichi-nichi, ip-pon gurai*

(3)   *uisukī, is-shūkan, botoru* "bottle" *ip-pon*

(4)   *bīru, ik-kagetsu, ni-dāsu* "dozen"

2.   *Tabako o ichi-nichi ni jup-pon gurai suimasu.*

(1)   *tabako, ichi-nichi, hito-hako*

(2)   *hamaki, ichi-nichi, ni-hon*

3.   *Hon o is-shūkan ni is-satsu gurai yomimasu.*

(1)   *zasshi, is-shūkan, ni-satsu*

(2)   *shigoto no shiryō, ichi-nichi, san'jup-pēji* "page" *gurai*

Drill 10 Substitute the underlined parts. Change the verbs accordingly.

e.g.,	A:	_Kōhī_ wa nomimasu ka.
B:	_Ē_, nomimasu.
A:	Dono gurai nomiasu ka.
B:	Sō desu nē... _Ichi-nichi ni go-hai_ gurai desu.
	A-san wa.
A:	Watashi wa _amari_ nomimasen.

(1) bīru, ichi-nichi ni ip-pon, takusan

(2) kēki, ichi-nichi ni hito-tsu, amari

(3) tabako, ichi-nichi ni hito-hako, zen'zen

Drill 11 Translate and substitute the underlined parts. Change the verbs accordingly.

1. _e.g.,_ my Japanese class, five students

    ⟶ _Watashi no Nihon-go no kurasu_ ni wa

    seito* "student(s)" ga _go-nin_ imasu.

*_Seito_ does not include full time students like college students. They are called
gakusei.

(1) our company, a thousand employees (_shain_)

(2) this area, three hotels

(3) this building, about a hundred people (_hito_)

(4) that park, a lot of _sakura_

(5) this area, a lot of good shops

2. _e.g.,_ this area, not many good restaurants

    ⟶ _Kono hen_ ni wa _ii resutoran_ wa _amari_ arimasen.

(1) this area, no _soba_ shop

(2) my French class, not so many good students

(3) this company, not so many foreign employees

Drill 12 Change the sentences for small talk using **[V/A/AN]**-_te_/-_de_

1. _e.g.,_ Kono hen ni wa ki "tree"ga takusan arimasu kara ii desu nē.

    ⟶ Kono hen ni wa ki ga takusan atte, ii desu nē.

(1) Kono hen ni wa ii mise ga takusan arimasu kara ben'ri desu nē.

(2) Kono hen ni wa kōen ga takusan arimasu kara ii desu nē.

2. _e.g.,_ Otaku wa gakkō kara chikai desu kara ii desu nē.

    ⟶ Otaku wa gakkō kara chikakute, ii desu nē.

(1) Kono hen wa eki kara chikai desu kara ben'ri desu nē.

(2) Midori ga ōi desu kara kirei desu nē.

(3) Bukka ga takai desu kara taihen desu nē.

3.   *e.g.,*   *Kono hen wa shizuka desu kara ii desu nē.*

   ⟶   *Kono hen wa shizuka de, ii desu nē.*

(1)   *Midori ga kirei desu kara ii desu nē.*

(2)   *Nihon-go ga (o-)jōzu desu kara ii desu nē.*

(3)   *Okusan ga ryōri ga (o-)jōzu desu kara ii desu nē.*

▦Drill 13   Using the dialogue as a model, practice the rituals for visiting someone's home — in western style as marked with * (in offering/accepting and asking and in not insisting the guest stay longer).

(1) — You are the guest —

pin'pon

You

Tape: *Donata desu ka.*

You: _____ .

Tape: *Chotto omachi kudasai.*

— At the entrance hall —

You

Tape: *Dōzo oagari kudasai.*

You: _____ .

— In the room —

You

Tape: *Dōzo okake kudasai.*

You: _____ .

Tape: **Kōhī ka kōcha demo ikaga desu ka.*

You: _____ .

Tape: **Satō wa iremasu ka.*

You: _____ .

Tape: **Miruku ka remon wa iremasu ka.*

You: _____ .

Tape: *Dozō.*

You: _____ .

*Tea, please.

*sugar
No, thank you.

*Milk, please.

small talk

The days have gotten shorter, haven't they?

7:00 a.m.   5:00 p.m.

You: _____ .

Tape: *Sō desu nē.*

leave taking

You: _____.
Tape: *Sō desu ka. Sore jā...

— At the entrance hall —

You: _____.
Tape: Shitsurei shimasu. Ki o tsukete.

You

(2)   Now you are the host/hostess
— Ms. Takahashi, your guest, rings the door bell —

You: _____.
Tape: Takahashi desu ga...
You: _____.

You

— At the front door —

Tape: Kon'nichiwa.
You: _____.
Tape: Ojama shimasu.

You

— In the room —

You: _____.
Tape: Shitsurei shimasu.

You

You: _____.
Tape: *Dōmo arigatō gozaimasu. Sore jā, kōhī
       onegai dekimasu ka.
You: * _____.
Tape: *Satō mo kurīmu mo kekkō desu.
You: _____.

small talk

Tape: Atatakaku narimashita nē. Mō sugu sakura
       mo sakimasu ne.
You: [EL] _____.

Leave taking

Tape: *A, mō ku-ji desu nē. Sorosoro shitsurei shimasu.*

You: * _____ .

Tape: *Dōmo ojama shimashita. Sore jā shitsurei shimasu.*

You: _____ .

Visiting a Japanese apartment *man'shon* — At the entrance

Kon'nichiwa.

Dōzo ohairi kudasai. "Please come in."

Shoes at the entry way

Drill 14 This is a dialogue about visiting a Japanese home — traditional style.

Express what you are supposed to say.

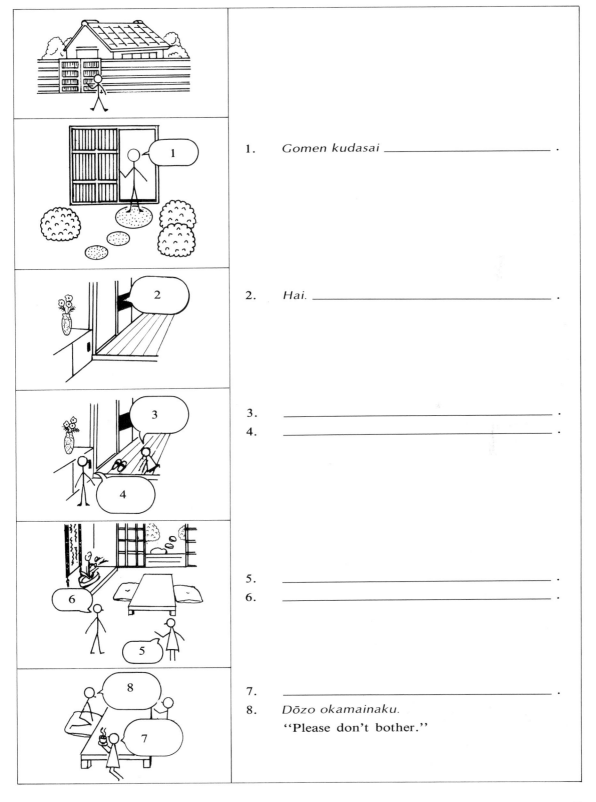

1. *Gomen kudasai* _____ .

2. *Hai.* _____ .

3. _____ .
4. _____ .

5. _____ .
6. _____ .

7. _____ .
8. *Dōzo okamainaku.*
    "Please don't bother."

[Small talk]

9. _____ .

10. _____ .

11. _____ .

"It's not so late."

12. _____ .

"But it's late..."

13. _____ .

"Is that so?"

14. _____ .

15. _____ .

"Not at all. Take care."

16. _____ .

"Please come again."

Culture Note 11 — *En'ryo*

There are certain key words in Japanese that unlock doors to whole blocks of Japanese culture and emotional psychology. One such word is **en'ryo**. It means something like diffidence or reserve or restraint in English, but like many words in Japanese, the usage is different from and wider than English.

We must first remember that diffidence is a major way of expressing politeness in Japan. This applies not only to verbal expressions but also to manner and manners as well. If you receive a gift, don't open it. It's too forward. If you leave the office before your colleagues, don't march out with your head held high, apologize for leaving earlier than everyone else and slink away. If you, your family, your possessions are complimented, parry it. It is against this background that the word **en'ryo** exists.
You don't impose yourself or your personality or your preferences on others. You hold back. If you drop in on someone without notice, and are offered tea or coffee, refuse. (**O-kamai-naku**, "Please don't bother.") You are not thirsty in the least. Of course, you expect that your wishes will be over-ridden and be served tea anyway. For the host to do otherwise is rude. So the guest refuses, several times if necessary and the host continues to press refreshments on you so that you may, eventually, let yourself be persuaded, with a great deal of reluctance, to partake, sparingly. But if you have been invited on purpose, then naturally it is very rude to have too much **en'ryo**. You expect and are expected to eat and drink. But in this case, your hostess shows **en'ryo**. Although she has spent the day cooking, she offers something beautiful and tasty saying "I'm sure you won't like this," or "We really have nothing in the house."

If you really do want to refuse, there seems to be no easy way. It becomes a battle of wits, matching **en'ryo** or offer, until one side gives in. Mind you, you will be pressed hard, with the host saying some such phrase as **Dōzo, go-en'ryo-naku** "Please go ahead, don't have **en'ryo**; *i.e.*, don't stand on ceremony." Whereupon you, the guest, may then give up and decide you will eat after all. Or, if you are successful, the host will have given in finally believing you when you say don't bother. A compromise, of a kind, is to give in, let the host bring the refreshments and then touch nothing.

The danger is when one half of the relationship is not Japanese. A Westerner will accept a refusal at face value. A Japanese, though prostrate with thirst, will have **en'ryo** and refuse your offer of a drink (with the firm conviction, however, that the drink will be forthcoming anyway). You, on the other hand, with a faint "Are you sure," refrain from pressing the guest for fear of being unpleasant and pushy and do not produce anything, even when you see your poor guest about to expire. The guest is offended and angry, you are upset and frustrated. East has great difficulty in meeting West here. "Why," you might ask, "can't the guest simply say yes or no in answer to a simple question?" But the guest can't. It is impolite. Could you force yourself to do something as impolite as, for example, extinguish your cigarette in the remains of your host's meal?

It is equally excruciating to contemplate directly giving one's preferences to the Japanese, whether it's tea or a pay raise. What to us is a chatty exchange, tea or coffee?, milk or cream or lemon?, how many sugars?, weak or strong?, is social anguish in Tokyo.

There is also the phrase. . . **wa go-en'ryo kudasai** ''Please have **en'ryo** (for. . .)'' In English, in the same situation where this phrase is used, we would say ''Don't. . .,'' ''Please refrain from. . . '' ''You can't. . .,'' *etc.* You hear this when you meet the psychological barrier. It is not that there is a law or a policy or even a custom prohibiting what you want. It is just that it is difficult for psychological reasons, so we'd prefer you to desist. People in authority can give a clear prohibition (. . . **te wa ikemasen, dame desu**, *etc.* ''You must not. . . .''), friends can demur (**chotto.** . ., *etc.*), but people in between, who are not friends, and who do not have clear authority, or the right to enforce authority, resort to **Go-en'ryo kudasai**. They are unwilling to help you now, so it's not worth your while, nor the destruction of relationships to pursue your request any further, no matter how trivial the actual barrier may seem to be.

Finally, **en'ryo** applies only in formal situations. The closer the relationship, the less it applies, until in the family you actually meet its opposite, self-indulgence — **amae**, another key word. Equally, it does not apply to ''non-relationships'' either, such as trains, stations, other public places, foreign countries and in some cases, regrettably, foreigners themselves. But in every country, your own included, you'll find ''funny people.'' In the meantime, beware of **en'ryo** in your more formal relationships and don't be too forward yourself. You'll get all the vibes of the traditional bull in a china shop.

No smoking sign
禁煙
(kin-en)
Otabako wa. . . **go-enryo** *kudasai.*
''Please refrain from smoking.''

Review Quiz (Lesson 22 — Lesson 24)

I. Complete the following sentences with the verbs listed below by changing the forms accordingly.

1. *Hirugohan ni (   ) ka.*
    Ē, (   ).
2. *Eiga o mi ni (   ) ka.*
    Ē, ii desu nē. Doko e   (   ) ka.
3. *Nichi-yōbi o-hima deshitara uchi e*
    shokuji ni (   ) ka.
4. *Nanika (   ) ka.*
    Ē, bīru wa dō desu ka.
5. *Rōma-ji de (   ) ka.*
    Ē, onegai shimasu.

   [*nomimasu,   aimasu,   ikimasu,   kimasu,   kakimasu*]

II. Fill in the blanks.

1. *Issho ni nomi (   ) ikimasen ka.*
2. *Do-yōbi (   ) dō desu ka.*
3. *Sumisu-san, kuruma (   ) kimasu ka.*
4. *Ten'genji Intā kara Shuto Kōsoku (   ) notte kudasai.*
5. *Nan-ji ga ii desu ka. Nan-ji (   ) ii desu kedo.*

III. What Japanese expressions would you use in the following situations?

1. When you invite someone to have a drink after work (around five o'clock) . . .
2. When you accept the invitation . . .
3. When you decline an invitation for Saturday . . .
4. When you don't want to be the one to decide when (to meet) . . .
5. When you invite someone to your home for dinner on Saturday . . .
6. When you offer help by drawing a map . . .
7. When you say that Saturday is all right with you . . .
8. When you ask for permission to interrupt somebody for a moment . . .
9. When you offer someone something to drink . . .
10. When you ask for a preference (out of three different kinds of drinks) . . .

Final Quiz (Lesson 1 — Lesson 24)

I.   Fill in the blanks.

1.   Sumisu-san, kochira (   ) Tanaka-san desu.
2.   Moshimoshi, Yamada-san (   ) otaku desu ka.
3.   Mikkusu-san'do (   ) tomato-jūsu onegai shimasu.
4.   Tsugi no shin'gō (   ) migi (   ) magatte kudasai.
5.   Sono akai sētā (   ) misete kuremasen ka.
6.   Ii desu (   ), chotto takai desu nē.
7.   Kyonen no shichi-gatsu (   ) Nihon (   ) kimashita.
8.   Karuizawa wa dō deshita ka.
     Yama (   ) kirei deshita.
9.   Kon'do no yasumi ni kazoku (   ) Nikkō e ikimasu.
10. Futsū depāto wa jū-ji (   ) roku-ji (   ) desu.
11. Gorufu wa dō deshita ka. Jitsu wa kaze (   ) ikimasen deshita.
12. Yoru wa taitei terebi (   ) mimasu.
13. Is-shūkan (   ) san-kai Nihon-go no ressun (   ) arimasu.
14. Shin'juku (   ) eiga o mimashita.
15. Nichi-yōbi wa taitei uchi (   ) imasu.
16. Kuyakusho wa ano shin'gō (   ) saki desu.
17. Kōshū den'wa wa eki no soba (   ) arimasu.
18. Sumisu-san shirimasen ka. Doa no tokoro (   ) imasu yo.
19. Kono den'sha wa Odawara (   ) tomarimasu.
20. Doko de aimashō ka. Doko (   ) ii desu kedo.

II.   Choose the most appropriate response in the following mini dialogues.

1.   Tanaka: Hajimemashite Tanaka desu. Dōzo yoroshiku.
     Sumisu: (1) Hajimemashite Sumisu-san desu. Dōzo yoroshiku.
               (2) Hajimemashite Sumisu desu. Dōzo yoroshiku.
2.   Inoue: Osakini shitsurei shimasu.
     Sumisu: (1) Sō desu nē.
               (2) Shitsurei shimasu.
3.   Suzuki: Kon'ban'wa. Samui desu nē.
     Howaito: (1) Sō desu nē.
               (2) Oyasuminasai. Sō desu nē.
4.   Tanaka: Shitsurei shimasu. [As he enters the room.]
     Howaito: (1) Iie.
               (2) Dōzo.
5.   Tanaka: Nikkō wa dō deshita ka.
     Sumisu: (1) Kuruma de ikimashita.
               (2) Yokatta desu yo.
6.   Sumisu: Ryokō wa tanoshikatta desu.
     Tanaka: (1) Sore wa yokatta desu nē.
               (2) Sore wa zan'nen deshita nē.
7.   Tanaka: Sumō wa suki desu ka.
     Sumisu: (1) Iie, kekkō desu.
               (2) Iie, amari suki ja arimasen.
8.   Tanaka: Nihon-go ga jōzu desu nē.
     Sumisu: (1) Hai, sō desu.
               (2) Iie, mada heta desu.
9.   Suzuki: Sumimasen, Tanaka-san wa doko deshō ka.
     Sumisu: (1) Erebētā no tokoro ni imashita yo.
               (2) Erebētā ni imashita yo.

10. *Tanaka:*   *Dōzo ohairi kudasai.*
    Sumisu: (1) *Shitsurei shimasu.*
                (2) *Dōzo okamainaku.*

III.   Express in Japanese.

   A.   *Use _____ **wa ikaga desu/deshita ka.***
      1.   Would you like a drink?
      2.   How do you like Japan?
      3.   How was your holiday?
      4.   How about (going to) Nikko?
      5.   How do you feel about the Japanese language?

   B.   *Use _____ **ga ii desu ka.***
      1.   What would you like (to drink)?
      2.   Where would you like (to go)?
      3.   When would you like (to go)?
      4.   Who would you like (to have for a teacher)?
      5.   What time would you like (to meet)?

   C.
      1.   I'm Tanaka from Mobil.
      2.   Mr. Smith, (this is) my wife.
      3.   It's fine weather, isn't it?
      4.   I'll see you on Monday.
      5.   Where do you come from?
      6.   I work for Mobil.
      7.   Where do you live?
      8.   Excuse me, how much is it?
      9.   Thank you for (inviting me) today.
     10.   (Table for) three people, (please).
     11.   (I'd like) a ham sandwich and coffee, please.
     12.   (Take me to) the north exit of Tokyo Station, please.
     13.   Turn right at the next traffic signal.
     14.   Could I see that black sweater?
     15.   Could I see that green one over there?
     16.   Are you planning to go somewhere for the holidays?
     17.   I'm going to Gotenba to play golf.
     18.   I read a book most (nights).
     19.   I (usually) have some fruit, a piece of toast and coffee (for breakfast).
     20.   I often eat lunch at a restaurant near my office.
     21.   I got up at six this morning.
     22.   I went to bed at 10:30 p.m. last night.
     23.   I wonder where the Mikimoto pearl shop is?
     24.   Is there [*Lit.* isn't there] a mail box around here?
     25.   (I wonder if you know) where Mr. Tanaka is?
     26.   I'd like to have the second one from the left.
     27.   How long does it take to get to Shin'osaka?
     28.   May I interrupt for a moment, Mr. Tanaka?
     29.   How long would it take altogether to get there?

30.   I wonder how much further it is to the last stop?

IV.   Answer the questions.

1.   *Itsu Nihon e kimashita ka.*
2.   *Nihon wa dō desu ka.*
3.   *Nihon no tabemono wa dō desu ka.*
4.   *Kekkon shite imasu ka.*
5.   *Okosan wa nan-nin imasu ka.*
6.   *O-shigoto wa nan desu ka.*
7.   *Kaisha wa dochira ni arimasu ka.*
8.   *O-sumai wa dochira desu ka.*
9.   *O-kuni wa dochira desu ka.*
10.   *Go-shumi wa nan desu ka.*
11.   *Terebi wa mimasu ka.*
12.   *Sumō wa suki desu ka.*
13.   *Puro-yakyū wa mimasu ka.*
14.   *Hon wa yomimasu ka.*
15.   *On'gaku wa suki desu ka.*
16.   *Don'na on'gaku o kikimasu ka.*
17.   *Asa nan-ji ni okimasu ka.*
18.   *Asa-gohan wa tabemasu ka.*
19.   *Nani o tabemasu ka.*
20.   *O-shigoto wa nan-ji ni owarimasu ka.*
21.   *Nihon-go wa ben'kyō shite imasu ka.*
22.   *Nihon-go wa dō desu ka.*
23.   *Shū ni nan-kai ressun ga arimasu ka.*
24.   *Kinō wa dokoka e ikimashita ka.*
25.   *Dō deshita ka.*
26.   *Kon'do no yasumi wa dokoka e ikimasu ka.*
27.   *Kyūka wa itsu desu ka.*
28.   *Kyūka wa doko e ikimasu ka.*
29.   *O-sake wa nomimasu ka.*

— Appendix —
USEFUL EXPRESSIONS

I. Telephone calls — **Den'wa**

Operators:	_X_ de gozaimasu.	"This is __X__ (May I help you?)"
White :	(Kochira wa)	"This is White from Mobil Oil. May
	Mōbiru Sekiyu no	I speak to Mr. Suzuki of the International
	[Company Name]	Finance Department please?"
	Howaito desu ga,	
	[Name]	
	Kokusai kin'yū-bu no	
	[Department]	
	Suzuki-san	
	[Name]	
	(1)onegai shimasu.	

1.
Operator:	Hai, shōshō omachi kudasai.	"Yes, hold on, please."
Suzuki :	Hai, Suzuki desu.	"Hello, Suzuki here."
White :	A, Suzuki-san, Howaito desu.	"Ah, Mr. Suzuki, this is White."

2.
Operator:	Anō, Suzuki wa tadaima (2)seki o hazushite imasu ⎫ orimasu ⎭ ga. . .	"Well, Suzuki is not at his desk right now. . ."
White :	(3)Jā, mata atode den'wa shimasu. Nan-ji ga ii deshō ka.	"I'll call back later. What time should I call back?"
Operator:	San-ji goro onegai shimasu.	"Please call back at about three."
White :	San-ji desu ne. Sore jā, dōmo.	"At three? Well then, thank you."
Operator:	Yoroshiku onegai itashimasu. Shitsurei shimasu.	"Thank you. [Lit. Please kindly do so.] Good-by."
White :	Shitsurei shimasu.	"Good-bye."

Variations for (1), (2) and (3):

(1)		Suzuki-san irasshaimasu ka.	"May I speak to Mr. Suzuki? [Lit. Is Mr. Suzuki in?]"
(2)	a)	gaishutsu-chū ⎧desu ga. . . ⎨de gozaimasu ga. . .	"He is out."
	b)	kaigi-chū ⎧desu ga. . . ⎨de gozaimasu ga. . .	"He is in a meeting."
	c)	hoka no den'wa ni dete ⎰imasu ⎱ ga. . . ⎰orimasu⎱	"He is on another line."
	d)	kyō wa yasumi desu ga. . .	"He has the day off today."

359

(3) *Ā, sō desu ka.*

   a) *Sore jā, Yamamoto-san wa irasshaimasu ka.*   "Then, is Mr. Yamamoto in?"

   b) *Sore jā, den'gon (o) onegai dekimasuka.*   "May I leave a message?"

   c) *Sore jā, kochira ni denwa o kureru yo ni itte kudasaimasen ka.*   "Could you please tell him to call me?"

   d) *Sore jā, matte imasu kara. . .*   "I'll wait."

Others:

Moshi moshi	"Hello."
Naisen no nī-gō-yon onegai shimasu.	"Extension 254, please."
Ban'gō ga chigaimasu.	"You have the wrong number."
Tanaka-san no otaku desu ka.	"Is this the Tanaka residence?"
Howaito desu ga, shujin/kanai onegai shimasu.	"This is White. May I speak to Mr./Mrs. White?"
Nanika (go-)den'gon wa arimasu ka.	"Can I take a message?"

II. Emergency calls

  110   Police (*Keisatsu*)

  119   Fire department (*shōbōsho*) and ambulance (*kyūkyūsha*)

Example   Calling the fire department to ask for an ambulance

Fire department:	*Hai, shōbōsho desu.*	"Fire department."
White	:	[1]*Kyūkyūsha onegai shimasu.*	"Ambulance, please."
Fire department:	*O-namae wa.*	"Your name, please."
White	:	*Howaito. Ho-wa-i-to desu. Amerika-jin desu.*	"White. Ho-wa-i-to. I'm an American."
Fire department:	*Ima doko desu ka.*	"Where are you now?"
White	:	[2]*Minami-Azabu 4-15-8 (yon no jūgo no hachi) Azabu Man'shon 101 (ichi maru/zero ichi).*	"Minami Azabu 4-15-8 Azabu Mansion 101."

After this, you should give the name, age and condition of the person who is ill, if you can. (If you can't, say **Nihongo wakarimasen.**)

Variations for (1):

(1)   *Kaji desu!*   "Fire!"

      Dorobō desu!   "Thief/Burglar!"

(2) Giving one's address

Reverse the usual English order and begin with the largest division of your address, proceeding on to your particular house/apartment number at the end.

English style:	Japanese style:
Bruce White	*107 Tōkyō-to*
Azabu Mansion, Apt. 101	*Minato-ku*
4-15-8, Minami Azabu	*Minami Azabu 4-15-8*
Minato-ku	*Azabu Man'shon 101*
Tokyo 107	*Burūsu Howaito*

III. Having something delivered

— Telephoning a neighborhood liquor shop —

Azabu Man'shon 101 no Howaito desu   "This is White of Apt. 101, Azabu
ga, Kirin bīru no kan'iri o san-dāsu   Mansion, could you deliver 3
todokete kuremasen ka.   dozen cans of "Kirin" beer?"

IV. Reservations, Appointments — *Yoyaku*

— Telephoning a dentist, hotel, *etc.* —

Yoyaku shi-tai-n desu ga . . .   "I'd like to make an appointment/
     reservation. . ."

— Theaters, stations, *etc.* —

Shi-gatsu tō-ka no "esu"-seki (wa)   "Do you have an "S" class ticket
arimasu ka.   for April 10?"

Shi-gatsu tō-ka no "esu"-seki (o)   "I'd like two "S" class tickets
ni-mai onegai shimasu.   for April 10."

V. Cancellations — *Torikeshi*

[Time] *no* [Reservation, *etc.*] *o*   { *kyan'seru shi-tai-n* / *torikeshi-tai-n* }   *desu ga . . .*

   yoyaku
     "reservation"   "I'd like to cancel. . ."
   yakusoku
     "appointment"
   ressun
     "lesson"

VI. At food stores

	[Item]		o	[Amount]	kudasai/ onegai shimasu
Niku-ya "Meat shop"	gyū (-niku) buta (-niku) tori (-niku) ramu maton hikiniku	"beef" "pork" "chicken" "lamb" "mutton" "ground meat"		-kiro "kilogram" -guram "gram" -mai -hon -wa	"I'd like to have"
	hamu sōsejī	"ham" "sausage"			
Sakana-ya "Fish shop"	maguro hamachi tai aji	"tuna" "yellow tail" "red snapper" "horse mackerel"		-hiki -mai/kire -sara	
	saba iwashi ika tako ebi	"mackerel" "sardine" "squid" "octopus" "shrimp/ lobster"			
	asari	"short-necked clam"			
	shijimi	"fresh water clam"			
	kirimi sashimi	"piece of fish" "raw fish"			
Yao-ya "Vegetable shop"	tomato kyūri nasu daikon kabu negi retasu kyabetsu jagaimo satsumaimo	"tomato" "cucumber" "egg plant" "radish" "turnip" "green onion" "lettuce" "cabbage" "potato" "sweet potato"		-tsu/ko -hon -yama -hako	
Kudamono-ya "Fruit store"	rin'go mikan oren'ji ichigo budō momo nashi kaki	"apple" "tangerine" "orange" "strawberry" "grapes" "peach" "pear" "persimmon"			

VII. At a post office — *Yūbin'kyoku*

1.

[Item]		o	[Amount]	*kudasai/onegai shimasu.*
100-en kitte	"100 yen stamp"		*jū-mai* "ten"	"I'd like to have."
hagaki	"post card"			
kōkū shokan⎫ *earoguramu*⎭	"aerogram"			

2.

Kore wa	[Means]	*de*	*ikura desu ka.*
	Kōkū-bin "air mail"		"how much is it?"
	funa-bin "sea mail"		

3.

[Means]		*de*	*onegai shimasu.*
sokutatsu	"express"		"please"
kakitome	"registered"		

4. Other vocabulary:

kozutsumi	"package"
kokunai	"domestic"
gaikoku	"overseas [*Lit.* foreign country]"
ichi-ban no mado-guchi	"No. 1 window/counter"

VIII. At a beauty parlor or barber shop — *Biyōin/Tokoya*

1.

[Service]		o	*onegai shimasu.*
shan'pū	"shampoo"		"please"
katto	"cut"		
burō	"blow dry"		
setto	"set"		
pāma	"permanent"		
torītomen'to	"treatment"		

2.

[Part]		*wa*	[How you would like it cut]		*kitte kudasai.*
mae	"front"		*sukoshi dake*	"only a little [trim]"	"cut please"
yoko	"side"				
ushiro	"back"				
ue	"top"		*mijikaku*	"short"	
			kono gurai	"this much"	

3. Other expressions:

Ue wa kiranaide kudasai.	"Don't cut any off the top, please."
Shan'pū wa kekkō desu.	"I don't need a shampoo."

Barber:	*Hige wa sorimasu ka.*	"Would you like a shave?"
Customer:	*Onegai shimasu.*	"Yes, please."
	or	
	Kekkō desu.	"No, thank you."

IX. Repairs/Alterations — **Shūzen** *or* **Sun'pō naoshi**

— At a dry cleaner's (*Kurīnin'gu-ya*), a photo shop (*Shashin-ya*), *etc.* —

Customer:	*Itsu dekimasu ka.*	"When will it be done?"
Clerk :	*Ashita no go-ji made ni dekimasu.*	"We'll finish it by five o'clock tomorrow."

X. At a bank — **Gin'kō**

kōza	"bank account"
kōza-ban'gō	"account number"
kōza o hiraki-tai-n desu ga. . .	"I'd like to open an account."
kyasshu-kādo	"cash card"
jidō shiharaiki	"automatic teller [*Lit.* automatic machine]"
tsūchō	"bank book"
nyūkin	"depositing money"
hikidashi	"withdrawing (money)"
kinyū	"updating bankbook"
kakunin	"confirm"
torikeshi	"cancel"
an'shō-ban'gō	"secret code number"

Other vocabulary:

furikomi	"money transfer"
furikomi-yōshi	"money transfer form"
furikomi tesūryō	"transfer charge/fee"

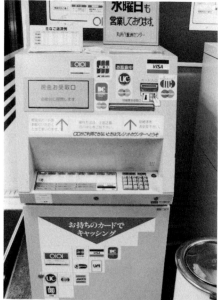

Automatic teller "Cash machine"

CITIES IN JAPAN

1	札幌	14	鎌倉
2	函館	15	箱根
3	青森	16	岐阜
4	盛岡	17	名古屋
5	秋田	18	奈良
6	仙台	19	京都
7	新潟	20	大阪
8	長野	21	神戸
9	富山	22	岡山
10	日光	23	広島
11	金沢	24	下関
12	東京	25	高知
13	横浜		

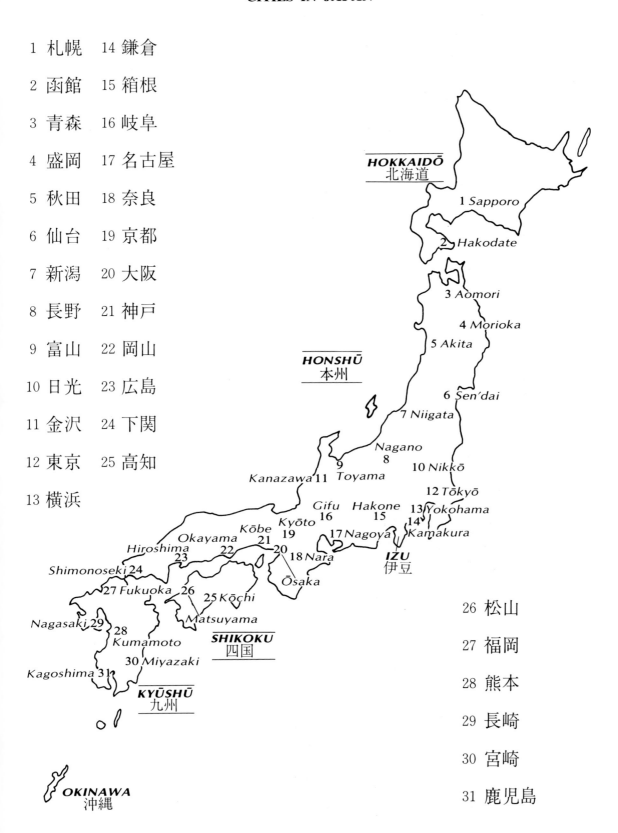

26	松山
27	福岡
28	熊本
29	長崎
30	宮崎
31	鹿児島

INDEX

itashimasu.	がいいたします		
Dōzo yoroshiku.	どうぞよろしく	Nice to meet you.	2

E

_e_	へ	[M] [Direction] to	75
_e_	え	painting	162, 240
_ē_	ええ	yes	18, 33
Ē, dōzo.	ええ、どうぞ	Yes, go ahead.	317
Ē, ii desu yo.	ええ、いいですよ	Sure.	270, 317
Ē, mochiron.	ええ、もちろん	Yes, of course.	317
Ē, onegaishimasu.	ええ、おねがいします	Yes, please.	314
Ē, . . . -te mo ii desu (yo).	ええ、…てもいいです（よ）	Yes, you may...	317
efu-emu	エフエム	FM	160
eiga	えいが	movies	123, 148, 159
eigagai	えいががい	cinema street	210
_Ei-go_	えいご	English	19, 160, 162
Ei-go no shin'bun	えいごの　しんぶん	English newspaper	160
eigyō	えいぎょう	the sales (department)	6
Eikoku, Igirisu	英国, イギリス	U. K.	23
Ei-teishoku	A ていしょく	set menu A	67
eiwa-jiten	えいわじてん	English-Japanese dictionary	233, 239
eki	えき	station	73
ekiin	えきいん	station employee	280
en'jinia	エンジニア	engineer	22
en'pitsu	えんぴつ	pencil	240
erebētā	エレベーター	elevator	226
essei	エッセー	essay	160
Esso Sekiyu	エッソ石油	Esso Sekiyu (Oil) Co.	3
esukarētā	エスカレーター	escalator	226
ētto	ええっと	let me see	311
eyashūtā	エヤシューター	air shooter	243

F

fairu	ファイル	file	240
fakushimiri	ファクシミリ	facsimile	240
Firipin	フィリピン	The Philippines	23
Fōdo-san	フォードさん	Mr. ／ Ms. Ford	27
fōku	フォーク	fork	63
fuben	ふべん	inconvenient	87, 178
fuben ja nakute	ふべんじゃなくて	not inconvenient	174
fujin-fuku	ふじんふく	women's clothes	225
Fujiya	富士屋	name of a shop	175
fuku	ふく	clothes	173
Fukuoka	福岡	place name	132
fukuzatsu	ふくざつ	complicated	87
-fun, -pun	…ふん, …ぷん	minutes	103, 256
fune	ふね	ship	124
Furan'su	フランス	France	23, 132
Furan'su-go	スランスご	French	162
Furan'su no eiga	フランスの　えいが	French movies	159
Fran'su-ryōri	フランスりょうり	French (style) food	171
Furen'chi (doresshin'gu)	フレンチ(ドレッシング)	French (dressing)	345
(o-)furo	（お）ふろ	bathroom	248
furuhon-ya	ふるほんや	used book store	292
furui	ふるい	old	292
futa-	ふた-	two	62
futa-ri	ふたり	two people	58, 62
futatsu	ふたつ	two	61

futatsu-me no	ふたつめの	the second (in the sequence)	205
futoi	ふとい	thick [cylindrical things]	87
futsū	ふつう	usually, usual	100, 192
futsu-ka	ふつか	2nd (of the month)	103
fuyu	ふゆ	winter	12

G

ga	が	but	33
ga	が	[Subject Marker]	114
gakkō	がっこう	school	79, 112
gakusei	がくせい	student [Neutral]	22
gakusei-san	がくせいさん	student [Honorific]	22
gamu	ガム	chewing gum	53
gasorin-sutan'do	ガソリンスタンド	gas station	215
-gatsu	…がつ	month	103
gen'kan	げんかん	entry way	248
getsu-yōbi	げつようび	Monday	14, 103
gin'kō	ぎんこう	bank	79, 112, 214, 275
gin'kōin	ぎんこういん	bank employee	22
Gin'za	銀座	place name	54
Gin'za Eki	銀座駅	Ginza Station	209
Ginza-sen	銀座線	The Ginza Line	124
go	ご	five	46
-go (ni)	…ご (に)	. . . later/after	113
go-ban-me	5ばんめ	the fifth (one)	237
gochisōsama	ごちそうさま	a feast	330
Gochisōsama deshita.	ごちそうさまでした	Thank you for the delicious meal.	329, 339
Go-gatsu	5がつ	May	12
gogo	ごご	p. m.	100
gohan, shokuji	ごはん，しょくじ	cooked rice, meal	168, 171, 176
go-kai	5かい	five times	153
go-kai	5かい	5th floor	224
Go-kai ni arimasu.	5かいに　あります	(It's) on the 5th floor.	224
Go-kai ni gozaimasu.	5かいに　ございます	(It's) on the 5th floor. [Humble]	223
go-kazoku	ごかぞく	(your) family	122
go-kiro	5キロ	five kilometers	285
goro	ごろ	around [Time]	113
Gomen'kudasai.	ごめんください	hello, excuse me	351
Gomen'nasai.	ごめんなさい	I'm sorry.	34, 64
goro	ごろ	approximately, around (time)	109, 113
go-roku-jikan	5、6じかん	five to six hours	256
go-rop-pun	5、6ぷん	five to six minutes	256
gorufu	ゴルフ	golf	23, 120, 123, 161, 339
go-ryōsin	ごりょうしん	(your) parents	122
-gō-sen	…ごうせん	loop road No. . . .	322
Go-shin'pai naku.	ごしんぱいなく	[*Lit.* Do not worry.]	339
go-shujin	ごしゅじん	(your) husband	122
go-shūkan	5しゅうかん	five weeks	108
Goten'ba	御殿場	place name	120
Goten'ba Intā	御殿場インター	Gotenba Interchange	323
gozen	ごぜん	a. m.	100
gozen'chū	ごぜんちゅう	in the morning	193
gurai	ぐらい	about	154
guramu	グラム	grams	246
gurē	グレー	gray	86
gurēpu-furūtsu	グレープフルーツ	grapefruit	176

H

hachi	はち	eight	46

I

N

Uiriamuzu-san	ウイリアムズさん	Mr./Ms. Williams	28
uisukī	ウィスキー	whisky	67, 335
ukagaimasu	うかがいます	visit [Humble]	313
umi	うみ	ocean	138
un'ten'shu	うんてんしゅ	driver	73
unagi	うなぎ	grilled eel	189
unagi-ya	うなぎや	one type of Japanese restaurants	306
uogashi	うおがし	fish market	180
uōkuman	ウォークマン	walkman (stereo cassett tape recorder)	163
uriba	うりば	place/counter where something is sold	222
ūru	ウール	wool	88
urusai	うるさい	noisy	87
ushiro	うしろ	in back of	206, 236
usui	うすい	thin (things like books), light (color), *etc.*	87
uta	うた	songs, singing	165
utsukushikatta desu	うつくしかったです	was beautiful	138
uun	ううん	O. K.	34

W

wa	は	[Topic *or* Contrast marker]	18
waei-jiten	わえいじてん	Japanese-English dictionary	239
wain, budōshu	ワイン，ぶどうしゅ	wine	172
wakaranakattara	わからなかったら	if you get lost,	326
wakarimasen	わかりません	don't know (*Lit.* don't understand)	109
wakarimashita	わかりました	was easy to find (*Lit.* understood)	327
wakarimasu	わかります	understand	201
wakarimasu ka	わかりますか	Do you know ?	205
Wakō	和光	first rate department store in Ginza	201
Wan	ワン	Chinese surname (Wang)	31
wāpuro	ワープロ	word processor	240
warui	わるい	bad	87
warukatta	わるかった	was bad	139
waruku arimasen	わるくありません	not bad	140
wa-shitsu	わしつ	Japanese style room	248
watashi	わたし	I	4

Y

Y no tokoro	Yの　ところ	place where Y is	223
Y no uriba	Yの　うりば	place/counter where Y is sold	223
yachin	やちん	(house) rent	115, 166
yakusoku, apoin'to	やくそく，アポイント	appointment	220
yakyū	やきゅう	baseball games	159
yama	やま	mountain (s)	134
yama (nobori)	やま（のぼり）	mountain climbing	23
Yamabiko	やまびこ	name of a bullet train	262
Yamada	山田	Japanese surname	6
Yamanakako	山中湖	Lake Yamanaka	187
Yamate Dōri	山手通り	Yamate Ave.	76
Yamashita	山下	Japanese surname	2
yao-ya	やおや	vegetable store	172
yappari	やっぱり	just as I planned, or thought	253
yasai	やさい	vegetables	173
yasashii	やさしい	easy	87
Yamashita Yoshio	山下芳夫	Mr. Yoshio Yamashita	7
yasui	やすい	inexpensive	80
yasukatta	やすかった	was cheap	139
yasuku nakute	やすくなくて	not cheap	174
yasukute	やすくて	cheap, less expensive	169

Z